VPN Applications Guide
Real Solutions for
Enterprise Networks

David McDysan

Wiley Computer Publishing

John Wiley & Sons, Inc.

NEW YORK · CHICHESTER · WEINHEIM · BRISBANE · SINGAPORE · TORONTO

Publisher: Robert Ipsen

Editor: Carol A. Long

Managing Editor: Micheline Frederick

Text Design & Composition: North Market Street Graphics

Library of Congress Cataloging-in-Publication Data:

McDysan, David E.
    VPN Applications guide : real solutions for enterprise networks / David McDysan.
        p.   cm.
    "Wiley Computer Publishing."
    ISBN 0-471-37175-0 (pbk. : alk. paper)
    1. Extranets (Computer networks).   2. Business enterprises—Computer networks.
  3. Internet (Computer network)   4. Computer networks—Security measures.   I. Title.

 TK5105.875.E87 M 37 2000
 650'.0285'46—dc21

                                                                          00-024456

Printed in the United States of America.

10 9 8 7 6 5 4 3 2 1

Wiley Networking Council Series

Scott Bradner
Senior Technical Consultant, Harvard University

Vinton Cerf
Senior Vice President, MCI WorldCom

Lyman Chapin
Chief Scientist, BBN/GTE

Books in the Series

Tim Casey, *ISP Liability Survival Guide: Strategies for Managing Copyright, Spam, Cache, and Privacy Regulations* 0-471-37748-1

Geoff Huston, *Internet Performance Survival Guide: QoS Strategies for Multiservice Networks* 0-471-37808-9

Geoff Huston, *ISP Survival Guide: Strategies for Running a Competitive ISP* 0-471-31499-4

Elizabeth Kaufman & Andrew Newman, *Implementing IPsec: Making Security Work on VPNs, Intranets, and Extranets* 0-471-34467-2

For more information, please visit the Networking Council Web site at www.wiley.com/networkingcouncil.

*This book is dedicated to my wife, Debbie,
and my parents, Lowell and Martha, for their
support and encouragement.*

Contents

networking council foreword

The Networking Council Series was created in 1998 within Wiley's Computer Publishing group to fill an important gap in networking literature. Many current technical books are long on details but short on understanding. They do not give the reader a sense of where, in the universe of practical and theoretical knowledge, the technology might be useful in a particular organization. The Networking Council Series is concerned more with how to think clearly about networking issues than with promoting the virtues of a particular technology; that is, how to relate new information to what the reader knows and needs, so that he or she can develop a customized strategy for vendor and product selection, outsourcing, and design.

In *VPN Applications Guide* by Dave McDysan, you'll see the hallmarks of Networking Council books: examination of the advantages and disadvantages, strengths and weaknesses of market-ready technology; useful ways to think about options pragmatically; and direct links to business practices and needs. Disclosure of pertinent background issues necessary to understand who supports a technology and how it was developed is another goal of all Networking Council books.

The Networking Council Series is aimed at satisfying the need for perspective in an evolving data and telecommunications world that is filled with hyperbole, speculation, and unearned optimism.

In *VPN Applications Guide: Real Solutions for Enterprise Networks* you'll get clear information from experienced practitioners.

We hope you enjoy the book. Let us know what you think. Feel free to visit the Networking Council Web site at www.wiley.com/networkingcouncil.

Scott Bradner
Senior Technical Consultant, *Harvard University*

Vinton Cerf
Senior Vice President, *MCI WorldCom*

Lyman Chapin
Chief Scientist, *BBN/GTE*

Acknowledgments

A book like this is not created in a vacuum. I would like to thank Vint Cerf for asking me to write this book as well as for the many helpful suggestions, corrections, and comments that he provided. I would also like to acknowledge Carol Long of John Wiley & Sons for helping to refine the outline, providing a careful review of each chapter, and making many helpful suggestions to improve readability. I also thank my wife, Debbie, for giving me the time to write this book along with her continual support and encouragement. I also gratefully acknowledge the reviewers from MCI WorldCom who carefully read the manuscript, corrected errors, and suggested clarifications. These reviewers were: Michael Conn, Chris Daniel, Jim Dalton, Paul Litzenberger, Henry Sinnreich, Lee Thomas, and Lei Yao. I would also like to thank John Wiley & Sons for providing the glossaries from the books *ISP Survival Guide* by Geoff Huston and *Implementing IPsec* by Elizabeth Kaufman and Andrew Newman so that the glossary in this book could be as complete and as accurate as possible.

This book does not reflect any policy or position of MCI WorldCom. The ideas and concepts expressed herein are those of the author or the cited references.

Preface

IP-based Virtual Private Networks (VPNs) are a hot topic and a rapidly growing industry in the tidal wave of Internet-driven businesses. However, the concept of VPNs is not something new; it is in fact over two decades old. Because those who cannot remember the past are condemned to repeat it, this book begins with a history of VPNs as background. We cover private network technologies, voice VPNs, and, of course, X.25, frame relay, and ATM data VPNs. Looking back over this history, one constant is that only enterprises are interested in VPNs—individual users need only public services. However, Internet-powered VPNs make this capability available to even small enterprises. Consequently, the focus of this book is on the networking needs of business and government enterprises. Other historically consistent drivers for enterprises are the need to remain competitive, to continually reduce costs, to improve productivity, and to expand operations on a global scale. One important technological response to the need to reduce costs and improve productivity is that of integrating voice, data, and video applications onto a single network infrastructure. Another recurring theme is the reduction of cost through shared usage by enterprises of a public network versus the inherently higher costs involved with a private network.

The worldwide adoption by enterprises of the Internet as the place to conduct business is a fundamental and profound change that creates new opportunities, as well as new challenges for enterprises in the twenty-first century. Therefore, the majority of the book focuses on IP-based VPN solutions that have stormed onto the scene in the late 1990s. This includes cost-effective dial-in access, tunneling, firewalls, authentication, encryption, routing, address translation, and switching technologies. The book presents a combination of business requirements and drivers, technology trends and enablers, summary technical descriptions and real-world applications of these technologies to enterprise networking problems. We draw parallels to trends or patterns that historically arose with prior VPN technologies, and we point out where the IP-based VPN technologies fundamentally differ from their predecessors. After introducing the technologies, the book presents several generic business case models that can help determine the most economical approach, depending on the characteristics of an enterprise. Armed with this knowledge, the reader can then decide which approach is best for a particular enterprise application.

Overview of the Book

The business of building and operating networks is expensive. Not only must the network operator purchase and install equipment, transmission facilities, and computer systems, but the operator must also hire and maintain a staff of experts just to keep the network running. In the past, large corporations and government agencies built and operated separate private networks for voice and data either because it was less expensive than purchasing services from a carrier or because no carrier service provided the required features. Beginning in the mid-1980s the situation began to change as carrier VPN voice services became more cost effective and feature rich than their private network counterparts. In the 1990s this trend spread to the replacement of private line-based data networks with frame relay and ATM virtual connections. Although these trends began in the United States, the rest of the world followed along a similar path a few years later.

During the latter half of the 1990s, the worldwide adoption of the Internet suite of protocols has placed Email and the World Wide Web in the mainstream of personal, business, and government transactions. Looking ahead to the next millennium, the convergence of voice, data, and video will usher in a new generation of applications running on a common IP-based infrastructure. As competition increases on a global basis, corporations and large enterprises must continue to improve productivity, protect sensitive information, and reduce costs. Increasingly, the ability to manage, disseminate, and prioritize information becomes the difference between successful ventures and failures. Therefore, the appropriate design and deployment of VPNs will play an increasingly larger part in the success of corporate and government enterprises.

This book briefly covers the history of private and virtual private networks, focusing on user needs, business drivers, and applications. It summarizes technology and protocol aspects at a high level and provides an extensive glossary and bibliography for the reader interested in further detail. The goal of the book is to help you think about enterprise application requirements and how to select the appropriate private, virtual private, or public network technology.

How This Book Is Organized

This book is organized into 10 chapters. The first two chapters provide an introduction and background for the remainder of the book. The next three then provide a roughly historical perspective regarding the business and technological phases of circuit-switched and connection-oriented packet-switching VPN technologies. The next four chapters cover the TCP/IP protocol suite and the protocols and architectures developed in support of VPN applications. The final chapter begins with a down-to-earth description of designing and implementing a VPN and ends with some speculation regarding the future of VPNs.

Chapter 1, *Introduction and Overview*, describes why enterprises were driven to build private networks in the first place and defines how a virtual private network differs from a private network. It then provides an introduction to the subject of VPNs, briefly describing the various approaches of circuit switching, connection-oriented packet switching, and connectionless packet switching. The chapter concludes with a discussion of the overarching business drivers and technology trends that stretch across the entire history of VPN technologies.

Chapter 2, *Private Network Technologies*, begins by defining the technology, economics, and network deployment fundamentals of the circuits that are the foundation upon which every private, public, and virtual private network is built. This includes the fiber-optic transmission, microwave, and satellite systems that interconnect the planet. It also addresses emerging technologies like Digital Subscriber Line (DSL), cable, and wireless that promise to extend broadband networking ever further. The chapter then describes how and why enterprises built private voice and data networks.

Chapter 3, *Circuit-Switched VPNs*, begins with an analysis of the business drivers and technology trends that first drove enterprises from their private voice networks to carrier-offered solutions. It describes the Intelligent Network (IN) architecture based on the Narrowband Integrated Services Digital Network (N-ISDN), summarizes the relevant standards, and describes typical carrier network implementations. The chapter concludes with several commonly encountered circuit-switching features and applications that are still quite relevant in the emerging Voice over IP (VoIP) applications of modern networks.

Chapter 4, *Early Connection-Oriented Data VPNs—X.25 and Frame Relay*, begins in a similar manner, with an analysis of the business drivers and technology trends that first drove enterprises away from their private data networks to carrier-offered solutions. A summary of the X.25 and frame relay protocols focuses on concepts that are still relevant to VPNs—for example, Closed User Groups (CUGs), traffic management, and congestion control. It concludes by highlighting the applications for which enterprises choose connection-oriented solutions.

Chapter 5, *Modern Connection-Oriented VPNs—ATM, MPLS, and RSVP*, continues the theme of the previous chapter, but advances it into the modern era of integrated networking ushered in by Asynchronous Transfer Mode (ATM). This chapter also introduces the MultiProtocol Label Switching (MPLS) and Resource reSerVation Protocol (RSVP) standards defined for operation with IP that are in essence connection-oriented, even though IP itself is in fact connectionless. We introduce a number of concepts in this chapter that are critical to IP-based VPNs as well, including Quality of Service (QoS), admission control, and constrained routing. The chapter concludes with several applications that apply to modern connection-oriented VPNs.

Chapter 6, *The Internet Protocol Suite*, starts with a review of the business drivers and technology enablers that have made the Internet the unstoppable force that it is today. A comprehensive summary of the TCP/IP protocol suite follows, including an introduction to the Border Gateway Protocol (BGP) and higher-layer protocols that are critical to enterprise VPN applications. It concludes with an overview of the global Internet architecture and explains why this can be an extremely cost-effective infrastructure for enterprise VPNs.

Chapter 7, *Building Blocks for IP-Based VPNs—Security, Quality, and Access*, points out that although a public network has many advantages, it also presents some serious challenges for an enterprise that has sensitive communication needs. The overlay technologies developed by vendors and standardized in the IETF fall into three basic categories. The first is that of providing security, which involves achieving authentication, confidentiality, and integrity. Next, providing guaranteed capacity at an acceptable level of quality is a challenge for a connectionless network, and additional protocol support is required. Finally, a public network potentially opens up an enterprise network to intrusion from the outside. Here, too, technologies can help control access to what is private and keep it separate from what is public.

Chapter 8, *Dial-In Access and Multiprotocol Tunneling VPNs*, pulls together the technological and business background from Chapters 6 and 7 and applies it to basic communication networking problems that many enterprises have. An important business driver is support of the user who travels frequently and, increasingly, individuals who use high-performance access technologies to remotely access the enterprise network from remote locations or their homes. The chapter summarizes the various protocols developed to authenticate and secure access by these types of users, citing the relevant advantages and disadvantages of each and the prognosis for industry adoption. It concludes with two business analyses. The first provides an objective view of how the size and activity patterns of the dial-in user population drive cost trade-offs for a telephony versus an ISP-based solution. The second compares usage of overlay IP-based VPN technology to that of a connection-oriented data VPN like frame relay or ATM based on the traffic pattern of an enterprise.

Chapter 9, *IP Security-Enabled and Routing-Controlled VPNs*, focuses on the latest set of IPsec standards defined by the IETF and also covers some network-based alternatives that are a hybrid of IP routing combined with network-based connection-oriented VPNs. Beginning with the business drivers and technology enablers, it summarizes the important technical aspects of IPsec and illustrates how an enterprise can effectively use this technology to protect against a wide range of security threats. The discussion then summarizes how the use of BGP extensions working in concert with MPLS can provide a VPN with security comparable to that of frame relay or ATM but with greatly reduced configuration complexity and greater flexibility. The chapter concludes with a discussion of how enterprises typically deploy the technologies described in Chapters 8 and 9.

Chapter 10, *The Future of VPNs*, concludes the book with some practical considerations as well as some speculation regarding the future role of VPNs. The first part of the chapter begins with a step-by-step description of how to analyze requirements, plan, and implement a VPN, including a short case study of an extranet implementation. It then concludes with some reflections on how the Internet has scaled and what challenges lie ahead before enterprises can make maximal use of IP-based VPNs. Finally, we conclude with some comments regarding the state of IP-based VPNs in the marketplace, the ever shifting technological landscape, and the changing role of the enterprise in society.

Who Should Read This Book

The primary audience is network designers, network architects, network decision makers, executives, and professionals interested in learning about VPN technologies. The secondary audience is protocol designers, network managers, and network administrators who are already well versed in the protocol details but seek a broader perspective. The ideal reader for this book would be a network designer tasked by executive management to improve productivity and reduce expenses by integrating the enterprise's separate voice and data networks. The reader should have a basic background in voice and data networking principles; however, the book provides sufficient background so that up-to-date knowledge of the protocols is not essential.

A reader wanting to get the entire historical perspective on VPNs should read the book from cover to cover. A reader interested primarily in IP-based VPNs could read Chapter 1, then skip to Chapter 6 and finish the book from there forward. The book provides clearly marked cross-references to both earlier and subsequent chapters to avoid repetition. This means that a reader interested in implementing a VPN could begin with Chapter 10 and follow the references backward from there according to his or her interest.

Summary

The history of VPNs shows a focus by enterprises on economics and response to the marketplace. The Internet changes these factors in significant ways that in some cases simplify matters, but in other areas make things more complex. In response to this new environment, the technology solutions developed to date for IP-based VPNs consist of a number of overlays on the otherwise elegant, inherently simple connectionless IP paradigm. Some technologies are rather complex, most notably those that provide for secure operation over the public Internet. The emerging Public Key Infrastructure (PKI) promises to automate many of these complex tasks, but stands at a critical phase of market adoption. Another critical challenge that the Internet faces is the fulfillment of delivering guaranteed capacity and quality for applications that require these attributes. These and other success factors will determine whether IP-based VPNs fulfill the market forecasts of triple-digit growth or whether they suffer a fate similar to that of a marginally successful technology with a lower growth rate. Clearly, connection-oriented packet-switching networks must also become more IP-aware, or else enterprises will not suffer the additional complexity that they add. Whatever happens, having a clear and balanced business as well as technical understanding of all aspects of VPNs is the best preparation for an uncertain, rapidly advancing future.

CHAPTER

1

Introduction and Overview

**I do not know which makes a man more conservative—
to know nothing but the present, or nothing but the past.**
—John Maynard Keynes

This chapter begins by providing a brief history of public and private networks as background. We then introduce the main topic of Virtual Private Networks (VPNs). Finally, we examine the business motivation and technology enablers for virtual private enterprise networks.

A Brief History of Public Communication Networks

In the beginning, all networks were public. A user connected to a public network could reach any other user served by that same network. The earliest networks supported telegraphy service via electrical signals transferred over a single wire. The earth provided the ground for the signal. Later innovations by Marconi in 1895 extended the media to radio frequencies, allowing communication to ships at sea. Operators manually keyed in messages using a simple digital code invented by the painter and sculptor Samuel Finley Breese Morse in 1836. The first telegraph message ("What hath God wrought!"), sent in 1844 between Washington, D.C., and Baltimore, Maryland, was a bellwether of the ensuing telecommunication revolution. The telegraphy protocol required that the sender identify a destination telegraph station and the name of the intended recipient. The operators communicated with each other and intuitively determined the best way to forward a message from station to station until it reached the destination. The basic concepts of packet switching and connectionless routing have their roots in telegraphy. Electronic mail utilizes a messaging forwarding paradigm remarkably similar to telegraphy.

The next major innovation in telecommunications was the invention of the telephone by Alexander Graham Bell in 1876. The earliest telephone networks dedicated a pair of wires to connect each pair of callers. This limited connectivity made sense when only a few people had telephones or wanted to call each other. When the maze of overhead lines in urban areas became unmanageable, entrepreneurs responded with an elegant solution—switching. The first step involved human telephone operators who connected parties using patch cords on a switchboard in response to routing determined via a dialogue with the calling party. The address of the destination was simply the name of the person with whom the caller wished to speak. Now the network looked like a star network with all the wires from each telephone subscriber going back to a central operator station. However, as the number of users grew beyond what a single operator could handle, the network topology became a cluster of stars. At this stage of network evolution, multiple operators had to communicate with each other in order to manually connect calls through several switchboards. Addressing also became more complicated, because common names like Smith and Jones created the potential for routing a call to an unintended party. The next major innovation was the assignment of numeric addresses and the means to automatically route telephone calls to the destination identified by the digits dialed by the caller.

MOTIVATION FOR INVENTION OF THE TELEPHONE SWITCH

History attributes the invention of automatic circuit switching to Almon B. Strowger in 1889 [Bear 76], a man who was actually one of two undertakers in a town of moderate size. Unfortunately, the wife of Strowger's competitor was the switchboard operator for that town. As the telephone increased in use, the relatives of anyone who died rang up the telephone operator to request funeral services. The operator, of course, routed the requests to her husband, not to Strowger. With his business falling off because of this arrangement, Strowger conceived of the electromechanical telephone switch and the rotary dial telephone so that bereaved customers could contact him directly.

Strowger's invention used the series of pulses generated by the rotary dial of a telephone to actuate a clever arrangement of rotors and switches that associated a series of digits with a particular subscriber's line. As testament to the fundamentally sound nature of this invention, Strowger switches are still in use in telephone networks today. You can hear the operation of the rotors making contact as an unmistakable clicking sound as the switch operates. A number of electromechanical innovations improved circuit switching over the years. However, until the availability of reasonably priced electronic circuits in the early 1960s, the switching was electromechanical and analog. Digital switching fabrics did not arrive until the 1970s with the introduction of cost-effective integrated circuit technology. Interestingly, by the time that analog switches were decommissioned, digital transmission had been in place for decades. During the middle of the twentieth century, engineers designed the electromechanical telephone switches to last for 40 years!

Early telephone networks employed analog transmission over metallic media. The transmission performance over relatively short distances was actually quite good. However, performance degraded over longer distances due to the phenomena of electrical noise. Clever engineering and careful attention to detail extended long-distance calling across greater and greater distances, highlighted by transoceanic communication in 1956. The introduction of microwave radio technology occurred in telephone networks after World War II. Unfortunately, you could readily tell the difference between a long-distance call and a local call by the noise level of the connection. Interestingly, the era of digital transmission was driven not by the need for better voice quality but by basic economics.

In the late 1950s, telephone engineers faced a challenging problem. The crowded bundles of cables lying beneath the streets of large cities were no longer able to satisfy increasing demand. Should the engineers replace these cables at considerable labor and construction expenses, or should they find some electronic means that efficiently used the existing cables? Fortunately for the digital network of today, they chose to develop a major innovation using emerging solid-state electronic technology that converted analog voice signals into digital samples and multiplexed these samples into periodic time slots. Although this technique was relatively expensive, it cost less than replacing cables or digging additional tunnels in major cities. Called Time Division Multiplexing (TDM), this technique has become the prevalent multiplexing method in all modern telecommunication networks. Many users are unaware that the network converts every voice conversation to digital data, transmits it an arbitrary distance, and then converts this data back to an audible signal. TDM makes the quality of a voice call essentially independent of distance. This invariance in performance as a function of distance results from digital repeaters that decode and regenerate the digital signal at periodic intervals to achieve extremely accurate data transfer.

Data communication is more sensitive to noise and errors than digitized voice, but reaps tremendous benefits from the deployment of TDM infrastructure in public networks. TDM technology delivered the earliest digital private lines in the 1960s. TDM also forms the basis of the Synchronous Optical Network (SONET) in North America and the Synchronous Digital Hierarchy (SDH) in the rest of the world. All of the VPN technologies described in this book run over this transmission infrastructure originally developed for voice.

Why Enterprises Build Private Networks

This section introduces some generic reasons that drive enterprises to build their own private networks instead of using public network services. As detailed in Chapter 2, *Private Network Technologies*, a private network is technology deployed by an enterprise connected by transmission facilities either leased from a public carrier or constructed by an enterprise itself. Subsequent chapters expand upon these themes in the context of specific VPN technologies.

One Size Does Not Fit All

In the early days of networking, there was a specific network for each type of service. Telegraph networks, telephone networks, and radio broadcasts were all separate. Building and operating any network was an expensive endeavor in those days, and hence the principal demand was for a single ubiquitous public service. Due to the large costs of the technology available in the nineteenth century and the first half of the twentieth century, only a single company could make a telegraph or telephone network a viable business in a particular geographic area. Hence, a natural monopoly arose for telecommunications. In general, number of subscribers determines the true worth of a public network. Just as the value of the telephone increased as more businesses and households adopted the technology, so does the value of the Internet increase with each new user.

Cutting Costs

If public networks have such great value, why would any enterprise ever want a private network? Two reasons: *control* and *economics*. Control involves several dimensions: privacy, priority, and connectivity. A recurring theme in this book is that, economics often plays a significant role in decisions that enterprises make regarding networking.

Economics plays a role for a private enterprise in a number of situations. First, if an enterprise can implement a specific service at a lower cost than a public tariff, then the justification is straightforward. Such was the case in the 1970s and 1980s when many corporations and government agencies interconnected networks of voice switches, called Private Branch eXchanges (commonly called PBXes) via private lines. Second, if the enterprise needs a capability not offered by the public network provider in given geographic regions, then it has no choice but to build its own network. For example, a network of computer front-end processors interconnected via private lines is the quintessential definition of a private data network. In fact, the Internet had its origin as a private data network, funded by a large enterprise—the United States Department of Defense's Advanced Research Projects Agency (ARPA).

Controlling Communication

When a large company operates a network on behalf of the public interest, the private interests of some enterprises (e.g., competing corporations) and government agencies handling sensitive information are subject to inadvertent compromise. Eavesdroppers may monitor transmission at telephone company offices via a variety of subterfuges. For example, it is easy to monitor microwave and satellite transmissions. Even transmissions over fiber-optic cables are subject to eavesdropping [Whyte 99]. Furthermore, the public network may not offer services or capabilities that a communication-intensive enterprise requires. Therefore, in the early days, only large corporations or government agencies could justify the expensive business of private networking. For example, corporations and government institutions built cable and microwave networks for their own campuses. Later, carriers used TDM technology to provide private lines to corporations so that they could construct their own networks.

Achieving Connectivity

The earliest private networks utilized microwave technology developed during World War II. Another communications technology derived from the space age also empowered development of private networks. Communication satellites enabled communication to remote areas of the world, broadcasts of television and radio programs around the world, and private networks as well. In the 1970s and 1980s, satellite communication networks competed with digital private leased lines, which in part helped drive down the costs of private networking. Beginning in the late 1980s, fiber-optic technologies have markedly increased available transmission capacity.

What Makes a Private Network Virtual?

Okay, now that we've described the difference between a public network and a private one, what makes a private network virtual? We first give some basic definitions and then introduce the types of VPNs discussed in this book.

A good VPN has the low-cost structure of a ubiquitous public network, but retains the capacity guarantees, quality, control, and security of a private network. How can a network design achieve these apparently contradictory goals? The answer lies in software-defined networking technology, sophisticated communication protocols, and good old-fashioned capitalism. This is the central topic of this book, understanding how good VPN designs preserve the economies of scale afforded by large public networks while simultaneously partitioning and segregating VPN users from one another and public network users at large.

Private Line-Based Networks

A typical enterprise private network has a number of sites interconnected via private lines, as illustrated in Figure 1.1. The boxes in the figure indicate the equipment located at each enterprise node, and the lines depict the private lines. The circles depict the central offices in the carrier's private line network. In a loose sense, the TDM switching performed by add/drop multiplexers and digital cross-connects can be considered a virtual network [Huston 99], however, we do not adopt this definition.

A fundamental attribute of any network is its topology, that is, the interconnection pattern of nodes and links. A tree network has the least num-

---

WHAT IS A VIRTUAL PRIVATE NETWORK?

A Virtual Private Network (VPN) attempts to draw from the best of both the public and private networking worlds. Such a network is *private* in the sense that the data an enterprise transfers over the VPN is secure. It is *virtual* in the sense that the underlying public infrastructure is partitioned to have some level of guaranteed capacity for each enterprise.

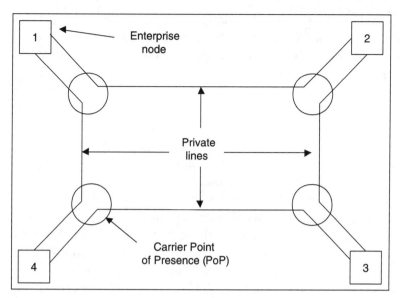

Figure 1.1   A typical private line network.

ber of private lines; however, it is not resilient to any failures whatsoever. A ring network is the network with the least number of private lines that is resilient to any single link or node failure. Therefore, each enterprise node must have at least two private lines, as shown in Figure 1.1, to provide a resilient network. Depending on traffic patterns and the economics of private line charges in relation to the equipment and operating costs, networks with partial-mesh topologies may be more economical than a ring network. Furthermore, enterprise nodes must perform tandem switching or routing in any topology that is not fully meshed. For example, traffic from node 1 to node 3 must traverse either node 2 or node 4.

If the public network does not support the capabilities required by the enterprise equipment, then there is little choice but to build a network using private lines or even privately owned transmission facilities. Examples of such applications are real-time control systems, telemetry and monitoring applications, high-performance cryptography, and high-quality video transmission systems. Chapter 2 describes the private line infrastructure on which all networks build and further details these private network applications.

However, if the enterprise equipment implements a standard protocol like switched voice, X.25, frame relay, ATM, or IP, then direct interfaces to a public network using these protocols may be more cost effective than a private network. This is, in fact, the primary topic of this book. The next few sections introduce the major networking technologies that enterprises have employed to construct VPNs using this approach. The presentation is in roughly historical order of enterprise adoption, namely, circuit-switched, connection-oriented, and connectionless.

Circuit-Switched VPNs

The first VPNs supported switched voice over a public network infrastructure. This design exploited the inherent separation of the functions that operate on the dialed digits from those that establish a connection from those that actually carry user information. Common Channel Signaling (CCS) allowed computers within switches to communicate with each other, as well as make requests from an outboard database. The outboard database knew the identity of the calling party, and could interpret the dialed digits using a private numbering plan. Therefore, an early VPN service allowed a carrier network to support the equivalent of a Private Branch eXchange (PBX) abbreviated dialing plan.

Figure 1.2 illustrates a simple example of a public network supporting two circuit-switched enterprise VPNs that have overlapping numbering plans. Boxes represent enterprise telephony equipment that use an overlapping three-digit abbreviated dialing plan. The shading of the equipment boxes indicates the two enterprises. All telephones at each enterprise node have a number of the form Nxx. The first digit N indicates the enterprise node site numbered 1 through 4. Thus, each site can have up to 100 telephones with this dialing plan. A single private line connects the enterprise equipment to a service provider switch, shown as a triangle in the figure. These switches interpret signaling messages received from the enterprise nodes by consulting a database, shown in the center of the figure. Because the switch knows the private line on which the call arrived, in this example, it knows the identity of the enterprise. The database contains a mapping indexed by the originating access line and the dialed number that returns the terminating access line. The arrows in Figure 1.2 show how the connection-switched VPN routes a call originating with the same dialed digits 333 from equipment located in the white- and gray-shaded enterprise nodes in the upper left-hand corner.

The separation of call control from database access in the first VPNs also enabled a number of other interesting call processing features. Dubbed the Intelligent Network (IN) in standards, this technique is widely used in support of features implemented in modern telephone networks around the world. Chapter 3, *Circuit-Switched VPNs*, describes the business drivers and technology utilized in voice VPNs and intelligent network-

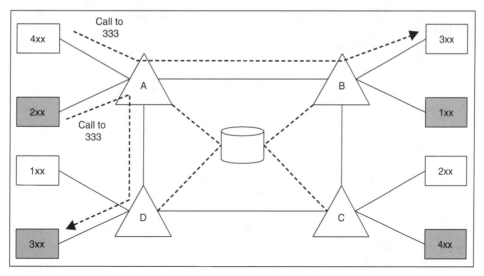

Figure 1.2   Example of two circuit-switched VPNs.

ing. We also summarize important aspects of the protocols involved and give some example applications of these features.

Connection-Oriented VPNs

X.25, frame relay, Asynchronous Transfer Mode (ATM), and IP's MultiProtocol Label Switching (MPLS) are all forms of connection-oriented label-switching protocols [McDysan 00]. A label is the header field of a packet, frame, or cell. Labels are unique only to an interface on a device, such as enterprise user equipment or a network switch. Figure 1.3 illustrates a simple example of the operation of a simple two-port label switch. Starting from the left-hand side, a label switch uses the label header from the packet received on an interface as an index into a lookup table in the column marked In. The lookup table returns the outgoing label from the column marked Out and the outgoing physical interface from the column marked Port. The switch routes the packet, frame, or cell to the outgoing physical interface using an internal switching fabric, and it switches the label to the outgoing label retrieved from the lookup table. The example in Figure 1.3 uses patterns for the packets to trace the result of the label-switching operation implemented by the lookup tables on the input side of each port. Of course, contention may occur for the output port in a label switch if multiple packets are destined for the same output. Typically, label switches must implement some form of queuing to handle this situation.

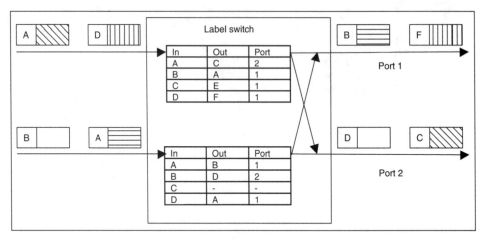

Figure 1.3   Illustration of label switching.

A connection-oriented label-switched network consists of a number of label switches implementing the foregoing basic function. Typically, these switches also implement a number of other features related to connection establishment, traffic control, QoS, congestion control, and the like. Some form of network management or signaling protocol establishes a consistent sequence of label-switching mappings in the lookup tables to form a logical connection that can traverse multiple nodes. We call such a logical connection a Permanent Virtual Connection (PVC) if a management protocol establishes the set of label mappings for a long period. We call the logical connection a Switched Virtual Connection (SVC) if a signaling protocol originated by the enterprise equipment dynamically establishes the label mappings on demand.

Figure 1.4 illustrates a public connection-oriented network supporting two disjoint VPNs. As in the previous example, shaded boxes represent equipment from different enterprises, and triangles represent public network label switches. The label-switched connection-oriented network implements disjoint virtual connections (either PVCs or SVCs) between different enterprise nodes, as indicated via dashed lines of different styles in the figure. Notice that a connection-oriented label-switched network looks very much like a private line network, but uses virtual connections instead of real ones. The important difference is that the service provider switches utilize label switching instead of TDM cross-connects to logically share trunk circuits between multiple-enterprise VPNs. Therefore, a connection-oriented VPN can be a plug-compatible replacement for a private line-based network. This has a number of advantages. First, the granularity of capacity

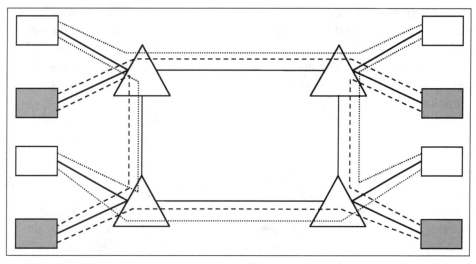

Figure 1.4   Example of two connection-oriented VPNs.

allocation is much finer with a label switch than that implemented in the rigid TDM hierarchy. Second, if the traffic offered by the enterprises is bursty in nature, then the network can efficiently multiplex many traffic streams together. Finally, the shared public network achieves economies of scale by utilizing high-speed trunk circuits that have a markedly lower cost per bit per second (bps) than lower-speed links do.

X.25 was the first connection-oriented data VPN. A number of service providers deployed X.25 beginning in the 1970s, including BBN, Telenet, and Tymnet. The technology still has significant global reach even in the year 2000. It combined the connection-switching and label-switching paradigms to establish logical connections on demand. X.25 pioneered a VPN concept called a Closed User Group (CUG). Frame relay followed X.25 by simplifying the protocol and hence improving the price-performance ratio in the late 1980s. Frame relay pioneered the important VPN concept of per-connection traffic management and some simple responses to congestion. Chapter 4, *Early Connection-Oriented Data VPNs—X.25 and Frame Relay*, summarizes the important business drivers, technology trends, protocols, and applications for X.25 and frame relay.

ATM was the successor to frame relay, focusing on a fixed cell size to ease hardware implementation and achieve high performance. Carriers such as Sprint, AT&T, and MCI began supporting ATM in the early 1990s. ATM borrows heavily from the signaling protocols of the narrowband Integrated Services Digital Network (ISDN), the traffic management concepts of frame relay, and automatic topology discovery from IP. ATM standards significantly extended the concept of Quality of Service (QoS) and more precisely defined traffic management, these being the hallmarks of ATM. ATM also introduced the concept of two levels of connection aggregation. Specifically, an ATM Virtual Path Connection (VPC) carries many Virtual Channel Connections (VCCs).

In many ways, MPLS is an enhancement of ATM: It provides most of the same capabilities and also adds some useful extensions. MPLS overcomes the inefficiency caused by the partial fill of the last fixed-length ATM cell when carrying variable-length packets. MPLS also supports a more flexible hierarchical aggregation of connections and supports loop detection as well. Chapter 5, *Modern Connection-Oriented VPNs—ATM, MPLS, and RSVP,* summarizes the important business drivers, technology trends, protocols, and applications for ATM and MPLS. The design of MPLS also allows tighter integration of connection-oriented flow management with IP routing protocols in support of VPNs, as described in Chapter 9, *IP Security-Enabled and Routing-Controlled VPNs.*

Connectionless VPNs

A connectionless protocol does not require a signaling protocol since it does not use connections to forward user traffic. Instead, a separate routing protocol distributes topology information such that each node can make an independent, yet coordinated, decision about the next hop on which to forward packets that have a particular destination address in the header. Unlike label switching, the addresses in packet headers must be unique throughout a set of interconnected networks, such as the Internet. Therefore, the indices into the forwarding lookup table are identical in every node in a simple connectionless network. Because each address must be unique, the forwarding table could become quite large. Connectionless networks like the Internet scale to large sizes by carefully administering address assignments so that their forwarding tables need only process the high-order prefix bits of the address. Although a number of connectionless protocols like SMDS, CLNP, DECnet, and others have been defined and are in use today, the de facto industry standard is the Internet Protocol (IP). Therefore, we focus on only IP-based connectionless protocols in this book.

In a connectionless network, a VPN is a logical overlay on a shared IP network of a different type. A shared IP network may be the public Internet or a network that supports IP routing protocols implemented specifically for use by enterprise customers. A secure IP VPN utilizes the concept of an encrypted tunnel implemented at the enterprise equipment connected to the IP network. A tunnel may exist at the link layer or the network layer as an association between two endpoints attached to a public network, therefore making it virtual. As described in Chapter 7, *Building Blocks for IP-Based VPNs*, encryption is a technique that scrambles information such that only the intended receiver can decode it, thereby achieving privacy. Since an IP network is connectionless, the packets between enterprise nodes may take different paths depending on conditions such as link failures or the configuration of routing parameters. The connectionless routing protocol synchronizes the forwarding tables in all the nodes whenever the state of the network changes. This fundamental difference in paradigms is what has allowed the Internet to scale the way it has in response to the tremendous demand that arose in the latter half of the 1990s.

Figure 1.5 illustrates a connectionless IP-based VPN for two enterprises. The enterprise nodes are shaded boxes, each with an IP address that has a prefix associated with the network router to which the private access line attaches. For example, the gray-shaded enterprise node has an address prefix A.2 connected to the network router with address prefix A. The figure illustrates the forwarding tables next to each network router. Note how these tables contain only the address prefix and the next hop link number, not the enterprise node address prefixes. Therefore, the enterprise equipment at the edge of the network implements the IP VPN functions. This architecture has a number of fundamental advantages. First, configuration changes to the enterprise VPN do not require changes in the core Internet. Second, because the Internet is a global public network, a

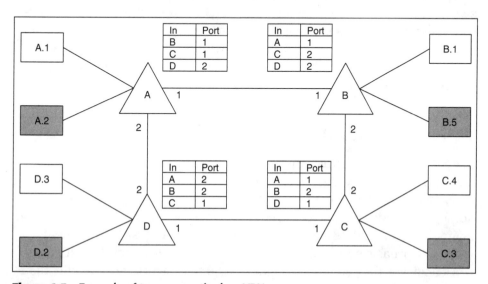

Figure 1.5 Example of two connectionless VPNs.

WHAT A VPN IS NOT

A VPN is neither an intranet nor an extranet. An *intranet* is a set of computers networked together that works like the Internet, but with the data accessible only to authorized users in a single enterprise [Wagner 97]. An intranet is an overlay on a shared IP network implemented by firewalls and enterprise-specific Web servers that employ password protection for an additional level of security [Minoli 97]. An *extranet* extends the concept by opening up portions of private data in an intranet to multiple enterprises, or even to the public [Baker 97]. A VPN provides some, but not all, of the infrastructure in intranets and extranets, and it does not provide support for enterprise-specific applications.

---

tunneled enterprise VPN can be implemented across multiple Internet Service Provider (ISP) networks.

Because the IP-based suite of protocols is the latest wave of communication networking innovation, the majority of this book focuses on this important topic. Specifically, Chapter 6, *The Internet Protocol Suite*, provides a high-level review of the public Internet as background. Chapter 7 then describes the basic building blocks used in constructing IP-based VPNs, namely security, connectionless QoS, and access control. Chapter 8, *Dial-In Access and Multiprotocol Tunneling VPNs*, then summarizes applications of these building blocks to dial-in and secure VPNs. It also compares the economics of the IP-based solutions versus those of circuit-switched and connection-oriented designs. Chapter 9 describes the application of the latest IP security (IPsec) standards to enterprise VPNs. This chapter also summarizes how service providers can support IP-based VPNs through the manipulation and use of information exchanged with enterprise sites using routing protocols.

Basic Economics of VPNs

In general, if the enterprise equipment technology and protocol matches that of the underlying public network on which the VPN exists, then the economics will be the most favorable. This occurs largely because the homogeneous design avoids the cost of selecting, purchasing, configuring, maintaining, upgrading, and operating separate conversion equipment.

The other basic economic cost reduction of VPNs is that the public network achieves the economy of scale of a large network more readily than most enterprises can. These scaling factors include the following:

- Statistical multiplexing of large traffic aggregates
- Lower unit capacity cost of high-capacity trunk circuits
- Lower amortized common equipment cost
- Better purchasing power for larger quantities of equipment
- Shared design, maintenance, operations, and support expertise

The remainder of this chapter introduces business drivers and environment along with technology trends and enablers.

Business Drivers and Environment

As the brief history of telecommunications presented earlier in this chapter illustrated, technology alone does not determine the path forward. Fundamental economic and social factors often play a pivotal role. These factors drive the business cases and establish financial requirements for enterprise communication network purchasing decisions. Each chapter in this book that introduces a VPN technique begins with a discussion of the associated business drivers and environment. This section provides some general background and introduces the terminology used in these chapter openers.

All enterprises have their own business drivers, requirements, and objectives. For commercial enterprises, these are largely economic. Government enterprises also have drivers and objectives, which are sometimes economic, but which span a broad range of other drivers and objectives (environmental, health, national security, safety, etc.). Similarly, nonprofit enterprises focus primarily on noneconomic objectives. However, fiscal responsibility is usually an important consideration in any enterprise, even if it is not the most important objective or driver. Therefore, in the business sections of this book, our focus is mainly on the economic impact of networking.

Government Regulation and Deregulation

A significant business factor in telecommunications networks is the role that government policy plays. Historically, governments around the world deemed the telephone network a monopoly and either made it a government institution or regulated the corporation as a public utility. Many European countries combined the postal, telephone, and telegraph services into an entity known as the PTT. After World War I, the United States government regulated AT&T as a public utility by setting the price for service so that the corporation achieved a fair rate of return. This approach had some advantages, but over time also created some significant problems.

Regulating the rate of return helped prevent monopolies from drastically overcharging customers; however, many experts believe that the resulting monopoly networks ended up being gold plated. Furthermore, in the United States, the company that delivered service to telephone customers also manufactured the equipment and sold it to itself. Because rate-of-return regulation involved the monopoly earning a percentage of its assets (called the *rate base*), the monopoly actually had significant financial motivation to make its network as expensive as possible. As technology advanced and the monopoly providers introduced more services, the regulations became increasingly complex. For example, one significant regulation at issue today is that of universal service—that is, providing at least minimal telephone service to everyone in the nation at an affordable price. A regulatory vehicle commonly used here subsidizes lower prices for residential customers by charging businesses higher prices. Obviously, when corporations began building private networks for their voice traffic, this offset the careful balance orchestrated by government regulators. Furthermore, the inertia of monopolies stifled innovation. For example, until the Carterfone decision in 1968, AT&T allowed customers to use only the telephone that it provided for connection to its network. The deregulation of telephone networks in the United States began humbly but resulted in the most profound antitrust settlement since the U.S. government dismantled John Rockefeller's Standard Oil monopoly in 1911 [Cantelon 92].

On the other hand, the Internet began on a different basis than telephone networks and is largely unregulated at the time of this writing. The Department of Defense (DoD) Advance Research Projects Agency (DARPA) established ARPANET in 1969 to interconnect government agencies and universities. The TCP/IP protocols were not put into general use until the Internet was formed in January 1983 and all host computers on the ARPANET and other DARPA-sponsored networks were required to use these protocols in lieu of the earlier ARPANET host-level Network Control Protocol (NCP). In 1986, the National Science Foundation (NSF) entered the picture and established another backbone called the NSFNET. In 1995, NSFNET was retired and in its place the NSF established a framework of Network Access Points (NAPs) allowing Internet Service Providers (ISPs) to compete on a fully commercial basis. While the deregulation of telephone networks is history, the extent of regulation applied to the Internet will have a critical impact.

> **THE BIRTH OF COMPETITIVE TELECOMMUNICATIONS**
>
> Jack Goeken filed a petition with the FCC in 1963 for Microwave Communications Inc. (MCI) to establish a microwave network for use by truckers along a highway between Chicago and St. Louis. The FCC finally granted a license to MCI in 1969. Bill McGowan gave the fledgling company financial backing and a sound business plan beginning in 1968. AT&T vigorously opposed MCI from the outset because MCI threatened the monopoly position it had held since World War I. Following a 12-year legal battle, Judge Greene delivered the Final Consent Decree that resulted in the breakup of the AT&T monopoly telephone network into AT&T long distance and the seven Baby Bells in 1984. This precipitated a wave of telecommunication deregulation that swept the globe, driving prices down for enterprises and residential users alike, and spurred a new wave of innovative services.

Government-Funded Innovation

Lest the reader think that all government activities are inherently counter-productive, sometimes government investment in technology creates major paradigm shifts that have huge benefits to industry and society. Frequently, the required investment is so large or the risk is so great that private industry cannot profitably engage in such speculation and hence the government takes on the risk. Many of these initiatives have little impact, and some fail miserably. A few have been hugely successful.

Sometimes, other circumstances also come into play. For example, war often delivers significant technological and industrial innovations. The wars of the twentieth century greatly accelerated the automotive, aeronautic, computing, and broadcast industries. Technical innovations include radar, microwave communications, jet engines, atomic energy, and rocketry. Let's look at a few examples of government initiatives that significantly shaped the world in which VPNs exist today.

Often, the resulting innovations only tangentially relate to the initial goal. Take for example the space race. Although the objective was travel to the moon and beyond, a principal benefit has been the acceleration of the microelectronics industry. The need for low-weight, low-power, high-performance electronics in space vehicles led to the development and refinement of the integrated circuit. The resultant availability of cost-effective microprocessors, memory, and associated communication circuitry is the very foundation of today's computer communication networks.

Another example is the investments by the U.S. government to interconnect university and government research laboratories described previously. Certainly, the government saw some return on the investment from the research programs conducted on its private computer communication network. However, the principal benefit occurred only after the government stepped out of the picture and made the network public. For a relatively small investment (when compared with the cost of war or the space race), the investments in the Internetting program as well as the Packet Network Research program resulted in a time-tested set of protocols that form the foundation of the Internet today.

Managing the Bottom Line

Progress marches ever onward, and the world of networking is no different. In a manner similar to the way that enterprises constructed private data networks over the telecommunications infrastructure developed for telephony, the industry is developing a new wave of technologies that overlay the basic suite of Internet protocols to construct VPNs. As we shall see, when the public network infrastructure of a VPN matches that of the enterprise equipment, then significant savings can occur. This is a recurring theme in the history of communication networks, with the Internet simply the latest frontier.

Successful enterprises are cost conscious. Even large government programs are subject to public scrutiny. For example, the Strategic Defense Initiative was simply too expensive and politically unpopular. In the highly competitive world of commercial enterprises, those that are not cost conscious fail on a predictable and regular basis. Standing still is simply not good enough. The maturation of computing hardware and the supporting software has ushered in the postindustrial information age. Enterprises now need to interconnect employees, databases, servers, affiliates, and suppliers in a rapidly changing business environment. Flexibility becomes an overarching requirement. Enterprises that do not adapt will not survive.

Innovation as a Necessity for Survival

Increased competition breeds the need for innovation. In traditional services and products, new, smaller companies grab market share by offering new and innovative services more rapidly or by offering traditional services or products at a lower cost. The incumbents sometimes cry foul, claiming that the newcomers are "cream skimming" the lucrative market segments. The newcomers counter that the incumbents are the "fat cats" who have all the cream. Although some monopolies do exist, either regulated or de facto, the pace of change is ever accelerating. For example, although Microsoft holds a dominant share of the Personal Computer (PC) operating system and application software markets in 2000, Bill Gates claims that this could change rapidly if Microsoft fails to introduce innovations to maintain its lead. It could happen! Look at the history of IBM's decline in market dominance in the computing and software industry.

The worldwide adoption of the Web is a great equalizer. Even a small enterprise can have a large impact and presence via the electronic Web that never sleeps. The user-friendly Web browser with downloadable plug-ins empowers distribution of new paradigm-shifting applications within days to weeks. The rapid adoption of electronic commerce will forever change the way business operates and government administrates. Enterprises are rapidly deploying Web-based intranet and extranet technology to reduce internal costs, in many cases replacing legacy mainframe-based systems.

Mergers and acquisitions occur at an ever increasing pace in the business world. If a huge number of start-up companies did not also spring up, the industry could conceivably collapse back into an oligopoly. A changing business environment where companies must combine operations and business units in a rapid and effective manner is one driver that creates a demand for new types of networking capabilities.

Addressing Global Needs

Communication networks continue to shrink the distances between nations, cultures, and time zones. The introduction of each new type of communication technology empowers the nearly instantaneous dissemination of new media types around the globe. Beginning with the first transatlantic telephone cable in 1956, the speed of transfer of news and breaking information fell from days to minutes. On the heels of the space age, communication satellites ushered in the era of video and multimedia distribution in the 1960s. In the late twentieth century, high-capacity fiber-optic transoceanic and transcontinental cables connect the planet, bringing the benefits of digital transmission to the corridors used by most enterprises.

This increase in high-performance connectivity enables enterprises to scale beyond national boundaries, particularly in the commercial and nonprofit sectors. It may also have an impact on governmental enterprises. Witness the lowering of national barriers in the European Union as an example.

Need to Protect Sensitive Information

Most enterprises have at least some sensitive information. Possible exceptions are nonprofit organizations and some government agencies. Most commercial enterprises have some sensitive information that would be of value to competitors. Enterprises trust the implicit security in private leased-line networks. In fact, a major impediment to the adoption of VPNs is ensuring that this new technology delivers levels of privacy and security comparable to those of private lines.

Toward this end, the fundamental security requirements of any VPN are as follows [Flanagan 97; Kaufmann 99; Kosiur 98; Schneier 95; Stallings 98a]:

Authentication. Validating that the originator is indeed who he or she claims to be.

Access control. Allowing only authorized users admission to the network.

Confidentiality. Ensuring that no one can read or copy data transmitted across the network.

Integrity. Guaranteeing that no one can alter data transferred by the network.

The VPN technologies studied in this book employ different methods to meet these requirements. These methods are sometimes implicit and in other cases are explicit. Security is a fundamental requirement for Internet-based VPNs. Chapters 7 through 9 cover the important topic of Internet security. Of course, good security begins with secure practices. For example, if the employees of your enterprise leave their user IDs, passwords, or encryption keys lying about, then all of the security technology in the world won't protect your sensitive information.

Quality of Service, Capacity, and Service-Level Agreements

Most enterprises believe that Quality of Service (QoS), traffic management, and prioritized or differentiated service will become an increasingly important driver in their evolving communication needs [Ferguson 98; McDysan 00]. Some applications (e.g., voice and video) have rigid required amounts of capacity and minimum levels of quality to operate acceptably. Other applications (e.g., Web browsing, file transfers, and Email) are elastic and can adapt to available capacity to a certain extent. However, even elastic applications result in lowered productivity, and increase effective cost to the enterprise, if certain minimum capacity and quality guidelines are not met. Normally, an enterprise may also need to prioritize or differentiate between these categories of applications to handle intervals of congestion.

The primary QoS measures are loss, delay, and availability. Voice and video applications have the most stringent delay and loss requirements. Interactive data applications like Web browsing and electronic collaboration have looser delay and loss requirements, but they are sensitive to errors. Non-real-time applications like file transfer, Email, and data backup work acceptably across a wide range of loss rates and delay. Availability requirements vary across enterprises. Normally, service providers charge a premium for high availability, because additional costs accrue to guarantee operation in case of failures (as we'll be examining in this book).

Capacity, also referred to as *bandwidth* (especially in the trade press), is fundamental to the traffic engineering of a VPN to deliver the required QoS. Some applications require a minimum amount of capacity to work at all—for example, voice and video. The performance of elastic protocols that adaptively change their transmission rate in response to congestion in the network improves as the capacity allocated to them increases. The Internet's Transmission Control Protocol (TCP), which carries Web traffic and file transfers, is an example of an elastic protocol. Other applications are elastic up to a certain point, after which adding capacity does not improve performance.

Finally, many network providers guarantee specific QoS and capacity levels via Service-Level Agreements (SLAs). An SLA is a contract between the enterprise user and the network provider that spells out the capacity provided between points in the network that should be delivered with a specified QoS. If the network provider fails to meet the terms of the SLA, then the user may be entitled a refund. These have become popular capabilities offered at additional cost by network providers for the private line, frame relay, ATM, or Internet infrastructures employed by enterprises to construct VPNs.

Technology Trends and Enablers

Technology often enables a paradigm shift in the networking decisions that enterprises make. Innovative enterprises recognize promising technology trends and try them in order to gain a strategic advantage. The chapters in this book describe technology trends and enablers applied to the specific VPN technique under discussion. This section provides some general background on network technology trends and enablers and introduces terminology used in subsequent chapters.

Wavelengths and Optical Switching

Dense Wavelength Division Multiplexing (DWDM) promises to deliver huge amounts of capacity in fiber-optic backbones [Ryan 98]. DWDM effectively allows reuse of existing fiber, avoiding the expense of approximately $40,000 to $80,000 per mile to install new conduit and cables. DWDM is rapidly driving down the cost of high-speed backbone capacity. Each wavelength in these fiber backbones operates at capacities of up to 10 billion bits per second, commonly expressed as gigabits per second (Gbps). Current implementations support over 100 wavelengths per fiber. This means that a pair of fibers can support over 10^{12} bps, or a terabit per second (Tbps). However, it is important to remember that these low costs apply only between points where the fiber backbone has add/drop multiplexers that provide lower-speed access. These multiplexers are necessary because the optoelectronic interfaces on switches and routers currently operate at maximum speeds of 1, 2.5, or 10 Gbps.

Most service provider networks currently employ TDM as the switching and grooming mechanism for the backbone. Electronics becomes the dominant cost of these systems. In fact, transmission systems have historically increased the capacity per wavelength in multiples of 4 once every four years. With DWDM enabling growth in the additional dimension of wavelengths, the old TDM architecture will not be able to keep pace with the backbone capacity. Therefore, engineers are busily developing space-division and wavelength optical switches that operate at higher-aggregate-capacity levels at even lower unit costs.

The cost of optoelectronic switching and routing equipment is also declining at a similar pace. On the optical side, routers and switches employ the same technology used in DWDM, hence achieving manufacturing volume and, consequently, lower unit costs. The continual improvement of electronic price-performance ratio also drives down the unit cost according to Moore's law. Another important factor in the growth of backbone router and switch capacity is the use of more sophisticated architectures that will deliver terabit-per-second capacities in the early part of the twenty-first century.

Overcoming the Limitations of Moore's Law

Although the price-performance ratio of electronics continues its precipitous fall that began in the early 1970s, it pales in comparison to the growth rate of Internet traffic. A popularly cited trend for electronic price performance is attributed to Gordon Moore, a cofounder of Intel Corporation. It's called *Moore's law* [Ferguson 98; Goralski 97; Whyte 99] after its author, who observed early on that doubling of semiconductor density, and hence processing power or memory capacity, occurred approximately once every 18 to 24 months. Subsequent analyses [McDysan 94; Goralski 97] show that this trend has continued for over 20 years! If we assume that the chip cost remains approximately the same (without accounting for inflation), then the cost per unit of processing power or volume of storage declines by approximately 25 to 33 percent per year. Although predicting the future based on past experience can be risky business, the historical trend of electronics price performance has been quite predictable.

However, the growth of the Internet exceeds that achievable by electronics alone as predicted by Moore's law. In other words, routers or switches using the same hardware architecture can double network capacity only in 18 to 24 months by using newer, faster components. If the service growth rate exceeds the capacity growth rate of the underlying technology, then designers must find other solutions. Fortunately, switch/router designers are drawing upon supercomputer interconnection and ATM switch designs developed over the past decade to achieve architectures that scale at rates faster than the underlying electronic technology.

Access—The Perennial Bottleneck

Although costs are rapidly falling on the backbone transmission network, getting traffic to the backbone sites in a cost-effective manner has been a long-standing challenge. A principal reason for the higher cost of access is that the traffic density is inherently lower where the network interconnects to enterprise locations. A fundamental aspect of achieving economy of scale on backbone networks involves aggregating traffic from a large number of low-speed access network facilities via a switch, router, or multiplexer onto a small number of high-speed backbone facilities.

Traditionally, a monopoly carrier provided the access service. In many areas of the world, the access technology is twisted wire pairs. Fortunately, applied communications engineering can deliver up to 56 kbps on much of the twisted wire plant. When a carrier employs specific testing and configuration procedures, a variety of Digital Subscriber Line (DSL) technologies deliver capacities ranging from several hundred kbps to several Mbps over the same twisted wire pairs. In general, the maximum speed achievable is inversely proportional to the distance from the enterprise to the service provider's equipment. Some larger enterprise sites are fortunate to have fiber-optic connections to one or more service providers.

Other alternative access technologies also exist. One that may be attractive for enterprises in remote locations that are some distance from a service provider's Point of Presence (PoP) is wireless data communication. Fixed, point-to-point wireless networks can deliver tens of Mbps of capacity. Unfortunately, due to limitations in available radio spectrum, this solution can only support a relatively small number of enterprise sites within a particular geographic region. Another, older technology for remote locations is to relay communications via satellite to a larger enterprise site that has economical access to a terrestrial access network.

Finally, although primarily applicable to residential broadband access, television cable networks may prove convenient for some enterprises. This is especially true for enterprises that plan to use a telecommuting paradigm in which information workers must be able to productively network from their residences. Of course, the QoS, security, capacity, and performance of any access method must meet the needs of the enterprise.

Integrating Voice and Data Services

Modern VPN technologies allow enterprises to cost effectively share expensive access facilities between voice and data applications. Voice over IP (VoIP), Voice over ATM (VoATM), and Voice over Frame Relay (VoFR) standards enable interoperation between various equipment manufacturers and carrier services. These technologies allow enterprise equipment to share access facilities connected to a public network for both voice and data, as shown in Figure 1.6. Enterprise users may employ legacy voice technologies like a Private Branch eXchange (PBX) or may use alternative VoIP technologies directly to their computer desktops. The data service connections may be routers with frame relay, Ethernet, or ATM interfaces. The enterprise voice and data ports may connect site to site only or also may connect into the carrier's public voice and data networks as shown in the center of the figure.

The VPN architecture may be either connection-oriented or connectionless, as described earlier. In either case, the networking protocols must ensure that voice flows have sufficient capacity and priority on the access line in order to deliver acceptable QoS. These protocols achieve additional sharing advantages by dynamically allocating the scarce access line capacity to voice only when calls are active or, in some cases, only when people are actually speaking. Chapters 4, 5, and 6 (on frame relay, ATM, MPLS, and IP) summarize the important protocols and benefits involved via supporting these functions.

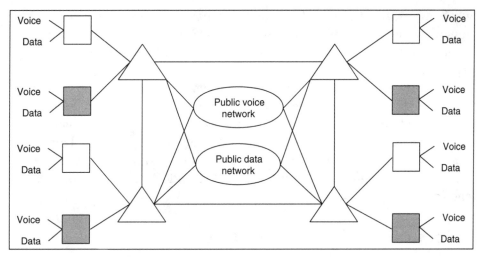

Figure 1.6 Illustration of integrated access.

Traffic Management, Queue Scheduling, and Congestion Control

As indicated in the previous section, most enterprises have some requirements for Quality of Service (QoS), guaranteed capacity, and predictable
performance for elastic applications. Fortunately, the VPN technologies
studied in this book either already have standardized means to support
these requirements or the means to do so are far along in the standardization process [McDysan 00].

Interestingly, the basic techniques employed by frame relay, ATM, and IP
share some common attributes. First, these protocols define the notion of
a traffic contract between the end user and the public network infrastructure. The contract states that the network will provide a specified QoS to
that portion of the user's data that conforms to a set of traffic parameters
that specify the peak rate, average rate, and burst duration. User data in
excess of this parameter-specified traffic profile may not receive the specified QoS. Within the network, a number of queue scheduling mechanisms
(e.g., priority queuing or weighted fair queuing) service frames, packets, or
cells according to a particular scheduling mechanism to achieve the
desired loss, delay, or jitter on a hop-by-hop basis. Finally, under certain
conditions, network elements may experience overload even when the
device performs traffic management and queue scheduling. This may be
caused by statistical oversubscription, failures of nodes or links, or unusu-

ally heavy traffic. Under these conditions, network elements must invoke congestion control functions to meet the QoS of higher-priority flows and ensure fairness among those flows contending for the congested resources.

Currently, ATM has the most completely standardized set of functions that support QoS, guaranteed capacity, and congestion control. Frame relay essentially supports a subset of these capabilities. IP has some relatively new standards in support of QoS, guaranteed capacity, and congestion control, and several others are in the standardization process. The chapters corresponding to frame relay, ATM, and IP detail the specifics for each technology.

A Cornucopia of Internet Protocols

A fundamental technological enabler for the next wave of VPNs is the rich set of Internet protocols originally developed for a research environment. The latter half of this book focuses on the impressive suite of protocols and applications already in widespread use today and discusses how they apply to VPNs. These include routing protocols that automatically configure the forwarding tables in network equipment and hence reduce operational costs. An important set of recently developed standards supports encryption of sensitive user information in order to meet the security requirements of VPNs. Other protocols provide reliable delivery of user information, support the real-time aspects of voice and video, or simply provide a datagram service. Other protocols and procedures allow enterprises to manage, measure usage, and determine the performance of the underlying IP-based equipment and services. Of course, protocols employed by Web browsers (Email, file transfers, and the like) are familiar to most users.

However, this is only the beginning of the story. The Internet Engineering Task Force (IETF) and other standards bodies continue developing standards for new protocols and applications at a mind-numbing pace. Chapter 10, *The Future of VPNs*, outlines some possible future directions applicable to VPNs in the ever expanding suite of Internet protocols.

CHAPTER
2

Private Network Technologies

**Private information is practically the
source of every large modern fortune.**
—Oscar Wilde

This chapter introduces the transmission and switching technologies used
to implement private networks. All of the VPNs studied in this book also
utilize these technologies as access or trunk circuits. In general, VPNs are
modern alternatives to the traditional private voice and data solutions
summarized in this chapter.

Private Transmission Media

Transmission media interconnect equipment in private networks, provide
access to public switching nodes, and interconnect public network sites.
These include private lines, digital subscriber lines, cable modems, satellite links, and fixed wireless links. In a sense, these transmission media
provide the plumbing out of which enterprises and service providers construct their networks.

Digital Private Lines

This section defines the basic technology employed by carrier networks in
support of digital private lines. This technology offers the best QoS and

capacity guarantees of any technology studied in this book. Delay is constant, and loss occurs only as the result of errors or an unavailable circuit. Such high-quality and absolute-capacity guarantees may be warranted for some applications. However, if the traffic generated by an enterprise is intermittent or not of a regular nature and if the applications can tolerate some variation in delay and loss due to queuing, then other technologies may be more economical.

Because the carrier's physical plant typically involves twisted pairs, coaxial cable, radio frequency transmission, and/or optical fiber, private line security is the benchmark against which we measure the other VPN technologies. The inherent security of a private line is primarily physical. Good enterprise-level physical security involves keeping the communication-wiring closet locked and providing access only to trusted personnel. Generally, carriers keep good physical security for their sites. One area of potential compromise would involve a criminal act of cutting the wires or fiber-optic cables and intercepting data and/or inserting fraudulent data. Although these things rarely happen, or at least are rarely publicized, an enterprise with sensitive information should consider encryption, which covers IP-based VPN technologies, as an additional security measure for extremely sensitive data even in private line or connection-oriented VPNs.

Time Division Multiplexing (TDM)

TDM converts voiceband analog signals into quantized digital samples at periodic sampling intervals. Figure 2.1 shows a simple example of TDM sampling two analog signals using 3 bits to represent each quantized voice sample and a frame that contains two time slots. The figure shows the quantized bit patterns corresponding to an analog signal level to the left of each analog time trace. The gray-shaded blocks indicate when the TDM multiplexer samples the waveform. The multiplexer places the quantized 3-bit value into the position in time in the TDM frame shown in the center of the figure. The sampling and mapping for the waveform shown at the top of the figure is placed in the first time slot in each frame, while an analogous sampling and mapping to the second time slot occurs for the waveform at the bottom of the figure. This is essentially the concept used in modern TDM systems, except that 8 bits per time slot are used as well as more time slots per frame. Subsequent sections detail the number of time slots per frame used in real networks and discuss some practical considerations involved in connecting devices with private lines.

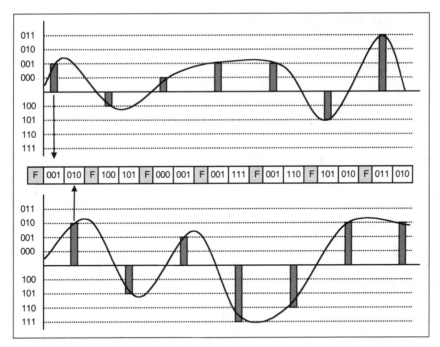

Figure 2.1 TDM support for digitized voice.

A channel bank is an example of a TDM device that takes a number of analog voice inputs, converts them into digital samples, and places them into time slots delineated by a framing pattern. Because samples occur 8,000 times per second, the frame period is 125 microseconds. A modulator sends bits on the physical transmission media at a specific rate, called the *transmission capacity* of the link. The framing pattern defines the starting bit position for a series of fixed-length time slots, each 8 bits long.

CONVERTING VOICE INTO DATA

In 1924, Nyquist proved that a receiver could reconstruct the original analog signal from digital samples taken at a rate of no less than twice the bandwidth of the original signal. Bandwidth is the frequency passband of an analog signal measured in units of Hertz (Hz). Thirty years later, telephone engineers employed the Nyquist sampling theorem to select a sampling rate of 8,000 samples per second for an analog signal bandwidth of approximately 4,000 Hz. Multiplying the sampling rate by 8 (or 7) bits per sample yields the standard 64-kbps (or 56-kbps) digital stream used in all TDM transmission, multiplexing, and switching systems. The digitized coding of each analog voice sample is called Pulse Code Modulation (PCM) [ITU G.711].

Plesiochronous Digital Hierarchy (PDH) Circuits

Because TDM operates in the time domain, an accurate clock is essential to achieve reliable data transfer. If adjacent switching nodes used different clocks, then the operation of mapping time slots received at one clock rate and transmitting them at another clock rate would eventually lead to buffer underrun or overrun. Consequently, the first carrier networks employed a *plesiochronous* (which means nearly synchronous) clocking scheme. Electronic technology could not easily operate at high speeds in the 1970s, so engineers designed schemes that combined a number of lower-speed signals into a composite higher-speed signal using several stages of multiplexing. These schemes consumed additional overhead bits to perform a procedure called *bit stuffing* to accommodate the small variations in digital signal rates resulting from independently running electronic oscillators.

Telephone networks initially employed the digital hierarchy to carry voice channels between switching nodes. Later, carriers offered the payload portion of these bit streams as private line services. As described in the previous section, a portion of the bits in each TDM frame are overhead (e.g., a framing pattern and other fields), and the remaining bits are available as payload. The bit rate commonly cited in many texts is the line bit rate. The payload available for nonvoice equipment is always somewhat less than the line rate. Table 2.1 lists the commonly employed line rates encountered in PDH systems around the world [ITU G.702; Goralski 97; McDysan 98b]. North America defines *hierarchical level x* as Digital Stream x (DSx). Only the DS1 and DS3 levels were commonly available in North America, beginning in the middle 1980s. These are frequently called T1 and T3 in the literature. The ITU-T-defined international levels are widely available in Europe; and the hierarchical level x is commonly referred to as Ex. Japan also has a set of PDH hierarchical levels, commonly known as Jx, as shown in Table 2.1.

Table 2.1 Commonly Encountered PDH Bit Rates

HIERARCHICAL LEVEL	NORTH AMERICAN LEVEL (DSX) (MBPS)	EUROPEAN LEVEL (EX) (MBPS)	JAPANESE LEVEL (JX) (MBPS)
1	1.544	2.048	1.544
2	6.312	8.448	6.312
3	44.736	34.368	32.064
4		139.264	397.2

The numerology and granularity of the PDH transmission systems is an important practical matter because the majority of the available private line circuits are of this type. A stand-alone 64-kbps circuit primarily exists within a higher multiplex level. North American convention also refers to a 64-kbps circuit as a DS0. Some carriers in North America offer a 56-kbps Digital Data Service (DDS), which is not related to the PDH hierarchy at all, but is a modulation scheme employed over twisted pairs connecting a network node directly to a customer. Of course PDH supports 56-kbps transmission by using 7 out of 8 bits in a time slot. Some equipment uses the eighth bit in a scheme called *robbed-bit signaling*. Historically, carriers also provided analog private lines over which enterprise customers could connect analog modems for digital data communications.

Synchronous Digital Hierarchy (SDH) Circuits

PDH allowed equipment manufacturers to achieve high transmission rates at lower cost by reducing the amount of electronics that operated at high speeds. However, this multiplexing increased the amount of network equipment. For example, in order to add or drop out lower level signals in the hierarchy, equipment had to demultiplex to successively lower levels in the PDH hierarchy, add or drop signals at that site, and then multiplex everything back together again for transmission to the next site. A long-distance private line traversing multiple sites required a significant amount of electronics at each intermediate site in addition to the switching required at the endpoints. As the performance of electronics improved, engineers devised a better solution. Called the Synchronous Optical Network (SONET) [ANSI T1.105] in North America and the Synchronous Digital Hierarchy (SDH) [ITU G.707] in the rest of the world, this evolution of the TDM technology required distribution of a highly accurate clock. In return, equipment could directly pull out and insert lower-rate signals and avoid the expensive intermediate levels of electronic multiplexing that PDH required.

Table 2.2 lists the commonly encountered SONET and SDH bit rates utilized in service provider network backbones, which are also available as a private line service in industrialized parts of the world [Goralski 97]. The North American SONET hierarchy defines the format of the TDM frame as a Synchronous Transport Signal (STS) and the optical characteristics of the signal via the Optical Carrier (OC) designation. The levels increase by a factor of 4 after the OC-3 level. The ITU-T designates levels of its hierarchy using Synchronous Transfer Module (STM). Although the SDH STM-N

Table 2.2 Commonly Encountered SONET and SDH Bit Rates

NORTH AMERICAN SONET	ITU-T SDH	BIT RATE (MBPS)
STS-1/OC-1	—	51.84
STS-3/OC-3	STM-1	155.52
STS-12/OC-12	STM-4	622.08
STS-48/OC-48	STM-16	2488.32
STS-192/OC-192	STM-64	9953.28

bit rate corresponds exactly to SONET's STS-3N bit rate, as shown in Table 2.2, these signals are not entirely compatible due to differences in the standards that define the meaning and use of the overhead fields.

SONET and SDH define mappings in support of the legacy PDH bit rates, albeit somewhat inefficiently in some cases. Hence, a carrier with a SONET or SDH network can support not only new high-speed private line services, but all of the old PDH rates as well. SONET and SDH networks have some additional benefits. For example, SONET/SDH rings automatically detect faults and restore within 50 milliseconds or less. Also, the performance monitoring capabilities of SONET/SDH are excellent.

An additional benefit widely used in service provider IP and ATM backbones stems from the fact that this TDM multiplexing technology allows devices to utilize approximately 97 percent of the line bit rate as a serial bit stream. Called a *concatenated payload* and designated as either STS-Nc or OC-Nc in SONET, this is the backbone transmission technology of choice for large private networks and public service providers.

Pricing Structure for Private Line Services

Dominant public carriers in the United States must file tariffs with the Federal Communications Commission (FCC). Public carriers in the United States began offering DS1 private line services only in the middle 1980s. Prior to that time, only analog private lines or 56-kbps digital private lines were available. The charges for a private line are made up of components from the Inter eXchange Carrier (IXC) and the Local Exchange Carrier (LEC) [Pecar 93]. Figure 2.2 illustrates a private line from enterprise site 1 to enterprise site 2. Starting from the left-hand side, the LEC provides the connection from enterprise site 1 to the closest Point of Presence (PoP) defined in the tariff, which has a distance of L1 local miles. The next leg of the private line connects LEC PoP 1 to the closest IXC PoP 1, which has a distance of A1 access miles, so that the distance for the access circuit is L1 + A1 miles. As shown in the figure, the long-distance portion of the private line traverses LD miles from IXC PoP 1 to IXC PoP 2. A similar access arrangement connects IXC PoP 2 to enterprise site 2 via LEC PoP 2.

LECs charge a fixed and mileage-based fee for the private line. With the advent of competition and increased deployment driven by VPNs and Internet access, local private line charges have declined significantly over the last decade. For a DS1, local access charges are typically $300 to $600 per month plus $20 to $40 per mile per month in major metropolitan areas. Usually, there is also a nonrecurring installation charge for a DS1 on the order of $1,000. Long-distance charges levied by an IXC often have a fixed and mileage-sensitive component as well. Some carriers base the charges on city pairs [AT&T 94]. After falling precipitously—as much as 70 percent—after divestiture [Insight 96; Coffman 98], long-distance private line prices have been relatively stable over the past five years. In fact, the price has been increasing slowly since 1994 due to high demand. Typical IXC DS1 prices are $4 per mile per month plus a monthly fixed charge of $3,000 [Leida 98]. Typical IXC DS3 prices are approximately $50 per mile per month plus a monthly fixed charge of $22,000 [Leida 98].

Because monopoly public carriers were the first to offer private line services, the prices, commonly called *tariffs*, are regulated by government agencies in many countries. With the introduction of competition, prices can be 20 to 40 percent lower wherever a competing service is available. Also, as is the case with many things in the business world, an enterprise that purchases large amounts of private line service can receive significant discounts for multiple-year contracts.

Researching and analyzing private line tariffs is a challenging task. You can either do this directly from the tariffs filed by carriers with the FCC at www.fcc.gov or pay a tariff research and analysis service such as the Center for Communications Management Information at www.ccmi.com. The

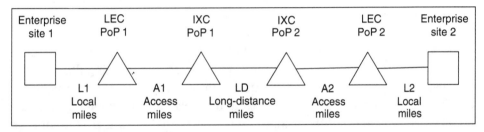

Figure 2.2   Tariff elements for a U.S. private line circuit.

foregoing figures are indicative of prices at the time of publication. Your enterprise may actually have to pay more or less, depending on geographic region, the precise location of enterprise sites, traffic volume, and the degree of competition in the local area.

Capacity and Cost Granularity of Private Lines

Although private lines provide the basic infrastructure for all of the VPN technologies described in this book, they have some significant disadvantages that newer techniques resolve. First, the rigid TDM hierarchy provides extremely coarse increments of capacity. For example, in North America the commonly available increments of capacity are a DS1 at 1.5 Mbps and a DS3 at approximately 45 Mbps. Whereas the DS3 bit rate is about 30 times that of a DS1, the cost ratio is only a factor of 5 to 10 times larger. Similarly, the OC3 bit rate is more than 100 times that of a DS1, but the cost ratio is only a factor of 10 to 20 times larger. In an analogous manner, the DS1 bit is 24 times that of a DS0, but the cost ratio is only a factor of 2 to 4 times larger. In response to the coarse granularity of the TDM hierarchy, the industry has developed inverse multiplexing technologies that combine DS0s into an aggregate bundle up to the capacity of an entire DS1 or E1 or that combine DS1s and E1s into an aggregate capacity of 12 to 16 Mbps. However, a nxDS1 or nxE1 multiplexer costs approximately $5,000. This additional equipment increases the effective cost of the private line. Even so, an inverse multiplexer may be justified if it defers expensive installation charges of fiber-optic facilities required for a DS3 or a SONET access line.

Figure 2.3 plots the cost per Mbps per mile per month for DS0, DS1, DS3, and OC3 private lines versus the private line bit rate. For a similar analysis applied to international private line tariffs, see McDysan 98a. The message here is clear: If an enterprise has a significant community of interest between two locations that can reasonably fill a high-speed private line, then the unit cost for capacity declines markedly. However, it is important to note that the total cost is the product of the link speed and the mileage times the cost per Mbps per mile per month. Therefore, only enterprises that can fill up high-speed private lines can reap this economic benefit. Because the TDM hierarchy is quite coarse, optimizing the cost of a private enterprise network with such granular capacity increments and different cost structures is a challenging network design problem. In fact, it is a theme throughout the remainder of this book that this private line

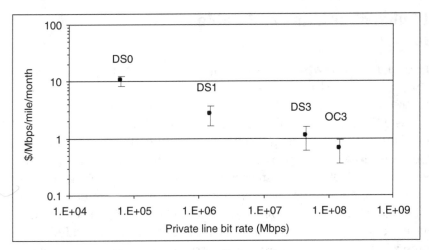

Figure 2.3 Private line unit cost versus line speed.

price structure that effectively provides bulk discounts is a fundamental economic driver for VPNs. This occurs because a VPN service provider can lease high-speed private lines or construct its own transmission facilities at a fraction of the cost that most enterprises could.

TDM technology allocates transmission capacity on a dedicated basis regardless of the actual traffic patterns. Some estimates place the utilization of private lines averaged over an entire week at only 3 to 5 percent [Odlyzko 98]. Of course, utilization during the busiest hour in an entire month may be as high as 50 to 70 percent. Typical of many enterprises is the fact that the busy hours in the late morning and the early afternoon during the business week comprise approximately 15 percent of the daily traffic. Most network designs address peak-hour demand, hence the low utilization when averaged over a week. Telephone network companies attempt to fill up their facilities by offering evening and weekend discounts to increase overall long-term-average utilization. In a similar vein, cost-conscious enterprises try to batch up data backups and large transfers to achieve similar economic benefits.

Finally, the provisioning of TDM private lines is at best a partially automated process in most carrier networks. Often, the coordination for ordering, configuring, and testing the various segments of a private line involves a significant amount of manual activities. Carriers must recover these costs via higher prices. Newer packet-switching technologies automate some of these manual processes which result in a more favorable overall cost structure.

Digital Subscriber Lines and Cable Modems

There are over 1 billion twisted pairs of copper wires entering buildings around the world today. Up until the late 1990s, these wires supported a maximum transmission speed of 56 kbps for analog modems or 128 kbps for ISDN Basic Rate Interface (BRI) service. With the advent of Digital Subscriber Line (DSL) technologies, much higher speeds are available for enterprises close to a service provider's PoP. Called xDSL for short, where x denotes the type of DSL as summarized in Table 2.3 [ADSL Forum; Tele-Choice xDSL], DSL technology utilizes state-of-the-art modem design to squeeze the maximum capacity out of the existing twisted-pair telephone lines. These technologies use one or more pairs of wires as indicated in the table. Some xDSL technologies are asymmetric, that is, the uplink speed and downlink speed may differ. The uplink is the direction from the subscriber to the network, while the downlink is the direction from the network to the subscriber. An asymmetric configuration is useful for applications like Web browsing, where the bulk of information transfer is in the downlink direction. However, most enterprise sites will require sym-

Table 2.3 Digital Subscriber Line (DSL) Terminology and Speeds

ACRONYM	FULL NAME	TWISTED PAIRS	UPLINK SPEED	DOWNLINK SPEED
HDSL (DS1)	High data rate Digital Subscriber Line	2	1.544 Mbps	1.544 Mbps
HDSL (E1)	High data rate Digital Subscriber Line	3	2.048 Mbps	2.048 Mbps
SDSL (DS1)	Single line Digital Subscriber Line	1	1.544 Mbps	1.544 Mbps
SDSL (E1)	Single line Digital Subscriber Line	1	2.048 Mbps	2.048 Mbps
CDSL	Consumer Digital Subscriber Line	1	64 to 384 kbps	384 kbps to 1.5 Mbps
ADSL	Asymmetric Digital Subscriber Line	1	16 to 640 kbps	1.5 to 9 Mbps
VDSL	Very high data rate Digital Subscriber Line	1	1.5 to 2.3 Mbps	13 to 52 Mbps

metric capacity. As seen from Table 2.3, xDSL achieves capacities that are an order of magnitude greater than the legacy analog modem and ISDN BRI access technologies using existing twisted pairs. There is a catch. Your enterprise must be no more than a few miles away from the service provider's PoP, because the achievable speed with DSL is inversely proportional to the distance.

The economics of xDSL are attractive, with charges ranging from $40 per month for a 384-kbps downlink to $120 for a 6-Mbps downlink. The xDSL modem costs between $200 and $400, and there is a $100 installation charge. The prices for symmetric services range from $100 for a 384-kbps link to $300 per month for a 1.5-Mbps link. Many carriers price the High data rate Digital Subscriber Line (HDSL) service at DS1 tariff levels. In areas with competition, HDSL effectively lowers the private line access charge by as much as 50 percent. Rates vary by geographic area and service provider and are not yet in equilibrium. In larger metropolitan areas, you may have a choice of service providers because regulators have unbundled the copper loop service, thus allowing competing carriers to offer xDSL service. Surf the Web. Many xDSL service providers advertise their prices on line.

Another alternative access technology uses the television cable plant [Medin 99]. Typically, cable modems operate at speeds ranging from 10 to 30 Mbps in the downstream direction, shared between all subscribers on that portion of the cable plant. This presents some security challenges for protecting sensitive data, because anyone can attach equipment and receive transmissions destined for subscribers on that portion of the cable network. It can also create congestion and low performance during periods of peak usage due to the need to share the downstream capacity. The bandwidth-limited and electrically complex upstream channel in today's cable networks remains a major barrier to realization of cable modem access for enterprises. Also, most office buildings do not have coaxial cable wiring, the necessary transport medium. Most experts believe that cable modem access targets primarily the residential market or the telecommuter. However secured cable modem access for telecommuters in an enterprise is an important access alternative.

Data access via cable modems may become the twenty-first century regulatory equivalent of telecommunications deregulation in the 1980s. In many parts of the world, the cable television operator has a geographic monopoly and is already regulated. Early experience indicates that where the cable operator offers cable modem service bundled with Internet access, other ISPs demand equal access via cable modem. In any event, competition between cable modem and xDSL technologies should inevitably benefit the enterprise through lower access charges.

Satellite and Wireless Media

Of course, some enterprises have sites in remote locations that are not close to carrier PoPs. In this case, other transmission media can provide cost-effective access. Satellite communications provide connectivity to almost any point in the world. Examples of enterprises with remote locations are natural resource exploration, military maneuvers, and expeditions into nonindustrialized parts of the world. Sometimes satellite communication makes sense as a backup media for highly reliable applications. The round-trip propagation delay of over 250 milliseconds with geosynchronous satellites makes interactive communication difficult, but it is acceptable for many data applications.

A more recent technology is fixed wireless access [Skoro 99]. These solutions can provide relatively high capacity to sites that cannot cost justify the installation of optical fiber. Because of limited radio frequency spectrum allocation, the total capacity in a particular geographic area is limited. We discuss this technology in greater depth in Chapter 10, *The Future of VPNs*.

Private Voice Networks

Beginning in the 1970s, many enterprises effectively built their own telephone networks to avoid expensive public telephone network charges for calls made between enterprise sites. This section outlines the technologies that enabled private voice networks and discusses the business drivers that drove large enterprises into the telephone network business.

Private Branch Exchanges (PBXes)

A Private Branch eXchange (PBX) is essentially a small telephone switch. The name derives from the fact that the PBX is effectively a branch of the public network. For example, a typical PBX may have a three- or four-digit internal dialing plan, with these digits corresponding to the last digits of the public telephone number. This type of numbering plan allows enterprise employees connected to a PBX network to call each other with abbreviated dialing while allowing people from outside to call in using the public numbering plan.

Typically, a PBX would have a set of access lines connected to the public telephone network and tie trunks to other PBXes in a private voice network, as illustrated in Figure 2.4. A *trunk group* is the telephony term for a set of circuits. The access lines connected to the local public network pro-

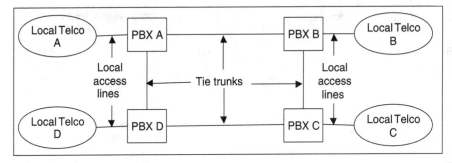

Figure 2.4   A typical private voice network.

vide local telephone calls, while the PBX routes calls destined for other enterprise sites over the tie trunks via dedicated private lines. Historically, the private network lowered long-distance charges significantly by routing calls to the closest serving PBX and paying only the local charges. After divestiture in 1984, the charges for leased lines decreased more rapidly than the cost of long-distance service. As a result, many enterprises constructed their own private voice and data networks.

Advances in electronics enabled cost-effective digital switching, and the Carterfone Act of 1968 allowed enterprises to connect equipment from competing manufacturers to the monopoly telephone network in the United States. Government deregulation and technology enabled competition for PBXes, which then spread to competition for telephone switch technology within the telephone networks themselves. It is important to note that the cost of the switching hardware was only 25 percent of a PBX; the remaining 75 percent of the costs were for software [Chorofas 90]. This is because PBXes support a broad range of sophisticated telephony services not supported by the public telephone network.

Cost Savings of Private Voice Networks

The principal savings that a private voice network achieved in the 1970s was reduced costs for long-distance calls between enterprise sites and for long-distance calls to the public network destinations within the enterprise's local calling area. With the impact of competition evident by the later 1980s the price of long-distance calls declined markedly. With this decline, the economic benefit of the tie trunk network diminished and stimulated the move toward voice VPNs.

The simple example shown in Figure 2.5 illustrates the economic trade-off involved in the deployment of private voice networks. We assume that

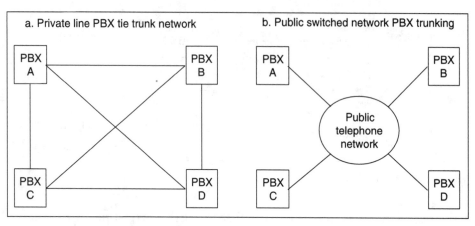

Figure 2.5   Tie trunk and switched PBX trunking.

the offered voice traffic is uniform between all sites, with an average of C calls in progress. Telephone engineers express the offered load in units of Erlangs, which is the average number of voice calls in progress. Figure 2.5a shows a network of four PBXes connected via private line tie trunks. Figure 2.5b depicts a network of the same four PBXes, each with a single access line group connected to the public telephone network. In the following we consider the general problem for an N node network where the private line network is fully meshed.

The most important quality aspect of voice network design is the blocking probability. Given the offered load of C Erlangs in the busy hour, telephone engineers use the Erlang-B formula $B(T,C)$ to size the number of circuits T required in a trunk group to meet the blocking probability objective [Kleinrock 75; McDysan 00]. A good approximation for a blocking probability on the order of 1 percent is $T \approx C + \sqrt{C}$ [McDysan 00]. For the private network case shown in Figure 2.5a, we assume that the price of each private line is $\$2L$ per month. That is, the combined costs of both access circuits equals the long-haul circuit cost. For both private and public network cases, we assume that the price of purchasing, installing, and operating each PBX port over the lifetime of the network is $\$P$ per month. Note that two PBX ports are necessary, one for each end of the tie trunk. Therefore, the overall cost of an N-node, fully meshed private line network with C Erlangs offered between each site is approximately as follows:

$$\$C_{PL} = N(N-1)\ T[2\$L + 2\$P]/2 \approx N(N-1)[C + \sqrt{C}][2\$L + 2\$P]/2$$

For the switched network case of Figure 2.5b, we must convert the busy hour traffic of C Erlangs into monthly minutes of use. Assuming that the busy hour comprises approximately ⅙ of the daily traffic and that an enterprise uses the voice network 5 days a week for 4 weeks in a month, this results in an average monthly usage of $M = 7,200$ minutes per Erlang between each pair of sites. The switched network still incurs the charges for PBX ports, but only requires the access line portion of the private line charge. Furthermore, since only one trunk group is required to access the public network, the economy of scale predicted by the Erlang-B formula means that only $N(N - 1)C$ ports are necessary when the number of sites N is large. Assuming that long-distance telephone service costs $\$S$ per minute, the monthly charges for the switched network case is approximately:

$$\$C_{SW} \approx N(N - 1)\ C\left[M\ \$S + 2\ \$P + \$L\right]/2$$

We now have an economic criterion on which to base a decision on whether to use a private line or a circuit-switched PBX trunk network design. That is, if the ratio $\$C_{PL}/\$C_{SW}$ is less than 1, then the private line solution is less expensive; otherwise the switched solution is cheaper. Forming this ratio from the preceding equations yields the following result:

$$\$C_{PL}/\$C_{SW} \approx \{1 + 1/\sqrt{C}\}\ \{(\$L + \$P)/(M/\$S/2 + \$P + \$L/2)\}$$

The first term in this formula represents the economy of scale achieved by the switched network over the private network as a function of the traffic C offered between each pair of sites. Note how this term approaches unity as C increases. The second term is the normalized cost Erlang for the private line solution divided by the public network cost, which we designate as the ratio X. Figure 2.6 plots the ratio $\$C_{PL}/\$C_{SW}$ against the offered intersite traffic C for several values of cost ratio X. The crossover point that justifies the cost of a private line between sites occurs when the value of the ratio $\$C_{PL}/\$C_{SW}$ becomes less than 1, as indicated by the horizontal line on the chart. The crossover point indicates the minimum amount of traffic C an enterprise must have between a pair of sites to economically justify the costs of a private line and the cost of purchasing and operating the additional PBX ports required to achieve the desired blocking probability.

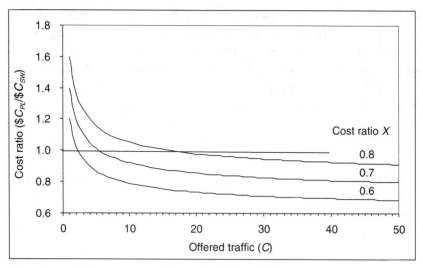

Figure 2.6   Private versus switched—decision criterion.

Extending the preceding analysis to partially meshed networks with nonuniform traffic requires a network design tool and an engineer who knows how to use it. In the 1970s and 1980s, many enterprises chose to take on this additional effort because communication costs were relatively high. With the introduction of circuit-switched VPNs in the mid-1980s, the cost ratio X increased and enterprises shifted their traffic to voice VPN services, as we'll discuss in Chapter 3, *Circuit-Switched VPNs*. In the 1990s, the availability of connection-oriented frame relay and ATM VPNs that delivered guaranteed capacity at a QoS level that supported voice effectively drove the cost ratio X down again, motivating enterprises to connect their PBXes via virtual tie trunks. Finally, the emergence of QoS-aware IP network services will likely drive the cost ratio down even further, motivating enterprises to install voice over IP technology. Furthermore, as we shall see, the capabilities supported by these newer VPN technologies are more flexible and have additional economic benefits.

Additional Benefits and Offsetting Expenses

An enterprise that takes on the business of being its own telephone company does achieve cost savings, as shown in the preceding section, as well as other benefits, but it also incurs some additional expenses. Enterprises achieve a number of additional benefits from their PBX-based networks. The principal benefit is the rich feature set offered by the PBX itself. Features include calling party identification, conference calling, voice mail, camp-on, callback, speed dialing, and many other productivity-enhancing capabilities.

As far as expenses go, the following are the principal expenses involved in running a private voice network. First, the enterprise must hire and retain staff for operations, troubleshooting, network planning, and augmentation as well as to support moves, adds, and changes. Second, the enterprise must purchase, maintain, and upgrade the PBX hardware and software. Finally, the enterprise must carefully manage the network design to minimize private line charges and thus obtain the economic benefit. An overprovisioned tie trunk network can actually cost more than switched long-distance voice service.

Integrated Services Digital Network (ISDN)

The International Telecomunications Union (ITU), formerly known as the Consultative Committee for International Telegraphy and Telecommunications (CCITT) began standardizing the Integrated Services Digital Network (ISDN) in the early 1970s. Targeting simultaneous support for voice, fixed image, and data, ISDN built upon the circuit-switched telephony paradigm to dynamically establish connections with capacity doled out in increments of the basic 64-kbps time slot of the TDM hierarchy. The principal focus of standards activity was that of developing a comprehensive signaling protocol. Intended to place features and capabilities in the public network instead of in customer equipment, the CCITT labored for many years before producing the first set of comprehensive standards. Unfortunately, these standards were the result of some compromises, which required other bodies to select from the options presented in the CCITT recommendations. Furthermore, because the standard took so long to develop, the leading PBX manufacturers all had their own proprietary implementations by the time the standard eventually emerged.

PBX manufacturers implemented ISDN and proprietary extensions that supported data switching for interconnection of PCs during the 1980s. Enterprises tried these solutions, but found them difficult to configure and expensive to use. During this same time, competing local area network technologies emerged and overshadowed the ISDN-based integrated voice data PBX. We describe these competing technologies in the next section.

The standard ISDN protocol suite allowed transport of proprietary information elements in the signaling messages to support vendor-specific features. ISDN enables the potential for a much richer feature set than the transmission of tones between PBXes, and this justifies the additional complexity of the signaling protocol. Users adopted ISDN on a broader scale in Europe and other industrialized parts of the world than they did in the United States. Part of the reason for this difference in adoption patterns was higher private line prices and lack of competition in Europe compared to the United States. The ISDN 128-kbps Basic Rate Interface (BRI) actually experienced something of a renaissance in the mid-1990s as an early high-performance access technology. Now, the faster and less expensive xDSL technology displaces the deployment of ISDN BRI.

Private Data Networks

This section summarizes the background of the early data networks that were entirely private since no public data service was available. Enterprises first constructed these networks in the late 1960s to connect terminals in remote locations to expensive mainframe computers. As the cost of computing declined, the need to interconnect mainframes arose. Starting in the mid-1980s, the adoption of the personal computer and local area networking by enterprises created a need to distribute computing and databases, which precipitated the development of another type of private data network. The rapid development of this technology resulted in the deployment of a number of incompatible protocols, which created a market for multiprotocol routers. The adoption of the Internet protocol suite as the de facto industry standard is the latest chapter in the continuing saga of private data networks. However, some of the tactics taken by enterprises in deploying private IP-based networks present additional challenges for IP-based VPNs.

Mainframe Computers and Early Data Networks

In the 1970s, computers were expensive. The hardware and software developed by International Business Machines (IBM) were the de facto standard. An enterprise might have only one large mainframe computer located at its headquarters. Furthermore, most of the data was text based. Initially, the terminals worked only a line at a time, which required messages of between 1 and 80 characters. Full-screen terminals had 24 lines of 80 characters, that only require 1,920 bytes of data to represent. For comparison purposes, a 640×480 display with 256 colors requires over 300,000 bytes of data to represent. The data communication bit rate requirements of the character-oriented terminals were quite modest. For example, 300 or 1200 bps modems were commonly used for dial-in access. Analog modems operating at 2.4 to 9.6 kbps over analog private lines satisfied branch office requirements supporting multiple terminals, while 56-kbps links supported those sites requiring higher capacity. Furthermore, analog lines allowed implementation of a shared media topology. Modems at a number of sites tapped onto an analog line and the head-end controller polled each site in round-robin fashion to share the expensive analog line. For the typical low-volume, intermittent-terminal-to-mainframe traffic, this level of performance was adequate.

A tree network constructed from private lines with multidrop analog lines at the periphery as shown in Figure 2.7 was a commonly employed topology in private data networks of the 1970s [Cypser 78]. Starting at the top of the figure, one or more mainframe hosts at the central computing site are connected to one or more communication controllers, which are also referred to as Front-End Processors (FEPs). The communication link between the mainframe and the FEP was a high-speed proprietary electrical channel that transferred characters between the devices. Terminals could be connected directly to the communication controllers, but most terminals were connected to *cluster controllers* that interfaced to the FEPs via digital private lines or via modems operating over analog private lines at speeds of up to 56 kbps. Terminals could have local connections to these cluster controllers, or they could be connected via an analog multidrop line modem, indicated by an *M* inside a box in the figure. This hierarchy collected data from and disseminated data to the distributed terminal devices, which included printers, card readers, and magnetic tape drives along with dumb cathode ray displays and keyboards.

By the 1980s, the advances in electronics and increased use of computing in enterprises created the need to interconnect mainframe hosts at multiple sites. IBM developed a Systems Network Architecture (SNA) that provided a data communications framework allowing enterprises to build large distributed networks by segmenting a larger network into multiple domains [Cypser 78; Tannenbaum 81]. Figure 2.8 illustrates the concept of domains used to build large SNA networks. The basic hierarchy exists within each domain, focused around the mainframe host, except when drawn in this way, it looks like a star instead of a tree. Over time, the advent of cost-effective minicomputers, workstations and PCs drove networks away from this mainframe host-centric architecture toward a distributed network design.

SNA supported higher communication link speeds to support larger numbers of terminal devices and graphics-capable terminals. This required

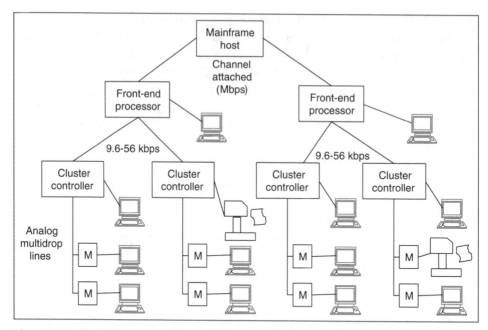

Figure 2.7 Typical 1970s mainframe data network.

improved protocols to route data between the hosts and terminal devices. The solution chosen by IBM designers was called *explicit routing.* Interestingly, token ring LANs, ATM networks, and emerging QoS-aware IP network routing algorithms all utilize the concept of explicit routing as a basis for establishing communication paths. SNA also defined a means to effectively aggregate a number of lower-speed links into a single logical communication link using a protocol called a *transmission group,* as illustrated in Figure 2.8. A similar concept occurs in frame relay, ATM, and IP protocols to combine multiple lower-speed links into one higher-speed aggregate. Another important data communications protocol concept pioneered by SNA was that of flow control, which IBM called *pacing.* This ensured that a high-speed device like a mainframe capable of transmitting at Mbps would not overrun a slow-speed device like a remote printer.

IBM's competitors tried to standardize a similar set of computer communication capabilities in the International Standards Organization (ISO) beginning in the 1970s. The resulting seven-layer computer communications model for Open Systems Interconnection (OSI) is well known but not widely adopted by the industry. In fact, the most widely implemented part of the protocol is the X.25 protocol suite, which we summarize in Chapter 4, *Early Connection-Oriented Data VPNs—X.25 and Frame Relay.* Although the specific protocol layers defined by the OSI model have in

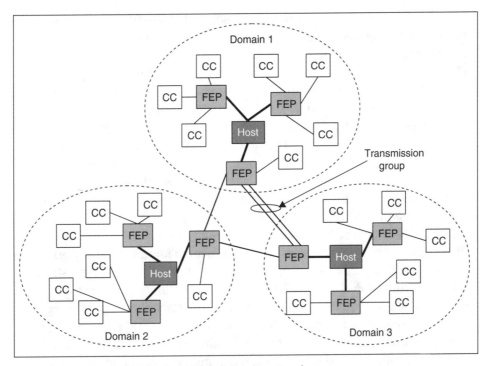

Figure 2.8   1980s multiple domain mainframe network.

large part not been adopted, the concept of protocol layering, originally developed in ARPANET research in the 1970s, is used in every modern data communications protocol.

As testament to these protocols designed by IBM, many corporations still utilize SNA networks for their mission-critical applications in the twenty-first century. Indeed, a significant challenge for VPNs is how well they match the reliability and stability of the current SNA-based private enterprise data networks.

Advent of PCs and Local Area Networks

With IBM's endorsement of the Personal Computer (PC) in 1982, enterprises began purchasing these machines as cheaper, multipurpose mainframe terminals, but more important, as stand-alone computing devices. As the number of applications grew and the associated databases contained an increasing wealth of information, enterprises needed to interconnect PCs to each other. Furthermore, peripherals like high-quality printers and large-capacity disk drives were expensive, and therefore enterprises had significant economic motivation to share these expensive resources. This was the business environment that drove the development and deployment of Local Area Networks (LANs).

Ethernet is by far the dominant LAN protocol used in enterprises today due to its low cost. Other protocols encountered in LANs are 4- or 16-Mbps token ring (first introduced by IBM), a 100-Mbps Fiber Distributed Data Interface (FDDI), and ATM-based LAN backbones [Saunders 96]. Token ring is often encountered in SNA environments. ATM LAN backbones are also being installed, because they offer superior traffic management capabilities in comparison with other LAN technologies. However, with the addition of QoS and traffic management capabilities to the Ethernet Standard, the need for ATM LAN backbones is diminishing.

Enterprise decisions to purchase and deploy PCs and LANs occurred outside the purview of the traditional mainframe Management Information Systems (MIS) organizations. Several factors drove this paradigm shift. First, the costs of PCs and LAN equipment fit within departmental budgets and hence did not require MIS approvals. Furthermore, these PC networks were initially justified as stand-alone systems that would not connect with the mainframes. Thus, an early shared-medium Ethernet LAN looked like the configuration shown in Figure 2.9. A number of PCs connect to the shared Ethernet media. Also connected to the Ethernet are a printer and a file server. Although the 10-Mbps shared Ethernet medium could run only at 30 to 40 percent load due to the operation of the Carrier Sense Multiple Access/Collision Detection (CSMA/CD) protocol, applications running on most PCs during the early days of LANs did not require a significant amount of capacity.

THE BIRTH OF LOCAL AREA NETWORKING

Dr. Robert M. Metcalfe and David Boggs invented Ethernet in 1973 at SRI International. Ethernet used the concepts of communication broadcast and collision detection pioneered in the ALOHA system, which was deployed to implement radio communication in the Hawaiian islands [Tannenbaum 96]. A multivendor consortium of DEC, Intel, and Xerox (abbreviated DIX) delivered the first Ethernet products in 1981. The DIX Ethernet specification defined operation at 10 Mbps over a 50-ohm coaxial cable, also called *thick Ethernet*. The term *Ether* refers to the broadcast media composed of a coaxial cable with "vampire" taps connecting each station. The IEEE refined the proprietary DIX standard, resulting in the adoption of the IEEE 802.3 standard. Related Ethernet standards define a common Media Access Control (MAC) protocol operating at 10, 100, and 1,000 Mbps over a variety of electrical and optical physical media.

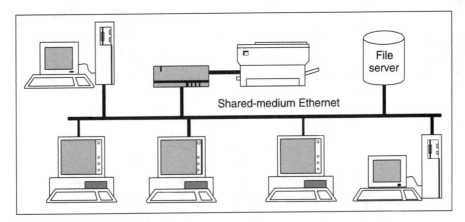

Shared-medium Ethernet

File server

Figure 2.9   Single segment local area network.

As the number of devices connected to a single LAN grew and the use of PCs exploded, the need to segment a single LAN to provide acceptable performance developed. At the same time, the need to interconnect LANs in order to share information across various departments arose. Furthermore, enterprises could improve productivity and reduce costs by interconnecting LANs to mainframe applications. In fact, a PC running 3270 emulation became a cost-effective, multipurpose replacement for the traditional mainframe terminal. In response to these business drivers, computer manufacturers invented proprietary solutions to interconnect computers on LANs using a technique called *bridging* [Perlman 92]. Bridges are a type of plug-and-play network device that interconnects LANs and, as a result, extends LAN reach and capacity. A bridged LAN connected many PCs to shared resources like file servers, printers, and gateways to mainframes, as illustrated in Figure 2.10. As PCs and LANs increased in importance, enterprises required that bridges support multiple communication paths so that any single failure would not result in a loss of connectivity. In addition, a translation bridge could connect dissimilar LAN technologies; for example, a bridge interconnects the token ring in the upper right-hand corner of Figure 2.10 to Ethernet LANs in other parts of the network.

Ethernet bridges utilized a Spanning Tree Protocol (STP) defined by IEEE standard 802.1D [IEEE 802.1D]. The STP technique met the plug-and-play objective, but at a cost. The protocol required bridges to exchange information about their neighbors, then automatically selected a tree topology rooted at the node with the lowest numerical bridge identifier. Unfortunately, all traffic flows up toward the root and then back down the tree if necessary until it reaches the STP-designated bridge serving the des-

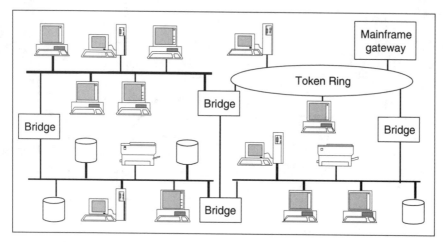

Figure 2.10   Bridged LANs and mainframe gateways.

tination LAN. In this way, STP prevents bridging loops. This worked fine in local networks where capacity was inexpensive; however, it could not make efficient use of expensive, wide area, private line capacity because the logical tree topology did not utilize all available links.

Multiprotocol Data Networking

The adoption of PCs and the deployment of LANs occurred at a breakneck pace in the 1980s. Although the IEEE standardized lower-layer protocols, the network-layer protocols necessary to make shared resources, like disk drives and printers, available to the PC user were the province of a number of competing manufacturers. In order to fill this need, a number of companies developed networking protocols to meet it, such as Novell Netware and BANYAN Vines. Unfortunately, LANs using different network-layer protocols could not work with each other. To further compound matters, the ISO had defined the ConnectionLess Network Protocol (CLNP), and the Internet Engineering Task Force (IETF) had defined the Internet Protocol (IP). The resulting zoo of network-layer protocols created the need for another type of device, which we know today as the *multiprotocol router.*

The commercialization of the multiprotocol router is largely attributed to Cisco Systems Corporation. Furthermore, the multiprotocol router overcame some of the performance issues with bridging by supporting a variety of Wide Area Network (WAN) protocols like X.25, ISDN, frame relay, or ATM. Figure 2.11 illustrates how routers interconnect LANs as well as different enterprise sites. Multiprotocol routers interwork seamlessly with

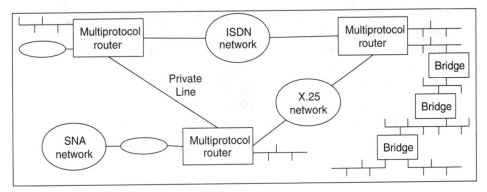

Figure 2.11   A simple private routed internetwork.

bridged networks, as shown in the right-hand side of the figure. Further-more, a router can send traffic over paths determined by a simple shortest-path routing protocol, which means that a router can balance traffic across available link layer connections better than a bridged protocol can.

These multiprotocol routers allowed devices connected to different net-works to interwork. We usually call such configurations an *internetwork*, or *internet* with a lowercase *i* for short. This differs from the public Internet with an uppercase *I*, which is the public service offered by the partial mesh of interconnected ISPs that provide access to the Web, deliver Email, and the like. Traditionally, multiprotocol router implementations employed general-purpose computers to process the header fields in each protocol to internet-work a wide range of ever changing protocols. The price-performance of such general purpose routers was worse than specialized machines employ-ing utilized special-purpose hardware optimized for a small set of specific protocols. Fortunately, IP has become the de facto standard, and the need for flexible software-based multiprotocol routing has diminished. This adop-tion of IP as the de facto standard has allowed router manufacturers to opti-mize their hardware designs for IP and, in turn, deliver machines with continually improving price-performance ratios.

Some enterprises face additional challenges when using the Internet for historical reasons. Instead of getting a unique IP address, many enterprises are assigned nonunique IP addresses. A 4-byte IP version 4 address is writ-ten down using a dotted decimal as A.B.C.D, where each position is a deci-mal number between 0 and 255 representing 8 bits of the address. In fact, some computing equipment comes with the default IP network address configured as network 10 (which was the address originally assigned to the ARPANET), that is, the IP address is of the form 10.*.*.*, where an asterisk (*) indicates any number between 0 and 255. A number of enterprises configured their IP addresses with these nonunique addresses because they believed that their network would always be private. When an enterprise wants to connect to the public Internet and still use these private addresses additional protocol support is necessary. Either Network Address Translation (NAT), as described in Chapter 7, *Building Blocks for IP-based VPNs*, or network-based VPN support, as described in Chapter 9, *IP Security-Enabled and Routing-Controlled VPNs*, can meet this need.

CHAPTER

3

Circuit-Switched VPNs

**Well, if I called the wrong number,
why did you answer the phone?**
—James Thurber

When Thurber posed this quip in a 1937 cartoon there was no caller ID service available. At that time, tracing a telephone call was a time-consuming procedure. The telephone network has changed markedly since then. This chapter describes the business drivers, technology enablers, protocols, architecture, and applications of circuit-switched VPNs, which were first introduced in the United States in the mid-1980s. These networks used circuit-switching protocols and the emerging technology of real-time transaction processing to reduce the cost of feature-rich voice communications below the break-even point that enterprises could achieve by building their own networks. Later, telephone companies offered similar services in local areas as well. Interestingly, the latest wave of circuit-switched VPNs entered Europe almost a decade later. A sophisticated set of intelligent network standards promises to extend VPN and other advanced circuit-switched features across multiple carrier networks. Although these services may seem rather old, one of the latest waves of VPNs, voice and multimedia over IP networks, strives to provide a similar set of capabilities using a similar architecture.

Business Drivers

Several regulatory and business factors drove carriers to develop VPN services for voice. These included lower prices for circuit-switched telephone calls, the unforeseen operational and management expenses of running a private telephone network, and the need for enterprise employees to access private network voice services from locations that were not on the network.

Impact of Deregulation and Competition

The division of AT&T into a long-distance company and seven Baby Bells had a profound impact on the cost structure of long-distance telephone calls. In 1983, a long-distance call between New York and Chicago during the business day cost $0.20 per minute. In 1984, the regulations resulting from the divestiture of AT&T split the charges for a long-distance call into three components: $0.03 on each end for local access, plus the charges for the long-distance portion of the call. In 2000, the total cost of a long-distance call is as low as $0.05 per minute. Around the same time, the charges for a local DS1 circuit declined markedly to approximately $1,000 per month. This pricing structure created a significant motivation for long-distance carriers to offer circuit-switched services to larger enterprise customers via dedicated private line facilities instead of paying the regulation-imposed, expensive, switched-access tariffs.

The deregulation of AT&T in 1984 precipitated the development of voice-oriented VPN services. Introduced as early as 1984, by 1986 AT&T, MCI, and Sprint all had rapidly growing virtual voice network services. Actually, Sprint's service used the acronym for Virtual Private Network (VPN) explicitly; but the industry now uses VPN as a generic term. Inter eXchange Carriers (IXCs) offered the majority of voice VPNs in the 1980s and 1990s. This occurred because most enterprise users had locations in more than one Local Access and Transport Authority (LATA), the geographic area within which regulators restricted a monopoly Local Exchange Carrier (LEC) to operate. Specifically, regulations restricted LECs to providing only intra-LATA services, whereas IXCs could only offer inter-LATA services. A commonly available intra-LATA service based on intelligent network technology is called *Centrex*. As a recurring practice, these regulatory conditions create opportunities for enterprise users and carriers to arbitrage tariffs to their own economic advantage. The process of deregulation temporarily creates these imbalances. However, regulators eventually recognize these situations and either modify regulations or else do away with regulations altogether and let competition decide on the appropriate pricing level. These boundaries will likely fall at some point in the twenty-first century, once the government verifies that LECs have truly opened the local markets to competition. Similar deregulation scenarios are playing out around the world as national governments open the telecommunications market to competition.

Unforeseen Expenses of a Private Network

Many of the initial business scenarios that enterprises developed to justify the deployment of a private voice network failed to take into account administrative, operational, and other expenses involved in keeping a network running. Furthermore, the PBX equipment was relatively new and sometimes required unanticipated upgrades. Enterprises required additional staff to monitor network traffic levels, to carefully scrutinize purchase of leased lines for tie trunk purposes, and to keep close tabs on the number of access circuits connected to the local telephone company. Traffic-engineering and capacity-planning activities are crucial to efficient, high-quality operation of a circuit-switched network. In all too many cases, enterprises never realized the projected cost-saving benefits. In other cases, the quality and blocking performance of a private voice network suffered in order to realize cost savings. For many enterprises, the loss of productivity and delays offset the savings realized by such frugal network design.

Need for Ubiquitous Access

Another increasingly important consideration for enterprises was controlling the cost of traveling personnel who called back to their home offices or other enterprise locations. Before the advent of voice VPNs, the only solution was to make a long-distance call over the public network. The rates charged by hotels for long-distance phone calls were exorbitant in the 1980s, even more so than they are today. In addition, a salesperson hesitated to ask for use of a customer's long-distance service to call the office because of cost. The initial services offered by companies like MCI and Sprint addressed the cost of long-distance service, but required customers to dial up to 24 digits in addition to the called party's number. In return for dialing these additional digits, customers received significant discounts over the prevailing rates. Thus, the marketplace was ripe for a service that allowed off-site enterprise users to call enterprise sites at reduced rates.

Increasing Need for Data Communication

In the 1980s, the ITU-T and various national standards bodies were busily defining the Integrated Services Digital Network (ISDN) that would support circuit-switched services in multiples of the TDM 64-kbps time slot. The economic drive for an enterprise to minimize telecommunication costs became increasingly important as data traffic levels increased. For periods of intermittent use, some enterprises found that a switched circuit was less expensive than a dedicated one.

Heightened Security and Productivity Needs

With the increasing importance of the telephone network in the operation of enterprises around the world, improved security and productivity become pivotal concerns. The possibility of outsiders calling into secure private networks from the public network is one such issue. Fraudulent users have broken into private voice networks and used them to complete free long-distance calls. Another pressing economic concern is controlling access by enterprise callers to expensive 900 or 976 pay-per-minute services, pay-per-use directory services, or unnecessary calls to time- and weather-related numbers. Knowing the identity of the calling party improves productivity by allowing the enterprise employee to more effectively screen calls and decide which to answer and which to route to voice mail. The software features within a PBX provided the means for an enterprise to address many of these issues, albeit in a proprietary manner. However, the public network had to overcome these issues and others in order to provide circuit-switched VPNs to enterprise customers.

Technology Trends and Enablers

Several advances in technology enabled the design and deployment of circuit-switched VPNs in the mid-1980s. These included computerized telephone switches, computers capable of high-performance transaction processing, and reliable data communication protocols.

SECURITY ISSUES IN PUBLIC TELEPHONE NETWORKS

Security has been an issue in the public telephone network for quite some time. Study of these problems is still relevant today because similar security issues have arisen in the Internet. The problems created by a few people abusing public networks is an issue that enterprises must address. Nuisance and threatening calls have long been a problem in the public telephone network due to the anonymity afforded by the traditional difficulty involved in tracing a call. In the mid-1960s, callers with a blue box that emulated the tones used on carrier backbones to signal connections could make free telephone calls [van Bosse 98]. The advent of the calling card in the 1980s created new opportunities for fraud because callers could just try combinations of digits until they found a valid card number. The telephone network has addressed these security issues by using improved signaling protocols, network intelligence, and monitoring customer calling activity for abnormal patterns.

Computerized Telephone Switches

AT&T deployed the first stored program control telephone switches in the mid-1960s. Continual advances and the advent of competition in the telephone switch marketplace ushered in rapid advances in the capacity and capabilities of digital switching systems in the early 1980s. Founded in the 1970s, Northern Telecom (now called Nortel Networks) rapidly advanced to become a major supplier of PBXes and carrier-class telephone switches by the mid-1980s. The increased processing power of these newer switches, magnified in some cases by a distributed processor design, delivered computing power that was heretofore unknown in a telephone network switch. Additionally, the continual decline in the cost of electronic and magnetic disk storage gave each successive switch the capability to offer increasingly sophisticated services. Indeed, some carriers rolled out early voice VPN services, using this additional memory and processing capacity as a "switch-based" VPN. Other carriers exploited the emerging technologies described in the next two sections.

High-Performance Transaction Processing

The mid-1980s saw the maturation of the PC, and ushered in the era of the cost-effective minicomputer that rivaled mainframe performance of only a few years before. The operating system software of some of these machines also enabled the processing of a large volume of transactions, each with subsecond response time. Some of these machines were capable of operating in a distributed environment, providing the inherent capability to scale to thousands of transactions per second. Additionally, the software, and in some cases even the hardware, provided fault-tolerant operation. As we shall see, the superior architecture utilized the increased processing power of telephone switches to conduct query-response transactions with regional high-performance transaction-processing computers. The telecommunications industry dubbed the resulting design as the *intelligent network*.

High-Performance Data Communication

Given the telephone switch with increased computing power and a remote high-performance transaction processor, the remaining problem was how to reliably interconnect these two computers and retain high levels of performance. Fortunate happenstance occurred here as well. The ITU-T had developed Common Channel Signaling (CCS) to reduce call setup times by several seconds in comparison with those achieved by in-band tone signaling. It also provided a standard for the data communication link between a switch and a transaction processor. The CCS suite of protocols built upon experience gained in SNA, X.25 networks, and the ARPANET.

Implementations and Protocols

This section describes how service providers construct circuit-switched VPNs using the technologies introduced in the previous section. The presentation uses a generic intelligent network architecture based on terminology from international standards.

Common Channel Signaling

Telephone switches used Channel-Associated Signaling (CAS) for almost 100 years. As shown in Figure 3.1a, CAS uses the same signal path to transfer digits used by the voice path over each trunk. The earliest automatic telephone switches used dial pulses, and later implementations used tones to more rapidly convey sequences of digits. Unfortunately, the time required to transmit a series of tones corresponding to a telephone number still required approximately one second. Therefore, the time elapsed from entry of the last digit by the caller to the start of the ringing tone (defined as *postdial delay*) was typically 10 to 15 seconds for long-distance calls that

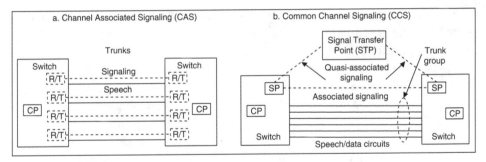

Figure 3.1   Types of telephone signaling.

traversed multiple switches. Additionally, the dynamic allocation of tone Receiver/Transmitters (R/T) via a Call Processor (CP) for the purposes of signaling was an expensive component of telephone switches. In addition, the use of tones limited the amount of information sent between switches.

Figure 3.1b depicts the Common Channel Signaling (CCS) solution to these problems. In essence, CCS provides a common digital data, message-oriented signaling channel for a trunk group of 64-kbps speech or data circuits. The digitized signaling messages travel at high speed either directly between switches in associated mode, or via an alternative transport facility in quasi-associated mode; for example, using a Signal Transfer Point (STP) as shown in the figure. CCS reduced postdial delay to only a few seconds and allowed the transfer of additional information between switches. It also reduced switch implementation cost by eliminating the need for tone receiver/transmitters on trunks, which had the additional benefit of preventing blue-box fraud. Finally, CCS enabled the use of messages between switches and external computers that were not directly associated with a trunk circuit.

Several standards have been defined for tone-based channel-associated signaling. AT&T defined a MultiFrequency (MF) standard, while the CCITT No. 5 signaling standard was defined for use on international trunks. Several variants of an R2 tone-signaling standard are still used in Europe. AT&T installed Common Channel Interoffice Signaling (CCIS) in the United States in 1976, and many operators deployed the ITU-T-specified Common Channel Signaling 6 (CCS6) internationally in the late 1970s. The version 6 signaling systems used a specific type of modem to digitally transfer signaling messages across analog or digital transmission facilities at speeds ranging from 2.4 to 4.8 kbps. The ITU-T and national standards organizations defined a new and improved version 7 by the mid-1980s. Called CCS7 internationally and SS7 in North America, these signaling systems are widely used in modern telephone networks.

SS7 has superior call setup time performance when compared to in-band signaling, and is critical to the implementation of value-added services. This was so important that, while presiding over the *United States versus AT&T* antitrust case, Judge Greene mandated interconnection of these signaling systems in the United States to provide equal access to all competing carriers in the late 1980s. Governments typically require equal access for competing carriers in deregulated telecommunications networks around the world. Although a number of national variants exist, SS7-based signaling has dramatically reduced call setup times and achieved a high degree of interoperability in the global telephone network at the end of the twentieth century.

A foundational aspect of the SS7 protocol is support for not only call-associated but non-call-associated signaling as well. Figure 3.2 illustrates the SS7 protocol stack [ITU Q.700; van Bosse 98; Russell 95]. The lowest part of the protocol stack is the Message Transfer Part (MTP), which has three levels as shown in the figure. MTP1 provides the physical signaling data link—for example, a 64-kbps digital transmission channel. MTP2 specifies the logical signaling link between two signaling points. It provides for message sequencing as well as error detection and correction via retransmission. MTP3 provides the interface to various signaling point user protocols. Most important, MTP3 provides for the logical addressing in an SS7 network

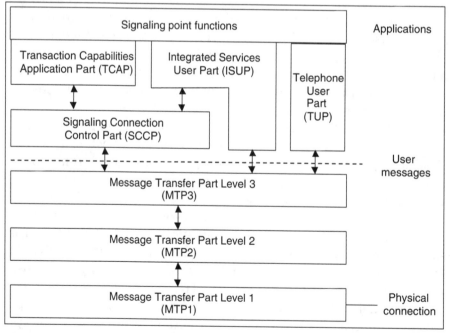

Figure 3.2   Signaling System 7 (SS7) protocol stack.

through the use of point-code assignments. Telephone network operators assign point codes to switches, STPs, and elements in the intelligent network. Point codes are assigned on a national and international basis. The 24-bit national point codes in the United States are assigned in a hierarchy. The high-order byte indicates the carrier, the second byte indicates a cluster, and the third byte indicates the actual signaling-point device. The 14-bit international point codes also use a hierarchical definition. The high-order 3 bits define a world zone, the next 8 bits define a particular national network, and the last 3 bits define a specific signaling point in that network.

The higher-layer protocols in the SS7 protocol suite support specific capabilities. The Telephone User Part (TUP) handles traditional telephone calls and provides functions for operating and maintaining trunk circuits in carrier networks. The Integrated Services User Part (ISUP) supports all of the functions that TUP does, but also supports narrowband ISDN. Both TUP and ISUP support trunk signaling. Subscribers utilize different, yet related, protocols to signal their requests to the network. In N-ISDN this is called the Digital Subscriber Signaling System 1 (DSS1) [ITU Q.931]. The SS7 suite of protocols supports signaling between switches and between carrier networks in an end-to-end digital circuit-switched network.

The Signaling Connection Control Part (SCCP) supports the transfer of messages that are not related to a specific trunk. In combination with the three MTP levels, SCCP provides a service to higher-layer protocols analogous to OSI layers 1 through 3. The Transaction Capabilities Application Part (TCAP) provides a standard interface to higher-level transaction-based applications. TCAP is a query-response protocol that provides a basic infrastructure that enables a broad range of transaction-oriented services using the client-server paradigm made popular by advances in distributed computing technology. TCAP is the foundation upon which most intelligent network is built. TCAP supports several other features, such as segmentation of long messages into lengths compatible with the SS7 network and the ability to return specific error codes in response to unsuccessful queries. Due to this alignment of protocol layers, it is possible to use protocol stacks other than MTP and SCCP (e.g., TCP/IP) to support TCAP.

Let's now take a look at how circuit-switched networks utilize the capabilities enabled by common channel signaling in typical telephone network deployments.

Call Processing and Intelligence

The first Stored Program Control (SPC) telephone switches employed special-purpose computers optimized for telephone call processing. Furthermore, these SPC switches had limited storage due to the high cost of memory. Therefore, up until the mid-1980s, telephone switches contained three basic software functions, as shown in Figure 3.3a. The first function was that of *basic call processing*, including recognition of off-hook and on-hook indications from the subscriber, collection of dialed digits, playing of tones and announcements, and routing according to the public network numbering plan. The second function included *service logic* that provided some customizable features on a per-subscriber or per-port basis. The third function provided for the storage and retrieval of subscriber-specific *service data*. The fourth function was that of collecting, storing, and transferring *billing data* to invoicing systems.

Competition drove the industry toward a new architecture for telephone networks. A new service that carriers offered in the United States in the early 1980s was the calling card. A North American telephone user had to first dial a 10-digit access number, the 10-digit destination number, and then the card number, which could be up to 14 digits. Because the convenience was so great and the savings so significant compared to collect calling or long-distance charges levied by hotels, many subscribers dialed up to 34 digits instead of 10 to save money. Although the stored program controllers could hold vast amounts of data, storing millions of calling card authorization numbers in every telephone switch in the network was not a cost-effective design. Therefore, service providers kept the service database containing the card authorization numbers in a computer system separate from the basic call-processing logic in the switches accessed for each card call.

Figure 3.3b illustrates this new architecture. The telephone switch still implements the call-processing function, but extends this logic to determine when to access a remote computer. Generically, we call a modern

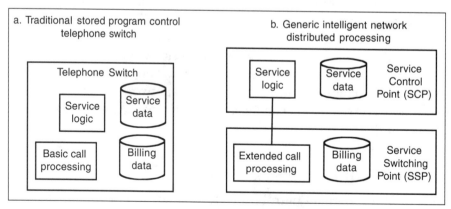

Figure 3.3   Evolution of call processing and intelligence.

telephone switch a Service Switching Point (SSP). The remote computer contains the service program logic and a means to access the service database. We call this function a Service Control Point (SCP). This architecture supported not only calling card services, but also a large number of other advanced services, in particular, circuit-switched VPNs. Many carriers leveraged the commercial high-performance, reliable minicomputers that were emerging at the time to cost effectively implement this architecture in the mid-1980s. As is often the case, when something becomes popular, the need arises to standardize the interfaces and protocols to promote interoperability and competition in the hardware and software industry that supports telecommunications. The next section briefly summarizes the history and direction of these standardization efforts.

Intelligent Network Architectures

In the late 1980s, standards bodies defined architectures and protocols to support intelligent circuit-switched networks. Bellcore (now called Telcordia) developed standards for the seven Baby Bells in the United States, calling the first set of standards the Intelligent Network 1 (IN/1). However, the first set of standards was too broad, so Bellcore broke the overarching architecture into phases of an Advanced Intelligent Network (AIN). As of the year 2000, AIN 0, AIN 0.1, and AIN 0.2 have been defined. The ITU-T began its efforts to standardize international intelligent networks in 1989. The ITU-T breaks the phases for its IN features and services into Capability Sets (CS). As of the year 2000, both CS-1 and CS-2 are standardized. AIN 0.1 and AIN 0.2 are closely aligned with CS-1 and CS-2, respectively.

Figure 3.4 illustrates the physical network elements defined in the Bellcore AIN intelligent telephone network architecture. A Service Switching Point (SSP) is a telephone switch as described in the previous section. An Intelligent Peripheral (IP), for example, a voice menu response system, may attach to some SSPs as shown in the figure. A Signal Transfer Point (STP), usually deployed as a mated pair for reliability reasons, interconnects multiple SSPs for the purpose of common channel signaling. The STPs also interconnect the SSPs to Service Control Points (SCPs). Normally, the link topology design connecting SSPs, STPs, and SCPs will survive any single link or node failure. A Service Management System (SMS) provides carrier, and in some cases end-customer, access to manipulate the service database implemented in an SCP. The SMS also collects statistics. Finally, a Service Creation Environment (SCE) provides the means for service providers, and in some cases end users, to define, test, and configure intelligent network services.

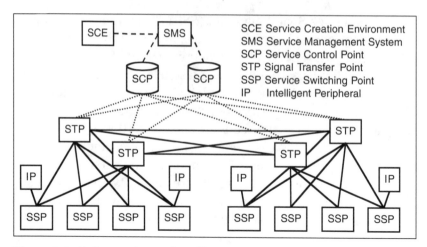

Figure 3.4   Bellcore Advanced Intelligent Network (AIN).

The ITU-T defines the intelligent network architecture in terms of a logical framework organized as a set of planes. Specific entities reside within each of these planes. The physical distribution of these functions can vary based upon implementation. Figure 3.5 illustrates the four planes and principal functions in the Intelligent Network Conceptual Model (INCM) defined in ITU-T Recommendation I.312/Q.1201 [ITU Q.1201]. Starting from the top, the *service plane* is the view of concern to enterprise users and service providers. It consists of a number of services composed of generic service features. Each Service Feature (SF) is composed of one or more Service-Independent Building blocks (SIBs) in the *global functional plane*, as shown in the figure. Basic call-processing generates a Point of Initiation (POI) for these SIBs at trigger points in the basic call model (e.g., off-hook or receipt of specific digit patterns). The SIBs then execute a set of service logic, possibly invoking other SIBs, eventually resulting in a Point of Return (POR) to the invoking basic call-processing logic. One or more Functional Entities (FEs) in the *distributed functional plane* implement each SIB, as shown in Figure 3.5. An FE consists of one or more Elementary Functions (EF), such as off-hook recognition or digit reception. The Functional Entity Actions (FEA) combine these elementary functions and interact with each other to implement the SIB using logical Information Flows (IF), as shown in the figure. The lowest-level *physical plane* consists of Physical Entities (PE) that each implement one or more functional entities. This is the level where equipment manufacturers determine the packaging and composition of the higher-level functional planes.

ITU-T Recommendation Q.1211 defines these concepts and their relationships for CS-1, while Recommendation Q.1221 defines these components

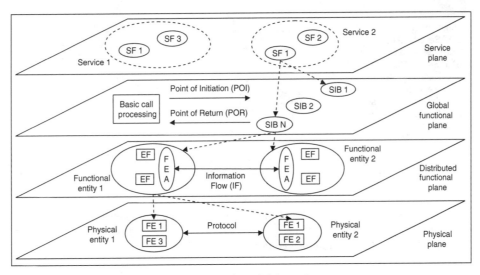

Figure 3.5   Intelligent Network Conceptual Model (INCM).

for CS-2. Figure 3.6 illustrates the Functional Entities (FEs) and their relationships as defined for CS-1 in ITU-T recommendations Q.1211 and Q.1214.
These descriptions are based on a set of Service Independent Building
blocks (SIBs) defined in ITU-T recommendation Q.1213. The scope of CS-1
covers only single-ended, single-point-of-control services. We first describe
the real-time functions involved in the establishment of circuit-switched
calls. The Call Control Agent Function (CCAF) provides user access to the
network (for example, via off-hook detection). The Call Control Function
(CCF) is closely coupled to the Service Switching Function (SSF) for IN-
capable switches, as shown in Figure 3.6. The CCF controls call processing
and establishes network connections. A non-IN-capable switch does not
have an SSF. The CCF supports a bearer path and a non-IN connection control information flow, as shown in the figure.

The SSF supports IN triggers and provides access to other IN functions,
as shown in the figure. An IN trigger is a point in a call that initiates a
sequence of other functions. When the SSF encounters a trigger, it formulates a standardized query to the Service Control Function (SCF) based
upon the call state and information received from the CCF. The SCF may
invoke Service Data Functions (SDFs) and/or Specialized Resource Functions (SRF) before finally returning a response to an SSF query. Examples
of SRF resources include DTMF tone transmission/reception, speech
recognition, and generation of synthesized speech. An SRF interfaces to
the CCF and the SCF, as shown in Figure 3.6, to perform functions like
playing a prompt tone or message and collecting digits entered by the call-

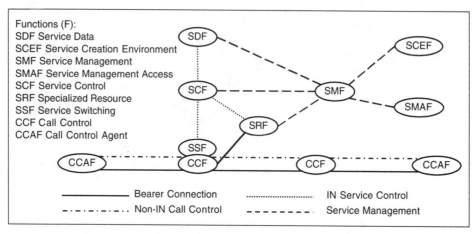

Figure 3.6   ITU-T CS-1 logical IN architecture.

ing user. As described later in this chapter, the interaction between the SRF and the user as controlled by the SCF is the basis of many intelligent network services employed by circuit-switched VPNs.

The remaining functional entities shown in Figure 3.6 support the non-real-time management, provisioning, and operation for CS-1 services. The Service Management Function (SMF) supports provisioning and operation of the real-time SSF, SCF, SDF, and SRF functional entities. The Service Management Access Function (SMAF) provides the capability to remotely access the SMF. The ITU-T IN architecture includes the concept of service creation, which the Service Creation Environment Function (SCEF) provides for the definition, development, testing, and input to the SMF. The interface between the SCEF and the SMF includes service logic and service data templates.

Figure 3.7 illustrates some possible mappings of the CS-1 functional entities into physical entities, as described in ITU-T Recommendation Q.1215, which are a superset of the Bellcore-defined AIN physical network elements. A Service Switching Point (SSP) is a traditional telephone switch that contains the CCAF, CCF, SSF, and often SRF functions. An Intelligent Peripheral (IP) contains only the SRF—for example, an Integrated Voice Response (IVR) system. A Service Control Point (SCP) contains both the SCF and the SDF, whereas a Service Data Point (SDP) contains only the SDF. A Service Management Point (SMP) contains the SMF and the SMAF. Finally, a Service Creation Environment Point (SCEP) contains the SCEF. ITU-T Recommendation Q.1218 defines the physical and logical protocol interfaces between these physical entities using the SS7 protocol stack described earlier. The last section in this chapter gives some representative

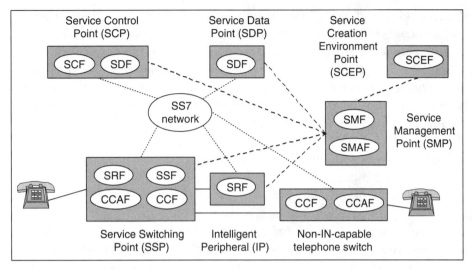

Figure 3.7   Example CS-1 physical architecture.

examples of circuit-switched VPN services implemented using the ITU-T capability set model overlaid onto this physical architecture.

Capability Set 2 (CS-2) adds support for mobility and broadband services. In addition, it supports services that involve several parties or multiple points within a call [ITU Q.1221]. CS-2 also facilitates interconnection of intelligent services that traverse multiple service providers. Of particular interest to enterprises is a Global Virtual Network Service (GVNS). ITU-T recommendations Q.1221 through Q.1225 and Q.1228 through Q.1230 define the components of the INCM planes and the interface protocols involved in CS-2. CS-2 adds a few new functional entities to those defined in CS-1. The Call-Unrelated Service Function (CUSF) handles activities unrelated to a call, such as allowing a user to configure his or her services via the Service Control User Agent Function (SCUAF). The CUSF interfaces to the SCF for real-time control and the SMF for management interactions. More important, CS-2 also defines the means for linking together a sequence of Service Control Functions (SCF) or Service Data Functions (SDF) as a result of a single trigger event.

Voice over Data and Intelligent Networking

Because the previous descriptions covered traditional circuit-switched voice, the reader might ask: What is the relationship, if any, to the emerging deployments of voice transported over data networking protocols like

IP, frame relay, and ATM? Interestingly, many of the same intelligent network concepts still apply. Voice over data usually involves encoding speech using techniques that are more complex than the Pulse Code Modulation (PCM) method described in Chapter 2, *Private Line Technologies*. These encoding techniques generate packets that represent human speech. By restricting the source to human speech and not any type of analog signal, some of these encoding techniques require bit rates as low as 5 kbps [Minoli 98a; Minoli 98b]. However, the overhead of packet framing, ATM Adaptation Layer (AAL) and cell fields, or IP reduces efficiency, in some cases rather significantly. Hence, the actual bit rate required on an access line or within a network backbone can be substantially higher than the packetized speech coding rate [McDysan 98b].

The generic industry name for the device that interfaces between the circuit-switched voice network and the voice over data network is a *gateway*. Figure 3.8 illustrates some representative scenarios where a Voice over Data (VoD) gateway interworks with circuit-switched voice services [Kozik 98]. Starting from the left-hand side of the figure, a telephone set connects to VoD gateway A, which converts speech into packets, and relays signaling information to destination VoD gateway B. The encoding and transport of the speech packets, as well as the signaling protocols, differ for IP, frame relay, and ATM. Although TCAP was defined for operation over the SS7 protocol stack, as noted earlier, any protocol stack that provides comparable functions will do. In particular, TCAP over TCP/IP is one such possible variant. In this example, VoD gateway A used TCAP over

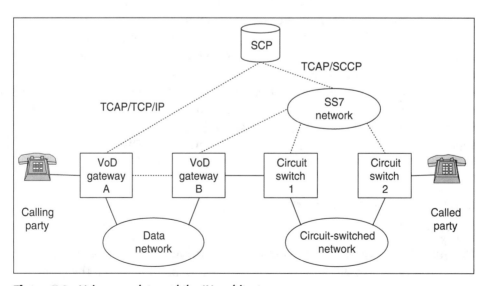

Figure 3.8   Voice over data and the IN architecture.

TCP/IP to query the SCP to determine that VoD gateway B was the appropriate point for handing off the call to the circuit-switched network to reach the called party. VoD gateway B has a TDM interface to circuit switch 1 and uses standard SS7 signaling to hand off the call. The circuit-switched network uses standard procedures to deliver the call to circuit switch 2, which serves the called party. The circuit-switched network may also access the same SCP depending upon what specific features the original request contained or the state of the network.

Of course, many other scenarios are possible, and these are being standardized in the industry. They include the provision of trunks connecting traditional circuit switches via VoD gateways, interworking between VoD gateways using different protocols, and end-to-end voice connections where the gateway actually resides in the end user's computer. Also, the points where a VoD gateway accesses an IN service point may differ. Furthermore, some VoD services require nontelephony services. For example, an important advance in the VoIP technology is the potential for users to enter names instead of dialing impersonal numbers dictated by the rotary dial legacy of the telephone network. At present, standard telephone network solutions only provide identification of the calling party by number or name. This requires a server that supports resolution of names into IP addresses along with support for other nontelephony services like multimedia.

Circuit-Switched VPN Applications

This section describes the principal applications of circuit-switched VPNs. Many of these services are based upon the CS-1 and CS-2 standards; however, service providers may implement them in a proprietary manner or provide additional services [Briere 90]. We focus primarily on the standards-based services in this section. CS-1 and CS-2 define support for many telecommunications services; however, our focus is on those capabilities most commonly utilized by enterprise VPNs. The CS-1 and CS-2 standards specify the logical primitives, their interactions, and the actual messages and protocol interactions in great detail. This section presents a high-level view using the time-sequence diagrams of the message exchanges between physical entities as defined in ITU-T Recommendation Q.1218.

On-Net and Off-Net Access Methods

Figure 3.9 depicts the various means that an enterprise VPN user can employ as originating or terminating access methods for circuit-switched

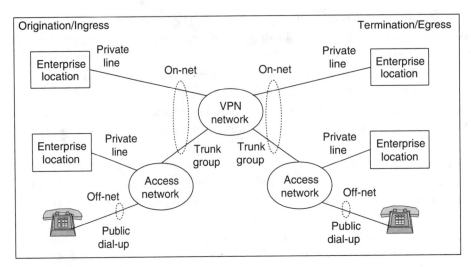

Figure 3.9   On-net and Off-net calling scenarios.

calls. Most VPN services are still offered by a single provider's network, as shown in the center of the figure. For example, for regulatory reasons in the United States, Inter eXchange Carriers (IXCs) provide the majority of VPN services. For economic reasons, an important means of connecting an enterprise location to the VPN is via a private line. As an alternative access method, a Local Exchange Carrier (LEC) provides a private line to the enterprise location, which supports local public calls as well as VPN calls. Sometimes regulations allow only the LEC to complete local calls. This switched access method provides an important capability because the access network provider authenticates the identity of the calling location or end user and passes this to the VPN network provider via the common channel signaling protocol associated with the trunk group connecting the networks. In a similar vein, the access network provider ensures that calls terminated over a switched access network reach the intended destination. Telephone networks in the United States employ these means to implement switched access using presubscription to a specific IXC or use of a 101XXXX dialing prefix on a call-by-call basis to indicate the desired IXC network. The public dial-up access method differs from the switched method in that the access network does not provide authentication of the calling party identity to the VPN network provider. Examples of such a public origination would be use of a pay phone, calls from a residence, or calls from some other establishment that are not part of the enterprise's circuit-switched VPN. Circuit-switched networks must provide additional means to authenticate a calling user before providing access to enterprise VPN services from a publicly dialed origination. Another distinction for the

Table 3.1   On-Net and Off-Net Voice VPN Combinations

VPN CALL TYPE	ORIGINATION/INGRESS	TERMINATION/EGRESS
On-net-to-on-net	Private line/switched	Private line/switched
On-net-to-off-net	Private line/switched	Public dial-up
Off-net-to-on-net	Public dial-up	Private line/switched
Off-net-to-off-net	Public dial-up	Public dial-up

public case is on the termination, or egress, side of the call. A public termination that is off the enterprise VPN (i.e., off-net) is handled differently than one that is on the enterprise VPN (i.e., on-net).

Table 3.1 summarizes the four possible VPN call types in terms of the origination (or ingress) and termination (or egress) methods. The high-level objective is that all VPN services should be supported independently of the access method. However, some service features are specific to the ingress and egress methods involved with a particular call.

The distinction between on-net and off-net origination and termination has some significant security and economic implications for an enterprise. The implicit authentication of on-net callers is an important security aspect of any VPN. The need to authenticate off-net callers is primarily economic, because the potential exists for off-net callers to fraudulently use an enterprise VPN for off-net-to-off-net calls.

Private Numbering Plans

A Private Numbering Plan (PNP) provides a group of enterprise users the capability to place calls using digit sequences that have different structures and meanings than those employed by the public numbering plan between interfaces that are part of the VPN. These users may be either on-net or off-net, as previously defined. CS-1 calls PNP service Abbreviated Dialing (ABD). It allows an originating enterprise user to dial other users in the same enterprise using only the extension number of the called party. Typically, many enterprises use four-digit extension numbers. The use of abbreviated dialing does not apply only to call placement, but can also apply to supplementary services such as call forwarding and conference calling. CS-1 also defines support for a range of VPN services. The broadest definition is that of a distributed virtual PBX. CS-2 defines a Global Virtual Network Service (GVNS) that extends a switched VPN service across multiple networks.

Figure 3.10 illustrates a simple example of how CS-1 physical entities support a private numbering plan call. This is one of the simplest types of

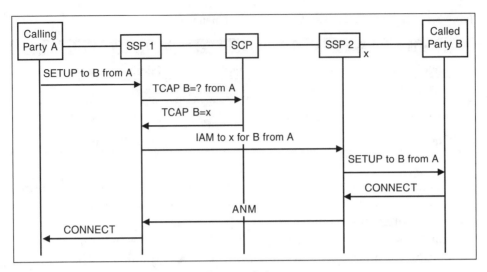

Figure 3.10   Example of private number translation.

IN transactions because it involves only a single query-response pair between the originating switch (SSP) and the IN translation database contained in the SCP [ITU Q.1219]. Many IN services, such as freephone (i.e., 800 or 888 numbers in the United States), credit card, Universal Personal Telecommunications (UPT), as well as VPN services use this simple paradigm. Starting from the left-hand side of Figure 3.10, calling party A requests establishment of a call to B using a private numbering plan. The example uses ISDN messages, but the service works with other telephony signaling protocols as well. The first Service Switching Point (SSP 1) receives this call request and formulates a TCAP query to the Service Control Point (SCP). The SCP has a database that maps the Private Numbering Plan (PNP) for each enterprise to its own internal numbering plan, which is shown as the SSP and port number in this example. Thus, the SCP returns a response indicating an internally routable address x for the private address B which corresponds to a port on SSP 2 as shown in the figure. SSP 1 then formulates an SS7 Initial Address Message (IAM) indicating this routable address along with the original called party number B along with the calling party's number A. The telephone network routes the call request until it arrives at the destination switch SSP 2. Here, the last switch formulates a SETUP message to called party B. The called party answers by responding with a CONNECT message, which the telephone network propagates back toward the originator using the SS7 Answer Message (ANM). Finally, the originating switch SSP 1 informs the calling party

A that the call was answered using the CONNECT message. Parties A and B can now exchange information over the circuit-switched connection. If any error occurred during the call-establishment phase, the switches would clear the call attempt.

If the called party B is a toll-free number, then carriers implement a similar translation procedure. The decoupling of call processing from database transactions enables a broad range of innovative services. For example, an enterprise can have multiple locations answering a single toll-free number in a load-balanced manner. This group of destinations answering a toll-free number may be a mix of on-net and off-net interfaces. Note that most modern digital telephone switches propagate information about the calling party, which is the basis of Caller ID–type services. Caller name identification services require a switch to translate the calling number into an alphanumeric character string corresponding to the calling number. In this way CCS and IN help reduce the occurrence of nuisance or threatening telephone calls.

In response to the Telecommunications Act of 1996, telephone carriers in the United States must support Local Number Portability (LNP). This means that a user can change service provider yet keep the same telephone number. Keeping the same public telephone number can be very important for an enterprise, because changing the number creates additional expenses and potential loss of business. Implementation of LNP requires that one or more switches in the telephone network must consult an SCP via a TCAP query response to determine which carrier will provide services to the local telephone number.

Originating and Terminating Call Screening

Call screening has two flavors: one used on the originating side of a call and the other employed at the terminating side of a call. As defined in CS-1, Originating Call Screening (OCS) allows the enterprise user to specify whether outgoing calls are allowed or disallowed according to a screening list applied to the called party number. The screening list may change as a function of time of day and may also support an optional override feature that allows the calling party to enter an authorization code if OCS does not permit the call. The screening list may contain prefixes of public or private numbering plans that are either allowed or disallowed. In a similar vein, CS-1 defines Terminating Call Screening (TCS) as the ability for an enterprise user to specify whether incoming calls are allowed or disallowed according to a screening list applied to the calling party number.

Figure 3.11 illustrates the application of call screening applied separately at the originating and terminating switch. Starting from the left-hand side, A places a call to B. The originating switch SSP 1 formulates a TCAP query to an SCP asking if a call to B is allowed from A. If the SCP responds that the call is allowed, then SSP 1 routes the call across the telephone network to switch SSP 2 that serves B. At the terminating switch, call screening may also be invoked, in which case the TCAP query to what could very well be a different SCP asks if B will allow (or not allow) the incoming call from A. If the call attempt passes this terminating screening test, then SSP 2 advances the call by sending a SETUP message. From here on out, the called party B either answers the call attempt with a CONNECT message or rejects the call attempt with a RELEASE message. In some cases, the network may be able to perform both originating and terminating call screening using a single query.

The maintenance of screening lists can be a significant administrative burden if the set of allowed or disallowed numbers is large. As indicated in the previous example, call-screening profiles could be kept for each individual subscriber. Thus, an important service feature allows VPN administrators to define generic screening lists that apply to classes of users. For example, most users might not be granted the privilege to make international calls. Originating call screening implements this policy by disallowing any calls with an international dialing prefix based upon the privilege determined by the authenticated calling party address.

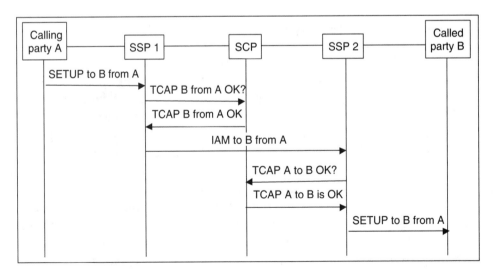

Figure 3.11   Examples of call screening.

Authorization and Accounting Codes

CS-2 defines User Authentication (UAUT) as a feature that confirms the identity of a user to the network and confirms the identity of the network with the user. UAUT utilizes information exchanged between the network and a user, such as authentication data provided by the user through digit entry or a computer terminal. A VPN network should ensure that multiple simultaneous switched access calls using the same user authorization profile are not in progress, as this is a likely indicator of the presence of fraud. CS-2 also defines Flexible Origination and Termination Authorization (acronyms FOA and FTA) features. FOA and FTA occur at any time prior to the point when an IN switch would authorize a call attempt. These features allow a service provider or an enterprise user to define nonstandardized customized algorithms. Let's look at several examples important to enterprise VPNs.

Off-net access is a popular feature for circuit-switched enterprise VPNs. Figure 3.12 illustrates a simple example of off-net-to-on-net calling with authorization. Starting from the left-hand side, calling party A places a call to an access number X served by SSP 1. Typically, the access number X is a toll-free (freephone) number. SSP 1 plays a prompt tone or a message indicating that the calling party should enter a destination address, which in this example is the public address B. SSP 1 then plays another announcement or tone indicating that the calling party should now enter an autho-

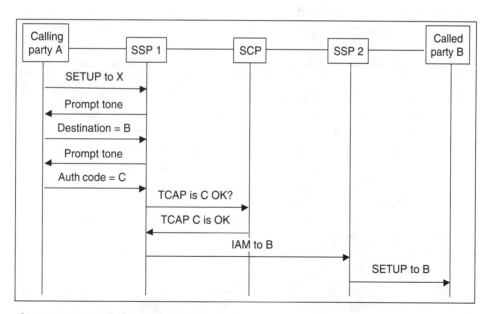

Figure 3.12 Example of off-net authorization.

rization code or calling card number. The originating node SSP 1 then formulates a TCAP query to validate the authorization code C. If the SCP indicates that the authorization code is valid, then SSP 1 routes the call through the network. Note that SSP 1 could have handed the call off to an Intelligent Peripheral (IP), which would then perform this query-response dialog with the calling party and return the result to SSP 1.

Obviously, a private numbering plan feature could readily be combined with this authorization feature to implement off-net-to-on-net calling. Optionally, the authorization code C could be mapped to an identification of the calling party (or at least the party who pays the bill for the calling card number) and passed by the SS7 network to the destination.

Account codes are another important feature utilized in many circuit-switched VPNs, because many enterprises bill back their clients for telephone usage. The use of account codes as digit sequences entered by the calling party in a query-response dialog similar to the one just described allows the service provider to offer customized billing based on the entered account code. An enterprise can then use this billing information, usually provided in computer-readable format by the carrier, to generate invoices to its clients.

Overflow and Internetwork Routing

Intelligent network protocols can also be involved in the determination of call routing. Since the IN architecture separates the database and any logic

---

CALLING CARD FRAUD AND CARRIER SOLUTIONS

Soon after carriers began offering calling cards with authorization codes, unscrupulous people found ways to make calls without incurring charges. One basic attack involved an individual calling the carrier's access number and repeatedly trying authorization code numbers. Some of the early services that used dial-up public network access had extremely short authorization codes, which meant that it was relatively easy for fraudulent users to hit upon a valid code. The greatest sources of fraud were generated from prisons, as one might expect, but also somewhat unexpectedly from college campuses. Carriers responded by increasing the length of authorization codes, by encouraging customers to keep their codes secret, and by vigorously prosecuting violators. They also implemented sophisticated systems that detect callers trying to crack codes via repeated attempts or that detect unusual usage patterns that could be indicative of fraudulent use. Nonetheless, fraud is still an issue for public dial-up services that use authorization codes.

from the switch itself, a number of routing features are feasible. For example, CS-1 defines User Defined Routing (UDR) as the ability for an end user to route calls to private line on-net egress, switched on-net egress, or off-net egress by time of day. The routing list can apply to single lines or directory numbers or else to groups of lines or numbers. The CS-2 Customized Call Routing (CCR) feature allows one network to access another public or private network to complete a call. The accessed network then has complete control of the call from that point onward, allowing for convenient update of other features like call forwarding, screening, or user-defined routing.

Figure 3.13 illustrates a simple example of overflow alternate routing. Starting from the left-hand side at step 1, an Initial Address Message (IAM) signals a call attempt to station 1234 on VPN xyz. The terminating switch determines in step 2 that the preferred route choice, a private line trunk group terminating directly at the enterprise PBX serving station 1234, is busy. The terminating switch formulates a query to the SCP in step 3 asking for overflow routing instructions. The SCP returns an indication that public overflow is available for the requested station and VPN in step 4. In this example, the public number is completely different from the private number. The terminating switch then attempts to place the call over the local public network in step 5.

A number of CS-2 features support internetwork services. Historically, a single carrier offered a circuit-switched VPN network, but the CS-2 standards will enable circuit-switched VPNs that span multiple countries and

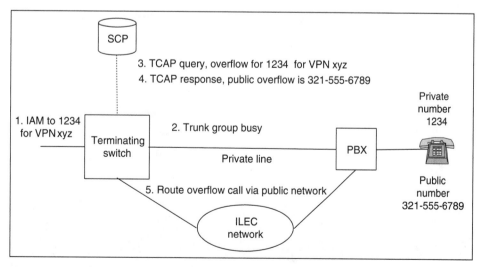

Figure 3.13   Operation of overflow alternate routing.

carrier networks. These protocols include the ability to route toll-free (freephone) numbers, communicate charging information, and identify the carriers involved in the call across multiple networks—things that cannot be done today.

Feature Interaction

We saw several cases, even in the simple examples used in this chapter, of how features can interact. A significant complexity arises when a user subscribes to multiple features. A set of rules called *feature interaction* determines the order in which certain service features can be invoked on the same call, specifies the order in which features can be used, and specifies rules for handling conflicts.

CHAPTER

4

Early Connection-Oriented Data VPNs—X.25 and Frame Relay

To the old, the new is usually bad news.
—Eric Hoffer

X.25 networks changed the data networking paradigm in the late 1970s by providing virtual access to a public network as an alternative to leased lines interconnecting mainframes and terminal clusters. The emergence of LAN-based applications in the late 1980s drove the need for a higher-performance solution, which has been addressed by frame relay, ATM, and most recently, IP-based VPNs. While X.25 was strictly a data-only solution, frame relay added support for voice. ATM, or more specifically Broadband ISDN (B-ISDN), was the ITU-T's vision for an all-encompassing network that supported not only voice and data, but video and every other service as well. However, as you'll see in the last half of this book, engineers are developing IP-based solutions that have not only most of the capabilities of B-ISDN, but more as well. This chapter introduces the realm of data-oriented VPNs. X.25 was the earliest protocol to support VPNs, followed by frame relay and then ATM and MPLS. Chapter 5 describes ATM and MPLS, and Chapters 6 though 9 cover the important topic of IP-based VPNs.

Business Drivers and Requirements

This section describes the environment and the factors that drove enterprises to use X.25 and frame relay networks. Economics were a driver, but the fundamental difference between data and voice communications played a role as well.

Inflexibility and Cost of Private Lines

As described in Chapter 2, *Private Network Technologies*, the digital hierarchy of TDM private lines is inflexible. Only a specific set of rates is available, and the destination is always fixed. Furthermore, in the 1970s, there was little competition, and the cost of private lines was relatively high, especially internationally. Enterprises responded by optimizing private line-based networks to interconnect remote terminals and Input/Output (I/O) devices to mainframes. Proprietary networks built on private lines dominated the data communications marketplace in the 1970s. The need for more cost-effective, flexible solutions drove the development of X.25 and frame relay.

Bursty Traffic of Interactive Data Applications

Traffic in early computer communication networks was extremely bursty. In other words, much of the time, no data was flowing to or from the enterprise user. The typical application involved a user inputting keyboard data ranging from a few characters to a few lines, then forwarding the information to a mainframe. Ordinarily, the mainframe responded with data ranging from a few lines to a full-screen display. An interval of user "think time" separated these interchanges, resulting in a traffic pattern whose peak rate was much higher than the long-term average. Although these transactions contained large amounts of data, the accurate and timely transfer of information was much more productive than it was for voice or facsimile communications. However, because the nature of terminal-to-computer communications was so intermittent, usage of a dedicated private line network was difficult to justify economically.

Human nature changes more slowly than technology does. As evidence of this fact, the same paradigm of bursty communication occurs in the use of many Web browser applications. Compare the following description with the terminal-mainframe scenario just described. Web browsing involves a user inputting a set of data that ranges from a single mouse click to multiple entries in a form and then submitting the inputs to a Web server. The server responds by returning an updated Web page, which, like the mainframe scenario, usually represents much more data than the user input. Sometimes, user commands initiate the playback of an audio or video clip or begin a file transfer. What has changed from the days of terminal-mainframe computing to the Web-fueled content of the Internet today is the user's power to unleash bandwidth-hungry and QoS-dependent applications. Indeed, some Web browser applications (e.g., audio and video playback) have traffic that is of a constant rate that is not bursty at all.

Emergence of Data Applications

Many initial computer applications were simply replacements for manual processes. The additional expenses of computer hardware, software, and support specialists more than offset the productivity gains provided by computerized transaction processing. Evolving from accounting, order processing, and inventory management applications, the realm of computer-based applications grew to encompass more and more of an enterprise's mission-critical functions. In fact, Email is in effect a replacement for interoffice memoranda, and file transfer is a replacement for copying and distributing documents.

Once the information was entered in the computer system, the effort of reentering data and the potential for introducing errors was also reduced. A paradigm shift occurred when enterprises began developing applications designed for data from the ground up. These new applications leveraged the enterprise's accumulated databases, providing better visibility for management and a competitive edge for those that mastered the new technology. Since computing was a relatively new industry, these applications were manufacturer-specific. It was during the 1960s and 1970s that the International Business Machines (IBM) emerged as a dominant supplier for enterprise computing and application software needs.

However, this newfound well of productivity enhancements brought with it some problems. One particular problem may well be the catalyst that drives the replacement of many of these older applications with new ones. In the 1960s and 1970s, electronic memory and disk storage was expensive. Since most programmers expected that later versions would replace their work, a common storage-saving convention was to employ only the last two digits of the year. Unfortunately, a number of these programs still support mission-critical, time-sensitive applications (mortgages, insurance, etc.). As a result, the computing industry had to retrofit these programs to handle rollover to the year 2000 or else replace the applications.

Declining Cost of Computing and Memory

A business trend that drove usage from X.25 toward frame relay was the continually declining cost of computing and memory capacity. The declining cost of mainframes and the advent of minicomputers stimulated the need for X.25. The adoption of the personal computer offered huge amounts of distributed computing and allowed many functions to be more economically implemented in the end systems than in network data switching equipment. Careful usage of expensive memory in end systems as well as network nodes was a hallmark of X.25. The decreased cost of memory enabled deployment of relatively large buffers in end systems and frame relay switching equipment.

Technology Trends and Enablers

This section summarizes the changes in technology that ushered in X.25 and frame relay. These included enhancements on many fronts: transmission performance, reduced cost of computing and memory, and advances in the design of the data communication protocols themselves.

Impact of Transmission Media on Performance

The microwave and satellite transmission networks of the 1970s and 1980s were much noisier than the modern fiber-optic-based networks. Many parts of private data networks and public X.25 networks used modems to convey digital data over noisy analog transmission facilities. Noise is the enemy of digital communication networks because it causes errors. In the world of computing, errors are unacceptable. As a result, a large part of early data network design dealt with handling errors and reliably delivering data to the destination.

Let's look at why errors have such a large impact on computer communications protocols. An entire packet must be received without any errors for an application to use it. Assuming that a packet has B bytes and the link Bit Error Rate (BER) is p, then the probability that a packet is received correctly is as follows:

$$\text{Prob[correct packet]} = (1 - p)^{8B} \approx 1 - 8\,B\,p$$

where the approximation is valid if the BER p is less than the exponent $8B$.

Figure 4.1 plots the preceding formula for the probability of correct packet reception versus line BER for a packet size of $B = 1,000$ bytes. We see that if the BER approaches the inverse of the packet length in bits (i.e., $\frac{1}{(8B)}$), then the probability of the destination receiving a packet correctly approaches zero. Since transmission BER generally increases with the distance traversed, the earliest data communication networks often performed error detection and retransmission on a hop-by-hop basis just to correctly deliver packets between adjacent packet-switching nodes. Of course, as digital communications technology evolved by utilizing sophisticated coding techniques to improve BER performance on radio frequency links or via the use of effectively noise-free fiber-optic transmission media, the probability of correct packet reception approached 100 percent over increasingly larger distances. This was a fundamental advance in digital data communication technology shift that enabled a move from X.25 to simpler link-level protocols like frame relay, ATM, and MPLS.

While the deployment of fiber-optic communication technology reduced the error rate significantly, it also increased the available transmission rate by orders of magnitude. This created another challenge for data communication protocols. Usually, higher-layer protocols have a window of packets that can be sent before receiving any acknowledgments. The sender sends sequence-numbered packets until this window size is reached. The receiver acknowledges receipt of a sequence-numbered packet by responding with a packet indicating the next sequence number that it expects. If the receiver misses a packet, then the sender detects this through a time-out while wait-

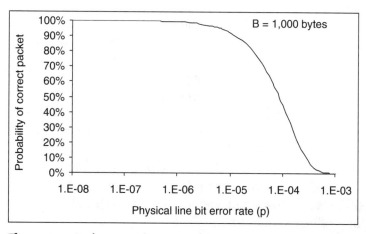

Figure 4.1   Packet reception versus bit error rate.

ing for an acknowledgment and retransmits the lost packet and all subsequent packets. The literature commonly calls this a *Go Back N* retransmission strategy since the transmitter must repeat some number N packet transmissions in order to recover from a lost packet. As long as the network seldom lost a packet or the number of retransmitted packets was small, this scheme worked fairly well.

Of course, communication occurs with finite propagation delay and the delays of electronics. These delays comprise approximately 1 millisecond for each 100 miles of distance traversed in typical private line networks. Thus, a packet traveling across the United States encounters approximately 30 ms of delay τ for one direction. Therefore a protocol had to have a window size of W packets large enough to keep the transmission facility of rate R busy as follows:

$$W = 2\tau R/(8B)$$

The term $2\tau R$ is called the *bandwidth-delay product*. It represents the number of bits in transit on the round-trip network path connecting two hosts. Higher-layer protocols often implement a Go Back N retransmission strategy because it is simpler, so the impact of lost packets due to errors or congestion becomes significant when W becomes large. In other words, the impact of errors or congestion on throughput becomes significant for networks with a large bandwidth-delay product. This first occurred in satellite networks where the delay τ was over 250 ms, and later in fiber-optic networks where the bit rate R grew to hundreds of Mbps and more. In fact, all protocols have required extensions of the sequence number fields to support the larger window sizes dictated by the increased network bandwidth-delay product.

Let's look at the impact of packet loss on the throughput of a Go Back N retransmission protocol. Assume the probability of the data network losing a packet due to errors or congestion is a constant value Pr[loss] that occurs independently for each packet. This simple model does not capture the effects of congestion overload that causes clumps of lost packets to actually affect throughput less than do random errors. However, the effect on throughput may not be shared fairly by multiple flows traversing the same congested point [McDysan 00]. Observe that, at worst, each packet loss event causes the sender to retransmit W packets. Therefore, the effective throughput is approximately the inverse of the average number of times such a worst-case retransmission scenario occurs [Bertsekas 92; McDysan 00; Stallings 98b], as follows:

$$\text{Throughput} = (1 - \Pr[\text{loss}])/(1 + W\Pr[\text{loss}])$$

Figure 4.2 plots the Go Back N retransmission protocol throughput versus the window size W for representative values of network packet loss $\Pr[\text{loss}]$. For small values of packet loss, the throughput is nearly flat, even for large window sizes. This occurs because retransmissions occur infrequently. As the probability of packet loss increases, throughput decreases markedly for larger window sizes. This phenomenon occurs because the sender frequently retransmits a packet multiple times in order to deliver it successfully to the destination. This simple example assumes that the physical transmission link is loaded at 100 percent. The throughput measure is the effective end-to-end information transfer capacity delivered to the higher-layer applications at the hosts, which, after all, is the true measure of productivity for an enterprise.

Refinements of this Go Back N strategy allow the receiver to selectively reject or acknowledge packets. The best-case performance of selective retransmission approaches that of the probability of correct packet reception shown in Figure 4.1. These selective retransmission protocols are optional in most standards, and hence are not widely implemented. However, if your enterprise network has noisy or lossy subnetworks and operates with large bandwidth-delay products, then use of these advanced retransmission techniques in the host software should improve throughput performance significantly.

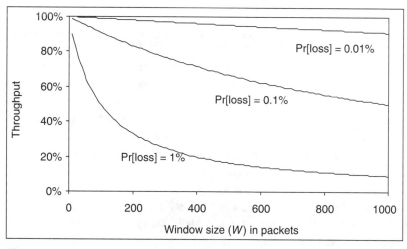

Figure 4.2   Throughput versus window size.

Continuing Improvements in Packet Switching

Packet switching arose from government-funded initiatives in the early 1960s. In fact, the name *packet* was coined by Donald Davies at the United Kingdom's National Physical Laboratory [Huston 99]. By the mid-1970s, computer manufacturers had developed and deployed a range of proprietary, incompatible data-networking technologies. Various bodies and government institutions initiated activities to standardize this new technology.

Two competing design philosophies for packet switching arose in the 1970s: connection-oriented and connectionless. The connection-oriented approach is used by many data communication protocols. The ones this book describes are X.25, frame relay, ATM, MPLS, TCP, and RSVP. This chapter and the next summarize the connection-oriented approach. Chapter 6, *The Internet Protocol Suite*, covers the connectionless approach. However, TCP, RSVP, and MPLS are all connection-oriented protocols that provide important services over the Internet Protocol. Therefore, the actual enterprise use of IP-based protocols is actually a hybrid of connection-oriented and connectionless applications, all running over the common connectionless IP infrastructure.

Layered Data Communications Protocols

Webster's New World Dictionary defines a *protocol* as "a set of rules governing the communications and the transfer of data between machines, as

THE BIRTH OF PACKET SWITCHING

In the 1960s Paul Baran and a small team of researchers at the RAND corporation were designing a resilient voice communication network that could survive the frightening devastation of a nuclear war [Baran 64]. The requirements on the network were stringent. The network had to reliably deliver critical messages in an environment where nodes and links could fail during the transmission of a message. In hindsight, the answer is surprisingly simple. Switches segmented a message into many smaller pieces, wrapping routing and protocol information around each piece. The result is a *packet*: a sequence of data fields containing addressing and handling instructions in a *header* that switches use to deliver the end-user information *payload* to the intended destination(s). The handling instructions ensured the correct and accurate delivery of the original message to the addressed end-user destination.

in computer systems." As a means to divide and conquer the design of complex protocols, engineers arranged data communications into logical layers that passed messages between themselves. This layering convention was created by ARPANET researchers in the early 1970s and adopted by the International Standards Organization Open System Interconnection (OSI) Reference Model. The OSI Reference Model refers to the messages passed between such layers as an *interface.* Each layer has a specific interface to the layer above it and the layer below it, with two exceptions: the lowest layer interfaces directly with the physical transmission medium, and the highest layer interfaces with the end-user application. Although many of the OSI standardized protocols are not widely implemented, the basic concept of protocol layering and terminology is widely used in the explanation of data communication protocols. Specifically, Chapter 6 describes how the Internet Protocol suite utilizes a similar layered concept. This book uses this proven technique to summarize the basic semantics and concepts involved in protocols in support of VPN applications.

Computer communication networking is primarily concerned with the lowest three layers: physical, data link, and network (as shown in Figure 4.3). Devices implementing these protocols may realize these layers in software, hardware, or a combination of the two. Typically, hardware implementations achieve much higher speeds and lower delays than software ones do; however, with the ever increasing performance of microprocessors this distinction blurs at times. An end system or host implements all of the protocol layers. X.25 corresponds directly to the lowest three layers of

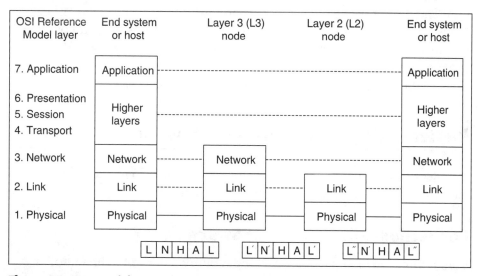

Figure 4.3 Layers of data communication protocols.

the OSI Reference Model which is due to the fact that the OSI standards adopted X.25 after it was developed. Frame relay corresponds to a subset of Layer 2 but it is not part of the OSI suite. ATM and MPLS also correspond to a subset of Layer 2, whereas IP corresponds to Layer 3. The literature commonly refers to these types of networks by the OSI layer number. For example, frame relay and ATM are frequently called Layer 2 (or L2 for short) protocols, and IP is called a Layer 3 (L3) protocol.

Figure 4.3 indicates physical connections as a solid line, and logical interfaces or protocols appear as a dashed line. The protocols communicate with each other via overhead fields carried with the packet headers (and sometimes a packet trailer as well), as indicated by the lettered boxes at the bottom of the figure corresponding to packets exchanged between adjacent nodes. The notation used here is L for link, N for network, H for higher layer, and A for application. Normally, the link layer has both a header and a trailer, as shown in the figure. Higher layer protocols normally have only a header. Nodes operating at lower-protocol layers perform functions and communicate with peer-level protocols in other nodes via changing bit patterns within the protocol overhead fields in the headers (and trailers). Figure 4.3 indicates this operation by showing the changed link layer protocol header and trailer as L, L′, and L″ as the packet traverses this simple network from left to right. Similarly, a Layer 3 node makes changes in the network-layer protocol header as shown by the change from N to N′ in the packet at the bottom of the figure.

The essence of data communication protocols lies in understanding what information these protocol headers (and in some cases trailers) contain. The details of the format and meanings of these protocol overhead fields are the stuff of standards, and therefore this book gives an overview of only the most important aspects. The text provides references to the relevant standards and to other books that provide more in-depth explanations of the inner workings of the protocols themselves.

Implementation and Protocol Specifics

This section summarizes the important aspects of X.25 packet switching and frame relaying as applied to enterprise VPNs.

Connection-Oriented Packet Switching

Connection-oriented packet switching requires the establishment of an end-to-end path between the origin and destination before transferring any data. The connection may be provisioned via administrative methods or established dynamically via a signaling protocol. In any event, the connection is established as an ordered set of links by means of intermediate nodes in a network. Once established, all data travels over the same preestablished path through the L2 or L3 network. The fact that data arrives at the destination in the same order as sent by the originator is inherent to the operation of a connection-oriented protocol.

The connection-oriented packet-switching standards introduced another useful concept in the modeling of protocol architectures. This was the notion of protocol planes (see Figure 4.4). In particular, the Narrowband ISDN (N-ISDN) standards introduced the concepts of user, control, and management planes. Each of these planes was composed of a stack of protocols operating in a coordinated manner. In particular, the planar model neatly captured the concept of a control plane signaling protocol that would establish a user plane path for the switching of time-slot or packet-level data through an ordered sequence of nodes. We use a variant of this planar model in Chapter 6 to describe how routing protocols operate to establish forwarding tables in a connectionless network.

This simple example illustrates one of the key trade-offs between a connection-oriented and connectionless network infrastructure. The nodes in a connection-oriented network must exchange and process multiple messages prior to transfer of any data, whereas in a connectionless network, all of the information necessary to relay a packet from end to end is contained in the network-layer protocol header. In a connection-

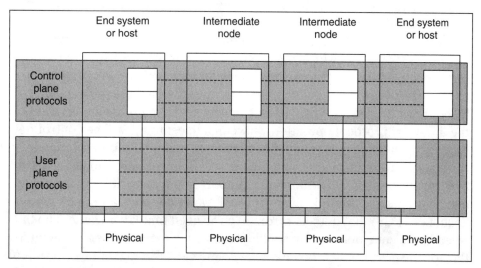

Figure 4.4 User and control plane interactions.

oriented network, the packets can be shorter than in a connectionless network because the path is already established. However, if the information flow is short-lived (for example, in a typical Web transaction), then the overhead of the connection-establishment message processing is not justified. Indeed, the Web could not operate at the scale it does today if network nodes had to process connection messages every time a user visited another Web page. On the other hand, longer-lived information flows (e.g., telephone calls, videoconferences, training sessions, or interactive multimedia conferences) are well served by the connection-oriented paradigm.

X.25 Packet Switching

Beginning in the late 1960s, computer manufacturers implemented proprietary protocols. In response to industry demand for data communication solutions that supported a multivendor environment, the Consultative Committee for International Telegraphy and Telephony (CCITT) standardized the first international physical-, link-, and packet-layer protocols in 1974. Collectively, these protocols are known as X.25 [Black 95a; ITU X.25; Tannenbaum 81]. The link layer of X.25 was based on the High-level Data Link Control (HDLC) standard, which extended the capabilities of the Synchronous Data Link Control (SDLC) protocol utilized in IBM SNA networks. X.25 provided reliable data communications over the noisy, unreliable transmission media prevalent in the 1970s and 1980s. Of course, the birth of the Internet occurred at approximately the same time as the deployment of X.25. But first let's review the connection-oriented protocols since the Internet Protocol can run over any other underlying protocol—connection-oriented or connectionless.

Figure 4.5 illustrates the principal fields in the X.25 link and network-layer packets for the user plane protocols. The link layer uses the HDLC flag sequence '01111110' to delimit the beginning and end of a frame. Bit- or byte-stuffing procedures support the transfer of a flag sequence in higher-layer protocol fields. The link address field supports supervision of the link-level protocol operation between adjacent nodes. The control field operates in information transfer, supervisory, and unnumbered formats. In the information transfer format, the control field contains link-layer send and receive sequence numbers that support hop-by-hop acknowledgment and flow control. The link-layer protocol trailer contains a Frame Check Sequence (FCS) that detects errors in a received link-layer frame. The link-layer frame concludes with a trailing flag, which may also be the beginning flag for the next frame. The link-layer frame carries a higher-layer protocol payload, as indicated by the shaded region in Figure 4.5. The X.25 network

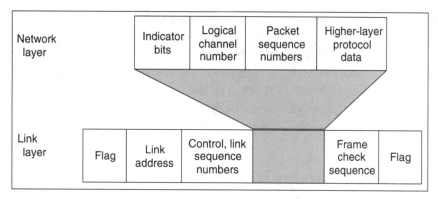

Figure 4.5 Important X.25 link- and packet-layer fields.

layer has several indicator bits that perform various functions. In particular, the Qualifier (Q) bit separates user plane data from control plane packets. The 12-bit Logical Channel Number (LCN) field supports up to 4,095 separate virtual connections on an X.25 interface. The packet sequence numbers are used for end-to-end acknowledgment and flow control.

X.25 control plane procedures allow for administrative establishment of a Permanent Virtual Circuit (PVC) or a Switched Virtual Call (SVC). The X.25 standard does not require that intermediate nodes use the X.25 protocol; however, we assume that X.25 packet switches use this protocol to illustrate some of the basic properties of X.25. The X.75 standard specifies the interconnection between X.25 network service providers.

The X.25 link layer is responsible for reliably delivering link-layer frames on a hop-by-hop basis using the send and receive sequence numbers in the link-layer control field. The packet sequence numbers in the network-layer header provide a means for end-to-end acknowledgment, but also provide an elementary form of traffic management described later. Memory was a precious commodity in early implementations of host computer communication interfaces and X.25 packet switches. Therefore, X.25 allowed hosts and packet switches to negotiate a maximum window size for each logical channel number. This meant that an LCN with a larger window size could send more data without an acknowledgment. The window size also provided a means to allocate precious buffer capacity in end-system interface cards as well as within packet switches within the X.25 network itself. Another level of traffic control occurred as part of the SVC process. If the network could not support the additional traffic, it blocked the call request.

X.25 packet switching enabled statistical multiplexing of multiple logical users onto a single physical circuit. Buffers in the packet switches reduced the probability of loss during rare intervals when many users transmitted simultaneously. Beginning in the 1970s, a number of service providers (such as Telenet, Tymnet, and monopoly telephone carriers) built networks to offer X.25 service. By the 1980s, X.25 networks connected the entire planet. X.25 packet switching still serves many user communities via public networks in less developed areas of the world. Most legacy manufacturers of WAN equipment support the X.25 protocol. In some cases, vendors just entering the market do not support X.25.

X.25 Closed User Groups (CUGs)

X.25 SVCs implemented an early form of data VPNs. The optional Closed User Group (CUG) facility allowed users to form communities of interest to and/or from which access was restricted [ITU X.25]. CUGs provided access control during the establishment phase of X.25 SVCs. Each X.25 user device could belong to one or more CUGs. A CUG defines a set of X.25 users that can communicate with other users in the same CUG. Within a CUG, the following options allowed further control of the types of calls that user devices could place:

- CUG with incoming calls barred prevents the user from accepting calls from other users.
- CUG with outgoing calls barred prevents the user from placing calls to other users.

Communication outside a set of CUGs subscribed to by the user is determined via subscription to the following optional facilities:

- CUG with incoming access accepts calls from any other X.25 user.
- CUG with outgoing access allows the user to place calls to any other X.25 user.

A simple use of CUGs allowed an X.25 network provider to segregate enterprises by assigning devices from each enterprise to a different CUG, as shown in Figure 4.6a. In the example, three enterprises labeled A, B, and C denote users by the enterprise letter and a user number. The circles indicate the allocation of a CUG index to each enterprise. This requires a minimal amount of configuration. When enterprises must communicate with each other, the situation becomes more complicated, as shown in Figure 4.6b. In order to allow all possible combinations of sets of users in one enterprise to interact with those in other enterprises, seven CUG indices are now required. As the number of cooperating enterprises increases, the complexity of CUG administration becomes unwieldy. An alternative tech-

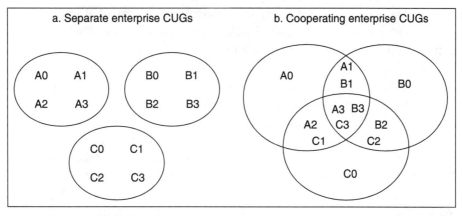

Figure 4.6 Applications of closed user groups.

nique called *address filtering*, or *screening*, is a better solution in this case, as described in Chapter 3, *Circuit-Switched VPNs*. Chapter 7, *Building Blocks for IP-Based VPNs*, applies this CUG model to firewalls, while Chapter 9, *IP Security-Enabled and Routing-Controlled VPNs*, applies the CUG model to an MPLS network controlled by IP routing protocols.

An X.25 user specifies a CUG index in an SVC call request message. If the SVC and the CUG index are valid, then the network converts the CUG index to an interlock code that is unique within the provider's network or within a set of interconnected provider networks. The interlock code is sent as part of the call request message across the network to the switch serving the called party destination. At the destination, the switch validates that both the calling and called parties belong to the CUG indicated by the interlock code. If valid, the network then converts the interlock code into the corresponding CUG index and delivers the call request message to the called party. The called party then either accepts or rejects the call attempt. If CUG validation fails at any point within the network, then the call is rejected.

Frame Relaying

Frame relay began as a movement within the standards bodies to streamline X.25 packet switching for operation over high-performance digital transmission media that connected powerful computer systems [Black 95b; Goralski 99; McDysan 98b]. In a sense, frame relay is the evolution of X.25 achieved by shedding retransmission on a hop-by-hop basis and eliminating end-to-end flow control. Removal of these processing-intensive functions allowed frame relay to operate at much higher speeds than X.25 could. Consequently, end applications experienced higher throughput with comparable reliability since hosts were performing retransmission and flow control already—implementation of these functions in the packet-switched network was redundant. Higher-layer protocols, for example, TCP, recovered lost or corrupted data when operating over frame relay networks.

Frame relay provides an upgrade to existing packet-switch technology by supporting speeds ranging from 64 kbps through nxDS1/nxE1 and all the way up to DS3/E3 speeds. Frame relay fills a technology gap between X.25 and ATM and, at the same time, provides a smooth transition to ATM. In fact, frame relay trunking over ATM and frame relay interworking with ATM, available from many service providers, are two options that smoothly facilitate this transition.

While frame relay has its origins in ISDN protocol standardization efforts [Black 95b], it broke onto the scene as a separate networking protocol [ITU-T Q.922]. The Frame Relay Forum was instrumental in driving vendors and carriers toward implementation agreements that made frame relay one of the fastest-growing carrier services in the early 1990s. WilTel offered the first commercial Permanent Virtual Connection (PVC) frame relay service in 1991, followed by carrier deployments around the world.

Figure 4.7 shows the principal fields of the frame relay Protocol Data Unit (PDU). Like X.25, frame relay uses the HDLC flag bit pattern to delimit the beginning and end of a link-layer frame. Frame relay also employs the same FCS as HDLC. However, if a frame relay switching node detects an errored frame, it simply discards it; leaving any required retransmission to higher-layer protocols. Frame relay adds a few important elements to HDLC. First, a Data Link Connection Identifier (DLCI) serves a role similar to X.25's Logical Channel Number, but in a range of header options that support 10, 16, or 21 bits of DLCI addressing. Frame relay also introduced the use of two other traffic control functions through the use of specific header bits for Discard Eligibility (DE) and Congestion Notification (CN), as described later in this chapter.

The Forward Explicit Congestion Notification (FECN) and Backward Explicit Congestion Notification (BECN) bits indicate to the receiver and sender, respectively, the presence of congestion in the network. Specifically, the network sets the FECN indicator in frames that traverse the net-

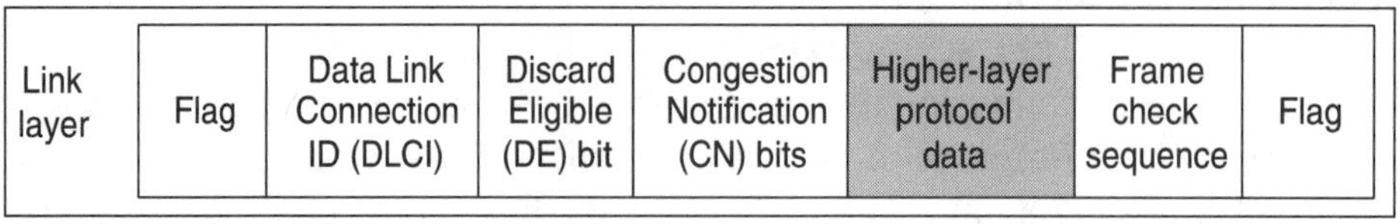

Link layer	Flag	Data Link Connection ID (DLCI)	Discard Eligible (DE) bit	Congestion Notification (CN) bits	Higher-layer protocol data	Frame check sequence	Flag

Figure 4.7 Frame relay protocol data unit.

work from receiver to sender to indicate congestion in the sender-to-receiver direction to the receiver. Receiver-based flow control protocols, such as DECnet, use FECN to initiate congestion-avoidance procedures. The network sets the BECN indicator in frames that traverse the network from receiver to sender to indicate congestion in the sender-to-receiver direction to the sender. That is, the network sets the BECN indicator in frames traveling in the opposite direction on the same virtual connection to those in which it sets the FECN indicator. Therefore, BECN aids senders, who can then dynamically change their source transmission rate.

The Discard Eligibility (DE) bit, when set to 1, indicates that during congestion conditions the network should discard this frame in favor of other frames with a higher priority—for example, those with DE bit set to 0. Note that networks are not constrained to discard only frames with DE set to 1 during periods of congestion. Either the user or the network may set the DE bit. The network sets the DE bit when the received frame rate exceeds the Committed Information Rate (CIR) specified for a particular virtual connection.

As in X.25, the DLCI need only be locally unique and frame relay need not be used between switches. Frame relay standards dub the interface between the user and the network, appropriately enough, the User-Network Interface (UNI) and the interface between networks the Network-Network Interface (NNI). Frame relay PVCs provide comparable security to private lines, but also provide more granular capacity allocation.

Early Traffic Management Capabilities

This section summarizes the traffic management capabilities important to VPNs that the X.25 and frame relay network services pioneered.

X.25 Flow and Admission Control

X.25 had two levels of windowed flow control: the link level and the end-to-end level. In the earliest implementation, the maximum window size was only 7 packets in length. Furthermore, X.25 required only that network service providers support packets of length up to 128 bytes, although some providers supported larger packet sizes. Finally, the relatively slow speed links connecting X.25 packet switches resulted in substantial store-and-forward delays. For example, transmission of a 128-byte packet at 9.6 kbps takes approximately 100 ms. Thus, the round-trip delay after traversing four or five such packet switches could exceed a few seconds if impacted by queuing delays and/or large distances. For the maximum end-to-end window size of 7 packets of length equal to 128 bytes, the maximum throughput was therefore only a few kbps. If the delay increased due to queuing within the X.25 network, then senders were limited by the end-to-end window size.

The send and receive sequence numbers in the X.25 packet layer provide flow control between the packet-layer source and the Destination End Systems (or DTEs). The packet-layer sequence number is incremented modulo the packet-layer sequence number modulus. X.25 currently defines packet-layer sequence number modulus values of 8, 128, and 32,768. The destination uses the packet-layer receive sequence number in a packet-layer acknowledgment to indicate the packet-layer send sequence number expected in the next packet from the other endpoint of that virtual circuit. Therefore, the packet-layer receive sequence number acts as an acknowledgment for all packets up to packet-layer receive sequence number minus 1. X.25 defines a separate value of the window size at the transmitter, which controls the maximum number of packets it can send without receiving a packet-layer acknowledgment from the destination. Similarly, X.25 defines a window size at the receiver, which controls how many packets the receiver will accept prior to generating an acknowledgment. Of course, the window size must always be smaller than the packet-layer sequence number modulus.

X.25 SVCs allowed a network provider to perform admission control on call request packets, blocking call attempts if the network was congested. X.25 PVCs had no such connection-level congestion control mechanism. However, an X.25 network could throttle back the input rate on selected ports by delaying link-level acknowledgments. None of these methods were ever standardized because the interaction with higher-layer protocols was never worked out.

Frame Relay Traffic and Congestion Control

With the higher speeds achievable in frame relay networks, protocol designers added more sophisticated traffic and congestion control features [ANSI T1.617; Goralski 99; McDysan 98b; ITU I.370]. Since frame relay provided a VPN solution that was similar to a private line, an important traffic management feature was a precise definition of the capacity of a virtual connection. Frame relay standards define the capacity of a virtual connection identified by a DLCI at an interface as the Committed Information Rate (CIR), which is the information transfer rate the network commits to transfer during normal conditions [ITU-T.370]. The conventional method for illustrating CIR uses a plot of the total number of bits transmitted on the vertical axis versus a time interval T on the horizontal axis, as shown in Figure 4.8. The access line rate AR determines the maximum number of bits that can be transmitted in an interval, as well as the slope of the cumulative bits transmitted when a frame is being sent. Frame relay standards define CIR as committed burst size Bc (expressed in bits) over a measurement interval of T seconds duration. Or, in equation form: CIR = Bc/T.

The dashed line in Figure 4.8 has a slope equal to CIR. Frames are sent at the access rate AR (as indicated by the line labeled "Transmitted frames") corresponding to the frames shown at the bottom of the figure. If the number of bits received during the interval T exceeds Bc, but is less than an excess threshold Bc + Be, then the frames associated with those bits are marked as Discard Eligible (DE) as shown in the figure. The bits that arrive during the interval T in excess of Bc + Be are discarded.

There is no standard for setting the interval T. If T is too small and the length of a single frame exceeds Bc, then those frames will be marked DE or discarded. If T is too large, then the required buffering to guarantee CIR may yield large variations in delay or be uneconomical. Selecting a value of T on the order of the round-trip delay results in good TCP/IP throughput over frame relay. Coast-to-coast round-trip delays across the continental United States are on the order of 100 ms across many frame relay networks.

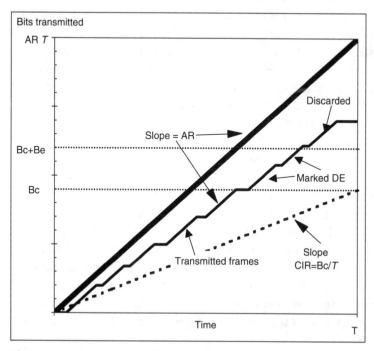

Figure 4.8 Frame relay traffic control.

Network providers offer different pricing plans for frame relay services. A typical pricing scheme entails a fixed monthly charge for each PVC and then an additional monthly charge based on the CIR. This pricing has an important consequence on economical VPN design, which will be discussed later in this chapter. Some service providers support a DE service at substantial discounts to the CIR service. Some carriers also provide billing based on actual traffic delivered to the destination. Customer network management, performance measurements, and service-level agreements are offered by some providers.

The DE bit in the frame relay header provides an effective means to respond to congestion. Either the customer or the network may set the DE bit. The customer can set the DE bit to mark some frames at a lower priority, for example, in a two-level video coding scheme [McDysan 00]. Normally, the network provider ingress switch sets the bit DE in frames exceeding the CIR. The frame relay standards state that if a network node is congested, then it should first discard the frames with the DE bit set, thereby delivering a higher quality of service to those frames that fall within the contracted CIR.

Frame relay also implemented some congestion indication and response functions in its protocol header. Frame relay switches indicated congestion by using 2 bits in the header, one for the forward direction and the other for the backward direction. Frame relay switches set the Forward Explicit Congestion Notification (FECN) bit in frames traversing a congested link in the direction from the sender to the receiver as an indication to receiver-based flow control protocols. Frame relay switches set the Backward Explicit Congestion Notification (BECN) bit in frames on DLCIs traveling in the opposite direction of a congested link as an indication to transmitter-based flow control protocols. An increase in the frequency of FECN and BECN bits received is the indication of network congestion provided by frame relay. At present, little use is made of the frame relay congestion notification by higher-layer protocols in intermediate systems. Since a significant portion of the traffic carried by frame relay networks is IP, the CPE router can do little else with the FECN/BECN bits but delay or discard the traffic. Unfortunately, there is no standard method for the CPE router to convey the FECN/BECN congestion notification to the IP-based application that could provide flow control. Although this may seem wasteful to not use information provided by a lower-level protocol, the capability for IP to run over any lower-layer protocol is a fundamental design principle of the TCP/IP protocol suite.

Store-and-Forward Performance

The packet-switching functions of X.25 and frame relay have some important implications on the performance experienced by VPN applications. A fundamental performance aspect is store-and-forward delay introduced by packet switching. Figure 4.9 illustrates the basic operation of store-and-forward packet switching in a configuration with a source and destination terminal and $N = 2$ switching nodes. In this space-time diagram, the spatial flow of packets occurs from left to right as time progresses from top to bottom. Starting from the upper left-hand corner, the terminal sends a packet of B bytes at the link rate of R bps. The first bit of the packet arrives after a propagation delay of P seconds at the first packet switch. However, the last bit of the packet arrives after a serialization delay of $8B/R$ seconds. Furthermore, since packet traffic is bursty, there will sometimes be a queue of packets awaiting service. Thus, this simple model assumes that a queuing factor of $Q > 1$ applies to the average packet transmission time required for each hop. A commonly used model for this queuing factor is $Q = 1/(1 - U)$, where U is the aver-

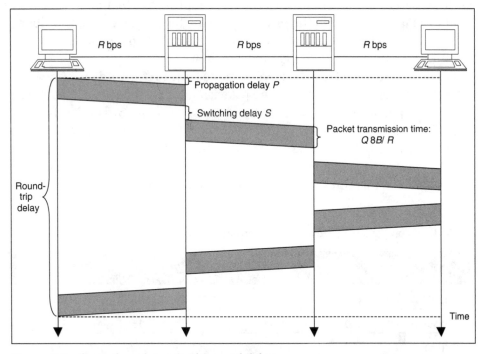

Figure 4.9   Illustration of store-and-forward delay.

age link utilization [Kleinrock 76; McDysan 00; Stallings 98b]. The packet switch could not begin processing until it had received the entire packet and confirmed that it was error-free. The packet switch then had to determine the next hop and perform any other processing, requiring a switching delay of S seconds. This process occurred hop by hop across the packet-switched network until the packet reached the destination, which also required a switching delay S.

Extrapolating this simple example to a generic N switch network connected by links with identical propagation delay P results in the following expression for the end-to-end round-trip delay:

$$RTD = 2(N + 1)[P + Q \, 8B/R + S]$$

Table 4.1 shows the resulting RTD for an $N = 5$ node network with all links of equal speed R operating at $U = 70\%$ utilization, ignoring propagation delay (i.e., $P = 0$). All nodes, including the destination terminal, have the same switching delay S. The values given in the table are illustrative. Implementations vary and have changed over time. The point is that as speeds increase and the switching performance of each node improves with each iteration of technology, the RTD approaches that of speed-of-light propagation delay in the physical line media. For example, in a fiber-optic cable, the propagation velocity of light is only approximately two-thirds of the velocity of light in a vacuum.

Frame relay allowed an intermediate node to begin forwarding a frame after the header fields were received [Black 95b]. This reduced a component of store-and-forward delay for low-speed links. The penalty paid for this decreased delay was that if the frame had any bit errors, then capacity on the links was wasted. If the line error rate was low, then this wastage was minimal. However few implementations used this technique, opting instead for cell-based transmission to reduce the store-and-forward component of delay.

Table 4.1 Comparison of Store-and-Forward Round-Trip Delay

PARAMETER	X.25	FRAME RELAY	IP SOFTWARE	ATM	IP HARDWARE
B (bytes)	128	256	256	53	256
R (Mbps)	0.56	1.5	45	150	600
S (ms)	~100	~10	~20	<1	<1
RTD (ms)	1273	175	242	12	12

Principal Applications

This section describes the principal enterprise VPN applications supported by X.25 and frame relay networks.

Private Line Network Replacement

Because X.25 was so richly featured, it carried almost any other protocol. It supported SNA, IP, DECnet, and many proprietary protocols. Such broad support came at a cost, since X.25 replicated some capabilities of the higher-layer protocols. The principal gain of X.25 and frame relay network deployments for most enterprises was economic. Figure 4.10a illustrates a comparison of a typical private line-based design, while Figure 4.10b shows a comparable X.25 or frame relay VPN design. The figure shows major nodes as squares connected by thick, high-speed trunks. It shows smaller, secondary nodes as circles connected by thinner, lower-speed trunks. As discussed in Chapter 2, *Private Network Technologies*, a private line often has several cost components corresponding to the local and long-haul service provider. Each link between nodes in the private line network could be composed of up to three segments. The X.25 or frame relay VPN design replaces the long-haul private lines with shorter-distance access lines connected to switching nodes within an X.25 or frame relay network, shown as a cloud in Figure 4.10b. Since the enterprise need only purchase a shorter-distance access line, the costs of the long-haul private line segments are eliminated. The X.25 or frame relay network provides a comparable long-haul packet- or frame-based transport service instead.

Many enterprise VPNs operating over X.25 or frame relay utilize circuit-switched access as a backup capability, as indicated by dashed lines in Fig-

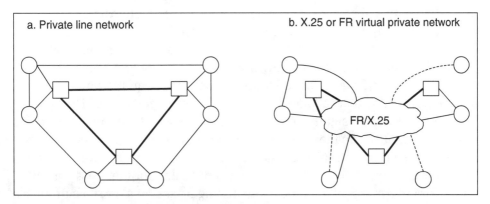

Figure 4.10   VPN replacement of private line network.

ure 4.10. In some cases, the primary access may also be an on-demand dial-up connection for small or single-user sites. Figure 4.10b illustrates these dial-up connections as dashed lines. Typically, if the time period employed for dial-up access is less than a few hours per day, then dial-up access is economically justified. In general, whether a private line or a connection-oriented VPN design is more economical depends upon many factors, such as location of the enterprise sites, prevailing tariffs for private line and VPN services in each geographic region, and traffic patterns. Circuit-switched access involves two stages. First, the user device signals the network and requests a connection to a device. After establishment of the circuit-switched connection, the X.25 or frame relay protocol can then operate. In other words, after the signaling protocol connects the circuit, it looks like a dedicated access line.

Cost-Effective Hierarchical Networks

X.25 and frame relay network support the basic security requirements of privacy, authentication, and integrity because data on an access line is limited to connectivity established by the virtual connections. Figure 4.11 illustrates a typical X.25 or frame relay VPN configuration. At the top of the figure, two large sites contain servers and databases for the enterprise. A high-speed virtual connection connects these sites via a high-speed access line. At the bottom of the figure, many smaller client sites connect to an X.25 or frame relay network via lower-speed dedicated access lines or a circuit-switched access method. Each smaller site with a dedicated access line is interconnected via a pair of PVCs to each of the two larger sites for reliability. Observe that any single failure of a large site, access line, or network switch leaves the virtual private network intact. If the access line to a smaller site fails, then only that site is affected. Since public X.25 and frame relay services often have a per-PVC charge, this hierarchical design is often quite economical when the underlying enterprise paradigm is client-server based. Chapter 8, *Dial-In Access and Multiprotocol Tunneling VPNs*, presents an economic comparison of this hierarchical design with an IP-based overlay VPN design.

The hierarchical design significantly reduces the required number of links compared with a full mesh of point-to-point connections. However, although this design significantly reduces the required number of connections, note that traffic may traverse additional, expensive access lines on its way to the destination. This may still save the enterprise money if the carrier passes on enough of its economies of scale. Another cost-cutting move for enterprises is to colocate switching nodes on a carrier's premises to avoid these additional access line charges.

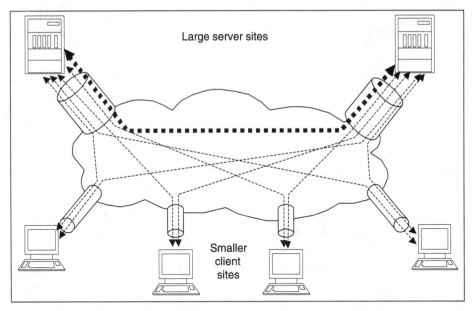

Figure 4.11   Typical X.25/frame relay VPN application.

Supporting Private Multiprotocol Networks

One of the early drivers for frame relay networks was the emergence of multiple network-layer protocols in local area networks. The IEEE and ISO standards organizations had defined a protocol header that supported multiprotocol encapsulation. In other words, this part of the packet header identified the protocol that was carried within. Service provider pricing was also a factor in this design. Typically, a provider charged for each Virtual Connection (VC). Therefore, the multiprotocol encapsulation scheme allowed an enterprise to run multiple protocols over the same VC, thereby reducing cost. Frame relay standards split the data link layer of the user plane into two areas: core services and user-specified services. Core services include basic frame relaying, status signaling, and SVC control. User-specified services include multiprotocol encapsulation specified in ITU-T Q.933 Annex E, IETF RFC 1490, Frame Relay Forum 3.1, and ANSI T1.617a.

Figure 4.12 illustrates an example of two network designs, with and without multiprotocol encapsulation. Each supports interconnection of SNA- and IP-based devices between every site. As shown in Figure 4.12a, the design without multiprotocol encapsulation required that the router at each site have two PVCs to every other site—one for SNA traffic and

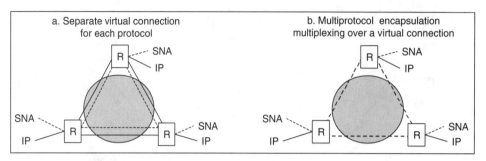

Figure 4.12   PVC usage and multiprotocol encapsulation.

another for IP traffic. If the routers employ multiprotocol encapsulation, then the additional header allows the router to multiplex many protocols onto the same virtual connection, as shown in Figure 4.12b. Because many providers assessed a charge for each connection, multiprotocol encapsulation resulted in a less expensive network. Separate connections for each protocol do provide at least one advantage: A specific amount of capacity can be dedicated to the traffic level for each protocol.

Frame relay also utilized control plane signaling in a new way to support data networks. The SVC signaling standards defined the STATUS ENQUIRY message for a user to inquire about the status of a particular connection. The network responded with a STATUS message. The initial developers of frame relay equipment used these two messages to construct a Local Management Interface (LMI) for PVCs. The STATUS message body contained 2 bits that indicated whether a specific frame relay DLCI was active (the A bit) and/or whether the PVC was new (the N bit). The LMI protocol operated as follows. Periodically, the user sent a STATUS ENQUIRY message to the network. The network responded with a STATUS message, which contained the status for each DLCI. If the user did not send a STATUS ENQUIRY message for a few polling intervals, the network declared the DLCI down and propagated this information to the LMI interface on the distant end. This allowed the protocol to detect access line CPE, or logical failures. Extensions to the status signaling protocol supported network interconnections. Because the maximum size of the STATUS message limited the number of DLCIs on an interface, network-network status signaling supported communication regarding only those DLCIs whose status had actually changed.

The standards developers also defined a means to resolve the higher-layer protocol address of the device at the other end of a PVC. Called an inverse Address Resolution Protocol (ARP), this action occurred for a new PVC or after a PVC that was previously inactive became active as determined via the LMI protocol. Basically, the router sent an inverse ARP message on the DLCI indicating its higher-layer protocol address. After the other end responded with an inverse ARP message indicating its higher-layer protocol address, the two routers had automatically discovered the protocol type(s) and the higher-layer protocol addresses of the device to which they were connected.

Integrating Voice and Data with Frame Relay

A serious performance issue occurs with frame-based protocols on lower-speed links when a long frame gets ahead of a short delay-sensitive frame. A long 1,500-byte Ethernet packet getting ahead of a short voice packet can delay it almost 200 ms on a 64-kbps link, as illustrated in Figure 4.13a. Interactive voice conversation becomes strained if the one-way delay is greater than 150 ms. For example, the one-way delay for communication via geosynchronous satellite is over 250 ms. What occurs when the delay becomes this large is that both people involved in the conversation can begin speaking before realizing that the other is already talking. The resulting collisions in conversation force repetition of sentences or phrases, greatly reducing the interactive nature of normal speech that we often take for granted. Therefore, packet voice and data cannot share the same link unless something is done to avoid the occurrence of long packets on low-speed links.

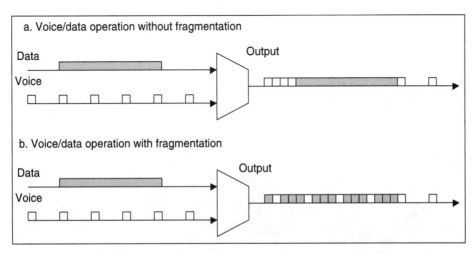

Figure 4.13   Frame relay fragmentation for packet voice.

The Internet Protocol defines a means for fragmenting packets; however, that method uses significant processor resources. Frame relay and other HDLC-based standards defined a simpler method where the user device and the network work together to fragment the large packets into shorter segments. A higher-priority packet, say a voice packet, then has an opportunity to interrupt a longer data packet, as shown in Figure 4.13b. For example, if the fragment size is 100 bytes, then the maximum waiting time reduces to approximately 15 ms on a 64-kbps link. The Frame Relay Forum FRF.12 implementation agreement specifies a protocol that breaks up long data frames into smaller segments and reassembles them at the destination. IETF RFC 2686 specifies a similar means to implement this function using the Point-to-Point Protocol (PPP) for use in IP networks. This avoids the problem of a long frame delaying shorter, urgent voice frames. The specification defines procedures for performing fragmentation across an interface between a user and a network or on an end-to-end basis.

The next chapter moves on to modern connection-oriented VPN protocols—specifically, Asynchronous Transfer Mode (ATM) and the Broadband ISDN protocol suite developed by the ITU-T, as well as the MultiProtocol Label Switching (MPLS) and Resource reSerVation Protocol (RSVP) developed by the IETF. As we shall see, these protocols borrowed heavily from concepts pioneered by X.25 and frame relay that were proven in real-world experience, but the designers refined or revised concepts that were either too vague, too complex, or ineffective. Furthermore, these modern connection-oriented protocols are blazing new trails that offer promising new features to enterprise VPN users.

CHAPTER

5

Modern Connection-Oriented VPNs—ATM, MPLS, and RSVP

He that leaveth nothing to chance will do few things ill, but he will do very few things.
—George Saville

This chapter describes the important characteristics of the more recent connection-oriented VPN technologies: Asynchronous Transfer Mode (ATM), MultiProtocol Label Switching (MPLS), and the Resource reSer-Vation Protocol (RSVP). These protocols are similar to X.25 and frame relay described in the previous chapter in many ways, but they also provide a number of enhancements and additional features. An old adage says that when your favorite tool is a hammer, then every problem looks like a nail. This set of connection-oriented protocols is like the familiar hammer, and some of the knottier networking problems look very much like nails. However, as we will see in the next chapter, a hammer is a poor choice of tool when the problem is more akin to a screw than to a nail.

Business Drivers and Requirements

The principal drivers for the continued development of improved connection-oriented VPN services are those of capacity reservation and quality. Simultaneously, the ever-increasing thirst for the newest wave of computers and applications swells demand, motivating improvements in efficiency and design.

Guaranteed Capacity and Quality

When an enterprise conducts important activities requiring communication services, sufficient capacity and quality are essential. These measures are extremely important to an enterprise, because they directly relate to the amount of money paid in exchange for the service provided. The principal measure of capacity is the information transfer rate provided by the network, expressed as bits, cells, or packets per second. We further qualify this measure in terms of a *peak rate* observed over short intervals and an *average rate* observed over longer intervals. The final measure of capacity is the *burst duration*. Taken together, these three measures—peak rate, average rate, and burst duration—form the basis of a capacity measure used in IP and ATM networks for defining offered traffic and allocated capacity. An agreed-upon measure of capacity and traffic in a packet- or cell-switched network environment is a critical component of the agreement between an enterprise user and the VPN service provider. The IP and ATM standards define such a measure via similar algorithms, dubbed the *token bucket* and *leaky bucket*, respectively, as described later in this chapter.

Along with capacity, the other important measure is that of quality, commonly referred to as *Quality of Service* (QoS). Quality takes on quantifiable attributes dependent on time scale. Performance for the interval required for service installation or updates is typically measured in weeks or days, whereas repair time objectives are often no more than a few hours. Other QoS measures such as loss, delay, and jitter are usually averages measured over seconds to hours. Availability is important QoS measure for mission-critical applications. For example, extended periods of downtime can have significant financial implications for some enterprises.

Some applications, such as video and video, are quite sensitive to loss and jitter. Other applications, such as file transfer, Web browsing, and Email, are relatively insensitive to loss and jitter. Interactive applications require one-way delays on the order of 100 ms; however, broadcast applications can tolerate delays ranging from seconds to minutes. Web-browsing enterprise users tolerate delays of a second or so, whereas file transfer application can tolerate much longer delays. Applications like Email can tolerate delays on the order of minutes. Each application type has its own QoS profile, and an enterprise user requires that the service provider meet or exceed these objectives in order to achieve productive benefit. There are few things more frustrating to an information worker than a network that performs poorly or inconsistently.

The Need for Speed

The increased usage of a Graphical User Interface (GUI) in operating systems and applications creates the need for greater peak transmission rates in order to preserve response time. Many graphics-intensive applications were first used in local area networks, where high transmission speeds were economical. As enterprises distributed their operations and personnel, valuable information content also became distributed across many locations. This move away from the centralized information storage paradigm of the mainframe-computing era empowered by the PC and LANs created the need for high-speed wide area networking.

Furthermore, some applications, such as voice and videoconferencing, computerized animation, audio and video broadcast, and supercomputing, inherently require larger amounts of capacity than computer-based applications. Let's consider an example. The standard transmission rate for voice of 64 kbps is approximately equal to the highest achievable dial-in speed available for accessing the Internet. It is interesting to note that even when presented with a higher peak rate, a Web user transmits at this peak rate in a very bursty manner. For example, a Web user's computer connected via a 10-Mbps Ethernet to a router with access to a high-speed Internet connection may generate an average information transfer rate of only a few hundred kbps or so. This wide disparity between the peak and average rates occurs because the user session is a sequence of queries and network response intervals punctuated by relatively lengthy intervals of "think time." A high peak rate is essential to keep the response time at acceptable levels, especially for highly visual, data-intensive applications.

Digital transmission and encoding of high-fidelity audio signals requires capacity on the order of several hundred kbps—a value comparable to that used on average by a high-performance Web surfer of the late twentieth century. However, the relative bit rate required for video is several orders of magnitude greater than that required for audio. Early in the twenty-first century, multiple-window, multimedia-intense Web experiences will likely become commonplace, increasing the required capacity of the Internet. Government research and specialized industrial and entertainment enterprises have frequently been leading-edge users of advanced visualization technologies. Indeed, these applications were principal drivers for the development of ATM technology beginning in the late 1980s.

Continual Cost Reduction

A recurring theme of enterprise VPNs is the persistent drive to reduce costs. New technology frequently delivers reduced costs along with additional features. Both ATM and MPLS take a similar tack toward economical networking: Simplify the switching operation so that it is readily implemented in hardware. History has shown that purpose-built hardware manufactured in sufficient volume costs less than software-based implementations. Well-defined and stable standards are extremely important in this arena, since integrated-circuit manufacturers must sell millions of chips to offset design and tooling costs. Once the market reaches a critical volume, incremental costs for manufacturing additional chips are quite low. Ethernet is a good example of this manufacturing economy of scale.

The experience from X.25 and frame relay showed that a virtual circuit on a public network is frequently more economical than a real circuit interconnecting sites when the offered traffic either is bursty, is of multiple types, or has multiple destinations. This basic economic paradigm, combined with the promise of higher speeds and the consequent improved economy of scale, made further reductions in the cost of information transport possible. Finally, greater trunk speeds in ATM and MPLS networks should also result in higher statistical multiplexing gain ratios, which translates into lower prices.

Technology Trends and Enablers

In parallel with the business drivers, other trends in the world of technology enabled the evolution of more powerful connection-oriented VPN networking capabilities.

Making Switching Hardware Run Fast

The ATM and MPLS protocols addressed the performance problems of software-based routers by defining a standard method for switching information that was readily implemented in hardware. ATM focused on making the data unit a standardized fixed size, because it is easier for hardware to handle fixed-length data blocks than ones of variable length. In fact, most hardware implementations that support variable-length frames on external interfaces actually employ a fixed-length data block for switching and routing within the machine. The reason for this internal design choice is straightforward. With a fixed-length data block, there is no need to implement an additional counter in the hardware logic to track the boundaries of variable-length data blocks. As the first and last step of a complicated switching process, transforming between a variable-length frame on an external interface to and from the internal fixed-length data blocks is a relatively simple operation. A foundational aspect of ATM is that it exposes a standard fixed-length data block, called a *cell*, used by a switching machine on external interfaces. Actually, most ATM switches use an internal cell that is larger than 53 bytes to ease implementation and provide additional internal switching functions like multicast and traffic control.

ATM also resurrected a large amount of research conducted in the late 1980s and early 1990s concerned with applying earlier research on parallel supercomputing and shared-memory designs applied to the problem of building extremely large switching machines [Awdeh 94]. The effect of Moore's law, which consistently improves the speed, density, and price-performance of integrated circuits, coupled with advances in switching design, has kept network node capacity ahead of the computing and communication power available to the enterprise user. This combination of basic electronics and sophisticated design enabled the implementation of switching machines that occupy footprints that were a fraction of those of preceding technologies with comparable capacity. For example, the state of the art in the early twenty-first century supports switching and routing capacity on the order of 40 Gbps on a single 19-inch rack-mounted shelf. In comparison, a telephone switching system of comparable capacity in the 1980s occupied a small building. Larger label switches or routers consist of multiple shelves of this type interconnected using the techniques arising from the research of the late 1980s.

In the late 1980s, the ITU made the distinction between existing and next-generation communication protocols based solely on speed. The preceding Integrated Services Digital Network (ISDN) was dubbed the Narrowband ISDN (N-ISDN), while the new heir was christened the Broadband ISDN (B-ISDN). In ITU parlance, ATM is only a part of the overall B-ISDN infrastructure targeted to support integrated voice, data, video, and multimedia services [ITU I.211]. Initially, N-ISDN supported link speeds up to the 2-Mbps E1 rate, while B-ISDN supported all higher speeds. Although the link speeds supported by N-ISDN and B-ISDN now overlap because B-ISDN now supports DS1 and E1 rates as well as xDSL, there was never any concerted effort to increase the maximum speed of N-ISDN.

QoS and Traffic Management

A principal focus of the ATM layer of B-ISDN was that of supporting precisely defined measures of quality at well-understood traffic levels. Most industry experts acknowledge that the definitions and design principles resulting from this effort will form the foundation of QoS and traffic management in future networks as well. In fact, one of the principal drivers for MPLS was to align these capabilities with IP routing protocols, since many early Internet service providers utilized ATM as the backbone transport because of its traffic management capabilities. The ITU precisely defines QoS in terms of measurable events [ITU I.356] and also provides a standardized means for end users or service providers to measure the actual performance experienced on an individual connection basis [ITU I.610]. These definitions correspond to the generic concepts of loss, errors, delay, and jitter that are important to many applications, as discussed earlier in this chapter.

Two principal technologies support the delivery of different levels of QoS for connections that have a well-defined traffic level. The first technology involves a precise means for measuring the level of traffic offered by a user to the network. ATM standards precisely define a cell-based Generic Cell Rate Algorithm (GCRA), also known as a *leaky bucket* or virtual scheduling algorithm [ATMF TM 4.0; ITU I.371]. The IETF standards reference, but do not precisely define, a packet-based algorithm called a *token bucket*. The second technology centers around a buffering strategy that supports different levels of loss, delay, and jitter by means of multiple buffers that have a scheduling and admission policy. Since these two technologies are pivotal to the delivery of QoS for flows conforming to an agreed-to traffic level, we now examine each in more detail and summarize how they indeed deliver on the promise of QoS.

Both the cell- and packet-based traffic measurement algorithms utilize the concept of a bucket to illustrate their basic principle of operation. Some things may seem diametrically opposed at first glance, but end up being different views of the same underlying concept. The ATM leaky bucket and IP token bucket algorithms are an example of this apparent dichotomy; in fact, the two algorithms are quite compatible. We describe the high-level concept of these approaches with reference to Figure 5.1. These algorithms apply either to the peak rate or to the average rate. A traffic measurement system that monitors both the peak rate and the average rate must have two bucket-based algorithms operating on each traffic flow, one for the peak rate and another for the average rate.

Figure 5.1a depicts the operation of the cell-based leaky bucket algorithm in response to a series of cell arrivals shown along the time axis. The contents of the bucket are shown below the series of arriving cells. The example begins with an empty bucket on the left-hand side of the figure. Each cell arrival adds 3 units to the bucket, while the bucket leaks 2 units

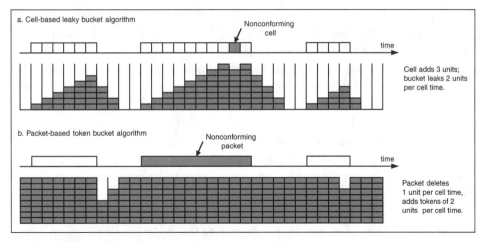

Figure 5.1   Leaky bucket and token bucket algorithms.

during each cell time. This means that a cell arrival adds a net value of 1 unit to the bucket while the absence of a cell arrival means that the bucket drains two units. The leaky bucket algorithm considers a cell arrival to be conforming if the addition of the fluid would not overflow the bucket. Therefore, the ninth cell arrival in the second burst is nonconforming, as shown by the shaded cell at the top of Figure 5.1a. All other cell arrivals are conforming, indicated by the white-filled cells. This is a problem if all the cells make up part of a single packet, because loss of a single cell within a series of cells representing a packet causes loss of the entire packet. ATM switches have developed means to address this issue, at the expense of additional complexity, by discarding all of the cells associated with a packet.

Figure 5.1b illustrates the operation of the packet-based token bucket algorithm in response to a series of packet arrivals that correspond precisely to the bursts of cell arrivals considered in the leaky bucket example. The token bucket algorithm adds 1 unit per cell time in this example. In fact, there is no standard for precisely how frequently an implementation must add tokens to the bucket. If implementations add tokens at markedly different rates, then they may determine different values of conformance for the same series of packet arrivals. However, if the implementation adds tokens frequently enough, such as on a per-byte basis or even at each cell time as in this example, this is not an issue. The token bucket algorithm in our example requires that the bucket contain 1 unit for each cell time of the arriving packet's total duration for that packet to be deemed conformant. Note that our example shows this determination occurring only after complete reception of the packet, a design that most MPLS encapsulation protocols require. As shown in Figure 5.1b, the first and third packets are conforming, but the second is not. In this example, the token bucket adds 2 units each cell time until the bucket is full.

Although these algorithms produce similar results, they determine conformance based on the bucket contents in an opposite manner. The leaky bucket must have empty space to accept a cell arrival as conforming, whereas the token bucket must be sufficiently full to consider a packet arrival as conforming. Aside from the case of partially conforming packets for the cell-based leaky bucket algorithm, a direct mapping between the leaky bucket and token bucket parameters has been standardized [RFC 2381].

A network node monitors traffic flows according to a leaky bucket or a token bucket algorithm, passing conforming traffic to the destination interface. The node may either discard nonconforming traffic or mark it at a lower priority. Alternatively, a network node or an end user may employ a bucket-based algorithm to shape traffic such that it precisely complies with a set of traffic parameters that specify the peak and average rates along with their associated burst duration. The switching fabric and port interfaces on the node must then perform additional processing on the cells or packets destined for a particular interface. The earliest network nodes implemented a single queue per interface. This meant that all traffic destined for that interface experienced the same level of loss, delay, and jitter.

Since the packets or cells of different flows may have different QoS requirements, network node designs evolved to support multiple buffers using the generic architecture illustrated in Figure 5.2. An implementation with a small number of buffers supports class-based queuing, and an implementation that provides a queue for each active flow performs per-flow queuing. Starting from the left-hand side, the switch or port first classifies arriving packets or cells to determine the appropriate buffer (or

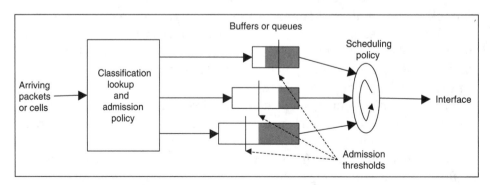

Figure 5.2 Multiple buffers managed by policies.

queue), as well as apply an admission policy. The admission policy often relates to a threshold that measures the fill of the target buffer, as shown in the figure. Once this function admits packets or cells to the target buffer, a scheduling policy determines when the buffer contents are transmitted on the outgoing interface shown at the right-hand side of the figure.

The operation of multiple buffers with different admission thresholds does indeed achieve the desired result of delivering multiple levels of quality. Figure 5.3 illustrates this concept for a simple switching node that has two buffers, each with a single threshold, as shown in Figure 5.3a. The shorter buffer has a higher priority, and the port services it in preference to that of the longer buffer. In the simplest case, this would be strict priority queuing. However, many devices implement other scheduling policies, such as Weighted Fair Queuing (WFQ) or round-robin service [Keshav 98b]. Furthermore, each buffer also has an admission threshold for traffic flows that have different loss objectives. These thresholds could support differentiation between conforming and nonconforming traffic, as determined by a bucket-based policing algorithm. Figure 5.3b qualitatively illustrates the resulting loss rate and jitter for each of these buffer partitions. Since buffer length bounds jitter and the port services the shorter buffer at the highest priority, the traffic served by this buffer experiences the best jitter and loss performance. Furthermore, the traffic that can occupy the entire buffer (H0) experiences lower loss but greater jitter than the traffic that can occupy only part of the buffer (H1) as determined by the admission threshold. Since the port services the longer buffer at a lower priority, loss and jitter are both greater. In an analogous fashion, the traffic served by the entire buffer (L0) has greater jitter but lower loss than traffic that can utilize only the portion of the buffer (L1) determined by the admission threshold.

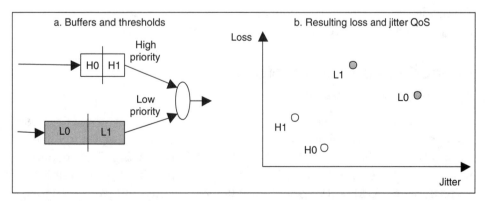

Figure 5.3 QoS resulting from multiple buffers.

The computation of the resulting level of loss and jitter is dependent on several factors, including the statistics of the offered traffic, the operation of the scheduling policy, and the threshold settings. Queuing theory gives exact results for only the simplest cases of offered traffic for simple scheduling and threshold policies. Simulation modeling is usually required to estimate these values for realistic implementations. The reader interested in further details should consult McDysan (00), Onvural (93), and Stallings (98b).

Packetization for Voice, Video, and Circuit Data

Another important technology enabler is the development of algorithms that digitally encode audio and video signals in packet format. These encoding algorithms have dramatically reduced the required digital transmission rate for audio and video signals while simultaneously preserving a high level of quality. Furthermore, in the case of ATM, the development of protocols that support synchronous TDM data over an asynchronous network enable B-ISDN to deliver on the promise of supporting N-ISDN applications in a seamless manner. For ATM, these algorithms rely on a set of protocols called ATM Adaptation Layers (AALs), as described later in this chapter. For IP, these protocols utilize other techniques as described in Chapter 6, *The Internet Protocol Suite*.

Implementation and Protocol Specifics

This section summarizes the salient points of ATM, MPLS, and RSVP technologies as they apply to enterprise VPNs. The presentation of the ATM-based protocols originating from the traditional ITU standardization alongside the IP-based protocols defined by the IETF affords a view of the many similarities and highlights the few important differences.

Connection-Oriented Protocol Relationships

Since the following material covers a number of related protocols, we use the concept of protocol layering from the discussion in Chapter 4, *Early Connection-Oriented Data VPNs—X.25 and Frame Relay*. The shaded portions of the left-hand side of Figure 5.4 illustrate the layered relationships between ATM and its adaptation layers with higher-layer protocols,

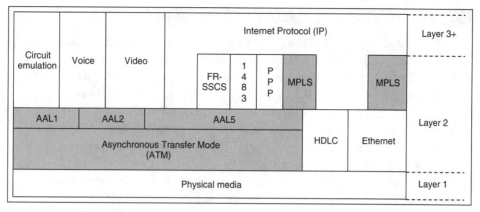

Figure 5.4   ATM, MPLS, and related protocols.

and the right-hand side of the figure shows where MPLS fits into this over-all layered schema. The left-hand side shows ATM-based support for voice, video, and generic data services, while the right-hand side shows support for IP-related protocols by ATM's AAL5 and MPLS. This drawing presents a road map of the topics covered in this chapter and the remainder of the book. All communication protocols run over some Layer 1 physical trans-mission medium, as shown at the bottom of the figure. Higher-layer proto-cols make the digital bit stream, cells, frames, or packets available to yet higher-layer protocols in the universal method of protocol layering. The OSI layer numbers on the right-hand side are valid for the Layer 2 proto-cols that support IP because these protocols all support data communica-tion in a standard way. Note that services shown on the left-hand side, such as circuit emulation in support of private lines, voice, and video, do not necessarily conform to the OSI layered model.

Starting from the left-hand side of Figure 5.4, ATM operates over a num-ber of physical media. In turn, higher-layer protocols do not usually inter-face directly with ATM, but instead utilize ATM capabilities through an ATM Adaptation Layer (AAL) protocol. An AAL converts between a stream of cells and the data format that the higher-layer protocol uses. For exam-ple, AAL1 [ITU I.363.1] supports the emulation of the bit stream provided by a private line service. AAL1 also supports the switching of Constant-Bit-Rate (CBR) voice, whereas AAL2 [ITU I.363.2] supports Variable-Bit-Rate (VBR) voice and video services. Initially, the ITU-T planned to standardize separate AAL3 and AAL4 protocols to support connection-oriented and connectionless data protocols, respectively, but the final AAL3/4 standard [ITU I363.3] supported both. Only the Bellcore-defined Switched Multi-

AAL5—THE SIMPLE AND EFFICIENT ADAPTATION LAYER

Although AAL3/4 provided the necessary functions for all types of data communication protocols, many implementers found that it was quite complex and inefficient. The computer industry responded with a proposal for a Simple Efficient Adaptation Layer (SEAL) in 1991 [Lyon 91] that had a simpler and more efficient design. The principal difference was that AAL3/4 provided for multiplexing of more than 1,000 flows over a single ATM Virtual Channel Connection (VCC), whereas AA5 relied on higher-layer protocols to perform their own multiplexing. The ITU-T and the ATM Forum, along with national and regional standards bodies, quickly adopted this concept and standardized the protocol now known as AAL5 [ITU I.363.5]. AAL5 rapidly became the AAL of choice for equipment manufacturers and service providers supporting packet data.

megabit Data Service (SMDS) uses the AAL3/4 protocol. Since SMDS is not widely deployed, it is not a viable VPN option in most regions of the world, and therefore we do not cover it in this book.

As shown in Figure 5.4, AAL5 carries IP packets, LAN frames, signaling messages, frame relay, voice, video, and a number of data communication protocols. AAL5 also carries voice; however, this simple two-dimensional drawing does not show this relationship. A Frame Relay Service-Specific Convergence Sublayer (FR-SSCS) provides for the trunking of frame relay over AAL5. The IP protocol can run directly over AAL5 or via a number of encapsulation protocols. Many early implementations utilized the multi-protocol encapsulation defined for bridging and routing in IETF RFC 1483, which applied the IEEE 802.2 standard for the Logical Link Control (LLC) SubNetwork Attachment Point (SNAP) used in LANs to AAL5. A more recent addition to the protocol suite is the Point-to-Point Protocol (PPP) commonly used for xDSL access to the Internet. Moving to the right-hand side of the figure, we see that MPLS operates over AAL5, HDLC, and Ethernet. Of course, Figure 5.4 shows that IP and MPLS can operate directly over HDLC or Ethernet as well.

Since the ATM-based B-ISDN supports a large number of services, the stack contains a number of different protocols tailored to specific applications. The scope of B-ISDN contains even more protocols and relationships than those shown in Figure 5.4; however, Figure 5.4 and the accompanying description summarize the most important protocols and their relationships for our purposes. A number of books describe the ATM-related protocols in various levels of detail. The reader interested in further information should consult Black (95c), de Prycker (95), Goralski (95), McDysan (98b), and Stallings (98b). The reader will see in Chapter 6 that a different, yet still relatively intricate, protocol suite adopts a similar layered model to support voice, data, video, and multimedia services to IP. We now summarize the important aspects of the ATM cell, the AALs, and the MPLS header as they relate to the requirements of enterprise VPNs.

The ATM Cell

The fundamental unit of multiplexing and switching in ATM is the fixed-length 53-byte cell. Standards bodies chose a constant-length ATM cell to achieve simplicity and high performance. As shown in Figure 5.5, the ATM cell has 5-byte header and 48-byte payload components. All switching and multiplexing operations use only the contents of the header field. An ATM device transmits the bits from these cells in a continuous stream over one of a number of standardized physical transmission media. As covered in Chapter 1, *Introduction and Overview*, when we defined the basic concept of label switching, the cell header has local significance only, identifying the destination port on the switching device using the label-swapping technique. As in many other protocols, ATM defines an extensive list of acronyms, with the most important shown in Figure 5.5 and described in the following text.

ATM implements two levels of multiplexing using the header field. The highest level is the Virtual Path Connection (VPC), as specified by the Virtual Path Identifier (VPI) field. The lowest level is the Virtual Channel Connection (VCC), as specified by the combination of the VPI and the 16-bit Virtual

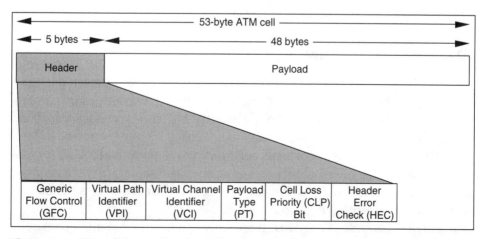

Figure 5.5   ATM cell format: header and payload.

Channel Identifier (VCI) fields. The VPI and VCI have significance only on a single local ATM interface, since each ATM device may translate the VPI and VCI values from input port to output port along the path of an end-to-end connection. Therefore, in general, the VPI and VCI values on the input and output ports of the same device differ. The sequence of VPI and VCI mappings performed in the switches along the route forms an end-to-end connection. The 4-bit Generic Flow Control (GFC) field allows a multiplexer to control the rate of an ATM terminal. Although B-ISDN standards define GFC, few devices implement it. The format of the ATM cell between network nodes, called the Network-Node Interface (NNI), redefines the 4 bits in the GFC field to increase the VPI field to 12 bits as compared with the 8 bits defined at the User-Network Interface (UNI). The 3-bit Payload Type (PT) indicates whether the cell contains:

- User data
- VC-level Operations And Maintenance (OAM) information
- Explicit Forward Congestion Indication (EFCI)
- AAL information
- Resource Management (RM) information

The Cell Loss Priority (CLP) bit indicates the relative priority of the cell similar to the Discard Eligible (DE) bit in frame relay, as defined in Chapter 4. Network nodes may discard cells with the CLP bit set during periods of congestion. The contents of the cell header are critical to proper operation of ATM. Therefore, the header contains a 1-Byte Header Error Check (HEC) field that is capable of correcting all single-bit errors and detecting double-bit errors in the 5-byte header field. The HEC does not perform error checking on the cell payload field.

ATM Adaptation Layers (AALs)

As previously introduced, the AAL maps between the data format and services required by higher-layer applications such as private line circuit emulation, voice, video, frames, and packets. The AAL protocol does this using specific fields within the 48-byte payloads carried by a sequence of ATM cells. Therefore, all AAL protocols require that the underlying ATM service deliver a sequence of cells to the destination in the same order transmitted by the sender. Since AAL5 is the simplest AAL protocol and it is the one used by IP, we describe it as an example.

Figure 5.6 illustrates how AAL5 maps between a variable-length packet from a higher-layer protocol and a sequence of cells. Starting at the top of

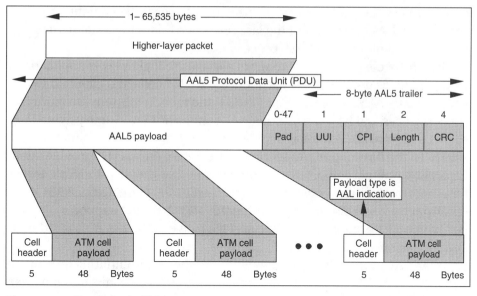

Figure 5.6 Simple and efficient AAL5.

the figure, AAL5 supports transfer of a higher-layer protocol packet ranging in length from 1 to $2^{16}-1$ (i.e., 65,535) bytes. As shown in the middle of the figure, the AAL5 protocol forms a Protocol Data Unit (PDU) from this higher-layer packet by adding a variable-length Pad field and an 8-byte trailer field. AAL5 uses the Pad field to construct a PDU that is an exact multiple of 48 bytes. The 8-byte trailer contains four fields, as shown in the figure. The AAL5 protocol transparently conveys the User-to-User Information (UUI), while the Common Part Indicator (CPI) is currently unused but is reserved for future capabilities. The 2-byte Length field gives the number of bytes in the AAL5 payload so that the receiver can remove the Pad field. Finally, the 4-byte Cyclic Redundancy Check (CRC) field detects errors in the AAL5 PDU. The sequence of ATM cells corresponding to an AAL5 PDU is shown at the bottom of the figure. The transmitter segments the AAL5 PDU into 48-byte payloads and places them sequentially in ATM cells sent over a VCC. The receiver reassembles this sequence of cells and extracts the higher-layer packet for delivery to the higher-layer application. One aspect of AAL5 that makes for a more efficient implementation of this Segmentation And Reassembly (SAR) process violates the strict protocol layering concept of the OSI Reference Model. As indicated in the figure, the payload type field within the ATM cell header for the last cell in the sequence of cells corresponding to the AAL5 PDU contains an AAL indication. The transmitter sets this value so that the receiver can save received cells, examining the payload type to determine when the reassembly process should begin. This simple convention means that the receiver need only process the contents of sequence cells after receipt of the last cell, since this is the point in time when the complete reassembly process can occur.

AAL protocols provide a number of services to higher-layer applications using the fields defined within sequences of ATM cells and capabilities supported by ATM. Table 5.1 summarizes the most important attributes of these services and how the various AALs support them. Some private line services require the accurate transfer of the bit timing clock from the source to the destination. As seen from the table, only AAL1 provides this capability. Another important attribute is whether the AAL supports transfer of information at a constant or variable bit rate. Here again, AAL1 differs from the other protocols by being the only AAL that supports constant-bit-rate applications. The service provided by the AAL is either a continuous bit stream as done by AAL1 or a packet-type service as done by all other AALs, as indicated in the table. Another differentiating attribute is whether the AAL multiplexes multiple flows together. As discussed earlier, the complexity of flow multiplexing is one the principal differences between AAL3/4 and AAL5. However, in some cases this complexity is warranted and therefore AAL2 supports flow multiplexing as well for voice or video connections carried between the same endpoints by an ATM VCC. Finally, there are differences in how the AALs support error correction and detection. AAL1 is the only protocol that provides an optional Forward Error Correction (FEC) service for use over noisy channels. Many data communication protocols require error detection, and here both AAL3/4 and AAL5 support this capability.

The AAL protocol is only part of the set of capabilities provided by the ATM infrastructure. The additional capabilities that completely describe the service are the traffic parameters and the required Quality of Service

Table 5.1 Important Attributes of ATM Adaptation Layer (AAL) Protocols

ATTRIBUTE	AAL1	AAL2	AAL3/4	AAL5
Timing transfer	Yes	No	No	No
Bit rate	Constant	Variable	Variable	Variable
Service provided	Bit stream	Packet	Packet	Packet
Flow multiplexing	No	Yes	Yes	No
Error correction	Yes	No	No	No
Error detection	No	No	Yes	Yes

(QoS). We now define these additional elements and then illustrate how they work together in conjunction with the AAL protocols to support specific higher-layer applications.

ATM QoS and Service Categories

Although ATM precisely defines the concept of QoS, it unfortunately does so in a rather complicated way. The ATM Forum decided to clarify QoS for end-user applications by defining a range of service categories, identified by simple acronyms, that combine the characteristics of the bit rate and in some cases a quality specification. Specifically, the ATM Forum Traffic Management 4.0 specification [ATMF TM4.0] defines the following ATM-layer service categories:

CBR   Constant Bit Rate

rt-VBR   Real-time Variable Bit Rate

nrt-VBR   Non-real-time Variable Bit Rate

UBR   Unspecified Bit Rate

ABR   Available Bit Rate

ITU Recommendation I.371 defines a related set of ATM Transfer Capabilities (ATC), unfortunately using a different set of acronyms. Table 5.2 summarizes the traffic parameters, attributes, application characteristics, and network design guidelines for each of the ATM service categories defined by the ATM Forum. See ATMF TM4.0, Lamberelli (96), McDysan (98b), and Stallings (98b) for further description of the application of ATM service categories. First, the bit rate is either constant or variable. The bit-rate characteristic of the CBR service category immediately narrows down

Table 5.2 ATM Service Category Attributes and Applications

ATTRIBUTE	CBR	RT-VBR	NRT-VBR	UBR	ABR
Bit rate	Constant	Variable	Variable	Variable	Variable
Real-time	Yes	Yes	No	No	No
Statistical multiplexing	No	Possible	Possible	Possible	Possible
Adaptive	No	No	No	No	Yes
Example applications	Circuit emulation	Voice, video	Interactive data	Batch data	Elastic data

the set of eligible AALs to AAL1, as seen from Table 5.1. The other service categories can utilize any other AAL. The CBR and rt-VBR service categories have an application requirement of real-time support, which means that the delay, as well as jitter, must be small. An ATM network cannot statistically multiplex CBR connections, although it may be possible to do so with all of the other service categories. Only the ABR service category requires that the source adaptively change its transmission rate in response to feedback from the network.

Example applications for CBR are voice, constant-rate video, and Circuit Emulation Service (CES). Examples of bursty, delay-variation-sensitive sources well served by the rt-VBR service category are voice and variable-bit-rate video. Applications of nrt-VBR include packet data transfers, terminal sessions, and file transfers used in an interactive manner. The UBR service category, also called *best effort*, supports applications such as LAN interconnection, transport of IP over ATM, and batch data traffic. Since ABR has a minimum rate that can expand if the network is not congested, good candidate applications are LAN interconnection, high-performance file transfers, database archival, non-time-sensitive traffic, and Web browsing.

The principal ATM QoS parameters are Cell Transfer Delay (CTD), Cell Delay Variation (CDV), and Cell Loss Ratio (CLR). These are cell-specific variants of the generic quality measures of delay, jitter, and loss. Propagation delay often dominates CTD, whereas queuing behavior impacts CDV in even moderately loaded networks. The effects of queue service strategy and buffer sizes dominate loss and delay variation performance in congested networks. The CLR is simply the ratio of lost cells to total transmitted cells. Note that cells may be lost due to transmission errors or congestion. ATM signaling protocols allow the end application to signal specific values for these QoS parameters, whereas permanent connections use the traditional allocation-of-impairments model used in private line network design.

ATM parlance defines a traffic contract as the QoS parameters and a set of traffic parameters using the leaky bucket algorithm described earlier in this chapter. The traffic parameters must specify the peak rate of a connection and for some service categories the average rate as well. The parameters for a single leaky bucket define the peak-rate case, while the specification of a combined peak rate and average traffic rate requires a pair of leaky buckets. The acronyms assigned to these traffic parameters form a widely used shorthand defined in the following manner:

■ A mandatory peak-rate leaky bucket defined by a Peak Cell Rate (PCR) with units of cells per second in conjunction with a Cell Delay Variation Tolerance (CDVT) with units of time

- An optional average-rate leaky bucket defined by a Sustainable Cell Rate (SCR) with units of cells per second in conjunction with a Maximum Burst Size (MBS) with units of cells

Table 5.3 indicates the particular QoS and traffic parameters that the specification of each ATM service category requires. As described, every service category requires specification of the peak-rate parameters (PCR, CDVT), but only the rt-VBR and nrt-VBR service categories require specification of the average rate parameters (SCR, MBS). Only the ABR service category uses the Minimum Cell Rate (MCR) parameter, which specifies a lower bound on the average cell rate that an ATM network should guarantee to such a connection. ABR also utilizes a number of additional parameters as defined in [ATMF TM 4.0].

The ATM service categories also differ in terms of the QoS parameters that require specification, as shown in the last three rows of Table 5.3. All service categories except UBR have some specification for loss (i.e., CLR). The network should deliver low level of loss for the ABR service category if the sending application responds in a timely manner to feedback from the network. The remaining maximum delay (CTD) and jitter (CDV) specifications apply only to the CBR and rt-VBR service categories. These are precisely the QoS parameters that are critical to the use of interactive and high-quality voice, video, and multimedia applications.

We now introduce related aspects of MPLS and RSVP, which embody concepts similar to ATM, but utilize a different set of terminology. Although subsequent chapters further describe application of these protocols, presentation of parallel concepts in this manner helps the VPN designer to compare and contrast the ATM-related capabilities with those defined specifically in support of IP networking. For example, the following sections show the parallels between the ATM cell header and the MPLS header in terms of establishing connections at multiple levels.

Table 5.3 Required ATM Service Category QoS and Traffic Parameters

PARAMETER	CBR	RT-VBR	NRT-VBR	UBR	ABR
PCR, CDVT	Yes	Yes	Yes	Yes	Yes
SCR, MBS	No	Yes	Yes	No	No
MCR	No	No	No	No	Yes
CLR	Yes	Yes	Yes	No	Low
Max. CTD	Yes	Yes	No	No	No
Max. CDV	Yes	Yes	No	No	No

MultiProtocol Label Switching (MPLS)

A proposed IETF standard [RFC MPLS] specifies the stand-alone 4-byte MPLS packet label shown in Figure 5.7 inserted between the link and network layer protocols. For example, the Point-to-Point Protocol (PPP) and Ethernet use this label format. The IETF MPLS working group is also defining other forms of labels, for example, direct use of the ATM VPI/VCI fields and the frame relay DLCI. The 20-bit label value is the index used in the forwarding table by a Label Switch Router (LSR). Earlier drafts of the MPLS work defined the 3-bit experimental field as a Class of Service (COS) field. However, the differentiated services (diffserv) reuse of the IP header's Type of Service (TOS) field now handles this function, as described in the Chapter 7, *Building Blocks for IP Based VPNs*. This experimental field may support other traffic management functions, such as conformance marking, discard priority indication, or congestion indication. MPLS uses the notion of label stacking to implement hierarchical multiplexing with an arbitrary number of levels that is an extension of the two-level ATM virtual path and channel multiplexing hierarchy. The Stack bit in the MPLS label indicates whether any other labels are stacked below it. And MPLS LSR processes only the label at the top of the stack. In support of connectionless networking, the 8-bit Time To Live (TTL) parameter supports loop detection and removal of old wandering packets through the network.

One of the initial uses of MPLS will be within ISP backbones, replacing ATM as a more efficient IP-aware, traffic-engineering-capable underlay. MPLS is approximately 15% more efficient than ATM and AAL5 when carrying typical IP traffic [McDysan 98b; McDysan 00]. ATM provides all MPLS capabilities except for the TTL field. However, since ATM is connection oriented, routing loops don't occur in proper implementations. Several standards efforts are also under way to make MPLS-powered networks interwork with ATM-based networks. However, MPLS also has the potential to become an IP-friendly, connection-oriented VPN infrastructure, effectively becoming the next protocol in the evolutionary sequence of X.25, frame relay, and ATM. Initially, these types of solutions will be supported via a single ISP in a manner similar to frame relay and ATM net-

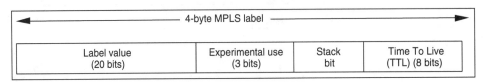

Figure 5.7 MPLS: encapsulation, header, and payload.

works. We describe an example of this technique in Chapter 9, *IP Security-Enabled and Routing-Controlled VPNs.*

Integrated Services and the Resource reSerVation Protocol (RSVP)

The Resource reSerVation Protocol (RSVP) uses the token bucket defined earlier in this chapter to describe the traffic parameters associated with a flow of IP packets identified by specific values in the packet header. Although IP is a connectionless protocol, RSVP is a connection-oriented protocol that has much in common with ATM signaling protocols. This section introduces the terminology of the integrated services concept along with the RSVP signaling and admission control protocol by using an analogy with ATM where applicable or a description of capabilities unique to this set of IP-based protocols and capabilities.

The set of integrated services (intserv) [RFC 2475] and RSVP-related RFCs defines two levels of service: *controlled load* and *guaranteed quality of service.* These differ from the current level of service provided by the Internet, which is called *best effort.* IETF RFC 2211 defines the controlled-load service for packets within a flow that conform to the token bucket traffic specification (Tspec). In a similar manner, RFC 2212 defines the guaranteed quality of service capability for packets that conform to a

THE DAWN OF QOS AWARENESS IN THE INTERNET

Although the IP packet header contains fields that could support different types of service, the actual implementation of the Internet up to the end of the twentieth century offered only a single level of quality—best effort. Available capacity, as well as the delay, jitter, and loss performance experienced by applications, depended on the instantaneous load and state of the network. Network designers controlled quality to some extent by provisioning links and routing parameters based on historical traffic patterns. When the Internet users were researchers, universities, and government agencies, best-effort performance sufficed because much of the communication was non-real-time, for example, Email and file transfer. Interestingly, the use of a limited multicast backbone called MBONE to broadcast portions of IETF meetings over the best-effort Internet of the early 1990s was a principal driver for adding QoS awareness to IP [RFC 1633]. The adoption of IP as the base protocol for emerging voice, video, and multimedia applications in a Web-empowered world drove the development of the integrated services concept, of which RSVP is the primary protocol.

token-bucket-measured Tspec. As defined in RFC 2215, two parameters completely specify the token bucket: an *average rate r* and a *bucket depth b*. The full RSVP Tspec starts with the token bucket specification and adds three additional parameters: a *minimum-policed unit m*, a *maximum packet size M*, and a *peak rate p*.

RFC 2211 defines the end-to-end behavior observed by an application for a series of network elements providing controlled-load service in terms of the behavior visible to applications receiving best-effort service "under unloaded conditions" from the same series of network elements. Although this definition may seem somewhat vague, it is not. Specifically, RFC 2211 states that "a very high percentage of transmitted packets will be successfully delivered by the network." RFC 2211 also states that "the transit delay experienced by a very high percentage of the delivered packets will not greatly exceed the minimum transit delay." Furthermore, the specification requires that the network attempt to forward nonconforming packets on a best-effort basis.

RFC 2212 defines an additional desired service (Rspec) parameter for Guaranteed QoS that specifies the actual service rate delivered by the network along with some additional parameters that bound the actual delay delivered to the flow. Interestingly, the guaranteed QoS protocol bounds the maximum delay encountered by an individual flow by exchanging information in RSVP messages. However, Guaranteed QoS does not control minimum or average delay. As noted earlier in this chapter, applications like video and audio playback require bounded delay variation, which guaranteed QoS supports.

Some experts believe that the approach of marking the service category in a connectionless manner using the differentiated services (diffserv) byte in the IP header, as described in Chapter 7, covers QoS support for connectionless IP-based VPNs. However, other experts believe that the announced demise of RSVP is premature, and they predict a renewed interest in this protocol when Microsoft includes RSVP support in Windows 2000 and NT 5.0. Cisco has been actively working with Microsoft to ensure that these RSVP-enabled workstation and LAN capabilities work seamlessly with routers. Certainly, some type of connection-oriented protocol is important to perform admission control on a session-level basis where network resources are scarce—for example, on access lines.

Switched and Permanent Virtual Connections—SVCs and PVCs

Connection-oriented network protocols use one of two basic methods to establish a connection. A Permanent Virtual Connection (PVC) exists where network management or provisioning actions establish a connection and leave it up indefinitely. A Switched Virtual Connection (SVC) involves a network that allows user application to signal for the dynamic establishment and release of connections. These connection-establishment techniques all involve three basic processes: connection request signaling, admission control, and routing. As shown in Figure 5.8, the processing for PVCs is often centralized, whereas SVC signaling is often distributed. Figure 5.8a shows a single processor (the square) controlling a network of five nodes interconnected by trunks (solid lines). The processor has control connections to each of the nodes, as shown by dashed lines. A PVC connection may be established by physical wiring, equipment configuration commands, service provider provisioning procedures, or combinations of these actions. These actions may take several minutes to several weeks, depending on exactly what actions must be performed. Once the network establishes a PVC, the user may transfer data. Usually, PVCs are established for long periods of time, as determined by a contract or service agreement.

In the case of an SVC service, only the access line and the associated address are provisioned beforehand. A signaling protocol plays a controlling role in SVC services, usually implemented on processors collocated with the switching function, as shown in Figure 5.8b. The originating user requests that the network make a connection to a specific destination identified by an address using the signaling protocol. The network determines the physical (and logical) location of the destination based on the address signaled by the originating user and attempts to establish the connection through intermediate nodes (if necessary) to the destination. The network then indicates the success or failure of the attempt back to the originator using the signaling protocol. There may also be a progress indication to the originator, alerting it of the destination or other handshaking elements of the signaling protocol. Usually, the destination utilizes signal-

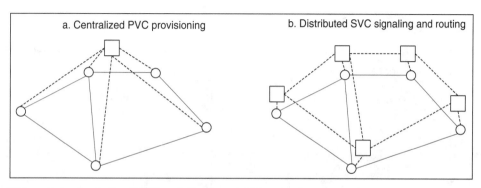

Figure 5.8 Centralized PVC and distributed SVC control.

ing to either accept or reject the call. In the case of a failed attempt, the signaling protocol usually informs the originator of the reason that the attempt failed. Once the connection is established, the user can then transfer data. Networks employ SVCs to efficiently share resources between dynamically originated and released connections. End users favor the use of SVCs because they can dynamically allocate expensive bandwidth resources without a prior reservation.

A simple way of explaining an SVC compares it to a traditional telephone call. After subscribing to the service, the calling party "picks up the phone" and "requests" a connection to a specified destination address using the SETUP message, as shown in Figure 5.9a. The network indicates progress— for example, a ringing tone—using the CALL PROCEEDING message. The network then either establishes the connection with a CONNECT message or rejects it with a RELEASE message. After connection establishment, the devices send data until one of the parties releases the connection using the RELEASE message. The RELEASE COMPLETE message completes the handshake between parties and confirms disconnection.

Although ATM, RSVP, and MPLS use different protocols to perform the signaling function, the overall result is essentially the same. Figure 5.9b illustrates this using a simple example of RSVP signaling. In RSVP, the sender advertises the fact that it has something to transmit using the PATH message, which is sent via the underlying IP network to a number of destinations using the multicast capability inherent in IP. One or more receivers

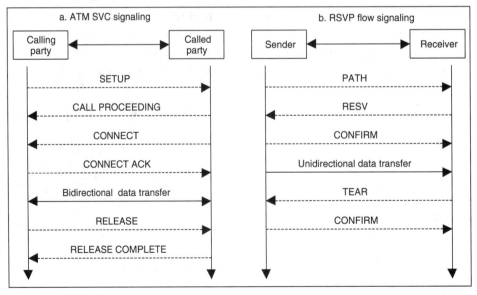

Figure 5.9   Example of ATM and RSVP signaling.

may request to receive this information using the RESV message, to which the sender and originating nodes may optionally respond with a CONFIRM message. This differs from telephony and ATM, where the receiver initiates the signaling protocol sequence, because the step of the receiver determining the sender's address is implicit. RSVP makes this step an explicit part of the signaling protocol sequence. This apparent difference in the sender-versus receiver-initiated operation does not preclude interoperation between ATM and RSVP, however, as we show later in this chapter.

A fundamental difference between RSVP and ATM signaling is that RSVP is *soft-state*, while ATM is *hard-state*. This means that the RSVP PATH and RESV messages must be sent periodically, nominally once every 30 seconds in order to hold the reservation. This additional messaging traffic of the soft-state technique is inefficient for a long-lived flow. The benefit of the soft-state approach is that errors are automatically corrected. Recognizing the occurrence of long-lived flows, the IETF is standardizing a hard-state version of RSVP. Interestingly, this hard-state version of RSVP is one of the label distribution techniques being standardized for MPLS. Another difference is that ATM signaling supports establishment of bidirectional connection, while MPLS and RSVP signaling only support unidirectional connections.

Admission Control and Statistical Multiplexing

Different admission control approaches involve the relationship between the average rate for the virtual connections on a user-network or network-network interface and the interface transmission rate. The first is called *undersubscription* (or underbooking), where the sum of the average rates associated with the connections on an interface is no more than the interface rate. If users conform precisely to average rate, the admission control is straightforward—unfortunately, real-world applications often send at less than the contracted average rate. This motivates the second method which is called *oversubscription* (or overbooking), where the sum of the average rates exceeds the interface rate.

In undersubscription, the fact that the sum of the average rates on an interface is not greater than the transmission rate ensures predictable, lossless performance. On the other hand, undersubscription can result in lower utilization if all connections rarely utilize their full average rate.

In the oversubscription case, there is a possibility of loss since the sum of the connection average rates exceeds the interface rate. The probability of loss depends on the statistics of the individual connections and buffer capacity of the switch ports. The oversubscription technique relies on the averaging of a larger number of smaller connections in a technique called *statistical multiplexing.* Typically, oversubscription achieves higher utilization than undersubscription does, at the expense of a higher loss rate. Properly engineered networks achieve relatively low loss levels on the order of no more than one lost packet in thousands or tens of thousands.

Figure 5.10 illustrates a typical application of oversubscription in the traffic engineering of a service provider network. An access interface has a number of connections or flows that have many different destinations within the network. Furthermore, each interface has traffic arriving to it from many other ports in the network, as shown in the figure. Oversubscribing the access interface allows any individual flow to operate at a rate up to the access interface rate. Of course, the various flows cannot operate at their full rate simultaneously since the interface speed limits their aggregate transmission rate. However, most traffic has significant variability in destinations and hence oversubscription is widely used in connection-oriented networks. It is also a fundamental concept in the operation of a connectionless network.

An oversubscribed access interface supports a number of virtual connections or flows whose sum of average rates A_i (written as ΣA_i) exceed the interface rate R. This means that the average probability of activity p of any connection on the interfaces within the core of the network is $p < R/\Sigma A_i$. For the example shown in Figure 5.10, if $A_i = R$, then $p < 1/3$. On a network trunk interface serving N virtual connections or flows, the required capacity C is bounded as follows [McDysan 00]:

$$N\,p < C < N\,p + \alpha\,\text{SQRT}[N\,p\,(1-p)]$$

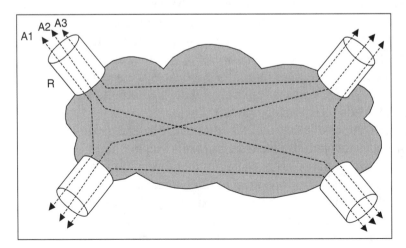

Figure 5.10 Statistical oversubscription.

The *statistical multiplexing gain G* is defined as the number of connections supported N divided by the required capacity C. Hence, the statistical multiplexing gain G is never more than $1/p$. In other words, the best-case statistical multiplexing gain requires allocation of capacity equal to the sum of the average connection rates. The lower bound on the required capacity C results when the buffer capacity of the interface is much greater than the burst size of the connections. This is the most efficient mode of operation, but can result in substantial variability in delay. The upper bound on C is the worst case, where the buffer capacity of the interface is comparable to that of the connection burst size. This results in bounded delay variation; however, the probability of loss is determined by the parameter α as determined by the normal distribution. The loss probability for the normal distribution is approximately $EXP(-\alpha^2/2)/2$.

Peak-rate admission control is a variant that applies to ATM, RSVP, and MPLS since these protocols define a peak rate in addition to the average rate. Instead of operating on the average rate as previously described, peak-rate admission control checks to see if the sum of the peak rates exceeds the interface rate. Peak rate allocation makes sense for connections where the peak rate equals the average rate—for example, in CBR applications such as circuit emulation or high-quality video. However, experience in trial and operational ATM networks has shown that peak-rate admission control sometimes results in extremely low interface utilization for bursty data traffic.

QoS-Aware, Capacity-Constrained Routing

Every PVC provisioning and SVC connection-processing protocol must perform the function of route determination, or routing for short, in conjunction with admission control. A routing protocol that must consider quality and capacity constraints is a problem of nontrivial complexity. Simple examples of this are shown in Figure 5.11. A well-understood problem is that of routing subject to optimization of a single criterion (e.g., the number of hops). The solution is known as the *Dijkstra algorithm*, covered in Chapter 6. Figure 5.11a illustrates the optimal route between nodes A and E when the optimization criterion is the number of hops. All traffic flows along the shortest path from A through C to E, potentially overloading these links. Figure 5.11b illustrates the case where the optimization criterion is also the number of hops, but each flow requires one unit of dedicated capacity. A number identifies the available capacity on each link. At most three connections requiring one unit of capacity can be supported by this network. However, each connection takes a different route.

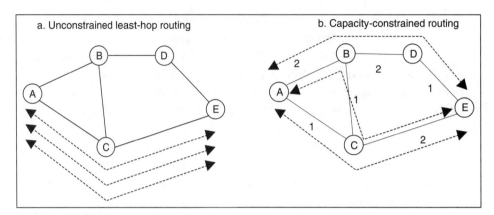

Figure 5.11   Unconstrained and constrained routing.

A number of algorithms and implementations have been developed over the years to solve the constrained routing problem in an efficient manner. However, at the time of this writing, there was no known optimal solution. The ATM Forum's Private Network-Network Interface (PNNI) specification defines a set of messages and gives some implementation guidelines for a constraint-based routing algorithm. Important concepts implemented via PNNI are source-generated routing and "crankback" of attempts to earlier points along the route when the constraints required by the connection request cannot be met. The IETF plans to develop a Constrained-Routing Label Distribution Protocol (CR LDP) for MPLS. This is an active area of work in the MPLS working group. See www.ietf.org/html.charters/mpls-charter.html for more information and the status, of constraint-based routing standards development.

Principal Applications

Modern ATM, MPLS, and RSVP connection-oriented networks can implement all the applications, described in Chapter 4, that their X.25 and frame relay predecessors can, but they can also support several important new ones. Furthermore, MPLS enables some additional IP-aware VPN approaches, which will be covered in Chapter 9.

Integrating Voice, Data, and Video

Virtually all carriers provide some form of public ATM service, enabling users to capitalize on a basic advantage of ATM—integrated physical and service access that reduces a significant cost component for many enterprise networks. The development of ATM nxDS1/E1 inverse multiplexers, CPE access products ranging from DS1 to OC-N speeds, and xDSL has extended many of ATM's benefits to users who currently employ separate TDM-based networks for voice, data, and video.

Figure 5.12 illustrates how ATM provides integrated access for voice, data, and video applications over a single access line. The configuration involves ATM-based, multiservice multiplexers connecting voice, video, and data applications at a number of enterprise locations over a single access line. The carrier's ATM network may interconnect these multiservice multiplexers to each other using PVCs or SVCs, as shown in Figure 5.12a.

Alternatively, or in conjunction with this site-to-site enterprise connectivity, the multiservice multiplexer may also connect to an edge switch within a service provider network providing access to specific services as illustrated in Figure 5.12b. Since multiple services share the same physical access circuit, savings in network interface equipment, a reduced need for access line capacity, and lower wide area networking charges often result. When used for integrated access, the provider's edge switch performs circuit emulation to split off the TDM traffic destined for the telephone and private line networks. Simultaneously, customer devices can access the Internet, or a public frame relay service, using protocol interworking, as shown in Figure 5.12b.

Hierarchical Connection-Oriented VPNs

A commonly encountered enterprise ATM VPN design carries VCCs over VPC PVCs provisioned on a public ATM network, as shown in Figure 5.13. Starting with Figure 5.13a, the network has three best-effort QoS (i.e., UBR service class) VPC PVCs that interconnect the three enterprise ATM switches. This VPC trunking design allows the enterprise switches to

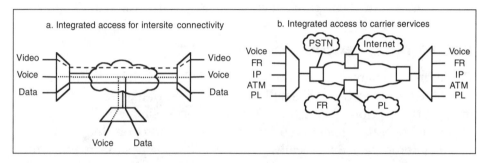

Figure 5.12 Integrated access architecture.

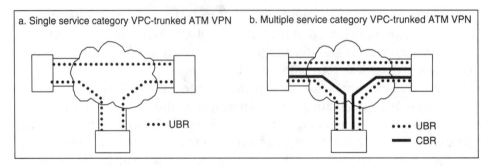

Figure 5.13 Hybrid public-private VPC-trunked network.

dynamically allocate capacity to individual VCCs out of the overall VPC capacity. Of course, each VCC has the same QoS as the VPC. An enterprise network requiring multiple levels of QoS can subscribe to multiple VPC trunks, each provisioned with a different QoS, to interconnect enterprise nodes. Figure 5.13b illustrates this case by adding a CBR service category VPC between each of the three sites. The enterprise ATM switches select the appropriate VPC based on the QoS requirements on the individual VCC connection requests. The network administrator could make this decision statically in the case of a PVC network, or the end users can make it dynamically if the enterprise ATM switches implement SVCs. For example, the users of this network could use LAN emulation over the UBR VPCs and on-demand videoconferencing over the CBR VPCs. This example illustrates another advantage of public networking, namely, combining multiple logical connections onto a single physical User-Network Interface (UNI) connected to the public network.

The label-stacking capability of MPLS allows implementation of a similar capability. However, as noted earlier, MPLS can support an arbitrary number of levels of aggregation hierarchy. Thus, a service provider can perform additional levels of aggregation to achieve greater economies of scale and efficient statistical guarantees of QoS. ATM and MPLS networks can also implement a form of enterprise-level hierarchy, as described in Chapter 4.

Interworking between RSVP and ATM

Earlier in this chapter, we showed that the IETF's token bucket and ATM's leaky bucket algorithms are simply different ways of expressing a deterministic description of a traffic flow. Furthermore, since RSVP and ATM signaling are both connection-oriented signaling protocols, they can indeed interoperate. Specifically, IETF RFC 2381 defines the mapping of the various parameters between ATM and RSVP as well as the specific signaling procedures and parameters that invoke them. Table 5.4 illustrates the mapping of these signaling protocols, algorithms, and parameters. Although these parameters are well defined, selection of specific values for these parameters to deliver acceptable application performance is still a challenge. One solution to this issue has been the development of parameter packages for well understood applications, like voice.

The interworking between RSVP and ATM allows IP-based applications to use RSVP signaling, with capacity reservation and QoS delivered by an ATM SVC network. Figure 5.14 illustrates a simple example of these protocols working together. Starting from the left-hand side, an IP sender transmits a PATH message, which is conveyed over best-effort connections via an ATM network to one or more receivers. Intermediate IP/ATM routers at the source and destination edges of an ATM network may process the PATH message. They will either pass it along or drop it, according to the network policy in effect at the time for the flow advertised by the PATH message. An IP receiver requests a reservation for the transmission using the RESV message, which the source and destination IP/ATM routers will normally process according to network policy.

The source IP/ATM router translates the "backward" RESV message into a "forward" ATM SVC request, and passes on the RESV message to the IP sender once the connection is established, as determined by receipt of the CONNECT message. The IP/ATM routers may transmit a CONFIRM message to the IP receiver. The IP/ATM routers detect refreshed RESV and PATH messages, but do not reestablish the SVC since it does not require refresh. The sender has the capability to send data unidirectionally over the ATM

Table 5.4 Interworking between RSVP and ATM

PARAMETER/PROTOCOL	IP	ATM
Signaling protocol	RSVP	SVC (Q.2931)
Traffic parameters	Token bucket peak (p), rate (r), bucket (b) Maximum packet size (M) Minimum policed unit (m)	Leaky bucket PCR, CDVT, SCR, MBS, MCR
QoS parameters	Delay	CDV Loss, delay, jitter
Service classes	Best effort Controlled load Guaranteed service	UBR nrt-VBR, ABR CBR, rt-VBR
Conformance	Treat excess as best effort	Mark excess using CLP

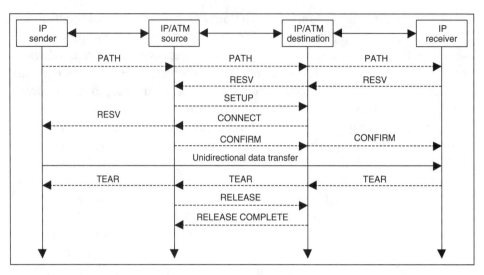

Figure 5.14   RSVP/ATM signaling interworking example.

SVC until either the sender or the receiver issues a TEAR message. If the application requires bidirectional communication, then the mirror image of this protocol must be replicated for the other direction. The IP/ATM routers translate a TEAR message into the disconnect handshake of the RELEASE and RELEASE COMPLETE messages that terminate the ATM SVC. Of course, the routers need not operate over an ATM network; however, the hard-state paradigm of ATM is better suited to long-lived flows than the soft-state approach currently standardized for RSVP, as noted earlier in this chapter.

This concludes our coverage of private circuit switched and connection-oriented VPNs. The remainder of the book focuses on connectionless, IP-based VPNs. Chapters 6 and 7 introduce the concepts, protocols, and architectures of IP and the extensions necessary to construct VPNs, respectively. After Chapter 8 explains how IP protocols provide secure dial-in access and LAN-LAN connections, we compare the relative economics and trade-offs involved in connection-oriented versus connectionless alternatives as a function of enterprise traffic and demographic characteristics. Chapter 9 includes a description of how IP routing protocols can work together with MPLS to automatically configure a connection-oriented VPN.

The Internet Protocol Suite

The man with a new idea is a crank until the idea succeeds.
—Mark Twain

The Internet Protocol, commonly referred to as IP, is the foundation of the emerging electro-optical computerized network of the twenty-first century. Actually, when we talk about IP, it is not a single protocol, but a set of cooperating, ever increasing suite of protocols built on top of IP. This chapter provides the business and technological background of the IP protocol suite and summarizes the aspects of these protocols important to enterprise VPNs. Because the Internet is in large part a public network, additional protocols and overlay network designs are essential to providing the privacy and virtual capacity guarantees of VPNs. Chapter 7, *Building Blocks for IP-Based VPNs—Security, Quality, and Access*, describes additional techniques as background helpful to understanding the expanding universe of IP-based VPN technologies that will be covered in the remainder of the book.

Business Drivers and Requirements

As covered in Chapter 1, *Introduction and Overview*, the Internet may well be one of the best venture capital investments made by the United

States government. In fact, the U.S. Department of Commerce [USDC 98] reported that the public's adoption rate for the Internet has been greater than it was for radio, television, and the personal computer. A few additional important factors contributed to the phenomenal growth rate of the Internet.

Killer Applications: Email and the Web

The embrace by the general populace of the Internet was largely driven by two user-friendly applications: electronic mail and the World Wide Web. Electronic mail, or Email for short, simultaneously empowers and endangers the network user. Invented almost three decades ago to allow programmers to exchange messages, over 225 million people were using Email in 1999 [Leonard 99]. Email empowers people by overcoming the traditional limitations of other communication techniques over vast distances and time zones. Using Email, far-flung families keep in touch, telecommuters work productively while leading balanced lives, and employees collaborate more effectively than ever before. Nevertheless, Email has a dark side as well. Attachments to Email messages can carry a host of vermin. Viruses lurking within attachments, or even the Email header itself, can disable a user's computer or even an enterprise's information infrastructure. Trojan horses can collect sensitive information (e.g., user IDs and passwords) from the user's computer. Furthermore, it is relatively easy to pose as someone else in an Email message on the Internet. Since enterprise users spend so much time and effort on Email, it is an important aspect of a VPN.

The second killer application of the 1990s was the user-friendly Web browser. Initially conceived as the means for physicists to exchange information regarding experiments and publications, the commercial success of businesses enabled by the browser is without precedent. The ranks of Internet users around the planet are expected to swell from almost 200 million in 1999 to over 500 million in 2003, in what *Newsweek* calls "the dawn of e-life" [*Newsweek* 99]. People shop, schedule travel, check weather forecasts, conduct research, bid in auctions, and meet on the Web. The types of information and services accessible by a Web browser are probably limited only by the human imagination. If your enterprise is heavily involved in a public Web presence, then the Internet is essential to meeting your goals. However, keeping sensitive information away from the public is important in a VPN. If even the Pentagon has difficulty keeping people out of its classified network, then you, too, should be concerned about the security of your enterprise's sensitive data.

The Value of Ubiquity

The value of a communication technology increases at greater than a linear rate because the real value is the size of the reachable community. The telephone network is extremely valuable for precisely this reason, because billions of locations are reachable. The Internet is rapidly moving up this value curve, with the number of users capable of access increasing at an unprecedented pace. Furthermore, after the number of users employing a certain communication technology reaches a critical mass, there is actually a disadvantage of not embracing the new technology. Sometimes new technologies are a fad—for example, the widespread use of citizens band radio in the 1980s. At other times, the trend is long term—for example, facsimile machines in the 1980s. An enterprise without a fax machine is at a disadvantage. Today an enterprise without Email and a Web presence is at a disadvantage.

The Internet became a household word beginning in 1995, when Netscape introduced the user-friendly, multimedia Web browser application. Microsoft soon followed with its Explorer application. A Web page became, like advertising, de rigueur for every enterprise. Retail stores, service industries, manufacturers, transportation companies, government agencies, and service providers vie for the attention of users surfing the Web. The days when the Internet was the haven of university researchers and government organizations are gone forever. If you want to check sports scores, review your stock portfolio, make travel reservations, purchase goods, or play computer games against other players—do it on the Web.

Changing Business Paradigms

A recurring theme in this book is that every enterprise, whether commercial or government, must continually look to reduce its cost basis to remain viable and prosper. Enterprises adopt new network technologies for one of two principal reasons: Either the new technology reduces cost or it enables new capabilities that change or extend the scope of the enterprise. Although the focus here is primarily on the cost of network infrastructure, cost also has other components. If a new technology makes enterprise employees more productive, opens new sales channels, or reduces administrative workload, then it saves money. Managers often look at these traditional economic measures when optimizing business processes.

Reducing the unit cost of communication services is fundamental to operating an enterprise; however, technology offers great challenges. Change can be disruptive, and existing businesses often have difficulty adapting to and managing the problems that arise [Christensen 97]. The Internet presented such challenges to incumbent telecommunication service providers; some did well by establishing separate divisions to run the new business, while others saw new entrants to the market dominating growth. The Internet also creates new ways of doing business (e.g., selling goods and services via Web portals as opposed to the traditional bricks-and-mortar retail outlets). Although sales and earnings of these new business outlets have not yet surpassed their more traditional predecessors, their stock market valuations certainly reflect the fact that investors expect them to grow at a much faster pace than their more traditional predecessors.

Technology Trends and Enablers

The introduction of Chapter 1 described some of the technology-related aspects of TCP/IP. Moore's law predicts a doubling in semiconductor price performance every 18 to 24 months. Access network capacity is the perennial bottleneck, driving the need for voice and data integration and increasing the importance of QoS and traffic management. The emergence of the Internet Protocol suite as the de facto desktop standard makes IP a paramount consideration for any modern enterprise. This section expands upon these themes by considering some of the technology trends and enablers that brought IP to this position.

IP over Anything

IP was designed from the outset to run over almost any communication network protocol. For example, it not only runs over private lines, Ethernet, X.25, frame relay, ATM, television cable, and telephone lines, but can be transmitted during the vertical blanking interval in a standard analog television signal. As a testament to the success of this design approach, some of these communication technologies were invented after IP was designed. However, not all of this happened overnight. In fact, the development of the technology and protocols that power the Internet has a history that reaches back to the late 1960s. A number of texts and Web sites provide accounts of this legacy. In this book, we provide only a brief history as background, focusing primarily on the state of affairs of protocols used in the Internet in the early twenty-first century. The reader interested in further details regarding the fascinating history and evolution of the Internet should consult [Hafner 98; Hobbes 99; Huston 99; Leiner 98; and Minoli 99], and www.isoc.org/internet/history.

WHO ACTUALLY INVENTED THE INTERNET?

Many people are credited as inventors of the Internet in one way or another. This brief summary offers some highlights. Bob Taylor was the director of the Information Processing Techniques Office (IPTO) at the Advanced Research Project Agency (ARPA) and funded the development of the first packet switches in 1969 by Bolt Beranek and Newman (BBN). Larry Roberts suceeded Taylor, leading and managing the initial ARPANET efforts. Donald Davies of the UK National Physical Laboratory coined the term *packet,* and convinced Roberts to use 50-kbps trunks rather than slower 2.4-kbps trunks to achieve lower latency. Leonard Kleinrock's dissertation work at MIT [Kleinrock 64] provided the theoretical basis for performance evaluation of packet-switching networks. Vinton Cerf and Bob Kahn wrote a seminal paper in 1974 [Cerf 74] proposing the concept of a network of networks, or an *internet.* Cerf also led the development of TCP/IP first from his research lab at Stanford and then as program manager at ARPA. This work eventually became what we now know as the TCP/IP protocol suite. Kahn worked on the development of packet switches at BBN and conceived many of the foundational concepts of TCP/IP. Al Gore is a latecomer in this crowd, laying his claim based on having supported high-performance computing initiatives while a senator and vice president of the United States. Gore held hearings and asked questions that led directly to the development of NSFNET that played a major role in the way the Internet evolved. Certainly another milestone is Tim Berners-Lee's development of the concept of the Web and its first implementations in 1989 in a research lab at CERN in Geneva, Switzerland. Others attribute Mark Andreesen's commercialization of the Web browser and the founding of Netscape as a pivotal landmark. Another important point in the history of the Internet was the government granting the request by Vint Cerf to connect the commerical MCI Mail network to the Internet in 1988. The first two commercial Internet services were launched in 1989 (PSINET) and 1990 (UUNET). Some credit the decision by the National Science Foundation (NSF) Division of Networking and Communications Research and Infrastructure (DNCRI) director Steve Wolff to get the government out of the Internet backbone business as the critical impetus for the emergence of the Internet as a commercial force. As we shall see, the Internet is a complex entity, with many interrelated parts and an evolving suite of supporting and overlay protocols. Therefore, it is incorrect to give sole credit to the famous individuals cited here for all of the inventions that comprise the Internet. Additionally, an ever growing group of hundreds of people that wrote standards and struggled through early implementations of the Internet should also be credited as inventors of the Internet we know today. As we shall see, much of this history and contributions by these individuals is recorded in the documentation produced by the IETF.

The U.S. Advanced Research Projects Agency (ARPA) began development of a packet-switched network as early as 1969, demonstrating the first packet-switching capability publicly in 1972. Named the ARPANET, this network steadily grew as more universities, government agencies, and research organizations joined the network. In 1969, Steve Crocker titled the minutes for the first Network Working Group meeting a Request For Comments (RFC) [Minoli 99]. The acronym stuck, and now all Internet documents are referred to as RFCs. Network designers introduced the Transmission Control Protocol/Internet Protocol (TCP/IP) in 1983, replacing the earlier Network Control Protocol (NCP). This is essentially the same TCP/IP standard in use today. The Internet has had several controlling bodies during its history, but now the Internet Engineering Task Force (IETF) formed in 1989 has the authority for developing technical standards for the TCP/IP protocol suite. See the Internet Society Web page at www.isoc.org for more information on the organizations involved with the evolution of the Internet.

Scalability of Connectionless Routing

Sometimes you will encounter the claim in the literature that IP is stateless and that only connection-oriented protocols such as ATM, require state information. Strictly speaking, IP is not stateless. The fact is that connection-oriented protocols require that each network node keep state on a per-connection basis, whereas connectionless protocols like IP require that network nodes only keep state at an address prefix level. Since the maximum number of potential connections is roughly proportional to the number of active end users, the state in connection-oriented network nodes grows at the rate of user population. On the other hand, the state required in a connectionless network node approach grows only in proportion with the size of the number of address prefixes. This is one of the fundamental reasons that service provider and enterprise networks based upon IP can scale up in response to rapidly increasing demand, while connection-state-oriented networks cannot.

Another inherent scalability advantage of a connectionless network is the fact that at any point in time a large number of relatively small flows share a trunk. This means that the concept of statistical multiplexing applied to ATM and frame relay, as described in Chapter 5 (*Modern Connection-Oriented VPNs—ATM, MPLS, and RSVP*), also applies to connectionless networks, but on a per-flow instead of a per-connection basis. When the number of flows becomes large, the statistical multiplexing efficiency approaches an optimal level. We use the formula for statistical multiplexing gain G from Chapter 5 to numerically show that bigger is indeed better. Recall that the maximum statistical multiplexing gain G_{max} is the inverse of the source activity probability p, which is simply the ratio of the average rate to the peak rate. The actual statistical multiplexing gain G depends not only on the source activity p, but also depends strongly on the number of flows N. Figure 6.1 plots the ratio of the actual gain G divided by the maximum gain G_{max} versus the number of flows N for several representative values of source activity p engineered for a packet loss level of 10^{-4}. As seen from the figure, scenarios with smaller values of source activity p approach the optimal operating point more slowly as the number of flows N increases than scenarios with higher values of source activity. This means that for very low activity levels, typical of human-machine interaction, that large number of flows are necessary for optimal operation.

As a calibration point, measurements performed on a public Internet backbone in 1997 showed that approximately 100,000 flows were active during busy intervals on an OC3 (155 Mbps) trunk circuit [Thompson 97]. Connection-oriented networks frequently have a smaller number of higher-capacity flows with higher utilization, and therefore may not approach statistical multiplexing optimality at the same level of network size that connectionless networks do. Furthermore, many of the flows on the Internet are relatively short-lived, lasting an average of 30 seconds or so. If you think about the situation for a moment, signaling the network for a new connection each time a user links to a different Web site is simply not practical.

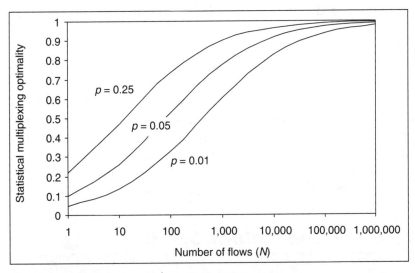

Figure 6.1 Statistical multiplexing gain efficiency.

Looking back at the analogy at the beginning of Chapter 5 (which introduced ATM, MPLS, and RSVP), the connection-oriented hammer is a good solution for applications that have long-lived flows requiring some special feature, such as guaranteed capacity or a specific level of QoS. When the problem is handling huge numbers of short-lived flows that work acceptably with best-effort service, the connection-oriented hammer solution does not scale well at all. Instead, a connectionless system composed of thousands of tiny motorized screwdrivers, each turning a tiny screw associated with each flow, is a far superior solution. However, when Chapter 10, *The Future of VPNs*, looks to the future, we predict that real-world enterprise applications will involve applications of both types, and a hybrid solution that combines protocols of both types may be the best long-term answer.

High-Performance Routers

As noted in Chapter 5 when we covered ATM, Internet service providers initially implemented their networks by connecting high-end enterprise routers using ATM switches. The reasons for this were twofold. First, ATM switches had higher interface speeds and larger overall switching capacity than software-based routers did in the mid-1990s. Second, ATM had traffic management capabilities that were far superior to anything available in IP. Manufacturers used commodity-integrated circuits based on the ATM standards, and so they achieved higher interface speeds and overall switching capacity at lower unit costs than routers could. However, the tremendous growth of the Internet motivated engineers to implement throughput-robbing functions in hardware. The result is that now routers can forward packets, perform flow classification, and even allocate capacity on a per-flow basis in hardware [Keshav 98a; Kumar 98]. Now the situation is reversed. Routers have higher interface speeds and larger aggregate switching capacity than ATM switches do. Furthermore, high-performance IP over SONET implementations [RFC 1619] running over MPLS achieve an efficiency improvement over ATM of approximately 15 percent [McDysan 98b; McDysan 00]. The higher interface speeds, larger switching capacity, and improved link utilization efficiency of modern routers enable large ISPs to achieve greater economies of scale, which benefits the enterprise that can make use of the current best-effort capabilities of the Internet.

Implementation and Protocol Specifics

Since the remainder of this book focuses on the IP-based VPNs, this section provides some technical background on the TCP/IP suite of protocols and the principal applications used by enterprises. The coverage here provides sufficient background information for our purposes. The reader interested in more details should consult Comer (95), Feit (98), Naugle (99), Simoneau (97), Wilder (98), or any of the newly published and highly rated texts covering TCP/IP. Of course, the reader can also get the details necessary to implement these protocols by referring to the Internet standards cited in the following sections.

The TCP/IP Protocol Suite

Although TCP/IP is incompatible with the ISO-developed layered protocols; it uses a similar protocol-layering concept, as illustrated on the right-hand side of Figure 6.2. The left-hand side of the figure shows the acronyms that represent many, but not all, of the layered protocols built atop the single network layer Internet Protocol (IP). IP is a connectionless protocol that forwards packets based on a globally unique address in the header. As we shall see, this requires that every system in the network have information about the best way to reach every other system in the network. The manner in which the IP solution scales to meet this fundamental requirement is the foundation of the Internet today. Routers send error and control messages to each other using the Internet Control Message Protocol (ICMP). ICMP also provides a function in which a user can send a ping (echo packet) to verify reachability and round-trip delay to a specific IP address. The IP layer also supports the Internet Group Management Protocol (IGMP), which provides for the multicast capability that is critical to some multiuser applications. The Address Resolution Protocol (ARP) directly interfaces to the data link layer. For example, ARP automatically maps an Ethernet Medium Access Control (MAC) address to an IP address.

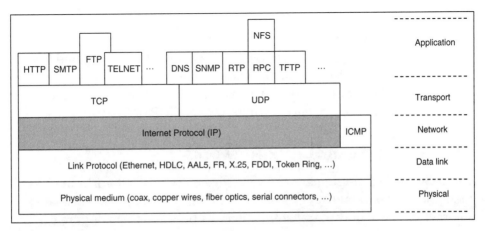

Figure 6.2 The Internet Protocol (IP) suite.

The User Datagram Protocol (UDP) and the Transmission Control Protocol (TCP) interface directly with IP, comprising the transport layer, as shown in Figure 6.2. Both TCP and UDP provide the capability for the host to distinguish among multiple applications through port numbers contained in their protocol headers. TCP provides a reliable, sequenced delivery of data to applications. TCP also provides for adaptive flow control, segmentation, reassembly, and congestion control as covered later in this chapter. UDP provides a lighter-weight, unacknowledged datagram capability that is useful to applications that don't require (or cannot use) the services provided by TCP; for example, voice, video, and audio.

TCP works over IP to provide end-to-end reliable transmission of data across the network. TCP controls the amount of unacknowledged data in transit by dynamically reducing either the window size or the segment size. A larger window or segment size achieves higher throughput if all intervening network elements have low error rates, support the larger packets, and have sufficient buffering. A number of applications interface to TCP, as shown in Figure 6.2. The Hypertext Transfer Protocol (HTTP) supports the popular World Wide Web application. The Simple Mail Transfer Protocol (SMTP) supports Email. The File Transfer Protocol (FTP) application provides for secure server login, directory manipulation, and file transfers. This was an early form of downloading files from the Internet, still employed by many Internet users. TELNET provides a remote terminal login capability, similar to the old command-line interface that dumb terminals used to communicate with a mainframe computer.

Some important applications employ UDP as a transport protocol. The Simple Network Management Protocol (SNMP) supports configuration setting, data retrieval, and alarm reporting, and it is the most commonly used protocol for collecting management data. The Real-Time Transport Protocol (RTP) defined in RFC 1889 provides real-time capabilities in support of voice, video, and multimedia applications. The Trivial FTP (TFTP) protocol provides a simplified version of FTP, which is intended to reduce implementation complexity. The Remote Procedure Call (RPC) and Network File Server (NFS) capabilities allow applications to dynamically interact over IP networks. Domain Name Services (DNS) provide a distributed or hierarchical name service running over UDP or TCP.

Building Blocks of TCP/IP Networks

Typically, only end systems at the very edge of TCP/IP networks implement the transport and applications layers, relying on the network-layer Internet Protocol only to transfer datagrams between them. Figure 6.3

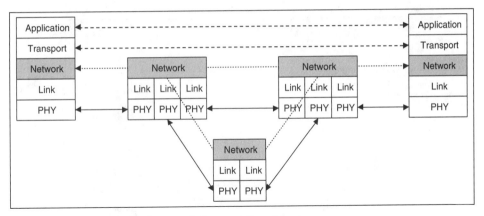

Figure 6.3   Transport- and network-layer relationship.

illustrates this concept by showing two end systems operating over an IP network—for example, a PC and a Web server. The network consists of three interconnected IP routers, two of which interface to the two end systems. The physical- (PHY) and link-layer protocols interconnect the end systems and the routers, while the IP network layer dynamically determines the path between the end systems in a process called *routing*, described later in this chapter. Note that packets communicated between the pair of end systems may not always traverse the same path, as shown by the dashed lines for the network layer in Figure 6.3. This occurs because when routers dynamically discover a better route, they change the path, potentially reordering the sequence of packet delivery and/or losing packets in transit. This means that the IP network layer provides a connectionless, best-effort datagram delivery service to the transport layer. The network-layer Internet Protocol does not provide in-sequence delivery, error control, retransmission, or flow control. If necessary, the transport- or application-layer protocols must provide these functions.

Routers in IP networks implement several interrelated logical functions. Figure 6.4 shows these functions in terms of a data flow beginning at the input side of a port on the left-hand side, through a switching fabric in the center, to the output side of each port on the right-hand side. Starting on the left-hand side of the figure, routers interface to a variety of LAN or WAN physical and link layer interfaces, often called *media encapsulation*. This means that routers naturally interconnect over private line, Ethernet, Token Ring, frame relay, and ATM networks. Next, a classification function determines whether to admit the packet or apply traffic policing as determined by an admission policy. Routers then logically implement a packet forwarding function, often using hardware in high-performance machines.

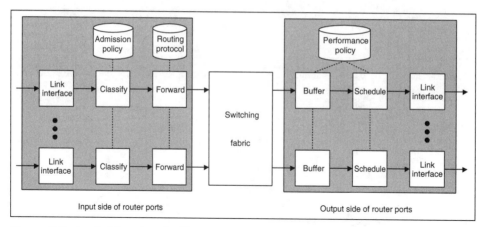

Figure 6.4 Logical functions inside a router.

The implementation of the forwarding function may either be distributed to each port card, as shown in Figure 6.4, or centralized. The packet forwarding function contains a lookup table determined by a routing protocol that identifies the physical interface of the next hop toward the destination. It does so based on the high-order bits in the packet's destination address and optionally upon other fields in the packet header. We describe this important function later in this chapter. The switching fabric function interconnects every port on the router and switches traffic from inputs to the output ports based on the result of the forwarding lookup. The switching fabric may be an electronic bus, shared memory, or a multistage complex of switching elements.

After the switching fabric delivers the packet to the output port, a performance policy buffers the packet and schedules it for transmission. Under periods of congestion, the buffer admission function may discard a packet, as described in Chapter 5. The scheduling function implements traffic shaping and capacity allocation across the various buffer pools. Commonly encountered variants of scheduling are class-based queuing and Weighted Fair Queuing (WFQ) on a per-flow basis. Finally, the output port places packets onto the outgoing interface by using the appropriate link- and physical-layer protocols. The output of a router goes to either an end system, a link-layer network like an Ethernet, or another router. If the next hop is another router, then the process repeats at each hop until the packet reaches the router connected to the destination link-layer network or end system.

A fundamental difference between frame relay and ATM VPNs and IP-based VPNs is that the IP-based solutions often involve multiple service providers, while the frame relay and ATM solutions often involve only a single service provider. The Internet experience of interconnecting and operating multiple loosely coordinated autonomous networks using automatic routing protocols enables this highly distributed mode of operation. The historical and functional breakdown of routing protocols involves those that operate within the interior of a service provider network and those that operate exterior to the enterprise or service provider network. Figure 6.5 shows a simple configuration of Internet Service Provider (ISP), enterprise networks, and end systems that illustrate these concepts. Physical or virtual circuits interconnect routers. Administrators must configure routers with a limited amount information—for example, address assignments, address prefix lengths, administrative link costs, and policy information. Routers employ an interior routing protocol within the domain of a single enterprise location or an ISP network, such as the Open Shortest Path First (OSPF) or the Intermediate System to Intermediate System (IS-IS) protocol. Interconnected networks often employ an exterior routing protocol, such as the Border Gateway Protocol (BGP). For example, ISPs use BGP to exchange information about how to reach specific IP address prefixes. In simple configurations, like directly attached networks or devices, manually configured static routing on the exterior of the network is adequate. More complex configurations (for example, the dual homing of enterprise site 2 to ISPs B and C) require an exterior routing protocol like BGP. Dual homing is important for enterprise locations that require high-availability service. This chapter illustrates these concepts using several examples.

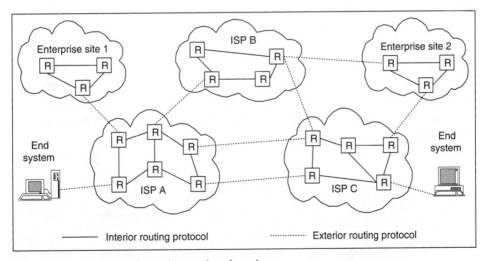

Figure 6.5   Interior and exterior routing domains.

This completes our introduction to the TCP/IP suite and its physical implementation. Next, we delve into IP packet format and addressing before summarizing the operation of dynamic interior and exterior routing protocols via some simple examples.

IP Packet Format and Address Usage

Figure 6.6 illustrates the principal fields of the IP version 4 packet header, with the most important functional fields shown via shading. A 4-bit version field supports a migration path for IP protocol updates. A 4-bit IP Header Length (HL) field specifies the datagram header length in units of 32-bit words, the most common length being five words, or 20 bytes when options are absent. If options are present (e.g., trace route or source routing), then the IP HL field indicates the total header length. The Type Of Service (TOS) byte field contains a 3-bit precedence field, plus 3 separate bits specifying other service attributes, along with two unused bits. The precedence field ranges from 0 (i.e., normal priority) through 7 (i.e., network control) indicating eight levels of precedence. The 3 individual bits request low delay, high throughput, and high reliability. Alternatively, recent standards redefine use of the TOS byte to indicate the level of differentiated service (diffserv) requested for the packet, as described in Chapter 7. The Total Length field specifies the total IP datagram length for the header plus the user data. The next 32-bit word contains an identification field, flags, and fragment offset fields that control fragmentation and reassembly of IP datagrams. Fragmentation allows IP to operate over link-layer connections that do not support a packet size as large as that generated by the source. Reassembly occurs at the destination, thereby reducing the complexity of intermediate routers. The 8-bit Time To Live (TTL) field specifies how many hops the packet can traverse before the network discards it to prevent packets from circulating indefinitely. The Protocol Type field identifies the higher-level protocol type (e.g., TCP or UDP). The Header Checksum field performs a simple parity error check on only the header fields. IP does not perform any error checking on the remainder of the packet, leaving this function to higher-layer protocols.

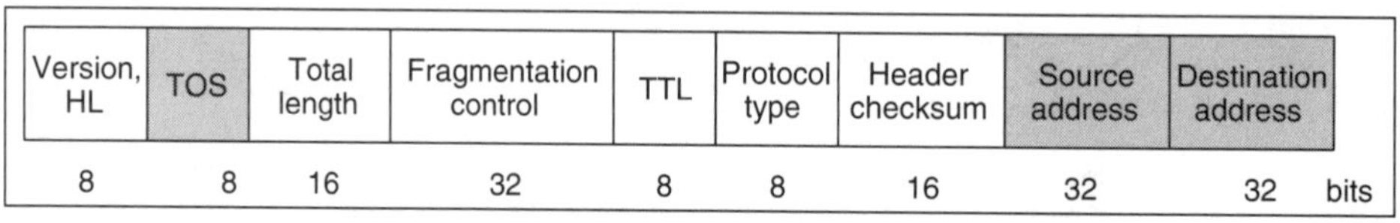

Version, HL	TOS	Total length	Fragmentation control	TTL	Protocol type	Header checksum	Source address	Destination address	
8	8	16	32	8	8	16	32	32	bits

Figure 6.6 Important fields in the IPv4 packet header.

The globally unique 32-bit IP address fields for the source and destination forms the foundation of the connectionless forwarding capability. If present, the Options field can specify security level, source routing, or request a route trace. Two types of source routing options give either a complete list of routers for a complete path or a list of routers that must be visited in the path. In the route trace, each intermediate router adds its own IP address to the packet header options field (increasing the IP Header Length field, of course). Optionally, the Options field can request that each router add a timestamp as well as its IP address when performing a route trace.

In response to rapid consumption of the IPv4 address space, the IETF standardized an updated version of IP, called IPv6. This occurred after standardization on an IPv5 protocol designed to support voice- and video-conferencing. The IETF issued the primary RFCs for IPv6 in December 1995. These include RFC 1883 for general definitions of IPv6, RFC 1884 for addressing, RFC 1885 for ICMPv6, and RFC 1886 for Domain Name Services (DNS) extensions. IPv6 was designed for easy transition from and interoperability with IPv4. It also contains the following additions and enhancements to IPv4:

- Expands the address field size from 32 to 128 bits
- Anycast addresses, which deliver packets to the closest node supporting that function
- Addition of a flowspec field for use by the Resource reSerVation Protocol (RSVP)
- Authentication, data integrity, and confidentiality options

Figure 6.7 illustrates the shorthand notation used for denoting 32-bit IPv4 addresses. The convention groups the 32-bit IP address into four 8-bit bytes, as shown in the figure. The decimal equivalent of the 8-bit byte is used in a *dotted quad notation* shown at the bottom of the figure. For example, bits 8 through 15 labeled x are equivalent to the decimal number X. Note that an 8-bit binary number takes on decimal values between 0 (for an all-zero bit string) and 255 (for a string of eight 1s). Let's look at a specific numerical example to illustrate the convention. The binary IP address 00001010.10100000.00010000.00000001 is equivalent to 10.160.16.1 in dotted quad notation.

Historically, IPv4 addresses were arranged in classes identified by letters ranging from A through D. Address Classes A, B, and C corresponded to use of the first 1, 2, and 3 decimal digits, respectively, in the dotted quad notation to represent the network portion of the address, while the remaining digits were available for assignment to hosts within that net-

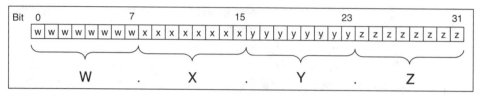

Figure 6.7   Shorthand IPv4 address notation.

work. However, this resulted in a Goldilocks' syndrome, where the Class A address space was too big for all but the largest enterprises and Class C addresses were too small for most enterprises. The resulting demand for Class B addresses drove the development of the IPv6 protocol, with its larger 128-bit addresses. Another technique developed at the same time, called Classless Inter-Domain Routing (CIDR) [RFC 1518; RFC 1519; RFC 1817], introduced a more flexible approach, as illustrated in Figure 6.8, that made more efficient use of IPv4 addresses. In essence, CIDR delayed the need to move to IPv6 addressing. CIDR defined a network address space using the familiar dotted quad notation in conjunction with a prefix length. The prefix length L identifies the number of high-order bits associated with a network, as shown by shading in the figure. A consequence of the prefix is that the remaining 32-L bits are all zero, as shown in the figure. Considering a specific numerical example again, the binary IP address 00001010.10100000.00000000.00000000 with prefix length $L = 19$ is equivalent to 10.160.0.0/19 in CIDR notation.

The previous class-based IP address structure is then a special case of the more flexible CIDR address prefix notation. Specifically, Figure 6.9 shows the correspondence of the traditional IP address classes to the ranges of addresses expressed in the generalized CIDR notation just described. The all 0s and all 1s address values are reserved, and thus the class-based IP address structure supported only 126 Class A networks, each containing up to 16 million hosts. Similarly, the Class B address space supported over 16,000 networks, each with approximately 65,000 hosts.

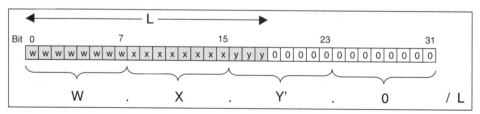

Figure 6.8   CIDR IPv4 address/prefix length notation.

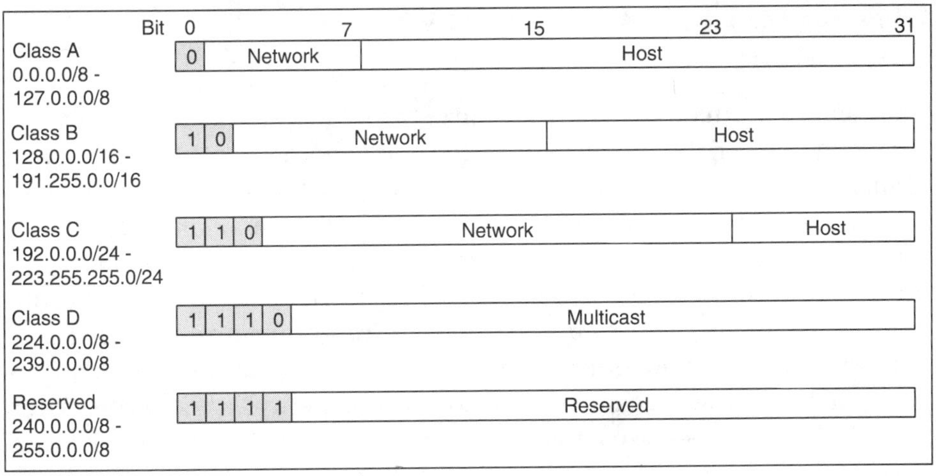

Figure 6.9 CIDR notation for IP address classes.

The Class C address space supported over 2 million networks; however, each network could have a maximum of 254 hosts. The Class D address space supports multicast, while the remaining block of addresses is reserved. Obviously, the modern CIDR notion of an address prefix allows a much more flexible assignment of address blocks appropriate to the needs of ISPs, enterprise locations, and individual users.

The original class-based assignment of addresses was not scalable, since routing table size was proportional to the number of organizations connected to the Internet [Li 99]. Fortunately, the careful assignment and alignment of CIDR address blocks by ISPs resulted in linear growth of the routing table size, whereas the overall size of the Internet has grown geometrically [Huston 99]. Chapter 10, *The Future of VPNs*, plots and extrapolates this trend. This occurred because ISPs allocate address assignments in alignment with the overall topology of the interconnected ISP networks. This results in a high degree of summarization of reachable IP address prefixes, which keeps the growth in routing table size manageable. Usually, ISPs allocate blocks from larger CIDR blocks and assign them to enterprise users. Because the ISP aggregates reachability information using CIDR address prefix notation, multiple smaller blocks allocated to enterprise users aggregate naturally into a small number of address prefixes advertised to other ISPs.

Usually, the Dynamic Host Configuration Protocol (DHCP) specified in RFC 2131 makes these details invisible to an end user by allocating an IP address and prefix length at the time of login or dial-in session establishment. However, address and prefix allocation are important activities for a LAN and enterprise WAN VPN administrator.

IP Routing: The Connectionless Cornerstone

The manner in which IP networks utilize the IP address header is somewhat complicated, but highly automated and quite resilient. The remainder of this section uses a simple network topology to illustrate the basic concepts involved in a network of interconnected IP routers. This algorithm forms the foundation of interior routing protocols like OSPF and IS-IS that are widely used within enterprise and ISP networks. The next section summarizes the important attributes of the exterior routing protocol used between ISPs and, sometimes, between enterprise locations and ISPs.

Figure 6.10 shows an example five-node router network, with each router identified by an uppercase letter. When a router is first installed, reboots, or becomes reconnected after a link or port failure, it runs a Hello protocol over the link. Neighbors exchange their identity, reachable IP address prefixes, and the administrative cost of the link via the Hello protocol when these events occur. When a node first starts up, it downloads the network-wide topology from a neighbor. However, in our simple example, we assume that all nodes start up at the same time. Figure 6.10a illustrates the exchange of a Hello message from router A to router B as Hi(A,2), indicating its identity and the fact that the administrative cost of that link has been configured as 2. We use the uppercase letter node identifier to represent the set of reachable IP address prefixes, which may be a rather long list in a real-world network. The result is that now each link has its own view regarding the cost of reaching the set of address prefixes associated with adjacent nodes contained in a local link state database, as shown in Figure 6.10b. For simplicity, this example sets the links cost symmetrically.

The next part of the routing protocol process is critical. It involves every node broadcasting its local link state information and reachable IP address

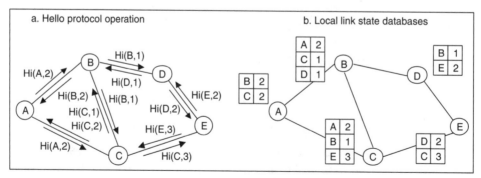

Figure 6.10 Hello protocol and link state determination.

prefixes to every other node within its own network. This process, refined by 20 years of network experience, is called *flooding*. Figure 6.11a shows how the link state and reachability information floods from router A to every other node. The flooding algorithm must minimize duplicated messages, although some repetition is unavoidable, as shown by dashed lines. Furthermore, the flooding protocol must ensure reliable delivery of the topology information using sequence numbering and retransmission. Once the topology data is flooded throughout the network, each node has an identical view of the administrative cost of each link in the network, as shown in Figure 6.11b. During normal operation, nodes flood information only about link state changes. This covers the case of a nodal failure by the neighbors flooding information about link state changes involving links connected to the failed node.

Because every node has an identical database of the network topology, distributed computation of the next-hop forwarding route is possible if each node uses the same algorithm. For a single metric, the most commonly used algorithm is the Dijkstra algorithm, which results in a minimum-cost spanning tree rooted in each node [Bertsekas 92]. Figure 6.12a shows the result of the Dijkstra algorithm for the shortest path between router B and every other node. Each router must break ties in a consistent manner—for example, by choosing the router with the higher IP address for the distributed algorithm to function correctly. An important property of the Dijkstra algorithm is that the segments of the minimum-cost spanning tree are the same regardless of the choice of the root node. Therefore, when a node independently determines the next-hop forwarding decision, a consistent end-to-end forwarding path results, as shown in Figure 6.12b. Now every router in the network knows the optimal next hop (in terms of lowest link cost) to reach every address prefix within the network running the interior routing protocol. These address prefixes are shown grouped

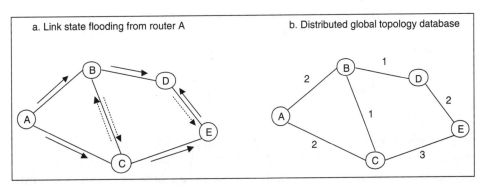

Figure 6.11 Flooding link state and global topology.

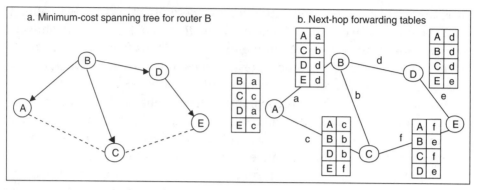

Figure 6.12   Dijkstra algorithm and per-hop forwarding.

(according to the node that advertised them using an uppercase letter as an index) to the next-hop link address (shown as a lowercase letter) in the forwarding table next to each router.

Whenever a link fails, becomes active again, or the IP address prefix reachability information changes, then the process repeats for the portion of the network that the change affects. The change is flooded throughout the network, and because every node eventually converges to the same topology database, its computation of the forwarding table yields the desired result. Usually, this process works smoothly and achieves convergence within a matter of seconds to minutes. However, if the link state changes too quickly, or changes at too many nodes, then the routing protocol does not have time to converge. Several problems may occur in this unstable situation. First, packets may loop through the same router(s) multiple times, potentially creating overloaded trunks and causing loss on other flows. Second, some packets may have no reachable destination whatsoever and end up going nowhere—a routing phenomenon called a *black hole*. Finally, if the nodes flood too much link state information, then the processors in the routers may become overloaded and crash, a situation that creates further flooding that can destabilize a network. For these reasons, routing protocols have timers to control the frequency of routing updates that can occur.

Policy-Based Routing—The Border Gateway Protocol (BGP)

In the early days of the Internet, one routing protocol ran the entire network. As the collection of interconnected networks grew, a need to better isolate administrative domains and provide policy-based routing arose. Initially, a protocol called the Exterior Gateway Protocol (EGP) fulfilled this role. Beginning in 1989, the IETF defined a series of versions of the Border Gateway Protocol (BGP) to replace EGP [Huitema 95; Steenstrup 95]. RFC 1771 defines the current version, BGPv4, of this widely used exterior routing protocol. Because BGP is fundamental to the interconnection of ISP networks that make up the global Internet and supports some important capabilities involving interconnection of enterprise sites to ISPs, this section describes BGP in some depth as background. We discuss the subject of how BGP supports VPNs in Chapter 9, *IP Security-Enabled and Routing-Controlled VPNs*.

BGP has its own set of unique terminology and acronyms. An important concept is that of an Autonomous System (AS), defined as a set of routers running an interior routing protocol that has a single exterior routing policy visible to other autonomous systems. Every AS operates its interior routing protocol independently of every other AS. Each AS has a unique 16-bit identifier assigned by the Internet registry. BGP does not communicate interior topology information between autonomous systems. Instead, it provides information regarding address prefixes that either are reachable within or by transit through the advertising AS. We refer to the use of BGP between border routers within an AS as *interior* BGP (iBGP) and the use of BGP between routers in different autonomous systems as *exterior* BGP (eBGP) [Huston 99].

BGP runs over a TCP session that provides reliable, in-sequence delivery of routing information. It has three phases of operation: BGP session establishment, Update message exchange, and BGP session termination. During session establishment, BGP peers in adjacent autonomous systems exchange Open messages which contain AS number identification, a keepalive time-out value, and optional parameters, such as authentication. BGP peers then periodically exchange Keepalive messages. Failure to receive a Keepalive message within the negotiated time-out value causes a BGP peer to declare the other party in the session unreachable, resulting in termination of the BGP session. Any routes learned from that peer over the BGP session then become unreachable as well. Following establishment of a BGP session, peers exchange Update messages regarding the current reachability of address prefixes, called Network Layer Reachability Information (NLRI). After this initial topology exchange, further updates to routing information are incremental.

BGP peers use the variable-length Update message shown in Figure 6.13 to exchange routing information. The message consists of three areas: withdrawn routes, optional path attributes, and a list of NLRI address prefixes associated with the path attributes. BGP identifies withdrawn routes and NLRI using the CIDR address/prefix length convention encoded as a 1-byte prefix length followed by one or more of the higher-order bits of the IP address prefix aligned to a byte boundary. This relatively simple message structure empowers BGP speakers to make local policy decisions regarding whether reachability to a specific IP address prefix with particular path attributes is advertised or whether a previous advertisement is withdrawn. The base-route selection policy selects the NLRI with the most specific (i.e., longest-length) address prefix match with the destination address in the IP header. In the event of more than one match of equal length, the default policy is to select the path with the least number of AS hops.

The principal features of BGP are contained in the path attributes field, which may be null for an Update message that contains only withdrawn routes. However, when the Update message contains NLRI information, some path attributes are *well-known mandatory*, whereas others are optional. In the optional category, the BGPv4 specification requires that all BGP peers recognize and process some *well-known discretionary* attributes for proper protocol operation, while others need not be recognized or processed for the protocol to still function correctly. The last category is further divided into those attributes that should be propagated to other autonomous systems, called *optional transitive*, and those that should not, called *optional nontransitive*. BGP defines seven path attributes, which we now describe. The remainder of the section will present examples that illustrate how an enterprise can apply these attributes to perform load balancing, preferentially select links, and achieve resiliency in configurations with dual-homed connections to one or more ISPs.

There are three well-known mandatory path attributes: ORIGIN, AS-PATH, and NEXT-HOP. ORIGIN identifies the source of the NLRI address prefix information. That is, was it learned via the interior or exterior routing protocol or by some other means (e.g., static configuration)? AS-PATH lists the *path-vector*, which is either the set of AS's traversed so far or an ordered

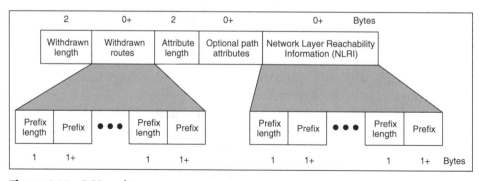

Figure 6.13 BGP update message contents.

sequence of AS's through which the NLRI address prefix information was obtained. At a minimum, it contains the AS number of the advertising BGP peer. AS-PATH provides a simple mechanism to avoid loops by requiring that each AS not forward an advertised route that already contains its own AS number. NEXT-HOP identifies the IP address of the border router that should be used to reach the NLRI address prefixes in the Update message.

Let's look at the simple example of eBGP in Figure 6.14 to illustrate the use of these mandatory path attributes. Routers in the four AS's are connected by ports labeled with their IP addresses. The Update message passed from the router in AS3 to the router in AS2 advertises NLRI for addresses 6.128.0.0/9 and 5.16.0.0/12 to AS2. ORIGIN indicates that these addresses were obtained through an Interior Gateway Protocol (IGP). AS-PATH identifies the path-vector as AS3 to indicate local addresses. NEXT-HOP identifies the IP address 3.2.1.2 of the port on the boundary router in AS3 that connects to AS2. AS3 also notifies AS4 of the reachability of address prefixes 6.128.0.0/9 and 5.16.0.0/12, indicating the NEXT-HOP of the router that connects it to AS4. AS4 then advertises this reachability to AS2, with ORIGIN indicating that these address prefixes were learned by EGP.

AS2 now knows of two routes to the address prefixes reachable by AS3. BGP policy decisions are a local matter. Since the traffic flows in the opposite direction of the BGP reachability advertisement, this process works correctly. The policy illustrated for AS2 in this example is use of the path with the least number of hops. Moving to the left-hand side of Figure 6.14, observe that the Update message from AS2 to AS1 advertises the NLRI reachability information regarding AS3 using the path with fewer hops, namely, the one directly via AS2. ORIGIN now indicates that the information was obtained by an Exterior Gateway Protocol (EGP), and AS2 adds its identifier to AS-PATH. NEXT-HOP now identifies the IP

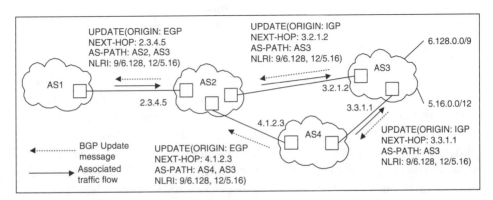

Figure 6.14   Example of BGP path vector usage.

address of the port on the router in AS2 that connects to the boundary router in AS1. The solid arrows in Figure 6.14 illustrate the flow of packets to address prefixes 6.128.0.0/9 and 5.16.0.0/12. Note that the traffic flow always occurs in the direction opposite to that of the BGP Update message and that traffic need not flow on every link that advertises reachability using BGP.

BGP has two well-known discretionary attributes: LOCALPREF and ATOMIC-AGGREGATE. LOCALPREF allows the advertising AS to indicate a ranking of local preference for routing traffic out of an AS when multiple links interconnect autonomous systems, as illustrated in the following example. It is used only for communication within an AS. ATOMIC-AGGREGATE is usually employed between ISPs to indicate that aggregation of address prefixes has occurred and that knowledge of the original NLRI has been lost. AGGREGATOR is the only optional transitive BGP path attribute, and it is used in conjunction with ATOMIC-AGGREGATE because it indicates the AS number and IP address of the router that performed the aggregation. There is one optional nontransitive path attribute called the multiple exit discriminator (MULTI-EXIT-DISC, or MED for short). It conveys the preference for traffic going from one AS to another. It can be used to load-balance traffic leaving an ISP destined for an enterprise network, as demonstrated by an example later in this section.

If an enterprise location is singly homed to an ISP, then static routing is sufficient. You will also see a single-homed AS, called a *stub AS*. An ISP may support a BGP connection for a singly homed customer for administrative reasons to avoid the burden of manually entering static routes. A stub AS often uses numbers from the private AS pool (AS 65412-AS 65535). When an AS receives an Update message with a private AS number, it advertises these routes to the other routers using its IGP. The use of BGP is essential when an enterprise network has multiple connections to an ISP or has connections to multiple ISPs. We will describe how this works later, but first let's look at how iBGP and the interior routing protocol work together within an AS [Huston 99].

As depicted in Figure 6.15, AS1 consists of multiple border routers that have an eBGP session with another AS. Border routers may be directly connected; however, they are frequently interconnected by other routers that run an Interior Gateway Protocol (IGP), such as OSPF or IS-IS, as shown by the shaded area in the figure. Each border router has an iBGP session with every other border router within an AS. This can be a significant issue in networks when the number of border routers N becomes large, since each router must support $N - 1$ iBGP sessions. ISPs overcome

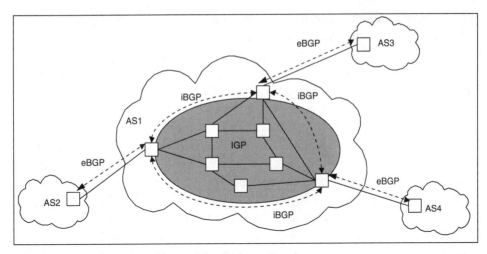

Figure 6.15 BGP and dual-homed enterprise networks.

this problem by configuring a smaller set of fully interconnected routers as *route reflectors*, effectively acting as a server that distributes routing information to other border router clients. Whether every border router runs iBGP or route reflectors are used, the net result is that every border router has a complete view of the path-vector and path attributes for reaching a set of IP addresses as learned from eBGP sessions with other AS's. This set can be as large as 100,000 entries when representing the entire Internet IP address space in an ISP network, or it can be considerably smaller in an enterprise network. Normally, the IGP is aware of only those IP addresses controlled by a particular autonomous system. This means that routers running IGP are unaware of the externally reachable IP addresses. When a router running only the IGP encounters an unknown address, it routes it to a border router, which has the additional BGP information necessary to make a better routing decision using a recursive routing lookup. A generic guideline is to minimize the number of exterior routes injected into the IGP, since this increases the size and complexity of the IGP routing tables. However, as we shall see, in some cases, some specific enterprise features require injection of exterior routes into the IGP.

An enterprise connected to an ISP using BGP can use the LOCALPREF attribute to indicate that a high-speed connection should be used in preference over a lower-speed link. Figure 6.16 shows an example of how this works. AS1a represents an enterprise network connected to an ISP represented as AS2. Two routers in enterprise network AS1a connect to the ISP via a low-speed link and a high-speed link. The ISP identified as AS2 connects two single-homed enterprise sites with address prefixes 1.2.4.0/22 and 1.2.8.0/22, represented as AS1b and AS1c, respectively. AS1b and AS1c advertise this information using an AS number from the private pool. The ORIGIN field indicates that the source of the routing information is unknown (?) because it was locally configured. The NEXT-HOP address of the IP address is the one that connects to the ISP.

The ISP autonomous system AS2 advertises reachability via a single hop to AS1a over both the low-speed and high-speed links, as shown in the center of Figure 6.16. AS2 indicates that the ORIGIN of these routes is internal, because the two enterprise sites used a private AS number. Within AS1a, router A adds a local preference value of 10 for these routes, based on configuration data, and uses iBGP to advertise reachability to these address prefixes to router B. In a similar manner, router B adds a local preference value of 100 for these routes, based on configuration data, and uses iBGP to advertise reachability for these address prefixes to router A. The NEXT-HOP field indicates the address of the border router to which other nodes should route packets. The IGP determines how best to reach these addresses internal to an AS. Now routers A and B both have the same view of local preference for the address prefixes corresponding to the remote enterprise sites. They use the local preference value to break the tie regarding the choice between the two single-hop paths to the address prefixes of the other enterprise sites, AS1b and AS1c. The result is that they route traffic over the high-speed link instead of the low-speed link, as indicated on the right-hand side of Figure 6.16.

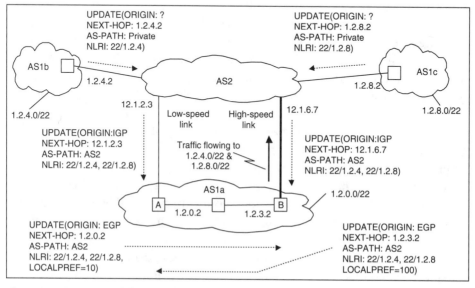

Figure 6.16 BGP and dual-homed enterprise networks.

Observe that if the high-speed link were to fail, then the Update message would not be received from AS2 over that link, and router B would communicate that it withdrew that route to router A. All traffic would then flow to the other enterprise sites over the low-speed link connecting router A in AS1a to ISP AS2. Of course, for the traffic flowing in the reverse direction from AS1b and AS1c to AS1a, the ISP must use the local preference attribute to achieve the same objective of using the high-speed link when available, but achieving resiliency by using the low-speed link when it is not.

BGP can also perform load balancing of a sort. However, it requires that an enterprise segregate its IP address space and have the ISP use BGP to advertise this reachability separately on each access link with a unique Update message that uses the multiple exit discriminator (MED) path attribute. Let's look at an example of this function for the same three enterprise sites described in Figure 6.16. In Figure 6.17, enterprise sites AS1b and AS1c supporting address prefixes 1.2.4.0/22 and 1.2.4.8/22 advertise their reachability to the ISP AS2 network as before. The difference now is that the ISP uses the MED to balance the load from enterprise site AS1a destined for the other enterprise sites. The two ports connecting ISP AS2 to enterprise site AS1a have different values of the MED for the address prefixes 1.2.4.0/22 and 1.2.4.8/22, as shown in the Update messages generated by AS2 in the middle of Figure 6.17.

The border routers within enterprise site AS1a distribute the MED information using iBGP to the border routers, as illustrated at the bottom of Figure 6.17. The border routers within AS1a use the MED as the tiebreaker to

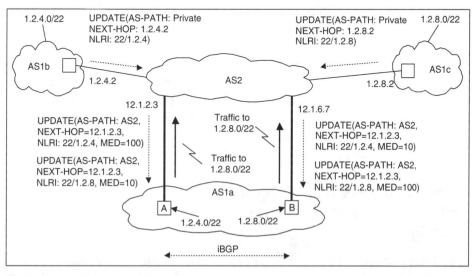

Figure 6.17   BGP support for load balancing.

decide between the equal-length AS-PATH alternatives to reach the address prefixes of other enterprise sites. In order to balance the load across the two connections from enterprise site AS1a to ISP AS2, the border routers A and B must inject the routes for 1.2.4.0/22 and 1.2.4.8.0/22 into the IGP for enterprise site AS1a. Now every router in AS1a knows the preferred exit based on the address prefixes for the other enterprise sites. The result is that within the AS1a cloud shown at the bottom of the figure, traffic destined for 1.2.4.0/22 from anywhere within AS1a uses the next hop 12.1.2.3 to AS2, while traffic destined for 1.2.8.0/22 from anywhere within AS1a uses the next hop 12.1.6.7 to AS2. If either of the access connections between enterprise site AS1a and ISP AS2 fail, the distribution of reachability between the border routers via iBGP and the subsequent injection into the IGP will result in all traffic flowing to the nonfailed connection.

Note that configuration of the local preference information described in the previous example would override the MED information received from AS2 in this example. Therefore, only one of these policies should be used for a particular address prefix. Furthermore, in order to achieve load balancing for traffic flowing in the opposite direction from AS1b and AS1c to AS1a, the enterprise AS1a would have to use the MED attribute to specify the preferred link for address prefixes served by routers A and B, shown at the bottom of Figure 6.17.

The application of BGP is not simple, even for the basic functions illustrated in the previous examples. The interactions when using multiple policies and optional attributes can become quite complex. Therefore, experts often characterize the application of BGP as more of an art than a science at this point. The previous examples illustrate only some of the typical uses of BGP for interconnection of enterprise sites to ISPs; however, other configurations are possible. ISPs have even more complicated issues to deal with, such as loop detection, address aggregation, and enforcement of transit agreements. See Huston (99), Huitema (95), Minoli (99), and Steenstrup (95) for more information and examples. Furthermore, the use of extensions to BGP (like the community attribute and VPN identifiers) provide additional capabilities, a subject covered in Chapter 9 when we discuss the means to support VPNs using BGP.

Connectionless UDP Support for Voice, Video, and Network Management

The User Datagram Protocol (UDP) [RFC 768] requires no message exchange between the sender and receiver before sending data, so we call it *connectionless*. This streamlined approach makes the connectionless IP

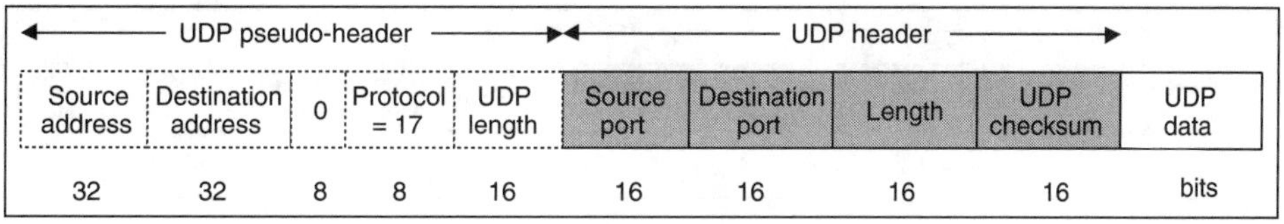

UDP pseudo-header					UDP header				
Source address	Destination address	0	Protocol = 17	UDP length	Source port	Destination port	Length	UDP checksum	UDP data
32	32	8	8	16	16	16	16	16	bits

Figure 6.18   User Datagram Protocol (UDP) header.

network service available to higher-layer protocols. The principal function performed by UDP, and a function performed by TCP as well, is that of application-level multiplexing using the header shown in Figure 6.18. The source and destination port numbers in conjunction with the source and destination IP addresses create a unique association between the sending and receiving application. The Length field gives the total number of bytes in the UDP Header and the UDP Data field. If used, the UDP Checksum field is the ones complement sum of the fields in the UDP Pseudo-header, Header, and Data fields. If used, it performs an error check on the data delivered to the destination application. If the UDP Checksum field is not used, it is set to zero, and no error checking is performed on the delivered data.

Furthermore, UDP is more efficient for transport of multimedia data—its header is only 8 bytes, whereas the TCP header is 20 bytes in length. However, there is a price paid for such simplicity in that the application layer must sometimes perform additional functions when operating over UDP. For example, as covered in Chapter 7 when we discuss overlay protocols required for IP-based VPNs, the Real Time Protocol (RTP) must perform additional timing and buffering functions that UDP does not when transporting voice and video. Additionally, since UDP has no congestion or flow control, unregulated applications can usurp capacity from better-behaved applications that obey the TCP flow control discipline.

Connection-Oriented TCP Support for Email, the Web, and File Transfer

Figure 6.19 illustrates the version 4 TCP packet format as specified in RFC 793 and RFC 1112. Because TCP performs more functions than UDP does, its header is longer and contains more fields. Like UDP, TCP employs source and destination port numbers to deliver packets to specific applications running on the source and destination hosts. The Sequence Number field identifies the relationship of this packet to other packets flowing in this direction of the TCP session. The Acknowledgment Number field identifies the sequence number of the next byte

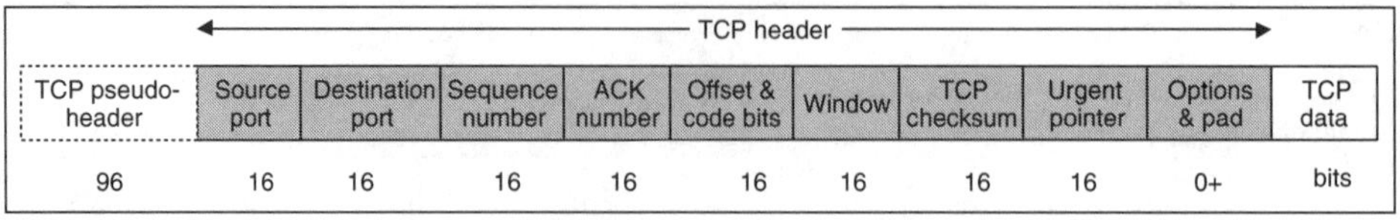

TCP pseudo-header	Source port	Destination port	Sequence number	ACK number	Offset & code bits	Window	TCP checksum	Urgent pointer	Options & pad	TCP data
96	16	16	16	16	16	16	16	16	0+	bits

Figure 6.19   Transmission Control Protocol (TCP) header.

expected at the receiver. The Data Offset field indicates the number of 32-bit words present in the TCP header, since options can make the length greater than the default value of five words, or 40 bytes. The Code Bits field contains six bits: URG, ACK, PSH, RST, SYN, and FIN. URG indicates whether the Urgent Pointer field is valid. ACK indicates that the Acknowledgment Number field is valid. PSH indicates that TCP should deliver data immediately to the destination (i.e., push) without waiting to fill a software buffer. RST resets the TCP connection. RST also rejects invalid segments and indicates refusal of a connection attempt. SYN is used at start-up to establish connections and synchronize sequence numbers. FIN releases a TCP connection. The Window field identifies the buffer space that the receiver has allocated to receive data for this TCP connection. The TCP Checksum applied across the TCP header, a TCP pseudo-header identical to the UDP pseudo-header, (except with Protocol = 6) and the user data detects errors. The Urgent Pointer field specifies the position in the data segment where urgent data ends. When present, the Options field provides additional functions, such as a larger window size, as specified in RFC 1323. Another popular option is selective retransmission as specified in RFC 1106. This option dramatically increases throughput in comparison with the default Go Back N protocol on links with errors or loss as described in Chapter 4, *Early Connection-Oriented Data VPNs—X.25 and Frame Relay.* The Options field may contain a Pad field that aligns the TCP header to a 32-bit boundary for more efficient host processing. Since TCP is a connection-oriented protocol, it has additional messages and a protocol for requesting a connection, as well as a means for a destination application to identify its readiness to receive incoming connection requests.

A TCP session uses the packet header to achieve end-to-end reliable, in-sequence data transfer. Furthermore, TCP dynamically adapts to network conditions using a flow control algorithm based on a variable-length sliding window. The tuning and refinement of TCP's dynamic window-based flow control protocol has been the subject of a great deal of research and operational refinement. The modern version, widely known as the Van Jacobson *slow-start* TCP algorithm [RFC 2001; RFC 2582], attempts to dynamically maximize throughput and prevent congestion collapse. A TCP sender keeps track of a local congestion window, which cannot exceed the window size reported by the receiver in TCP response packets. TCP implements flow control by dynamically adjusting this congestion window in response to acknowledgments (or the lack thereof) delivered by the IP network from the receiver.

Figure 6.20 illustrates a simplified example of dynamic TCP window flow control operating between a sender and a receiver connected by an IP network. The sender starts with a congestion window equivalent to the length of one TCP packet, sends packet segment 0, and then stops while awaiting an acknowledgment. The IP network delivers this segment to the receiver, which acknowledges receipt by the ACK 0 packet one Round-Trip Time (RTT) later, as shown in Figure 6.20. The RTT plays a significant role if it is larger than the time required to transmit a single packet, as is the case in our example. The TCP sender increases the congestion window to two, sends segments 1 and 2, and stops again while awaiting acknowledgment from the receiver. When the sender receives acknowledgments for

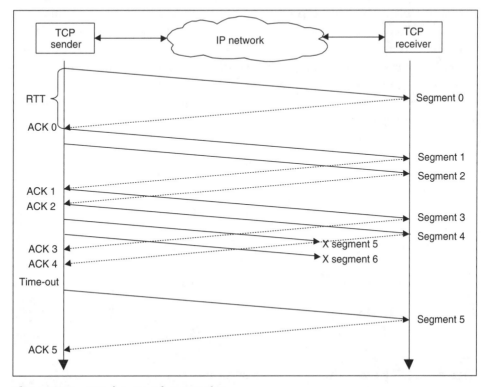

Figure 6.20   TCP data transfer operation.

both of these segments via the ACK 1 and ACK 2 packets, it increases the congestion window to four. At this point, congestion in the IP network causes loss of the fifth and sixth segments, as indicated by X in the figure. The sender detects loss by starting a timer immediately after sending a packet. If the timer expires before receiving an acknowledgment from the receiver, then the sender retransmits the packet. Upon such a retransmission time-out, the sender resets its window size to one and begins the process anew. The time-out may be immediate, but it is frequently set to 500 milliseconds in an attempt to piggyback an acknowledgment onto another packet destined for the same TCP endpoint.

Figure 6.21 illustrates the evolution of the TCP congestion window versus time measured in units of RTT. Observe that the result of TCP doubling the window within each RTT interval results in a geometrically increasing congestion window (i.e., 1, 2, 4, 8, and so forth during the start-up phase). After TCP detects a time-out, it enters the slow-start phase, which limits the interval of geometric increase to a threshold of one-half the congestion window achieved before the previous unacknowledged segment. After this point, TCP enters the congestion avoidance phase, in which the congestion window increases by only one segment for each round-trip time instead of doubling during the geometric growth phase as shown in the previous example. This linear phase is called *congestion avoidance.* Note that TCP uses byte counts and not segment counts, as shown in the examples. However, if all packets are of the same size, then our simple example using fixed length segments is accurate.

During steady-state operation, the congestion window at the sender evolves according to the sawtooth pattern shown in Figure 6.21. This oscil-

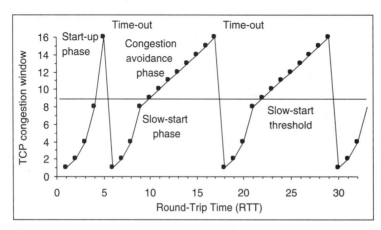

Figure 6.21   TCP dynamic window control operation.

WHY CLOSER IS FASTER ON THE WEB

Because the TCP adaptive windowing protocol operates in units of the round-trip time, locations that are closer together experience better response time performance. This phenomenon occurs because the TCP congestion window increases exponentially in units of the RTT. For example, a typical Web transaction involves 16 packets [Huston 99]. Observe that the sum of the congestion window values for TCP slow start for the first five RTTs is $1 + 2 + 4 + 8 + 16 = 31$. This means that TCP requires five round-trip times to transmit the 16 packets associated with a typical Web page. If the RTT is 100 ms, then TCP adds a noticeable ½ second delay to the response time. On the other hand, if the RTT is only 10 ms, then the 50 ms that TCP adds is barely perceptible. This is why many Web sites request that you identify the site closest to your location when downloading a large file. If your enterprise applications require downloads of large files from geographically diverse locations, consider replicating this data as part of the intranet or extranet aspects of the enterprise network to deliver consistent response time to your user community.

lating window behavior occurs when multiple TCP sources contend for a bottleneck resource in an IP network (e.g., a busy trunk connecting routers in an ISP or an access circuit connecting to a busy enterprise site). Because the Web's HTTP protocol runs over TCP, this phenomenon of oscillating throughput occurs during intervals of congestion on the Internet. During transient intervals, the TCP dynamic window protocol tends toward an equal allocation of bottleneck capacity to each session when the RTTs are equal. When the RTTs are unequal, TCP gives higher capacity to those sessions that have a shorter RTT delay.

When operating with automatically adjusted window sizes, the phenomenon of synchronization or phasing occurs all too frequently in real TCP/IP networks. In order to avoid congestion at router or switch ports, researchers at Berkeley invented an algorithm called Random Early Detection (RED) [Floyd 93]. The objective of this algorithm was to fairly distribute the effects of congestion across multiple user flows competing for a congested resource. RED does this by randomly discarding TCP traffic flows when the average fill of a buffer on a router port exceeds a predetermined threshold. Many routers now implement RED for TCP flows because it improves the overall performance observed by end users. For more information on RED, see Floyd (93), McDysan (00), Stallings (98b), and www.aciri.org/floyd/red.html.

User-Friendly Names Instead of Numbers—Domain Name Service (DNS)

Studies in the mid-twentieth century revealed that most people can easily remember sequences of only three or four digits. Telephone numbers are grouped into sequences of three or four digits because they are easier to remember that way. However, people remember names more easily than numbers. Indeed, a major factor in marketing and advertising is name and brand recognition. The TCP/IP suite defines a Domain Name Service (DNS) for this very purpose. Similar to a computer file system such as Windows or Unix, DNS uses a treelike structure for defining names and directory paths [Wilder 98]. The DNS style of names is familiar to anyone who uses the Internet (myenterprise.com, myenterprise.org, etc.). Web and Email applications further specify names usage. For example, www .myenterprise.com/mydirectory specifies a directory on a Web server, and myuserID@mail.myenterprise.com specifies a specific account on an Email server. The same DNS system handles the domain name part of each of these names.

DNS runs over either UDP or TCP; however, it usually runs over UDP. Formally, a DNS name is a sequence of alphanumeric labels, each potentially up to 63 characters in length, separated by periods [RFC 1123]. The maximum overall domain name length is 255 characters; however, most are considerably shorter. Ease of recall is an important consideration when choosing a name, so shorter is usually better. The rightmost label is the top-level domain name, whereas labels toward the left are successively closer to the user. DNS is an application-layer protocol used as a utility by a number of other application-layer protocols (FTP, HTTP, SMTP, and others). Up until the mid-80s, a single table on a centrally located server, called the *hosts file*, mapped names for every host domain on the Internet to its IP address prefix. The tremendous increase of network traffic and explosion of names as enterprises joined the Internet drove the distributed design of DNS, which replaced the centralized server architecture with a distributed name server database.

The Internet Assigned Numbers Authority (IANA) under contract to the ICANN (Internet Corporation for Assigned Names and Numbers) is responsible for overseeing policy for domain and address assignment. DNA delegates the assignment of domain names in the distributed hierarchical fashion illustrated in Figure 6.22 [RFC 1591]. The root-level name server keeps track of the IP address for the name server for each of the Top-Level Domains (TLDs) shown at the bottom of the figure. These TLDs

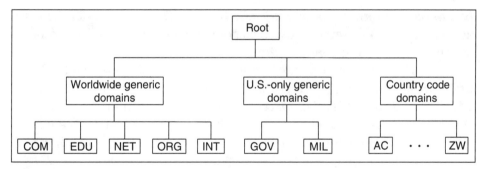

Figure 6.22   Domain name system operation.

are grouped into the generic categories shown in the middle of the figure. Each TLD may then have a hierarchy of names underneath it. Starting from the left-hand side, the worldwide set of generic domains consists of the following: COM for commercial entities; EDU for educational institutions, primarily four-year colleges; NET for network providers; ORG for organizations that don't fit in the other generic categories; and INT for organizations established by international treaties or international databases. The Internet began as a U.S.-funded research network, and the next set of U.S.-only generic TLDs reflect this history in that GOV represents U.S. federal government agencies and MIL represents the U.S. military. The last grouping of TLDs builds upon the definition of country codes defined in ISO standard 3166. At the time of this writing, these names ranged from AC for Ascension Island in the South Atlantic to ZW for Zimbabwe. As the Internet continues to grow, the commercial importance of names has grown as well. See www.icann.org and www.iana.org for current information on DNS name assignments and delegation structure.

In order to scale in response to the volume of transactions in the Internet requiring name resolution service, the DNS is implemented as a distributed database. At the highest level, 13 root name servers keep the authoritative record of which set of servers support the TLDs. Fundamental to the scalability of the distributed DNS database is the fact that other servers can maintain a cache of names previously resolved to addresses for a locally determined time-to-live period. Since the structure of the servers below the TLDs can mirror the label tree, a great deal of distribution, and therefore scalability, exists. Indeed, without this design, the tremendous transaction volume presented to the .com TLD could not be supported by a single server. The resulting distributed database system supports a hierarchy of administration. Because naming is so fundamental to user-friendly IP-based applications, all ISPs provide a public DNS as part of basic Internet access service. In fact, the IP addresses of a primary and secondary DNS server, as well as domain names for Email and other services, are required configuration entries for every host connected to the Internet. The distributed nature of administration enabled by the DNS architecture allows larger enterprises to provide their own DNS servers, which provide a first level of privacy by allowing only enterprise users to access internally used names. However, be aware that some DNS implementations have a potential security loophole if they accept unauthorized updates, because an update could direct queries to some other site masquerading as an enterprise site and collect sensitive data (e.g., user IDs and passwords). Initially, RFC 2065 defined some extensions to DNS to provide better security; however, the standard still required some revision to close the security loopholes [Feit 98].

Principal Applications

The Internet is a rapidly growing global phenomenon. It has grown faster than any innovation in the industrial and information ages, with the possible exception of the electric lightbulb in the late nineteenth century. New applications can achieve widespread usage within days to weeks over the Internet. This has several implications for the IP-based enterprise network, a topic introduced in this section and amplified in the remainder of the book.

The Global Internet

Internet service providers are in business for one reason—to make money, usually by increasing shareholder value. As in many emerging markets, logical niches emerge, and companies populate these using designs and technologies optimized for specific services. The Internet is no different in this respect. A generic classification of ISPs has emerged, first in the United States [Minoli 99], followed by similar trends in countries around the world [Huston 99]. We summarize the important characteristics of these ISPs in Figure 6.23. The generic categories of ISP services are access, transit, and value-added. Access-level ISP services often operate within a specific geographic region or country. Access services include dial-up over the Public Switched Telephone Network (PSTN), dedicated private line, xDSL, other data networks (X.25, FR, ATM, etc.), cable modem, and wireless. Sometimes an ISP specializes in one or more of these access technologies. Exchange points are sites established by either government or commercial agreement where ISPs can interconnect. ISP

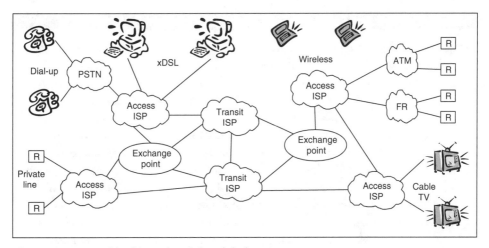

Figure 6.23   Provider hierarchy of the global Internet.

routers located at these sites peer with each other using BGP to exchange reachability information. A transit ISP service interconnects ISPs, sometimes on a country-level basis or, in the case of some large ISPs, on an international basis. Transit ISP service provides interconnection for ISPs, which when used in conjunction with exchange points provide access to the entire range of publicly advertised IP address prefixes. A transit ISP normally connects to all exchange points, whereas an access ISP may connect to only a few exchange points or rely on a transit ISP for interconnection to exchange points and other ISPs, as shown in Figure 6.23. Value-added ISP services include Email, Web hosting, firewalls, and VPN services, which the remainder of this book describes. An ISP network may implement one or more of these services.

The global Internet is an ever changing landscape of service providers as new companies start up, merge with each other, or are acquired. This phenomenon is not limited to the United States, as a similar evolution is occurring in different regions around the world. However, so far at least, the trends in the United States have been a good model and predictor for what has happened elsewhere in the world. For historical perspective on the evolution of ISPs, see Minoli (99) and Huston (99).

Electronic Mail, Commerce, and Library

The public Internet plays an important role for many enterprises. Users can exchange Email with individuals anywhere in the world. Furthermore,

DAWN OF THE PUBLIC INTERNET AND MERGER MANIA

The emergence of the public Internet did not begin in earnest until the 1990s. In fact, before then, usage was subject to Acceptable Use Policy guidelines that essentially allowed only government agencies and approved universities access to the government-funded Internet. This all began to change in 1987 when the Unix-to-Unix Copy Program (UUCP) and Usenet services were opened to commercial use, which spawned creation of UUNET. MCI Mail was allowed to connect to the Internet in 1989, followed shortly by many other commercial Email systems, thereby opening the floodgates for global adoption of Email. Prior to 1994, the National Science Foundation (NSF) ran the Internet backbone called the NSFnet. In 1995, the NSF introduced an alternative funding model, upgrading the network for interconnecting supercomputers to a very high speed Backbone Network Service (vBNS) and funding the establishment of four Network Access Points (NAPs). The NSF awarded a contract for the vBNS to MCI and awarded contracts for NAPs to Ameritech, Sprint, and Pacific Bell. Interestingly, all of these companies have either been acquired by or merged with other carriers.

the Internet is a rapidly growing sales channel for business-oriented enterprises. It also provides a means for companies to advertise their goods and services. The Internet can help reduce administrative costs by placing the data entry, verification, and think-time aspects of order entry and service parameter selection in the hands of the end user. This replaces the older, less efficient paradigm of two parties interacting over the telephone to place an order, update records, or complete a business transaction. The Web provides the automated means for the end user to peruse the choices at his or her own speed, requiring the expenditure of energy and time by only one person. Furthermore, careful design of the Web site by experts allows many more people access to the best set of information. In the classic telephone method, the level of expertise depended upon the particular agent the caller reached.

The tremendous volume of such information on public Web sites continues to grow and increase in quality based on real-world experience and user feedback. When the Web sites contain enterprise-specific information that is sensitive for one reason or another, we call the application an *intranet.* One level of security is that of user IDs and passwords. This is the same level of security used on many public domain Web sites. The next level of security is that of encryption and firewalls, topics covered in the next chapter. A more challenging activity is Internet use by multiple enterprises in a virtual private fashion, an application known as an *extranet.*

The premier example to date is probably that of the Automotive Network eXchange (ANX) connecting major automotive manufacturers and their suppliers as summarized in Chapter 9.

Shared Infrastructure for Internet-Based VPNs

As we saw in earlier chapters, a large public network becomes the underlying infrastructure for cost-effective VPN overlays. The Internet is the latest such public network infrastructure that forms the basis for virtual private enterprise networks. It will also soon to be the largest, assuming that current growth trends do not fall off markedly. The protocols, network configurations, and applications described in this chapter apply to public applications. In order to provide the additional features of privacy and virtual separation of enterprise users, additional protocols, technologies, and configurations are necessary. The next chapter introduces some of the foundational protocols and technologies used in IP-based VPNs—namely, encryption, authentication, QoS, and access control devices like firewalls and address translators. Chapter 8, *Dial-In Access and Multiprotocol Tunneling VPNs*, describes how an enterprise can use these standard techniques across the global Internet comprising multiple interconnected ISPs. Chapter 9 then focuses on the leading-edge IPsec-based VPN technique or those available as proprietary ISP-provided solutions.

CHAPTER

7

Building Blocks for IP-Based VPNs—Security, Quality, and Access

The difficulty lies, not in the new ideas,
but in escaping from the old ones . . .
—John Maynard Keynes

Some crucial building blocks for IP-based VPNs differ fundamentally from those used in connection-oriented VPNs. Furthermore, the promise of the open, public Internet is actually a threat to sensitive information and systems that are the heart of many modern enterprises. Three principal areas of challenge exist. The first involves making the public Internet or a shared IP network secure for private enterprise use. The second involves delivering the requisite capacity and quality that some applications require. Finally, there are the additional protocols necessary to support access to IP-based VPNs via the public Internet.

Business Drivers and Requirements

The foremost driver for additional functions in an IP-based VPN is that of security. In fact, some definitions of an IP-based VPN mandate encryption technology. Another significant requirement of many enterprises is that of providing secure, controlled access to remote or mobile users. Finally, IP is the latest networking technology that offers the promise of a truly integrated computing and communication solution. Although well suited to the empowering computing technology, IP requires additional support to meet the continuing user expectation for voice and video quality.

Privacy Problems in the Public Internet

Although IP serves the purpose of interconnecting a public worldwide network supporting shared networks and is planned to support an interplanetary network; the open, simple nature of the protocol presents several challenges for the private operation that many enterprises require. Many enterprises believe that physical security in itself is usually not sufficient. Connection to the public Internet is a two-edged sword. On the one hand, users have unparalleled access to everything and everyone in the world. On the other hand, anyone in the world potentially has access to an enterprise network and sensitive information contained in its computers and data stores. An important first step in the design of any security system is assessment of the threat model [Flanagan 97; Kaufman 99], as illustrated by the following questions. The answers to these questions and ones like them determine the level of security required by an enterprise.

- What would be the worst-case consequence if a competitor or an enemy had access to private or sensitive information?

- Is there a reason to keep information, such as financial reports, away from the public until a formal announcement is made?

- What is the time sensitivity of the data; is it valuable for a day, a week, a year, or a decade?

Although the vast majority of Internet users are not interested in the sensitive business of an enterprise, the few who are can create significant problems. The alarming increase in the number of stories in the trade press about industrial spies, saboteurs, hackers, and crackers who view breaking into systems as a challenge should convince any communications manager that security is a serious issue. The Internet opens to these unscrupulous types many avenues of entry into enterprise networks that were previously unavailable in private line or connection-oriented data networks. Compounding the issue is the fact that many places on the Internet allow an individual to assume another identity by *spoofing* the source IP address. A different sort of attack exploits the source routing option in the IP header [Huston 99; Ibe 99]. Here, the attacking host inserts its own address into the source route, effectively placing itself on the data path.

Problems with security are most evident in local area networks [Kaufman 99]. In this case, anyone who has access to an Ethernet segment can use a "sniffer" to look at the traffic passing by, picking off anything that looks interesting. The ability for unscrupulous Internet users to install remote sniffers on a computer in an enterprise LAN widens the security threat to a global extent. Furthermore, TCP and higher-layer protocols are also vulnerable to security attacks over the public Internet. Some of these protocols—for example, Telnet—require the end users to enter their user ID and password over a nonsecure communication link, leaving them open to compromise and sniffing from remote locations.

The list of potential security issues and compromises goes on and on. Email viruses can disable user machines and networks. Furthermore, hackers can generate *denial-of-service* attacks by overwhelming an enterprise machine with invalid requests for service. This can disrupt traffic or cause problems that are even more serious. In fact, a common hacker ploy involves flooding a machine with so many service requests that it crashes. Some operating systems keep unencrypted passwords in memory, and when they crash, they create a dump on disk of memory contents. A hacker can then peruse such a memory dump and employ the user IDs and passwords gleaned from it to break into other areas of the enterprise network [Meinel 99]. Another indirect security issue is that of external entities discerning information from the traffic pattern or from changes in it. For example, traffic patterns could indicate problems within an enterprise, a pending merger or acquisition, or release of a new product. Keeping the identification of the sender and receiver private is yet another challenge for the public IP-based VPN infrastructure.

Ideally, enterprises want one networking infrastructure that supports both public and private applications. However, access that is open to the public and controlled access to private information are often conflicting objectives. The business need for private communication over the Internet has stimulated the development of an overlay set of protocols and procedures that control access, authenticate user identity, guarantee confidentiality, and prevent the possibility of someone altering information traversing the Internet. Many of these solutions are now either standardized or in the standards process.

Need for Quality to the End User

As an increasing number of enterprise users employ computer-based communications technology, the quality standards set by the telephone network for voice and by television for video now apply to the new communications media. Information workers already conduct multimedia conferences combining voice, video, and collaborative applications in enterprise networks engineered to support these applications. Network planners have long had the vision of a single integrated network delivering every feasible service, beginning with N-ISDN, evolving to the ATM-based B-ISDN, and now targeted by the next generation of IP-based networks. Enterprises envision a number of benefits from a single network infrastructure, including reduced access charges, usage of a single switching and routing technology, and consolidation of staff currently supporting multiple networks.

Delivering the requisite quality is easiest in a homogeneous local area network by overengineering transmission and switching capacity. The challenge increases significantly when capacity is limited or distance increases. Although providing Quality of Service (QoS) to the end user is a difficult engineering problem, real-world applications demand a minimum level of quality. Other applications, such as non-real-time audio and video, are less demanding, and these have already made significant progress in Web-based applications. Since the underlying infrastructure of the Internet is a connectionless, best-effort network, the demand for quality has driven development of specific engineering solutions.

Technology Trends and Enablers

Where there is a need, people find a way. Such is the case for technology developed for virtual private overlays to packet-switched networks in response to the business needs for security, quality, and access. The emergence of the Internet as the dominant packet-switching network leverages the prior development of cryptographic technology, while protocols in support of quality and controlled access were driven by it.

Emergence of the Science of Crytography

The modern era of civilian cryptography began in 1970 when Dr. Horst Feistel invented the Lucifer encryption scheme while at the IBM T. J. Watson Research Lab. This scheme eventually became the root technology of the Data Encryption Standard (DES) developed in 1976. However, DES required that the sending and receiving parties possess the same secret key, making secure distribution of the key a significant challenge. Furthermore, a separate key was required for every party with which the sender wished to communicate. A seminal paper by Diffie and Hellman in 1976 [Diffie 76] pointed the way toward public key cryptography, which overcame the need for secure key distribution and also provided a practical means for authenticating the sender's identity. Another implementation of this concept, called the *RSA algorithm* after its inventors, Rivest, Shamir, and Adleman, was published in 1978. This is the encryption technology employed in popular Web browsers and other Internet-aware applications to ensure the confidentiality of sensitive data. Zimmerman released the first version of a commonly used encryption technique, called *Pretty Good Privacy* (PGP), as freeware in 1991. Consequently, PGP has become a de facto worldwide standard, probably because it is free. The science of cryptography is still an active area of research, involving people trying diligently to break existing codes and others striving to invent new encoding techniques that are even more difficult to break.

THE LONG HISTORY OF SECRECY

The history of people writing in such a way that others could not easily ascertain the recorded message is almost as old as writing itself [Brown 99]. The Greek word *kryptos,* meaning secret or hidden, is the root of a set of terms relating to cryptography. Initially, these coding schemes involved simple substitutions of one character for another. However, the differences in frequency of occurrence of different letter combinations made substitution codes easy to break. A contemporary example is the popular Cryptogram puzzles published in newspapers. Other schemes utilized permutations, or rearrangements of the order of characters, to achieve security of a sort, as is done in word scramble puzzles. The military was an early user of cryptography, because long-distance communications were by necessity written and subject to intercept by the enemy. After the Renaissance, people developed a number of innovations to overcome the loose security of substitution ciphers. These included ciphers that used a previously exchanged sequence of substitutions that made analysis much more complex, substitution of sequences of words for individual letters, and electromechanical encoders. Usage of cryptography expanded from the military to lovers, bankers, and criminals. Throughout history, many of these coding schemes were broken, most notably during wartime, often creating considerable loss for the party whose secrets were compromised. For example, the ability of the Allied forces to crack the codes of the Axis powers while maintaining security of their own codes had a significant impact on the outcome of World War II. Indeed, the science of breaking secret codes was founded in the early twentieth century and is known as *cryptanalysis.*

The applications of cryptography extend beyond those traditionally associated with the primary security functions of confidentiality, integrity, and nonrepudiation for private communications. Cryptography is also used for protection of copyrights and as a means to guarantee royalties, since the essence of entertainment and education is content, with economic value in proportion to the size and affluence of the audience. Researchers are also working on techniques that enable distributed voting, membership list management, digital cash, and even distributed gaming [Schneier 95].

The Scalable Evolution of QoS

Recall from Chapter 6, *The Internet Protocol Suite*, that the fundamental scalability of IP occurs because state in a connectionless routed network grows in proportion to the address prefixes assigned by ISPs. This stands in contrast to connection-oriented networks, where state grows in proportion to the number of users or user flows. However, the best solutions known for delivering QoS and traffic management are essentially connection oriented, even for IP-based networks, as discussed in Chapter 5, *Modern Connection-Oriented VPNs—ATM, MPLS, and RSVP.* Furthermore, determination of the traffic and QoS parameters for a connection is a complex problem that, so far at least, has been solved only for well-understood applications, like voice. The IETF has developed some solutions that offer some promise in applying the architectural philosophies that have made the TCP/IP suite of protocols scale so well. The first approach effectively pushes function into the end system, specifically, the Real-time Transport Protocol (RTP) that time-stamps and sequences packets so that the end system can remove most occurrences of jitter, loss, and reordering introduced by the Internet. The second approach reduces the state space by conveying all necessary information for QoS in the header for each higher-layer packet. Called *differentiated services* (usually abbreviated as *diffserv*), this technique redefines some fields in the IP header so QoS and traffic management can be performed on a per-hop basis.

Security—Keeping Important Information Private

Good security begins with plain old common sense. In the first place, if you want to keep a secret, don't advertise the fact that you have something to hide. Be sure that enterprise users don't leave private information lying about either: Establish and enforce policies that require putting it away in a safe place. Don't allow outsiders open access to the physical facilities of your enterprise. Keep user IDs and passwords in a safe place, and require users to choose passwords that are not easy to guess. Require users to periodically change passwords, and disallow reuse of the same password. Carefully screen password reset requests—require positive identification. Even these policies are not enough, because some of the most serious security threats come from within the enterprise itself. Although our concern in this book is primarily with the transport of sensitive information over a public IP network, be aware of the wider security issues involved in an enterprise.

As delineated in Chapter 1, *Introduction and Overview,* a complete security solution must meet four fundamental requirements: authentication, access control, confidentiality, and integrity. If someone tries to access this secure information, *authenticate* his or her identity. Once you've done this, carefully administer *access control* for enterprise users; give permission only to those users with a need to know. If you send information over the Internet, ensure its *confidentiality;* that is, no one should be able to read or copy this information. Furthermore, guarantee the *integrity* of sensitive information; that is, ensure that no one can alter information transferred over a public IP network. Finally, a secure network should confirm not only the source, but also delivery of the actual message, so that the sender cannot deny having sent it—an attribute called *nonrepudiation.* The following sections summarize the protocols and procedures developed for IP-based networks that meet these basic security requirements.

Cryptographic Systems

Encryption is the foundation of privacy in IP-based VPNs. A *cryptosystem* involves the transfer of any *plaintext* message between a pair of end users in a secure manner using the steps and process illustrated in Figure 7.1 [Schneier 95]. At the source, an *encryptor* uses a key to transform the plaintext into *ciphertext* before transmission over the Internet. The amount of ciphertext is usually equal to or greater than the amount of original plaintext. At the destination, a *decryptor* uses a key to transform the received ciphertext back into the original plaintext for delivery to user B. A foundational concept in cryptography is that although the encryptor and decryptor algorithms are publicly known, at least one of the keys must be secret. If at least one of the keys is not secret, then anyone could decrypt the message. At the top of Figure 7.1, a key management system provides a separate, secure method for distributing the key(s) for use by A and B. Many texts

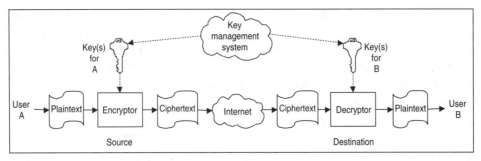

Figure 7.1 Components of a cryptosystem.

personalize A as Alice and B as Bob. Although this is cute and provides an amusing slant when describing the somewhat dry science of cryptography, we keep things generic because, after all, security is a serious issue. Instead, we suggest that you associate the generic users listed in the following descriptions with people, organizations, or functions in your enterprise that handle sensitive information. For example, instead of substituting Alice and Bob for A and B, think about accounting and billing, airplanes and bombs, acquisitions and buyouts, or any other enterprise-specific application terminology for which you have security concerns.

Two types of cryptosystems are in widespread use; each is distinguished by the way keys are distributed and used. The first, called a *symmetric cryptosystem*, uses an identical key at both the source and destination, as described next. The second, called an *asymmetric cryptosystem*, uses different keys at the source and destination, as discussed later in this section.

Symmetric Secret-Key Cryptosystems

In a symmetric cryptosystem like that shown in Figure 7.2, A and B must keep the single key secret from everyone else. Cryptologists call this a

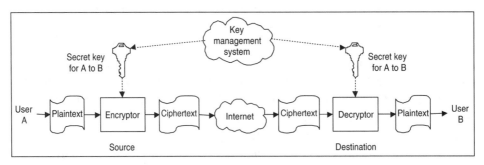

Figure 7.2 Symmetric secret-key cryptosystem.

shared secret. Furthermore, every combination of users wanting to exchange information should have a separate key for each direction of transmission, as shown in the figure; a single key is used for secure transmission from A to B. A separate key should be employed for secure transmission from B to A. When a separate key is used for each transmission direction, the receiver is able to authenticate the sender's identity. When communication between groups is required, a separate secret key can be used for each group. However, authentication of the individual sender is no longer possible in this case. Note that a symmetric cryptosystem necessitates distribution of a number of secret keys equal to the number of pairs of users requiring secure communication. Since distribution of secret keys is one of the more challenging problems in cryptography, symmetric secret-key systems are not a good solution for encryption between large numbers of users. However, since they have the best performance characteristics, they are a good choice for bulk encryption between enterprise sites.

Obviously, the power of the cryptosystem centers around the operations on the plaintext data performed by the encryptor and decryptor in conjunction with the keys distributed by the management system. Let's look at the functions inside the encryptor and decryptor of a typical symmetric cryptosystem to understand how these functions provide security features such as confidentiality, authentication, and integrity. These algorithms combine concepts from electromechanical rotor-based substitution cryptosystems of World War II along with permutations used in transposition codes. The Feistel cipher is the basis of DES, which combines a series of substitution and permutation operations, as illustrated in Figure 7.3 [Brown 99; Schneier 95; Stallings 98a]. Starting from the left-hand side, the algorithm begins with the plaintext message split into left- and right-hand parts of equal length. The DES standard requires permutation of the bits for hardware implementation convenience. DES has 16 rounds. Each round uses a function F to combine data with a permuted subkey K_n derived from the original secret key. The data is exclusive ORed with the result from the previous round. The *exclusive OR* function, shown by a circle with a cross inside it in the figure, is the bit-wise modulo 2 addition of its inputs. The function F is a complex arrangement of permutations, defined by "P-boxes," and substitutions, defined by "S-boxes." This technique implements the basic concepts of encryption postulated by Shannon in 1945, namely, confusion and diffusion. The function F generates *confusion* by making the relationship between the ciphertext and the key as complex as possible. The application of the exclusive OR function and swapping of the processing between the left and right halves of the mes-

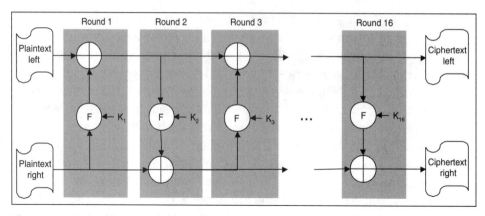

Figure 7.3 Feistel/DES encryption algorithm structure.

sage at each round achieves *diffusion* by making each ciphertext bit dependent on every bit of the input plaintext. The desired result is uniform statistics for the occurrence of each character in the ciphertext. Decryption is performed using the same algorithm, with the ciphertext as input and the plaintext as output.

Although the strength of a cryptographic algorithm is important, the principal measure of the security of a cryptosystem is the key length. In fact, a good cryptosystem should assume that the algorithm is known to the attacker and that only the key is secret. In general, the longer the key, the more difficult the cipher is to crack. A useful analogy for a key is to think of a combination lock [Fowler 99]. If the lock has three numbers with a range of 0 through 9 on the dial, there are only 1,000 combinations. However, if the lock has three numbers with a range of 0 through 99 on the dial, the number of combinations increases to 1 million. The lock with 100 numbers on the dial is 1,000 times more resilient to a *brute force attack* by a code cracker that tries every combination than the lock with only 10 numbers on the dial. Indeed, an important measure of the security of an encryption algorithm is the time required for a code cracker to decrypt a ciphertext message without prior knowledge of the key. A strong cryptographic algorithm makes the brute force method the best possible attack that a cryptanalyst can use. A weaker algorithm empowers attacks that could substantially reduce the amount of time required to crack a cipher.

Although the contents of ciphertext are scrambled by the encryptor, the fact is that an identical plaintext input results in the same ciphertext output for a given key. Longer keys improve the situation of simple character-by-character substitution, but still have this property for longer sequences of bits. For this reason, the practical use of encryption requires frequent modification of keys to foil cryptanalysis techniques that match repeated usage of letters in common language to patterns of bits occurring in the encrypted ciphertext.

The Data Encryption Standard (DES), developed at IBM and certified by the U.S. government in 1977, is a symmetric secret-key cryptosystem. Different versions have 40-, 56-, or 128-bit key length. Unfortunately, the 40- and 56-bit versions have been cracked in 15 seconds and 56 hours, respectively, using a PC controlling specialized hardware [Fowler 99]. The 128-bit version is currently considered *computationally secure,* or strong, meaning that the envisioned evolution of computer and hardware technology for many years to come will not be able to crack the cipher [Schneier 95]. In response to this threat, an enhancement called *triple DES* involves running DES three times with either two or three keys. A new government-approved algorithm is expected by 2002, which will entail an upgrade cost for encryption-based VPNs at that time. Another symmetric algorithm available with 40-, 56-, and 128-bit keys is RSA's RC4, which is utilized in Netscape's Secure Sockets Layer (SSL) and the default, exportable version of Microsoft operating system encryption for the Point-to-Point Tunneling Protocol (PPTP).

Unfortunately, cryptography has legal and political ramifications as well. Historically, the U.S. government imposed export restrictions related to the key length; this situation is evolving, but presents an additional system management challenge to keep track of the changing rules and regulations for multinational enterprise VPNs. Other foreign governments sometimes mandate that encryption users distribute a copy of their keys to them in a process called *key escrow.* The government concern is usually prevention of the use of encrypted communication for illegal activities. However, if the government's key escrow is compromised, then all of the enterprises with keys in escrow are compromised as well. Eventually, solutions that limit a single government agency to only a portion of the key may be developed. However, the overall approach of key escrow is problematic because in the end analysis it becomes an issue of trust [Schneier 95].

Asymmetric Public-Key Cryptosystems

In response to the issue of the large number of key pairs requiring distribution in a symmetric secret-key cryptosystem, Diffie and Hellman published a seminal paper in 1975 that led to the next generation of cryptosystems. The resulting asymmetric public-key cryptosystem design, illustrated in Figure 7.4, uses a combination of public and private keys. The key manage-

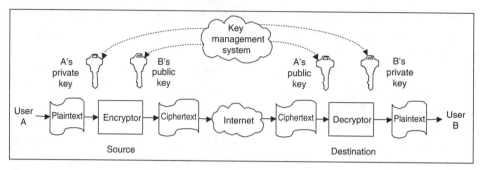

Figure 7.4   Asymmetric public-key cryptosystem.

ment system must securely distribute a private key to each user and also make public keys available to anyone. Compared with the symmetric approach that distributes a pair of private keys for every pair of users requiring secure communication, the asymmetric approach drastically reduces the amount of key distribution required. The two asymmetric cryptosystems in wide commercial use are both named after their inventors, Diffie-Hellman, and Rivest, Shamir, and Adleman (RSA). A number of popular software packages use the RSA encryption algorithm, including Microsoft's Internet Explorer, Netscape Navigator, Lotus Notes, and the IETF's Pretty Good Privacy (PGP) protocol which is used for securing Email communication. RSA is also widely used by IP-based VPN equipment and software manufacturers. The Diffie-Hellman and RSA algorithms differ in the way that they use the private and public keys, which has significant security and performance implications.

In the Diffie-Hellman approach, when A wishes to send a secure communication to B, the source first computes a shared secret key from A's private key and B's publicly distributed key, as shown in Figure 7.5. The encryptor uses this shared secret key to generate the ciphertext, which the Internet delivers to the destination. At the destination, the same shared secret key is computed using A's public key and B's private key, as shown in the figure. This computation of a shared secret using a privately held key unique to each user in conjunction with a public key associated with the other party is fundamental to public-key cryptography. This approach provides a means to perform secure key exchange of the public key, as described later in this section.

Since the Diffie-Hellman algorithm combines the public and private keys into a shared secret key, it has the performance of a symmetric cryptosystem. So far so good. However, the algorithm has at least one serious security issue, called *the man-in-the-middle* attack. One of the simplest means of distributing public keys is for the users to directly send them to each

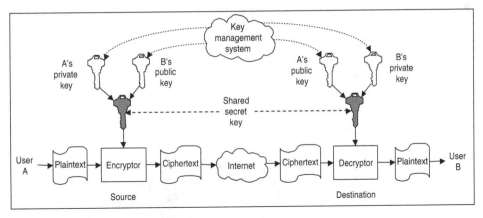

Figure 7.5   Diffie-Hellman public-key cryptosystem.

other over the public Internet. A problem arises if a malicious user C can intercept messages and insert his or her own instead. If user C substitutes his or her public key for A's and B's public keys in the cryptosystem of Figure 7.5, then users A and B are not aware that user C is in the middle. User C can then decrypt any ciphertext generated by A or B, since it has the same shared secret key. Worse yet, user C can substitute messages and masquerade as either user A or user B. The fundamental problem here is that the simple exchange of public keys over the public Internet does not allow users to authenticate the source of the public key. One solution is to use some other secure method to exchange the public keys and authenticate the sender before using Diffie-Hellman, for example, the RSA algorithm that we now describe. Another technique described later in this section involves certificates authenticated by a trusted third party.

The RSA algorithm uses public and private keys in another manner to prevent the man-in-the-middle attack, as illustrated in Figure 7.6. The key management system distributes a private key to each user and makes the corresponding public key available to anyone. The basic difference between RSA and Diffie-Hellman is that no shared secret key is used, but unfortunately, the processing performance required by RSA is often orders of magnitude higher than that required for symmetric algorithms like DES and Diffie-Hellman. However, because each user has his or her own private key, the man-in-the-middle attack is not possible.

The encryption technology used by RSA that makes it computationally feasible for only the corresponding private key to decrypt a message encoded by the public key is called a *trapdoor one-way* function. These are mathematical functions that cannot be easily reversed (i.e., one-way), unless a trapdoor is known (i.e., the key). The RSA definitions of keys and

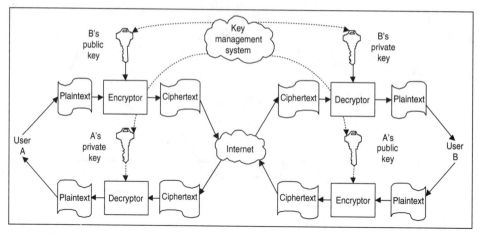

Figure 7.6   RSA public-key cryptosystem.

algorithms were revolutionary to the field of cryptography in the late 1970s. Instead of using complex combinations of substitutions and permutations as prior systems did, these systems had a basis in number theory, specifically, some results derived from Euler's theorem regarding prime numbers [Stallings 98a]. The RSA algorithm begins by a user selecting two very large prime numbers, p and q, on the order of 10^{75} to 10^{100}. The first part of the public and private keys is the product of these numbers, $n = pq$. All arithmetic is done modulo n; that is, only the remainder after dividing by n is retained from any calculation. The other parts of the keys require use of the Euler totient function, $t(n) = (p - 1)(q - 1)$. The public part of the key u is relatively prime with $t(n)$. That is, u and $t(n)$ have no common divisor other than unity. The private part of the key r is the inverse of the public part of the key u modulo n. That is, for any integer $X < n$, X^{ur} modulo $n = X$. In other words, the public key is $\{u,n\}$ and the private key is $\{r,n\}$. Let's look at how the RSA algorithm uses these keys to encrypt and decrypt messages. For a plaintext message segment M represented as a string of no more than $k = \log_2 n$ bits, the formula for the encrypted ciphertext C uses the public key $\{u,n\}$ as follows:

$$C = M^u \text{ modulo } n$$

The corresponding operation at the receiver decrypts a received ciphertext C using the private key $\{r,n\}$ to recover the plaintext M as follows:

$$M = C^r \text{ modulo } n = M^{ur} \text{ modulo } n = M$$

The RSA algorithm overcomes the confidentiality and integrity security problems that the man in the middle attack presents for the Diffie-Hellman algorithm. Unfortunately, it incurs a significant performance penalty since exponentiation is a conceptually straightforward, yet computationally intensive, operation. However, RSA does not allow the receiving user to authenticate the sender. In fact, any users who gain access to the destination user's public key can send secure messages claiming any identity they wish. This problem occurs in Email correspondence when the sender includes his or her PGP public key in a message. The next section describes additional algorithms that provide for authenticated identification of a sender and can detect modification of a message. As discussed earlier, the principal measure of security is the key length, and the processing load of the RSA algorithm increases with key length. A straightforward attack on RSA requires factoring out the numbers p and q that make up the factor n in the keys. This is a difficult problem if the values of the keys are selected according to specific guidelines.

As an example of an attack that is more effective than a brute force one, the computing time required to perform the exponentiation for encryption or decryption is a function of the number of 1s in the keys u and r. If a cracker can observe the compute time required for encryption or decryption, then a much more efficient attack than that required for brute force factoring of n is possible [Stallings 98a]. Although RSA and DES have enjoyed tremendous commercial success, progress marches ever onward, and the evolving science of cryptography is no different. Current research and IEEE P1363 standardization efforts in public-key cryptography now focus on elliptic curve cryptography, which promises equal security with less processing load [Stallings 98a].

THE SECRECY EMPOWERED BY HUGE NUMBERS

Currently, the number n in RSA keys should contain at least 1,024 bits to achieve reasonable security. The reader should observe that the value represented by such a key, 2^{1024}, is a huge number on the order of 10^{300} which is a 1 followed by 300 zeros. For comparison purposes, there are 10^{77} atoms in the universe, which has existed for 10^{17} seconds. This means that approximately 10^{200} numbers are necessary to describe the relative position in space and time of every atom in the universe for each nanosecond of its existence. This analogy provides some insight into why prime factors of such huge numbers are so difficult to find in brute force cryptanalysis attacks. The clever manipulation of such impressive quantities is fundamental to the science of cryptography.

Hashing, Digital Signatures, and Message Authentication Codes

A *hashing* function is a one-way mathematical function long used in computer science that transforms a long message into a relatively short, fixed-length *digest* that cannot easily be inverted to recreate the original longer message. A typical computer science application is transformation of a lengthy key into a fixed-length index. As an example, think of the images from a roll of photographic film exposed on top of each other. The combination of images will likely result in a unique photographic multiple exposure; however, it is usually quite difficult to extract an individual image. Obviously, the hashing function can transform different messages into the same digest, an event that computer scientists call a *collision*. However, messages containing written language, computer codes, or financial data are not equally likely, and therefore good hashing algorithms include a small likelihood that a commonly encountered message will result in an identical digest. In general, a good hashing function should produce each possible result with equal likelihood. The simple overlay of images is not a good hashing function, because if all of the exposures but one were taken in complete darkness, then the original set of images could be reconstructed from the multiple exposure.

Figure 7.7 illustrates the use of a hashing function to generate a message digest encrypted using the sender's private RSA key to generate a *digital signature*. The upper part of the figure illustrates the encryption of a plaintext message using any symmetric or asymmetric encryption algorithm, as described in the previous section. The shaded blocks and flow at the bottom of the figure illustrate the generation and verification of the digital sig-

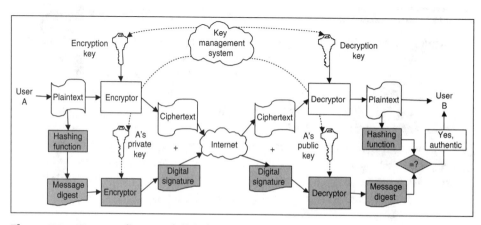

Figure 7.7   Message digest and digital signature.

nature. Starting at the left-hand side, user A employs a hashing function to generate a fixed-length message digest, which it encrypts using its own private RSA key to generate a digital signature. The Internet transfers the digital signature along with the ciphertext to user B, whose decryption algorithm returns the plaintext. In order to authenticate the sender of the received plaintext message, user B also decrypts the digital signature using A's public key to recover the original message digest. User B applies the same hashing function to the received plaintext and compares it with the decrypted message digest. If these results are identical, then user B has authenticated that user A did indeed send the associated plaintext message.

A number of hashing functions have been defined [Schneier 95], but only a few are in common use. Message Digest version 5 (MD5) addresses many issues with earlier versions, but now the revised version of the Secure Hash Algorithm (SHA-1) is the preferred hashing function due to its superior security. MD5 and SHA-1 produce a message digest of 128 bits and 160 bits, respectively. Note that a hashing function need not have a key, but the sender and receiver must agree to use the same algorithm. DES defines a Message Authentication Code (MAC) using Cipher Block Chaining (CBC) that performs a similar function to the digital signature previously described using the DES secret key shared between a pair of users [ANSI X9.17]. Another algorithm is the Digital Signature Standard (DSS), standardized by the National Institute of Standards and Technology (NIST) in 1991. The DSS algorithm uses a hashing function like the RSA-based algorithm, but it is based on discrete logarithms instead of encryption. Furthermore, it adds a public key associated with a group of communicating users and selection of a random number by the sender for the specific message in order to provide additional security. People continue to invent new cryptographic algorithms. Another promising approach is the Twofish encryption algorithm [Schneier 99].

Key Management Systems

So far, we've glossed over how keys are distributed to the end users in cryptosystems, representing this function as a cloud in the information flow diagrams of the previous sections. Since the secret or private keys are what provides security, proper key distribution and management is essential. Indeed, one of the initial objectives of asymmetric public-key cryptosystems was a completely distributed system for the exchange of secret keys. The most popular method is called the Diffie-Hellman key exchange algorithm, as illustrated in Figure 7.8. The algorithm begins by users A and B exchanging a large prime number p and a generator g over the public

Internet. The generator g is a primitive root of p, which means that g raised to successive powers taken modulo p generates all of the integers ranging from 1 to $p-1$, not necessarily in order. Now, users A and B generate random numbers x and y independently, as shown in the figure. Next, user A computes the value X and transmits it to user B, while user B computes the value Y and transmits it to user A over the Internet, as shown in Figure 7.8. Now, user A computes its secret key K from the value Y received from user B, while user B computes its secret key K' from the value X received from user A, as indicated in the figure. The fact that the results of these calculations are identical occurs because the order of exponentiation has no effect on the formula. Although anyone listening on the Internet knows p, g, and either X or Y, computation of either x or y involves calculation of a discrete logarithm, a complicated task for large prime numbers that provides the necessary security.

Unfortunately, this algorithm is vulnerable to the man-in-the-middle attack, described earlier in this chapter, because no authentication occurs. For example, a user C capable of intercepting every message that users A and B exchange can generate random variables and substitute its own values for X and Y in the key exchange. Thus, C can read every message without users A and B being aware that the security of their session has been compromised. The addition of digital signatures, or certificates as described later in this section, avoids this issue. The Diffie-Hellman key exchange protocol is useful for establishing temporary session keys, because using a new key for each session is a good security measure. The security of this algorithm also depends strongly on the means for determining random numbers.

The fundamental problem with the Diffie-Hellman key exchange algorithm is that of determining whether someone is actually who he or she

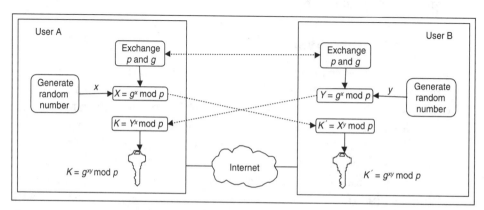

Figure 7.8   Diffie-Hellman key exchange algorithm.

claims to be. The X.500 series of standards developed by the ITU-T addresses this problem through an extensible infrastructure for registering and retrieving information associated with people, places, and a broad range of abstract objects. The organization of this information assumes a hierarchy of trusted Certificate Authority (CA) entities. The solution involves a digital certificate, or public-key certificate, issued by a trusted CA. A public-key certificate includes the following information as defined in ITU-T Recommendation X.509:

- Version number
- Certificate serial number
- Digital signature and signing algorithm employed
- Issuing authority's name and unique identification information
- Range of dates for which this certificate is valid
- User's name and unique identification information
- Public key and encryption algorithm for the certified user

The CA signs this information by using a hashing algorithm to generate the digital signature and then encrypt the entire set of information with its private key. The collection of subcomponents is called a *distinguished name*, which, when associated with the user's public key, becomes a *digital certificate*. A user can send this information (without the signature) to another user. The receiving user can generate the digital signature using the same hashing function and compare it to that derived by decrypting the public-key certificate using the CA's public key. This process makes forgery of the certificate extremely difficult. While the ITU-T originally specified X.509 certificates to enable authentication to X.500 directories, a number of other applications have emerged as well. For example, the Secure Sockets Layer (SSL) used in Web browsers employs the X.509 digital certificate approach.

A critical function of IP-based VPN administration is ensuring that only authenticated individuals receive specific keys, even if they are public keys. Increasingly, enterprises employ certification authorities for this purpose as well. Although this works well within a single enterprise, some issues occur in terms of scalability and authentication for exchange of information between multiple CAs. The idea is that the CAs are arranged in a hierarchy and that the root CA authenticates all of the lower-level CAs. The result is an inverted *tree of trust* and authentication relationships. In principle, at least, all that is needed is a copy of the root CA's certificate and a means to retrieve the certificates of all intermediate CAs and that of the CA whose signature applies to the certificate requiring authentication. In practice, however, a substantial amount of trust and processing load lies with the root CA and those CAs near the root. The IETF is actively developing standards associated with the X.509 Public Key Infrastructure (PKI) for the Internet that will address these issues.

Observe that the Diffie-Hellman key exchange is peer to peer, while the X.509 certificate model is a hierarchy of trusted authorities. Other models are possible—for example, the one used in PGP, where authenticity is guaranteed by a set of well-known users signing each others' keys in a face-to-face meeting. The resulting authentication is a *web of trust* comprising overlapping sets of users that have mutually authenticated the association of an identity with a specific public key. A public key may have multiple authenticating signatures. If you receive a key signed by someone that you trust, then with a high degree of certainty the user is indeed who he or she claims to be.

The longer-term objective of the IETF is to define a public key infrastructure that supports secure, authenticated distribution of keys in support of a suite of security protocols called IPsec. The target distribution protocol based on a subset of the ITU-T X.500 directory protocols is called the *Lightweight Directory Access Protocol* (LDAP). The key distribution protocol uses the Diffie-Hellman exchange as a basis, with additions designed to overcome its security weaknesses. We describe the key management system for IPsec, called *Internet Key Exchange* (IKE), after introducing the protocols and capabilities of IPsec in Chapter 9, *IP Security-Enabled and Routing-Controlled VPNs*.

Another approach that combines key distribution and authentication employed by a number of academic institutions is called *Kerberos*, named after the three-headed dog that Greek legend positioned as the guardian of the underworld, Hades. Kerberos is an authentication service designed for a hostile environment. This situation certainly applies to the computing and networking resources of a college, where users may not be who they claim, host addresses may be modified, or other security attacks may occur. Kerberos uses a centralized authentication service that requires client users to authenticate themselves with each service accessed. Version 5 is the most recent [RFC 1510], which extends the prior version 4, generated as part of Project Athena in the 1980s. It differs from other systems because it not only authenticates users, but also distributes encryption keys at the same time. After passing a logon/password authentication dialog, the Kerberos server issues a ticket and an authenticator to the user. The *ticket* contains a time stamp limiting its period of validity to a short interval—say 5 minutes—along with a session key, the user identification information, and identification of the encryption protocol. The ticket is encrypted using the server's public key. The time-stamped *authenticator*, encrypted by the session key from the ticket, contains an optional encryption key. A user wishing to access a server resource issues the ticket as part of its initial request. The server decrypts the ticket using the Kerberos server's public key, which validates the user's identity. The session then employs the encryption protocol identified in the ticket and the encryption key contained in the authenticator. A new ticket is required for each session that the user wishes to establish.

Note that use of Kerberos requires application modifications to use the key management protocol as part of access to every service. In addition, the centralized Kerberos server is a single point of attack that may be a security issue for some enterprises. However, it may see more widespread corporate use since Microsoft settled on Kerberos 5 as the basis for authentication in NT 5.0 and Windows 2000 [Kaufman 99].

QoS in a Connectionless Network

We covered the Resource reServation Protocol (RSVP) and MultiProtocol Label Switching (MPLS) in Chapter 5. Currently, support for these protocols is not consistently available across the many ISPs that make up the Internet, because they require close coordination of signaling and policy. In addition, these connection-oriented protocols require specification of a number of complex traffic and QoS parameters. The IETF has instead defined a simpler approach for differentiated services that reuses a part of the IP header on a hop-by-hop basis, which will likely see more rapid adoption by ISPs than that for RSVP and MPLS. Another approach is use of an overlay protocol. In particular, the Real-time Transport Protocol (RTP) adds sequencing and time-stamp information to packets carried by the Internet in support of real-time applications.

Differentiated Services (diffserv)

IETF RFCs 2474 and 2475 specify an approach, called *diffserv*, for the differentiated services in the Internet to provide different levels of QoS. The QoS measures currently specified in diffserv include responsiveness and availability. The diffserv standard requires that edge routers classify traffic based on TCP/IP header fields into microflows, with the resulting classification encoded into the 1-byte Type Of Service (TOS) field within an IPv4 or IPv6 header (see Chapter 6 for the IPv4 packet header format). Figure

7.9 shows the structure of the 1-byte diffserv field defined in RFC 2474. Because the diffserv byte is present in every IP packet header, each node can independently perform selective forwarding on a hop-by-hop basis without any other signaling. RFC 2474 requires that compliant implementations match the entire 6-bit Differentiated Services Code Point (DSCP) when determining which specific Per-Hop Behavior (PHB) to apply to the subject packet. As shown at the bottom of Figure 7.9, specific bit patterns within the low-order bits of the DSCP field determine whether the assignment policy is subject to standardization, experimental usage, or local usage. Enterprises or ISPs configure routers to use these PHBs to provide differentiated service from one edge of their network to the other. Currently, the specification of DSCP values, QoS, and PHBs on an end-to-end basis is an area of ongoing standardization activity.

RFC 2474 assigns DSCP values of the type XXX000 to a class selector codepoint, which provides backward compatibility to the IP Precedence field in the TOS byte. In general, packets with a class selector of a larger value should experience a higher probability of timely forwarding than packets having a class selector codepoint with a smaller value. Furthermore, an RFC 2474–compliant implementation must implement at least two independently forwarded classes of traffic.

Currently, the diffserv standard is unidirectional, allowing a microflow to have different levels of QoS in each direction. Anticipated service specifications include the concepts of a Traffic Conditioning Agreement (TCA) and a Service-Level Agreement (SLA) specified by parameters that may be qualitative or quantitative. The TCA and SLA may vary not only by direction, but also by geographic region and time of day. An example of a qualitative SLA is prioritization of one traffic flow over another. An example of

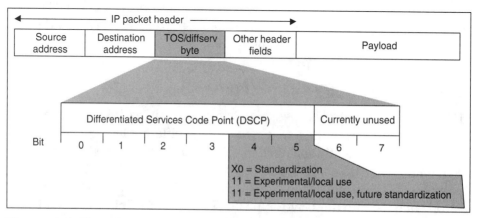

Figure 7.9 Diffserv definitions for IP TOS byte.

a quantitative TCA would be the traffic parameters analogous to those defined for RSVP in Chapter 5, namely, the peak and average rates along with a burst size. Quantitative SLA parameters are also analogous to RSVP, and include latency and packet loss.

An ISP must provision its routing and PHBs on a quasi-static basis using the traffic levels purchased by customers and measured traffic patterns. Examples of currently standardized PHBs include an assured forwarding group that specifies selective drop priorities and adaptive congestion avoidance [RFC 2597] and an expedited forwarding behavior [RFC 2598] that uses class-based queuing. An example of a basic service that an ISP could offer would be one with two qualitative SLA levels, namely, Expedited Forwarding and Default Handling. Initially, diffserv will be available only from a single ISP. However, as ISPs gain experience with diffserv, they will likely form service-level agreements between themselves. Only then will differentiated service spread across the Internet.

Real-Time Transport Protocol (RTP)

RFC 1889 defines the Real-Time Transport Protocol (RTP), which supports services with real-time characteristics, such as interactive audio and video. The functions provided by RTP include payload type identification, sequence numbering, time-stamping, and delivery monitoring. Typically, applications run RTP over the User Datagram Protocol (UDP) that provides port number-level multiplexing and checksum capabilities, as described in Chapter 6. RTP can operate in point-to-point or multicast modes. Since RTP is a protocol that runs only on end systems, it empowers the application to determine what to do with the sequencing and spacing of IP packets delivered by the underlying IP network. For example, a receiver may use the RTP sequence numbers to reconstruct the transmitted packet sequence or determine the location of a packet in a reassembly playback buffer. RTP operates in concert with the RTP Control Protocol (RTCP) to monitor delivery performance and convey some information about participants in an active session.

As stated in RFC 1889, RTP is a protocol framework designed with extensibility in mind. The base protocol implements a number of functions, which are best understood by examining the contents of an RTP packet as shown in Figure 7.10. The Flags/Options field contains information about the protocol version, presence of padding (for example, when block encryption is used), identification of header extensions, and enumeration of optional Contributing Source (CSRC) identifiers. It also contains a marker bit that may be used to delineate framing boundaries within

Flags/ options	Payload type	Sequence number	Time stamp	SSRC ID	CSRC ID(s)	Header extensions	Payload	Pad length
9	7	16	32	32	32		Variable	1

Figure 7.10   RTP packet contents.

the packet stream. The Payload Type field identifies the RTP payload format according to a profile associated with a specific assigned number. A single RTP stream uses only a single payload type. The next two fields provide QoS services to higher-layer applications over a connectionless IP datagram network. The source increments the Sequence Number field for each RTP data packet transmitted, beginning with a random value to complicate attacks on an encryption protocol with a known input plaintext. It may be used by the receiver to detect packet loss and to restore the transmitted packet sequence. The Time Stamp field indicates the instant at which the first byte of the RTP payload was generated, with time granularity determined by the profile. An application may use the time stamp to eliminate packet jitter introduced by the datagram network or to restore proper timing during playback. The Synchronization Source (SSRC) identifier identifies the sequence number and time-stamp grouping for use by the receiving application(s). Up to 32 CSRC identifiers follow this field if the application uses a mixer—for example, an audioconference. Optional header extensions precede the payload, which may be followed by a single byte indicating that the pad length in this option was specified in the Options field.

Let's look at a simple example of how RTP provides QoS support even when the underlying IP network does not, with reference to the packet sequences depicted in Figure 7.11. A source generates a series of sequence-numbered time-stamped RTP packets and transmits these into a best-effort IP network shown in Figure 7.11a. The sequence numbers are preceded by the # symbol, while the timestamps are indicated with the notation xx:yy, for example, seconds and hundredths of a second. The best-effort IP network introduces several impairments to this packet stream, illustrated in Figure 7.11b. RTP packets with sequence numbers 34 and 35 are reversed, and the time spacing is altered. Furthermore, RTP packet sequence number 38 is lost, and number 39 is substantially delayed. It is up to the application to determine what to do in response to lost packets. For example, in the case of voice or audio playback, the application often inserts a noise pattern. Normally, the receiving application imple-

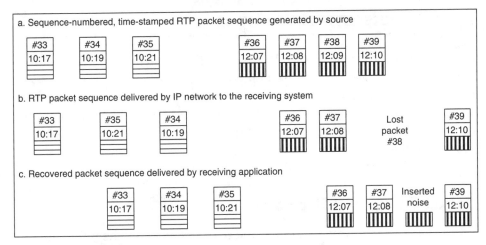

Figure 7.11 Example of application usage of RTP.

ments a playback buffer that assumes a maximum level of jitter caused by the underlying network. If the received packet jitter is less than this value, then the receiver can play back a delayed version of the original sequence of packets, as shown in Figure 7.11c. Notice how the packet stream is delayed by at least the differential time delay of the worst-case received packet in the example.

If RTP is used in conjunction with RSVP-, MPLS-, or diffserv-powered QoS, performance can actually be quite good. However, when an underlying QoS mechanism is not used, RTP performance may degrade during periods of congestion. RTCP provides a means for applications to measure performance and potentially reroute traffic under these conditions. For example, some voice over IP systems measure voice over RTP performance, and if it degrades too much, they route calls over more expensive telephone network circuits during periods of IP network congestion.

AUDIO, VIDEO, AND VOICE OVER THE WEB

If you've listened to music or a news report over the Web, then you've experienced the RTP protocol. Some near real-time video playback applications also use RTP. Voice over IP relies on RTP as well. Since most parts of the Internet are engineered with additional capacity to support restoration and growth, these real-time applications work acceptably most of the time. However, during busy periods when some point along the path is congested or under failure conditions, these applications may not work at all.

Access Tools and Techniques

Another important aspect of an IP-based VPN infrastructure is determining who has access to the enterprise computing and networking resources and how to make privately addressed hosts accessible to the public Internet. Chapter 8, *Dial-in Access and Multiprotocol Tunneling VPNs*, covers protocols that provide access control, as does Chapter 9's coverage of IPsec. This section introduces some foundational concepts and protocols as background to these discussions.

Packet Filters and Firewalls

A firewall stands between an untrusted network, such as the public Internet, and a trusted private network, such as a secure LAN, as illustrated throughout this section. There are several types of firewalls [Kaufman 99; Kosiur 98; Ibe 99]. The simplest is a packet filter that operates on specific fields within the IP packet header, such as the source and destination addresses and the protocol type. In some cases, firewalls may operate on fields within higher-layer protocols as well—typically the port number in TCP or UDP. A circuit or application proxy participates in the transport-layer session and the application-layer protocols on a packet-by-packet basis. Another approach is a firewall that performs stateful multilayer inspection that delivers capabilities similar to an application-level proxy at a lower cost. We briefly describe the operation of each of these types of firewalls.

As shown in Figure 7.12a, a *packet filter firewall* attempts to match the fields in every received packet against the configured set of rules. The figure shows simple IPv4 destination address prefix matching as an example. The rules can be set to deny certain types of matches or admit only certain

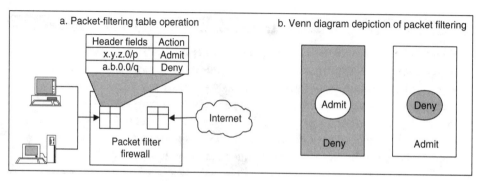

Figure 7.12   Packet filter firewall.

matches. If the number of rules is large, this can have a performance impact on the device implementing the packet filter. Filters can require a significant amount of configuration, so matching of the fields in a packet header is done on an address prefix or numerical range basis to keep the number of entries to a manageable level. An issue with packet filtering is that it is address based, and therefore cannot determine whether a user has been authenticated. Many places on the Internet do not authenticate the source IP address, hence address spoofing is a very real threat. Relying on a packet filter based on the source IP address is therefore not a secure solution. Packet filters can perform an important role in an enterprise VPN; for example, they can block access by certain types of potentially security-compromising protocols that utilize standard transport-layer port numbers, such as SNMP, Telnet, or FTP. Packet filters can also block security-compromising options in the IP header, such as source routing. As we shall see in Chapters 8 and 9, secure tunneling schemes encrypt higher-layer protocol information; therefore, filtering on the IP address and protocol type information may be the only security tool available in certain network designs.

Normally, the default action of a packet filter firewall is to either admit or deny a packet when no matching header field is found. Exceptions to selectively deny or admit packets matching a set of header field patterns are then an overlay to this default action. The resulting admission and denial policy in terms of the header field space can be represented as a Venn diagram, as illustrated in Figure 7.12b. Overlapping sets of packet filters configured at firewalls at multiple sites can be used to construct VPNs or Closed User Groups (CUGs), resulting in a capability similar to that defined for X.25, as described in Chapter 4, *Early Connection-Oriented Data VPNs—X.25 and Frame Relay*. The method of implementing the CUG between X.25 SVCs and packet filter firewalls differs. The filter approach has a higher degree of management and configuration complexity than the CUG interlock code approach of X.25. This is due to the fact that adding or deleting a site associated with a set of header field values requires modification of the filter tables in every other firewall in the VPN, while in a CUG interlock code approach only added sites require configuration.

More sophisticated firewalls operate at higher protocol layers, and thus can be used only in secure local area networks. They cannot operate in an environment where the IP payload is encrypted. These include circuit- and application-level proxies [Kosiur 98]. A circuit or application proxy usually sits between a secured LAN and the router that connects to the Internet, as shown in Figure 7.13a. A *circuit proxy firewall* often has two copies of

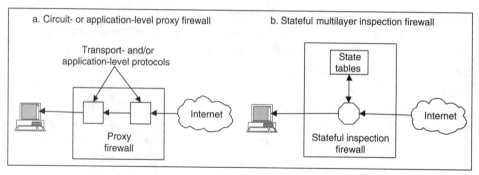

Figure 7.13 Higher-layer firewalls.

the transport-layer protocol (i.e., TCP and UDP), one for the secure LAN side and another facing the public Internet. It validates every session request and allows through to the other side (shown by the dashed arrow in the figure) only those that meet certain access rule criteria. An *application proxy firewall* operates in a similar manner, but also examines higher-layer protocol data. It also requires two copies of each application- and transport-layer protocol and transfers only data that meets the configured access control criteria.

The application-level proxy firewall is the most flexible and secure, because it examines all traffic in whatever detail may be required. However, performing a significant amount of processing on every packet degrades performance. The recently developed *stateful inspection firewall*, shown in Figure 7.13b, substitutes a single stage of processing for the two copies of an application running in a proxy firewall. This firewall is similar to an application-level proxy in terms of functionality, but it processes each packet only once via comparison with known bit patterns and the session state. The result is a firewall that has the security of an application-level proxy yet has higher performance.

Handling Private Addresses—Network Address Translation

Some networks using the IP-based protocol existed before the popularity of the Internet boomed. In fact, some of these networks were envisioned as completely separate private networks that would never interconnect to any other networks. Thus, designers of these networks did not bother to obtain a unique IP address block and instead reused IP address space allocated to other networks. Current administrators of an ever increasing number of these network islands now find users wanting connectivity to the Internet at large. Of course, one alternative is to obtain a valid, globally unique IP address block and reconfigure all of the workstations, servers, and routers in these network islands. However, IP address reassignment and reconfiguration is a disruptive and error-prone activity. Some of these network islands support applications important to the enterprise, so motivation arose to develop a solution in support of overlapping address plans.

Recalling the deployment of PBXs in private voice networks that led to the development of voice VPNs in the 1970s, as described in Chapter 3, *Circuit-Switched VPNs*, we note that a strong parallel exists with support for private IP address plans. Basically, the solution is translation of the nonunique private IP network address to a globally unique address at the source, which allows routing of the packet across the Internet and then performing the inverse of the translation at the destination. This is, in fact, exactly the approach that Network Address Translation (NAT) performs for private IP-addressed networks, as defined in RFC 1631. There are three types of NAT: static, many-to-many, and many-to-one [Brown 99]. *Static NAT* involves a one-for-one translation of the private IP address to a public IP address. This is useful for translating public IP addresses of a Web server into the actual private address of the device hosting the enterprise's Web site. However, it does not reduce the number of public IP addresses required. The *many-to-many NAT* capability assigns addresses from a pool of public IP addresses based on activity generated by a private IP-addressed host. This means that an inactivity timer is required, which can cause several problems. If the time interval is too short, then a user session may be disrupted. On the other hand, if the time interval is too long, then the number of public IP addresses in the pool must be larger. The net result is that the required number of IP addresses may not be significantly reduced. For these reasons, the many-to-many NAT capability is seldom used.

The *many-to-one NAT* protocol interacts with private IP-addressed hosts at the TCP or UDP port level instead of at the IP address level to dramatically reduce the size of the public IP address pool. We further explore the operation of many-to-one NAT with reference to Figure 7.14. On the left-hand side, four hosts on a LAN have private IP addresses ranging from 10.0.0.1 to 10.0.0.4. The many-to-one NAT function shares a single public IP address 49.4.5.6/32. It does this by mapping the host-assigned source ports in the TCP or UDP headers to unique ports. Let's walk through a simple interchange of packets between host 10.0.0.1 and the Web server 22.1.2.3. The host generates a packet with its own address, destined for the Web server with source port 2000 and destination port 80 (for HTTP). NAT substitutes the public IP address 49.4.5.6 from its pool for the source IP

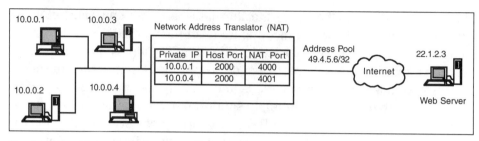

Figure 7.14   Network Address Translation (NAT).

address. It also allocates a unique port number for each combination of private IP address and host port number, substituting this for the source port number in the outgoing packet (4000 in this example). The public Internet uses the Web server address to route the packet, at which point the Web server responds by swapping the source and destination IP address and port number fields. This means that the destination IP address in the packet generated by the Web server is the NAT address, 49.4.5.6, and the destination port number is 4000. The Internet routes this packet back to the NAT, which indexes its translation table using the destination port number and determines that the target host is 10.0.0.1 port 2000. NAT then substitutes the host IP address 10.0.0.1 for the destination IP address and the host port 2000 for the destination port and transmits it on the LAN.

Note that NAT functions correctly, even if hosts access the same destination using the same host port number, by assigning a different NAT port number, as illustrated in Figure 7.14. Also, observe that in order for NAT to function, it must have access to the transport-layer port numbers. This requirement is similar to that for the proper operation of firewalls, and therefore constrains the placement of NAT and firewall functions to secured LANs in IP-based VPN networks.

This completes the overview of technologies, protocols, and techniques necessary to implement IP-based VPNs as described in the remainder of the book. Chapter 8 describes the various protocols and architectures for implementing IP-based VPNs by using remote dial-in protocols or tunneling over a public Internet that an enterprise may implement either directly or through use of a contractor. Chapter 9 focuses on the IPsec protocol suite and solutions within a service provider network that manipulate routing information to implement IP-based VPNs.

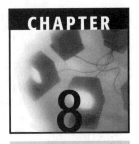

Dial-In Access and Multiprotocol Tunneling VPNs

It doesn't matter how new an idea is: what matters is how new it becomes.
—Elias Canetti

Chapter 6, *The Internet Protocol Suite*, and Chapter 7, *Building Blocks for IP-Based VPNs—Security, Quality, and Access*, provided background on techniques necessary to realize communication and security across the public Internet. Now, after introducing a few additional protocols that build on this foundation, this chapter describes enterprise VPN architectures built on top of the public Internet. After understanding these IP-based VPNs, this chapter concludes with an economic comparison to other VPN alternatives.

Business Drivers and Requirements

The factors that drive the public Internet described in Chapter 6 along with those that affect security, quality, and access control described in Chapter 7 are important to IP-based VPNs. Additionally, the needs of a mobile workforce and a means to leverage the economics of the world's largest network—the Internet—are important drivers for IP-based VPNs serving the dial-in and multiprotocol marketplace.

Empowering the Mobile Workforce

Despite the predictions by some networking visionaries, the advent of videoconferencing and other electronic communication techniques has not reduced the amount of travel for enterprise employees. These intrepid road warriors still travel as much as they ever did, but now communication networking allows them to be more productive while they are away from their home office. Furthermore, extension of high-performance access technologies to residential neighborhoods provides an option for an ever increasing number of information workers to telecommute. The benefits of telecommuting for an enterprise are several. First, the amount of office space required is less. In some businesses, telecommuting workers come into the office a few days a week and use shared offices, then work from home the remainder of the time. Social interaction and the dynamics of group meetings in the workplace have undeniable value; however, employees who sit at their desks and work at computers can just as easily do this at home. Second, the quality of life and productivity of a telecommuting employee can actually improve, especially if the physical commute involves long trips and traffic jams. In general, happy employees are more productive. Finally, telecommuting allows employees to time-shift their work patterns. For example, parents can care for children or people can attend to disabled family members, performing work for their employer during nontraditional business hours. A managerial challenge with telecommuting is that the means of monitoring employee progress and identifying problems differs from the traditional techniques, but many enterprises do not see this as an insurmountable issue.

An IP-based VPN offers one important capability that other VPN technologies do not: secure remote dial-in access from almost anywhere in the world. The set of protocols and procedures that enables this important differentiator is essential to an enterprise that has individuals who travel frequently, yet still require access to sensitive information. Since anyone can dial in, securing this front-door access method is an important consideration for an enterprise dealing with sensitive information.

Leveraging Economics of the Shared Internet

Since the global Internet will become by far the largest network ever constructed, significantly overshadowing the telephone, private line, and ATM networks, the opportunity to leverage this economy of scale for enterprise-specific VPNs is compelling. However, a proper business analysis must consider not only the benefits, but the costs as well. As we shall see, a principal benefit of an IP-based VPN for some enterprise traffic patterns is lower monthly recurring charges for access to the Internet when compared with telephone dial-up, private lines, frame relay, or ATM. Offsetting this benefit is usually the need for larger up-front capital expenditures for equipment necessary to secure the public Internet for VPN purposes. This economic analysis is amenable to determination of a payback period or return on investment. As described in Chapter 3, *Circuit-Switched VPNs*, voice networking encountered a similar situation in the late 1980s. Enterprises spent capital on PBXs to attain the benefit of the lower recurring cost for private lines compared with switched long-distance telephone charges. What they found, and what some enterprises are finding with IP-based VPNs, is that additional complexity and adoption of an emerging technology incurs additional cost. Hidden costs in IP-based VPNs include those for training, additional system management, hiring support staff expertise, and the need to upgrade security equipment and software [Fowler 99]. However, as analyzed at the end of this chapter, even after accounting for these additional costs, IP-based VPNs still look attractive to enterprises that have a large geographically diverse population of users generating bursty activity or when site-to-site communication is widely distributed.

Technology Trends and Enablers

The implementation of security techniques described in Chapter 7 in standardized protocols is an important enabler to IP-based VPNs. Several additional technology trends are important in IP-based VPNs.

Increasing Use of the Internet Protocol

Although many enterprises still run other proprietary network-layer protocols, such as IBM's SNA, Compaq's DECnet, Novell's IPX, and Microsoft's NETBEUI, they are moving to a primarily IP-based addressing environment. Some estimates place the total volume of non-IP traffic as high as 40 percent. The old adage of not fixing something if it isn't broken means that rewriting existing applications is often not justified. However, the fact is that most new applications are built atop IP because the latest technologies and features are available. Furthermore, most programmers and applications developers prefer to build new networking software applications using the TCP/IP protocol suite.

Positively Authenticating a User's Identity

As discussed in Chapter 7, a pivotal point of any security system is authenticating that users or entities are indeed who they claim to be. This process often begins with a human being attempting to gain access to a computer system. The security of the traditional login ID and password combination used since the beginning of computing hinges on selection of a difficult-to-guess-or-compromise password. This presents a dilemma to network administrators. If the password is easy for the user to remember, then it may be easy for an attacker to guess. On the other hand, if the password is complex, then the user may write it down somewhere, opening the avenue for an attacker to compromise security by obtaining this written record in some way. Of course, a clever attacker may also pose as an enterprise security administrator and request via a phone call that the user provide the password as part of a claimed need for network maintenance. Processes and procedures cannot handle all of these problems. Fortunately, technology is evolving to provide authentication mechanisms, in addition to the traditional login ID password combination, that promise to deliver much stronger security to enterprises whose information sensitivity justifies the additional expense. As described in this chapter, these techniques include special-purpose hardware installed in user computers, separate devices that generate security tokens, and adapters that analyze biometric data such as fingerprints or retinal scans.

Extending the Secured LAN via Tunneling

Another important technological advance has been the development and refinement of tunneling protocols that make the users and resources located at separate enterprise sites and authenticated remote dial-in users all appear to be on a single secured LAN. Two basic types of protocols and technology described in this chapter make this possible. The first is an access concentrator implementing protocols that authenticate users who usually access the enterprise VPN via remote dial-in. The second is a tunneling protocol implemented by a network server at each enterprise location. A *tunnel* is a means of carrying one protocol over another. The tunneling schemes covered in this chapter are capable of supporting IP and almost any other protocol as well. This capability allows an enterprise to focus on IP as an underlying infrastructure, yet still support legacy applications running over some other network-layer protocol.

Implementation and Protocol Specifics

This section describes the protocols that support secured dial-in access to VPNs as well as tunneling protocols that connect secured VPN LAN sites.

Generic Secure Dial-In Access Architecture

ISPs and some large enterprises deploy a device called an *access concentrator*, also known as a *Network Access Server* (NAS) or *Remote Access Server* (RAS), that connects an access network, such as the telephone network or xDSL links on one side and multiplexes this onto a high-speed connection to a router that connects to the Internet on the other, as shown in the left-hand side of Figure 8.1. When interfacing with the telephone network, the access concentrator contains a pool of modems into which users dial. The client computer runs an *authentication protocol* with the access concentrator during login. During the login procedure, the access concentrator runs an *access control protocol* with an authentication server, which may be collocated, but in general may be in some other location and accessed by the Internet, as depicted in the figure. If the requesting user is authenticated, the access concentrator allows the client access to the Internet. In the case of VPNs, the access concentrator establishes a session using a *tunnel protocol* to a network server that secures an enterprise LAN, as illustrated on the right-hand side of the figure.

It is important to keep this general architecture in mind as we delve into the sea of acronyms that accompanies the following protocol definitions. The authentication protocols covered in this chapter are the Password Authentication Protocol (PAP) and the Challenge Handshake Authentication Protocol (CHAP). The access control protocols covered are the

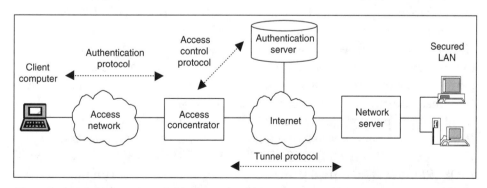

Figure 8.1   Generic secure dial-in access architecture.

Remote Authentication Dial-In User Service (RADIUS) and the Terminal Access Controller Access Control System (TACACS). Finally, the tunnel protocols covered are the Point-to-Point Tunneling Protocol (PPTP) and the Layer 2 Tunneling Protocol (L2TP). First, we begin with the Point-to-Point Protocol (PPP), which is the basis on which all of these protocols were developed.

Point-to-Point Protocol (PPP)

The earliest link-layer protocol designed specifically for the Internet by 3Com in the early 1980s to interconnect computers and routers was called *Serial Line IP* (SLIP), which the IETF documented in 1988 in RFC 1055. SLIP provides a means for delimiting IP packets on a serial link using specific characters. If the user data contains these specific characters, then SLIP uses a character-stuffing mechanism. Since the protocol was so simple, implementations readily achieved a high degree of interoperability, but SLIP supported only preconfigured IP addresses. Since SLIP required assignment of a scarce IPv4 address to every new Internet user, the IETF designed a better link-layer protocol for access to the Internet. The result was the standardization of the Point-to-Point Protocol (PPP) in 1994, as documented in RFC 1661, RFC 2153, and STD 0051. PPP supports IP as well as a number of other network-layer protocols over a wide range of link- and physical-layer protocols, for example, X.25 [RFC 1598], HDLC [RFC 1662], frame relay [RFC 1973], and ATM AAL5 [RFC 2364]. It also supports automatic configuration and management of the link layer using negotiation procedures, which involves one party proposing a particular option and parameters, followed by the other party either accepting the proposal or rejecting it.

PPP is a frame-based protocol that prefixes every network-layer packet with a 2-byte header that indicates the PPP frame type. During the link- and network-layer protocol negotiation phases, this prefix indicates that the packet contains control information. The PPP Link Control Protocol (LCP) automatically establishes, configures, and tests a data link connection. It negotiates parameters for authentication, maximum packet size, performance monitoring, and multilink operation. The optional authentication phase described in the next section occurs between the link establishment and the network-layer control phase. The PPP Network Control Protocol (NCP) is specific to each network-layer protocol, for example, IPv4 [RFC 1332], Novell IPX [RFC 1634], SNA [RFC 2043], Microsoft's Net-BIOS [RFC 2097], and IPv6 [RFC 2472]. The NCP does not run until the LCP has completed. ISPs employ PPP's IP Control Protocol (IPCP) [RFC

1332] to dynamically assign IP addresses to dial-in users, a design that stretches the limited IPv4 address space.

PPP also supports a number of other features, such as negotiation of header compression [RFC 2509], operation over multiple links [RFC 1990], bandwidth allocation for multiple links [RFC 2125], DES encryption [RFC 2419], and support for multiple traffic classes [RFC 2686]. For more information, see the referenced RFCs or [Wilder 98] for an overview. PPP also allows the network to authenticate the identity of users attempting to establish a connection. Furthermore, PPP is the basis of several tunneling protocols used in IP-based VPNs, described in the following sections.

Authentication Protocols—PAP and CHAP

The first level of authentication occurs when the user dials into the access concentrator. Two protocols are widely used to access the Internet, the Password Authentication Protocol (PAP) [RFC 1334] and the Challenge Handshake Authentication Protocol (CHAP) [RFC 1994]. We first describe the operation of PAP with reference to the space-time diagram of Figure 8.2. The authentication dialog begins with the client computer sending an authenticate request PPP message in the clear containing the user ID and password. The access concentrator employs the user ID and password to query a database, which may be local or remote, and determines whether the combination is valid (OK) or invalid (not OK). The access concentrator then returns an authenticate acknowledgment message (ack) if the query was OK, otherwise the not acknowledged (nak) message is sent. The protocol handles the case of lost messages by the client continually sending the authenticate request message until some form of acknowledgment response is received. PAP has several security problems. First, the password is sent in the clear, making the protocol vulnerable to sniffing and

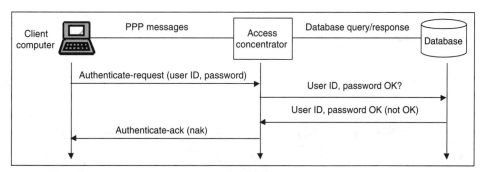

Figure 8.2   Dial-in user authentication using PAP.

replay attacks. Second, an attacker can exploit the retransmission mode of PAP and successively try to guess the password.

To overcome the security weaknesses of PAP, the IETF specified the CHAP protocol, first in RFC 1334, which RFC 1994 then made obsolete. CHAP replaces the two-way handshake of PAP with a more secure three-way handshake employing a shared secret, as illustrated by the space-time diagram of Figure 8.3. User identification occurs using a PPP LCP message during the link establishment phase, as shown in the figure. CHAP begins with the access concentrator sending a randomly chosen challenge string to the client protocol after the PPP link establishment phase completes. The client computer applies a hash function negotiated during the PPP link establishment phase (e.g., Message Digest 5, as described in Chapter 7) to the concatenation of the challenge string and the shared secret. The challenge response contains only the fixed-length hash value (e.g., 16 bytes for MD5). The access concentrator knows the challenge string that it sent and has the shared secret corresponding to the client computer's claimed user ID stored in its database. If the access concentrator's hash calculation matches that received from the client, then the authentication succeeds; otherwise, authentication fails. CHAP requires that the access concentrator drop the connection if authentication fails. CHAP handles lost packets by requiring the access concentrator to send the challenge string until it receives a response. Similarly, the client sends a hashed response until it receives either a success or a failure message response.

The principal advantage of CHAP over PAP is that the password (i.e., the shared secret) is not sent in the clear. Of course, the access concentrator must send a different challenge string in every message to prevent replay attacks. The access concentrator may execute CHAP at any time during a

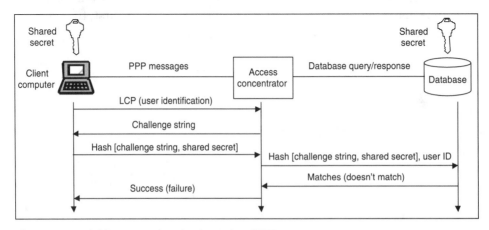

Figure 8.3 Dial-in user authentication using CHAP.

user session to verify that no one has hijacked the access connection. Since CHAP drops the connection upon authentication failure, it increases the time involved in a password-guessing attack, because each password attempt requires that the attacker make a new dial-in connection.

The principal disadvantage of CHAP, as well as of PAP, is that secure distribution of a shared secret to each client and a secured database are necessary. This can become a significant scaling issue for an enterprise with a large number of dial-in users. Finally, if the shared secret is a user-selected password, then the resulting security is as good as the difficulty of guessing the passwords, which can be a serious security problem if good password selection guidelines are not followed.

Extensible Authentication Protocol (EAP)

Earlier in this chapter, we lamented the inadequacy of passwords. However, most enterprises still rely on user IDs and passwords, as both PAP and CHAP do, which security experts call *weak authentication*. Is there any way to improve matters? Fortunately, the answer is yes. Increased security is possible if an enterprise uses at least one of the following methods, increasing the security level to *strong authentication* [Kaufman 99; Kosiur 98]. One approach employs a separate device that generates a token as part of the login and authentication process. Another technique involves using hardware that the user's computer invokes as part of the login and authentication process. Yet another approach takes an authentication technique commonly encountered in science fiction stories and moves it into the real world using analysis of biometric characteristics of the human body, such as fingerprints or retinal scans.

The hardware-based solutions take several forms. A *smart card* is separate microprocessor, about the size of a credit card, with memory in a package. Some are now integrated into computer keyboards or have adapters that work with a computer's floppy disk drive. Another packaging option is use of the PCMCIA card standard supported by many computers. Typically, these devices store the user's private key and Personal Identification Number (PIN). In some cases, these hardware devices have cryptographic processors that deliver performance improvements over software-based encryption.

The *token* authentication techniques require that both the user and the authenticating device share a piece of privately held secret combined with physical access to a corresponding hardware or software device that generates the token. These systems use a separate hardware or software mechanism that displays changing data that a user must enter as part of the authentication process during login. Two basic methods are used: PIN-based and time-based. In the PIN-based scheme, a separate card or software program uses a hashing function that takes a PIN number entered by the user and a challenge string generated by the authenticating network element to generate a response string. The user must then enter this response as part of the login dialog. Because the authenticating network element knows the user's PIN, the challenge string, and the hashing algorithm, only it can verify that the user has both the device and the PIN. On the other hand, time-based token systems employ a device that displays a character string that changes periodically, typically once a minute. The network administrator gives every user a device associated with his or her login ID and password. During the login sequence, the authenticating network element requests that the user enter the number displayed on the device. Since the clocks on the device and the authenticating server are synchronized, they generate the same character sequence. In either of these techniques, an attacker must obtain access not only to the user ID and password, but to the device that generates the token as well. This system is more secure because the period of potential compromise is limited by the fact that users know when a device is either lost or stolen. The network administrator can then disable access to the compromised devices and deliver a replacement to the user.

SCIENCE FICTION BECOMES SCIENCE FACT FOR AUTHENTICATION

Once the province of science fiction and spy stories, biometric devices and systems examine one or more distinguishing features of a person that should be both relatively unique and difficult to forge. Examples include fingerprints, retinal and iris scans, voiceprints, as well as hand geometry, facial images, and handwriting analysis. Fingerprints and retinal scans are unique and reliable schemes. Other techniques such as voiceprints, hand geometry, facial images, or handwriting are less reliable, because changes in the health or cosmetic appearance of the user may invalidate the recognition process. The amount of data that must be stored and analyzed for biometric analysis may be relatively large. This fact, combined with the relative cost of the devices that measure these biometric characteristics, indicates limited use for this application. However, recent cost reductions, particularly in the area of fingerprint scanner technology [Levine 99], are making this approach increasingly attractive to enterprises requiring strong authentication. Be aware, though, that legal issues may arise when using sensitive personal data, such as fingerprints, from enterprise users.

RFC 2284 specifies a PPP Extensible Authentication Protocol (EAP) that supports multiple authentication mechanisms, such as those previously described. The negotiation of authentication mechanisms occurs after the link establishment phase, which puts the authenticator in charge of the combination of two or more authentication mechanisms required to achieve strong security.

Access Control Protocols—TACACS and RADIUS

Cisco developed the Terminal Access Controller Access Control System (TACACS) protocol in the late 1980s [RFC 1492]. The latest version, called TACACS+ works much the same as the Remote Authentication Dial-In User Service (RADIUS) protocol specified in RFC 2138. The principal difference is that TACACS+ runs over TCP, while RADIUS uses UDP. Therefore, we focus only on the description of RADIUS in this section. When describing authentication protocols in the previous section, we intentionally made the database distinct from the access concentrator to show how these functions could logically be separate. RADIUS uses the client-server architecture illustrated in Figure 8.4 to physically accomplish this separation. Normally, the user interfaces to the RADIUS client using PPP. The RADIUS client (i.e., the NAS or access concentrator) determines whether to consult the RADIUS server during the PPP LCP PAP/CHAP negotiation phase. This example assumes usage of CHAP. Invocation of the RADIUS server may also occur by either configuration or failure to locate the specific user ID in its local database. The RADIUS client and server encrypt

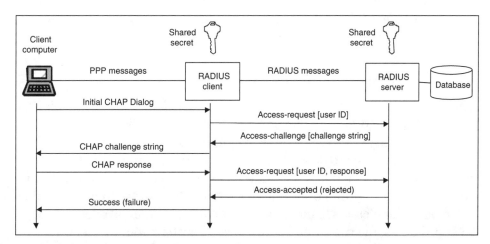

Figure 8.4 RADIUS client-server authentication.

transactions using the RSA algorithm and authenticate using an MD5 message digest with a secret shared between the client and the server. The client sends the user ID in an access-request packet to the server, which returns a random challenge string. The RADIUS client poses this challenge to the user via the CHAP protocol. The RADIUS client returns the user-generated response to the server along with the identifying user ID using another access-request message to the server. If the RADIUS server authenticates the user against the password stored in its database and the hashed value computed by the user, it returns an access-accepted message; otherwise, it rejects the attempt using an access-rejected message.

Enterprises can realize an important advantage from the separation of function created by the RADIUS client-server architecture: Namely, the ISP can implement the client using conventional access concentrator technology while the enterprise implements the server and thus has control over the user profiles and passwords. The ISP's access concentrator may directly contact the enterprise RADIUS server, or the ISP's RADIUS server may act as a proxy [Brown 99; Huston 99]. This design also eases the administrative burden of having to distribute user profiles and passwords to a set of distributed access concentrators. Of course, centralizing all of this information necessitates deployment of a primary and a backup server to achieve acceptable reliability. Also, beware of overloading a single RADIUS server, since time-outs may occur and result in failed user login attempts [Brown 99].

The RADIUS client-server architecture is also widely used for dedicated connections, such as xDSL or cable modem access. RADIUS also specifies an optional accounting function, as described in RFCs 2620 and 2621, that keeps track of the session establishment time, the number of packets and bytes sent and received, the termination cause, and other data. ISPs utilize this information for billing or network management purposes; however, an enterprise can use this data for similar purposes.

Tunneling Protocol Standards

Unfortunately, the term *tunnel* is somewhat misleading, since it implies a dedicated connection from one point to another. Tunneling is the scenario where two systems convey packets over another protocol. *Encapsulation* is another name used to describe this carriage of one protocol over another. As shown in Figure 8.5, sometimes tunneling involves carriage of one network-layer protocol by another. Although contrary to the inflexible OSI model that dictates higher-layer protocols only running over lower-layer protocols, the tunneling approach is consistent with the general concept of protocol layering. This figure illustrates the user-plane protocol

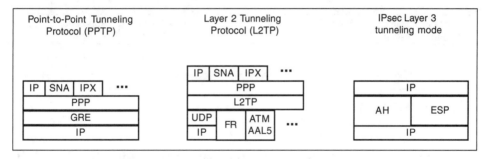

Figure 8.5   Illustration of protocol tunneling layers.

layering for the tunneling protocols described in this chapter and in Chapter 9, *IP Security-Enabled and Routing-Controlled VPNs*. A control protocol also exists for each of these protocols, but is not shown in Figure 8.5. PPTP and L2TP support IP as well as other protocols, such as IBM's SNA and Novell's IPX, as shown at the top of the figure. Both PPTP and L2TP utilize PPP, originally designed for dial-in applications, as the multiprotocol encapsulation technique. PPTP and L2TP use different methods to encapsulate PPP frames over another protocol. As seen from the figure, PPTP uses a modified version of Cisco's Generic Routing Encapsulation (GRE) header for carriage over IP, while L2TP uses its own header and then uses UDP over IP. Notice that L2TP may also operate directly over frame relay, ATM AAL5, or a number of Layer 2 packet-switching media.

Moving to the right-hand side of Figure 8.5, we show the IP security (IPsec) protocol layering options for operation in tunnel mode that has a similar layering of IP running over IP. Chapter 9 describes the header fields of IPsec in tunnel mode, which are the Authentication Header (AH) and the Encapsulating Secure Payload (ESP).

Point-to-Point Tunneling Protocol (PPTP)

Microsoft, Ascend, 3Com, ECI Telematics, and Copper Mountain Networks developed the Point-to-Point Tunneling Protocol (PPTP) as an extension of PPP used for dial-in connections. Microsoft bundles support for PPTP into NT 4.0 and Windows 98, as well as offering support as an add-on to Windows 95 [Microsoft 97]. This means that PPTP became a de facto standard for Layer 2 tunneled VPNs in the late 1990s for enterprises with PCs using Microsoft operating systems. We describe the capabilities of PPTP with reference to the packet format shown in Figure 8.6 [RFC 2637]. A

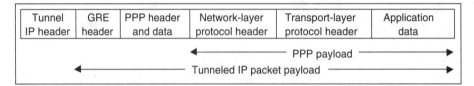

Figure 8.6   PPTP packet format.

PPTP packet rides over any protocol that can carry IP, since the Tunnel IP Header field corresponding to the devices at each end of the PPTP tunnel is standard. The tunneled IP packet payload begins with a modified version of a GRE header [RFC 1701; RFC 1702] that allows PPTP to handle protocols other than IP. This is an important feature, because many enterprises still have a number of applications running over network-layer protocols other than IP. The next field is the PPP header and data. This gives PPTP access to the protocol negotiation and features of PPP—for example, authentication and encryption. The remainder of the PPTP packet is the PPP payload, which is the original network-layer protocol header and application data. Optionally, the PPP payload can be encrypted. PPTP uses TCP to carry control packets for status inquiry and signaling information separately from the user data packets.

PPTP can be used to support dial-in users as well as LAN-to-LAN connections, as shown in Figure 8.7 [Brown 99; Fowler 99; Kosiur 98; Microsoft 98]. The figure shows PPTP tunnels as thick lines. A PPTP server has an IP address for each tunnel endpoint and stands between a secured LAN and the public Internet. It encapsulates packets received from the LAN that are destined for elsewhere using the PPTP packet format previously described, and it strips off the encapsulation from PPTP packets received from the Internet and delivers them to the LAN. PPTP servers can also filter packets, which, when used with IP address filtering, creates a simple firewall.

Dial-in users can access PPTP secured LAN resources using one of two methods, as illustrated at the top of the Figure 8.7. The first method provides access via a Network Access Server (NAS), which performs authentication using PAP or CHAP. Typically, an ISP implements the NAS function and shares it across many dial-in customers. If the NAS supports the PPTP protocol, then the client computer need only implement the PPP authentication protocol, as shown in the upper left-hand part of the figure. A disadvantage of this scenario is that the connection between the PPP client and the PPTP NAS is not encrypted. In the second method, if the NAS does not implement PPTP, then the client computer must establish a PPTP tunnel with the PPTP server, as depicted in the upper right-hand part of the figure.

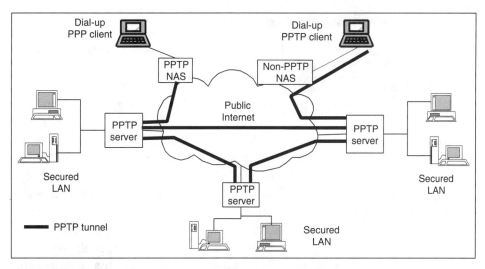

Figure 8.7 Dial-in and LAN-LAN usage of PPTP.

PPTP defines two modes for tunneling: voluntary and compulsory [Fowler 99; Kosiur 98; Microsoft 98]. A *voluntary* tunnel, also called client-initiated or service-independent, supports remote access to a VPN using PPTP. The dial-in PPTP client in Figure 8.7 voluntarily initiates a tunnel to the target PPTP server. Voluntary tunnels are an important mechanism for providing VPN access to remote users. A *compulsory* tunnel, also called involuntary, NAS-initiated, or service-dependent, has predetermined end-points defined by manual configuration and thus has better access control than a voluntary tunnel. A compulsory tunnel effectively makes the enterprise sites part of a single secured LAN. Because equipment establishes a compulsory tunnel without user interaction, they are transparent to the end users. Users can access only the set of sites interconnected by PPTP servers. Usually, they cannot access other parts of the Internet. The tunnels between the PPTP servers and the tunnel between the PPTP-enabled NAS in Figure 8.7 are examples of compulsory tunnels.

For encryption, PPTP uses Microsoft's Point-to-Point Encryption (MPPE) algorithm, which is based on the RSA RC4 symmetric cryptosystem. Compression is implemented using Microsoft's Point-to-Point Compression (MPPC) Protocol [RFC 2118], if this capability is negotiated via PPP at tunnel establishment time. The initial versions of Microsoft's implementation of PPTP used the password at the client and at the server in the computation of the shared secret key. Obviously, this approach is vulnerable to attackers who either sniff, guess, or otherwise compromise the password. A 40-bit session key is the default value for encryption, but a 128-bit key is available in countries where U.S. export regulations allow.

Layer 2 Tunneling Protocol (L2TP)

The Layer 2 Tunneling Protocol (L2TP) is the successor to PPTP standardized by the IETF in RFC 2661. L2TP also includes many of the features of the Layer 2 Forwarding (L2F) protocol developed by Cisco [RFC 2341]. We describe the fundamentals of L2TP with reference to the message format operating over a UDP/IP tunnel shown in Figure 8.8. The L2TP header contains a number of fields, many of which are optional (opt). The Flags field indicates whether the packet contains data or control information. Other flags indicate whether optional fields are present or absent, the protocol version, and message priority. The Length field indicates the total message length and is always present in control packets. The Tunnel and Session IDs are present in all control and data messages. These fields support multiplexing of many sessions over a single tunnel and support multiple tunnels over a UDP/IP transport-layer address or a Layer 2 virtual connection. The Ns and Nr send and receive count fields are used by the L2TP control protocol to ensure acknowledged in-sequence delivery of control messages. These are necessary because L2TP operates over the unreliable UDP protocol. The optional offset fields pad an L2TP message to a particular length, for example, when used with a block encryption algorithm.

Let's look at how all of these protocols work together to support secured dial-in access in a typical enterprise VPN architecture with reference to the space-time diagram shown in Figure 8.9. Starting from the left-hand side, the configuration at the top of the figure shows a client computer connected by the Public Switched Telephone Network (PSTN) to an L2TP access concentrator operated by the ISP offering dial-in service. The public Internet connects this dial-in ISP to the enterprise LAN shown on the right-hand side of the figure. The enterprise LAN consists of an L2TP network server connected to the Internet and a firewall that

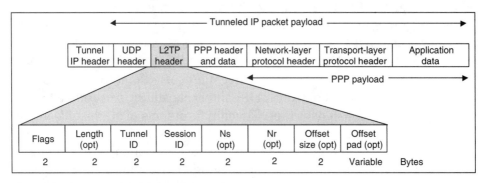

Figure 8.8   L2TP over UDP/IP message format.

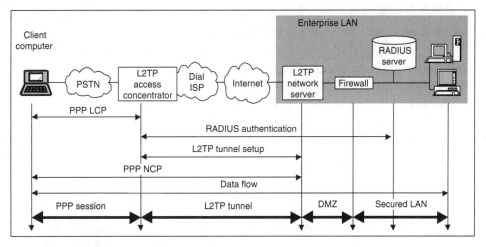

Figure 8.9 Secured remote access VPN.

secures the LAN resources, including a RADIUS server operated by the enterprise. The protocols operate in time sequence running from top to bottom. First, the client computer initiates link establishment using PPP LCP with the dial ISP access concentrator, which then authenticates the request using the RADIUS protocol in conjunction with the enterprise-operated RADIUS server. Once the user is authenticated by the RADIUS server, the L2TP access concentrator establishes a tunnel to the L2TP network server using the L2TP control protocol. The network-layer protocol can then be established between the L2TP network server and the client computer, because the PPP protocol packets are tunneled between these points. Finally, a client–to–secured LAN resource data path is established, composed of the segments shown at the bottom of the figure. A PPP session exists between the client computer and the L2TP access concentrator, which extends this session to the L2TP network server using an L2TP tunnel. The portion of the enterprise LAN between the L2TP network server and the firewall is known as the *Demilitarized Zone* (DMZ), because without the firewall-applied policy this portion of the LAN is not completely secure. Finally, the portion of the enterprise LAN inside the firewall is considered secure.

PPTP and L2TP have many things in common and a few important differences. Like PPTP, L2TP can carry not only IP packets but any higher-layer protocol that PPP supports. Since L2TP is based on PPP, it inherits all of the other capabilities described earlier in this section. In a manner similar to PPTP, the L2TP control protocol dynamically establishes a session between the dial-in access concentrator and a network server, or directly between network servers. L2TP also supports voluntary and involuntary tunnels in a manner similar to PPTP.

Unlike PPTP, L2TP does not define direct support for encrypting user data traffic. When running over UDP/IP, IPsec tunnel mode encryption can be used to secure an L2TP tunnel, as described in Chapter 9. Furthermore, higher-layer filtering on the network- and transport-layer headers of the PPP payload are not handled by the L2TP protocol; instead, this is a task that should be handled by a firewall.

Principal Applications

Now that we have introduced all of the VPN technologies, we can perform some economic and functional comparison analyses that indicate pivotal enterprise characteristics suited to one approach versus another. These analyses use approximate economic data, emphasizing instead the formulation of the problem and identification of critical decision parameters. Each comparison includes a listing of additional, less tangible decision factors that should also be considered.

Dial-In Terminal Servers versus Secured Internet Access

An enterprise has several alternatives for providing secure dial-in access to remote users. The choice depends on several factors; however, the economic criteria are the easiest to analyze. Figure 8.10 illustrates the two designs compared in this section. The traditional method shown in Figure 8.10a involves an enterprise deploying a terminal server, which has a pool of modems connected to a Public Switched Telephone Network—for

---

CAVEAT EMPTOR: LET THE BUYER BEWARE

Development of a solid business case requires careful research and an objective point of view. Beware of economic analyses generated by an equipment manufacturer or a service provider—keep in mind the source of the analysis and what benefit a particular conclusion has for them. Be sure that the assumptions apply to the enterprise application under consideration. Although IP-based VPNs are the latest, greatest technology available in the marketplace, not every enterprise can actually realize a benefit after taking real-world costs and practical network design considerations into account. As the old adage goes, if something sounds too good to be true, then it probably is.

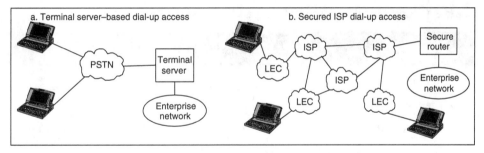

Figure 8.10   Terminal server and secured IP access.

example, using toll-free dial-in numbers that the service provider charges back to the enterprise. Remote users employ existing software on their laptops and log in to the enterprise network with security provided by user ID/password and optionally other authentication methods. The newer approach illustrated in Figure 8.10b involves the enterprise procuring a router that implements authentication and encryption functions in conjunction with additional software procured for each user laptop. The enterprise must also subscribe to an ISP account for each mobile user. One economic advantage of this design is that the mobile users need only make telephone calls through the Local Exchange Carrier (LEC) telephone network as opposed to making a long-distance call. However, the principal advantage is the statistical multiplexing of the Internet implemented as a set of interconnected ISPs that concentrates all remote traffic into the access line(s) to the secure router that guards the enterprise network resources.

The following analysis presents the basic economic trade-offs that favor either the terminal server dial-in design or the secured Internet design. Our model defines two parameters that model the size of the enterprise and the amount of remote access. The number of mobile employees E is obviously an important consideration, as well as the average number of minutes M per month that mobile employees spend dialed into the enterprise network. Furthermore, there are capital costs that are depreciated over a particular interval as well as monthly recurring costs, as summarized in Table 8.1. The costs listed in this table are not specific to any vendor and are based on a number of sources [Kosiur 98; TimeStep 99]. Specific numbers and design are approximate, and the numbers for a different choice of services and products in an actual network design may differ significantly from these values. However, this generic analysis does provide some insight into the applicability of different approaches based on the size and usage patterns of the enterprise's mobile workforce.

Table 8.1 Cost Model for Terminal Server and Secured ISP Remote Access

PARAMETER	TERMINAL SERVER DIAL-UP	SECURED IP ROUTER
Capital costs		
DS1 terminal server	$6,000	
DS1 secure router		$20,000
Depreciation interval (months)	36	36
Monthly recurring costs		
DS1 local loop	$700	$700
Phone call cost per minute	$0.07	
ISP charge per client		$20
ISP charge per DS1		$1,500
Software depreciation per user		$3

In order to compare these designs, the analysis must also size the capacity required for connection of the terminal server to the PSTN versus the capacity required to connect the secure router to an ISP. The capital costs of Table 8.1 model this on a per-DS1 basis in order to simplify the comparison. The other parameters of interest are the fraction of the traffic in the busy hour BH (e.g., 10 percent), the number of business days per month DAYS (e.g., 20), and the utilization U by the remote users of the dial-in circuit. The required number of DS1s X as a function of the utilization U is determined by rounding up the following formula to an integer:

$$X(U) = E \times M \times \text{BH} / \text{DAYS} /60 \times U$$

For the terminal server alternative, the utilization U is 100 percent, since the modem signal takes up an entire voice channel. On the other hand, the remote access via local dial-in to ISP has a utilization U that is considerably smaller, say 25 percent or even less. This means that the secure router design incurs significantly less expense for DS1 access lines. The capital cost contribution to the monthly cost for each alternative is X times the capital cost depreciated over the interval appropriate to that equipment. This may actually differ for the technologies considered; however, the following analysis does not consider that refinement. The remaining costs derive from the monthly recurring costs scaled for the number of employees E, their average monthly usage M, and the required number of DS1 access circuits X. The formula for the monthly cost for the terminal server-based solution is:

$$X\,(100\%) \times (\text{capital/interval} + \text{\$/DS1/month}) + E \times M \times \text{\$/minute/month}$$

In an analogous fashion, the monthly cost for the secure router-based solution is given by the following formula:

$$X\,(25\%) \times (\text{capital/interval} + \text{\$/DS1/month} + \text{\$/ISP/month}) + E \times \text{\$/user/month}$$

Figure 8.11 plots the monthly costs for the terminal server- and secure router-based remote access design cost models described here. The number of enterprise employees E is the parameter for the plot, illustrating the impact of enterprise mobile workforce size on economics for values $E = 200$ and $E = 2,000$. The other important decision parameter is the average monthly minutes M spent using remote access. For the parameter assumptions summarized here, the secure router solution requires only a single DS1 for 200 employees, which grows to only 2 DS1s for 2,000 employees. The higher depreciated capital costs and minimum monthly recurring charges per user make the secure router cost nearly independent of the average monthly usage M. On the other hand, the terminal server costs grow linearly with the average monthly usage per remote user. An important point to note from the figure is the point where the cost of the terminal server alternative crosses over that of the secure router solution. For a

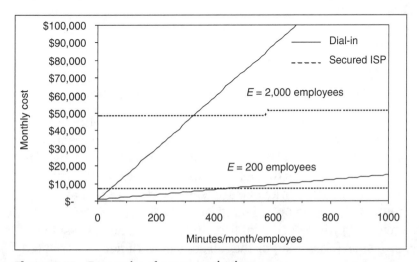

Figure 8.11   Economics of access methods.

smaller enterprise with 200 remote users, this crossover point occurs at approximately 500 minutes per month, or 25 minutes per business day. For a larger enterprise with 2,000 remote users, the crossover point decreases to 300 minutes per month, or 15 minutes per business day.

The general conclusions drawn from this analysis are twofold. First, enterprises that have either small numbers of remote users or remote users that generate little activity may find a terminal server alternative more economical. For example, if only the president and a few executives in your enterprise require remote access, then an IP-based VPN will be difficult to justify. Second, enterprises with large numbers of remote users, even if they generate small volumes of activity, may find the secured ISP alternative more economical. Another way to look at these alternatives is to monitor the long-distance dial-up charges generated by the road warriors in your enterprise. If the long-distance telephone charges for dial-up access are increasing, then looking at a secured ISP solution may save your enterprise a lot of money in the long run.

IP-based VPNs have several additional advantages over a terminal server-based dial-in network [Lombard 98]. They provide better security because they provide encryption and authentication. Additionally, they have superior performance because the voice calls are local and not long distance. They also allow users access to the enterprise VPN via high-speed Internet access, such as Ethernet connections in hotel rooms and airports, and telecommuting options, such as IP over cable TV or DSL. Therefore, if you plan to encourage remote access and/or telecommuting for a large user population using nontelephony access methods, then an IP-based VPN is essential. Of course, as summarized earlier, the secured ISP-VPN has some additional hidden costs involving training, management, and support that the preceding analysis does not quantify.

Connection-Oriented versus IP-Based VPNs

Although the frame relay and ATM connection-oriented VPN alternatives largely apply only to a single service provider, economic comparison between this alternative and an IP-based solution delivered by a single ISP is valid. If a single ISP provides the network for an IP-based VPN, then guarantees of quality and performance are feasible. Beware that an IP-based VPN built on top of the public Internet using services provided by several ISPs may not provide acceptable quality. Prior analyses assume a small number of sites [Kosiur 98] or that all sites in a connection-oriented VPN are fully meshed [Fowler 99]. Our model is more general than these approaches because the number of sites and the degree of meshing become parameters on which the network designer can base a decision. Specifically, the model assumes that many enterprise VPNs have an inherently hierarchical structure, as shown in Figure 8.12a, with H hub sites and B branch sites having routers with virtual connections (VCs). Chapter 4, *Early Connection-Oriented Data VPNs—X.25 and Frame Relay*, made this point when discussing the typical design for frame relay VPNs. Specifically, our model assumes that each branch site homes to two hub sites and that the hub sites are fully meshed. Therefore, a special case of this model is fully meshed when there are no branch sites (i.e., $B = 0$). An analogous IP-based VPN network has the same number of hub sites and branch sites, but requires the addition of overlay tunneling and/or encryption equipment, indicated by the boxes labeled O, as shown in Figure 8.12b. Both models assume that branch sites connect using a DS1, while hub sites connect using a DS3. Of course, the VCs connecting hub sites in the connection-oriented design are of higher speed than those connecting branch sites to hub sites, as illustrated by the thickness of the dashed lines in Figure 8.12a.

We can now compare the amortized capital and monthly recurring costs for these two alternatives using the economic assumptions of Table 8.2. As before, we have rounded off these numbers taken from a variety of sources. In the interest of brevity, this model does not show some costs that are identical for the scenarios, for example, router maintenance and support, access circuit install charges, and management of the router network. Also, note that different equipment and service providers can have markedly different prices as well as quality, performance, and support policies. The table first lists the capital costs for each alternative, followed by the monthly recurring charges, with the quantity required shown within braces to the right of the item. Each site requires a router, but the IP-based

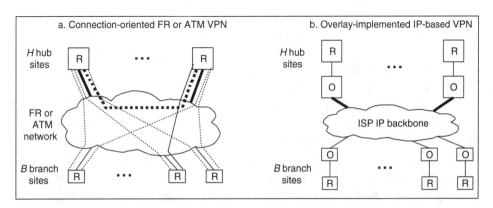

Figure 8.12   Connection-oriented and IP-based VPNs.

Table 8.2   Cost Model for FR/ATM and Overlay IP-Based VPN

PARAMETER	FR/ATM VPN	OVERLAY IP VPN
Capital costs		
DS1 router {B}	$3,000	$3,000
DS1 overlay security {B}		$4,000
DS3 router {H}	$10,000	$10,000
DS3 overlay security {H}		$20,000
Other overlay costs {1}		$50,000
Depreciation interval (months)	36	36
Monthly recurring costs		
DS1 local loop {B}	$700	$700
DS3 local loop {H}	$3,000	$3,000
DS1 port charge {B}	$1,500	$2,000
DS3 port charge {H}	$7,500	$10,000
High-speed VCs {H(H − 1)/2}	$2,500	
Low-speed VCs {2B}	$500	
Overlay support {B + H}		$1,500

VPN solution takes on the additional cost of the overlay security equipment. The overlay solution also assumes additional charges for licensing, network management, and initial installation and configuration. We assume that the depreciation interval is the same for both alternatives; however, the overlay security technology may not have an operational lifetime as long as the router technology.

Both alternatives have monthly recurring charges for local loops, but have different monthly per-port charges for the FR/ATM service versus an SLA guaranteed IP service from the ISP. Of course, these charges can vary significantly based on the service provider, geography, and size of the enterprise. In general, larger enterprises are able to negotiate significant discounts. The connection-oriented alternative has per-VC charges, with the high-speed ones supporting a full mesh of interhub connections and the low-speed ones used for resilient branch-to-hub interconnect. Finally, the model assumes an incremental operating cost for the IP overlay alternative. This analysis assumes that the enterprise takes on this cost, typically seen as the expense of hiring an employee skilled in this area or retaining a consultant on a part-time basis. The cost of outsourcing can be higher; for example, GTE Internetworking charges $2,500 per month per site to manage a firewall/security solution [Fowler 99].

A number of trade-offs occur in the overall cost of such a design, an important one being the degree of hierarchy present in the enterprise's traffic, and therefore in the network design. Figure 8.13 plots the monthly cost for a connection-oriented FR/ATM and overlay IP-based VPN network design versus the number of hub sites H for the economic parameters given in Table 8.2. The number of branch sites for every hub site reflects the degree of hierarchy in the network traffic. When all sites are hub sites the network is fully meshed since there are no branch sites, that is, $B = 0$. As the number of branch sites for each hub site increases, then we say that the network has more hierarchy or tends toward more of a hub-and-spoke traffic pattern. The figure plots the case where there are four branch sites for every hub site, or $B = 4H$. Notice from the figure that as the number of hub sites increases, the cost of the FR/ATM VPN solution becomes greater than that of the IP VPN solution. This occurs because the initial outlay for the IP VPN is spread out over more nodes in conjunction with the increasing PVC charges to connect the hub sites. The crossover point differs depending on the amount of hierarchy. For a fully meshed network, the crossover point occurs at about 5 hub sites, while for a network with a moderate degree of homing with 4 branch sites per hub site this crossover does not occur until about 8 hub sites.

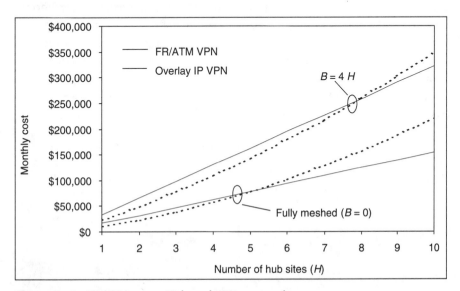

Figure 8.13 FR/ATM versus IP-based VPN economics.

An important conclusion from the preceding analysis centers on the traffic patterns of the enterprise. If a significant portion of the traffic goes between a large number of branch sites to a few hub sites, then a connection-oriented VPN is probably more economical. Access to the public Internet can then be secured via firewalls and private addressing handled by Network Address Translation (NAT) devices at these hub sites. On the other hand, if the enterprise has a more distributed traffic pattern, then it will recoup the additional up-front investment through savings on monthly VC charges. Further savings occur because a hierarchical design causes traffic to traverse expensive access circuits twice for traffic flowing between branch sites or between a branch site to the headquarters and back out to the public Internet. A fully meshed or connectionless design requires that the traffic traverse the access link once. However, increased meshing of the connection-oriented VPN design increases overall cost. The IP-based VPN design is inherently fully meshed and has essentially a constant capital cost for any traffic pattern. An IP-based design will have administrative costs proportional to the number of tunnels or security associations requiring configuration. However, QoS and traffic management for frame relay and ATM networks are often superior to those of the public Internet and many ISPs. Therefore, an important criterion in selecting an ISP is ensuring that the performance of its IP backbone be comparable to that of a frame relay or ATM alternative.

Chapter 9 covers other IP-based VPN solutions developed by the industry. The first involves a comprehensive IP security (IPsec) protocol suite that builds on the authentication and tunneling infrastructure described in this chapter and also tackles the knotty problem of cryptographic key management and distribution posed in Chapter 7. Like the technologies and protocols described in this chapter, IPsec is an overlay solution on top of the public Internet. However, a solution based within a provider's network is also possible. The next chapter summarizes some developments for network-based IP VPNs in this space.

CHAPTER

9

IP Security-Enabled and Routing-Controlled VPNs

It is easy to be brave when you are far away from danger.
—Aesop

This chapter describes the IP security (IPsec) protocol suite standardized by the IETF in the late 1990s as the latest technique to construct VPNs over the public Internet. It also briefly describes a few proprietary network-based solutions to illustrate alternative service provider-based approaches for implementing IP VPNs. The chapter concludes by describing several scenarios for IP-based VPNs that put together the technologies and protocols described so far in some representative deployment scenarios.

Business Drivers and Requirements

This section highlights some of the important business drivers and enterprise requirements for IP-based VPN offerings from manufacturers, outsourcing companies, or as a managed service delivered by a network provider.

Competition among Security Vendors

Over 60 manufacturers were offering IP-based VPN solutions as of 1999 [Brown 99; Fowler 99]. (Consult the Telechoice VPN Web page at www.vpdn.com or the VPN Consortium Web page at www.vpnc.org for a partial listing.) Competition is a powerful stimulus for improved price performance, and the implementations of tunneling, encryption, firewalls, network address translation, and related products are no exception. Standards also help reduce costs in that performance-intensive functions implemented in commodity integrated circuits drive down the cost of hardware. Standards further reduce costs in the increasingly expensive software component of modern telecommunications equipment. A major thesis of this book is that enterprises continually seek to drive down costs and improve productivity, and lower hardware and software costs of the IP-based overlay solutions is an important driver.

Outsourced and Service Provider VPNs

Like the PPTP and L2TP tunneling solutions described in Chapter 8, *Dial-In Access and Multiprotocol Tunneling VPNs*, the IPsec solution described in this chapter is also an overlay technology. An enterprise may install this hardware and software itself or contract with an external party to do so. The contractor need not be a service provider and may instead be a specialist in configuring and managing IP-based VPNs. If an enterprise outsources the task of designing, installing, and maintaining an IP-based VPN, it realizes a benefit by avoiding the expense and effort of hiring and maintaining expert staff in these new areas. Generally, outsourcing is best for a smaller enterprise or for one that cannot justify developing a core competency in IP-based VPNs. However, an outsourcing vendor will generally be more expensive than an in-house solution for a larger enterprise or an organization that has a business interest in developing expertise in IP-based VPNs—for example, vendors and service providers.

Technology Trends and Enablers

We've already described many of the technology trends and enablers regarding IP-based VPNs in earlier chapters. An important aspect described in this chapter is the extensible set of standards defining the IPsec protocol suite. However, technology does not stand still, and new ideas and ways of doing things continue to arise. The continual conflict between interoperability of standard solutions and the innovation of proprietary advances is an ever present tension in the world of IP-based VPNs.

Security Standards and Public Key Infrastructure

As described in Chapter 7, *Building Blocks for IP-Based VPNs—Security, Quality, and Access*, a number of encryption and authentication algorithms have been invented over time. As computer technology advances and as the skill of hackers and crackers improves, the security of any algorithm diminishes over time. Therefore, a protocol that seamlessly allows the negotiation of the use of new and improved algorithms for these important security functions was a fundamental requirement in the development of the IPsec standards. Of course, the standards also require that every implementation support a few specific, publicly available protocols in order to achieve interoperability.

The essence of cryptographic security is distribution of a secret key. Encryption algorithms use these keys to scramble information transferred between two parties in such a way that make the task extremely difficult for anyone but the intended receiver(s) to understand it, modify it, or alter the identification of the sender. Of course, the critical and most challenging part in this strategy is secure distribution of the secret key. Here again, technology has come to the rescue with the standardization of the Internet Key Exchange (IKE) protocol.

The Good and Bad Things about Standards

The good thing about standards is that once they are complete and all the bugs are worked out, an enterprise has considerable flexibility of choice regarding equipment and service providers. The bad thing about standards is that it usually takes quite a while to formulate, debug, and realize interoperable implementations. For example, the IP suite of protocols has been three decades in the making. This two-edged sword cuts both ways in IP-based VPNs. Because security has long been a focus for IP VPNs, a suite of protocols called IPsec now addresses a comprehensive set of capabilities for overlay technology on the public Internet. Unfortunately, there are still a number of interoperability issues to be resolved, such as compatible subsets, interworking with existing applications, traffic engineering, and network management techniques.

The good thing about a nonstandard proprietary solution is that it is usually available much earlier than a standards-based solution. The bad thing about a proprietary solution is that an enterprise does not have an alternative supplier, and the resulting lack of competition can increase cost, limit scalability, or reduce options. The benefits of a proprietary solution are early availability of a capability that may differentiate the enterprise in its field. The downside is that the equipment or service supplier may not support the product adequately, may charge a significant premium, or may not evolve quickly to a standards-specified solution in an effort to protect market share. Nonetheless, there is a place for both standard and proprietary solutions because the requirements of enterprises around the world are so diverse.

Implementation and Protocol Specifics

This section describes the structure, protocols, and application of the IPsec protocol suite in enterprise networks. It also describes use of routing and label switching within a service provider network to provide IP-aware VPN capabilities similar to frame relay and ATM, which may be all certain enterprises require.

IP Security Protocol Suite (IPsec)

The IETF designed the IPsec protocol suite to address the known issues involved with achieving secure communications over the Internet. IPsec reduces the threat of attacks based on IP address spoofing and provides a standardized means for ensuring data integrity, authenticating a data source, and guaranteeing confidentiality of information. Furthermore, it tackles the complex problem of key management head on. The prognosis is that consumers, businesses, and government organizations will begin to trust the Internet more now that this important set of standards is finalized and a public-key management infrastructure is in place. Experts expect IPsec to play an important role not only in enterprise VPNs, but also in electronic commerce and in individual end-user communication.

IPsec refers to a suite of three interrelated security protocols implemented by modification to, or augmentation of, an IP packet in conjunction with an infrastructure that supports key distribution and management. An interrelated set of RFCs published by the IETF referenced herein specifies the details of IPsec. We give only an overview in this section. For books that cover IPsec in more depth, see Kaufman (99) and Stallings (98a). Figure 9.1 depicts the IPsec protocol suite as shown in RFC 2411. RFC 2401 describes the overall IP security architecture, and RFC 2411 gives an overview of the IPsec protocol suite and the documents that describe it. The three protocols shown in the middle of the figure make up

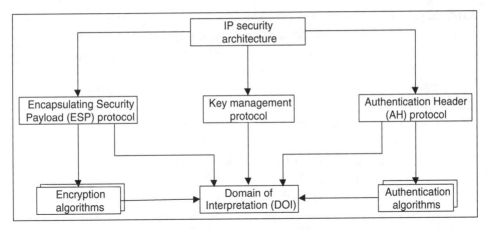

Figure 9.1   IP Security (IPsec) protocol suite architecture.

IPsec, with the names identifying the function performed. The two primary protocols involved in the transfer of data are called the Authentication Header (AH) [RFC 2402] and the Encapsulating Security Payload (ESP) [RFC 2406]. The AH protocol provides source authentication and data integrity verification using a header field, but does not provide confidentiality. AH also supports an optional mechanism to prevent replay attacks. The ESP protocol uses both a header and trailer field to provide confidentiality via encryption. ESP may also provide data integrity verification, source authentication, and an anti-replay service. Since both the AH and ESP protocols utilize cryptographic methods, secure distribution and management of keys is a fundamental requirement. IPsec specifies that key management may be manual or automatic. The automatic key management protocol specified for IPsec, called Internet Key Exchange (IKE), involves the mechanism for creating a Security Association (SA) between a source and a destination for the AH and ESP protocols. An IPsec-capable device may implement AH, ESP, or both. The Domain of Interpretation (DOI) ties together all of the IPSec group's documents by specifying all the mandatory and optional algorithms, attributes, parameters, and identifiers for the protocols of IPsec. It is the master database of all IPsec security parameters that systems negotiating a security association can reference.

The AH and ESP protocols operate in either transport or tunnel mode as defined by the parameters of an SA. In *transport mode*, they provide security by creating components of the IPsec header at the same time the source generates other IP header information. This means that transport mode can operate only between host systems. In *tunnel mode*, IPsec creates a new IP packet that contains the IPsec components and encapsulates the original unsecured packet. Since tunnel mode does not modify the original packet contents, it can be implemented using hardware or software located at an intermediate point between the source or destination system. This means that either the end system or an intermediate system can implement tunnel mode. Since the tunnel mode implementation is often a separate piece of equipment, the outer IP packet address usually does not correspond to the actual source or destination of the innermost packet, thereby providing an additional level of security.

At least three placements of an IPsec implementation using these modes are possible [RFC 2401; Kaufman 99]. First, IPsec tunnel or transport mode may be an integral part of a host's networking protocol software. Second, IPsec tunnel mode may be implemented by software and/or hardware added to a host's IP stack. Finally, IPsec may be implemented in an intermediate system, usually called a *security gateway*, which is completely separate from the source and destination host systems. Typically, this class of device serves a community of users, similar to the tunneling protocols described in Chapter 8.

Security Association (SA)

For both the AH and ESP protocols, the source creates a simplex connection to the destination called an SA before transferring any data. For duplex data communication, the pair of communicating parties must set up an SA in each direction for each IPsec protocol employed. By exchanging messages, the source negotiates an SA uniquely identified by the following information:

- A 32-bit connection identifier called the Security Parameter Index (SPI)

- The destination IP address for the simplex connection

- A security protocol (AH or ESP) identifier

Since the AH and ESP protocol overhead information contains the SPI, and the destination IP address is always present, this information taken together uniquely identifies an SA. IPsec systems may establish multiple SAs and use these for different purposes based upon a *Selector* function that operates on the combination of source and destination IP address, protocol type, the transport layer (i.e., UDP or TCP) port number, or other criteria.

RFC 2401 defines two means in which IPsec SAs can be bundled: *transport adjacency* and *iterated tunneling*. Figure 9.2 illustrates these bundles as well as the use of transport and tunnel SA modes by end-system hosts (H)

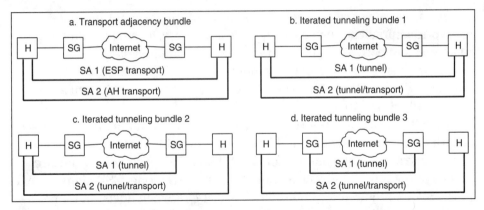

Figure 9.2   IPsec Security Association (SA) bundles.

and intermediate Security Gateways (SG). Because the transport mode exists only between a pair of hosts, there is only one transport adjacency bundle, as shown in Figure 9.2a. Here, a separate SA exists for the AH and ESP protocols. The remaining three bundles cover the various combinations of tunnel and transport mode for two security associations. Note that RFC 2401 only requires support for the last two bundles. Figure 9.2b illustrates a bundle where the tunnel endpoints are the same, which would usually be separate for AH and ESP. Figure 9.2c shows a bundle where one security association tunnel exists between hosts, but another exists between a host and a security gateway. A commonly encountered use of this bundle is host access via a dial-in access concentrator or Network Access Server (NAS). Figure 9.2d illustrates a commonly encountered bundle, in which one SA tunnel exists between hosts and another exists between hosts. In either of these tunnel mode bundles, the SAs may be either AH or ESP. An example of this bundle is the interconnection of secured LANs via IPsec security gateways used in conjunction with additional security on a host-to-host basis.

As we will see, the AH and ESP protocols have a number of options. As defined in RFC 2401, the parameters associated with an SA defines whether these options are used and the parameters that control them. The IPsec SA model defines two databases: the Security Policy Database (SPD) and the Security Association Database (SAD). SPD specifies policies that determine the disposition of all IP traffic inbound or outbound from an end-system host or security gateway IPsec implementation. This determines what IPsec processing the device applies on a packet-by-packet basis using criteria defined by the Selector function. SAD contains parameters that are associated with each (active) security association. The parameters include encryption algorithm, hashing algorithm, authentication mode for digital signatures, key generation information, SA lifetimes, encryption initialization vectors, source addresses, sequence number parameters, and path MTU information. For outbound packets, the SPD points to an entry in the SAD. For inbound packets, the destination address, IPsec protocol type (i.e., AH or ESP), and the SPI identify the appropriate SPD entry.

RFC 2401 requires support for only the subset of combinations of IPsec security associations shown in Figure 9.3, which illustrates how each packet carries the information for the AH and ESP protocols in the two modes of operation. In transport mode, either AH alone, ESP alone, or AH plus ESP are required for end-to-end security between hosts. In tunnel mode, the security gateway encapsulates the entire inner IP datagram and adds either AH or ESP overhead information. As discussed later in this section, the AH protocol has only a header component, whereas the ESP protocol has both a header and a trailer component. Any of these combinations can apply to the bundles shown in Figure 9.2. We later describe how specific combinations of these protocols and modes address specific enterprise security needs.

In summary, the establishment of the SA configures certain information in databases at each pair of systems implementing IPsec. The AH and/or ESP overhead information conveys additional information on a per-packet basis that is used with the SA-established databases. If the addition of the AH and/or ESP fields increase the packet size above the Maximum Transfer Unit (MTU) size of some link along the path, then IP must fragment the packet. To handle this case, IPsec requires that the source perform all IPsec operations before determining whether fragmentation is necessary and that the destination device reassemble the packet before applying any IPsec functions. This is an improvement over earlier packet-by-packet encryption devices that did not work correctly when the intervening network fragmented packets. Let's look inside the overhead information car-

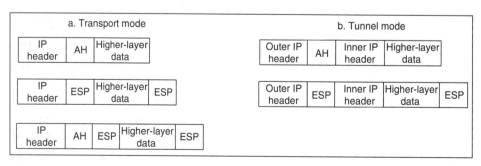

Figure 9.3   Required combinations of IPsec SAs.

ried by the AH and ESP protocols and their usage in the transport and tunnel modes in conjunction with SA distributed database information to understand their function and application to enterprise VPNs.

Authentication Header (AH)

The AH can be used in either transport mode or tunnel mode, as shown in Figure 9.4 applied to IPv4. See RFC 2402 for information on the specifics applied to IPv6. In transport mode, the AH follows the host IP header and precedes any higher-layer data, as illustrated in Figure 9.4a. In tunnel mode, the original IP packet is considered the payload of the AH protocol. In this case, as shown in Figure 9.4b, the source inserts the authentication header after the newly created outer IP header corresponding to the source before and the inner IP header addressed packet being tunneled. The Next Header field identifies the payload type following the authentication header field, which may be an IP header, a higher-layer protocol like UDP or TCP, or an IPsec ESP header. The Payload Length field indicates the total length of the AH in units of 32-bit words. The SPI field in combination with the destination IP address and the AH hashing protocol uniquely identifies the SA for the datagram. The Sequence Number field is a counter that the sender increments to allow the receiver to detect replay attacks. If the receiver compares this optional sequence number to a windowed range, it can detect an attacker replaying a previously authenticated packet.

The Authentication Data field contains the Integrity Check Value (ICV) for the entire packet and has a length that is an integral multiple of 32 bits, including padding if necessary. The AH protocol uses a secure hashing function to compute the ICV using the entire packet, except for fields that

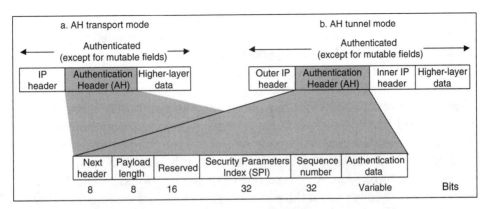

Figure 9.4   IPsec AH packet format.

may change or are mutable, as indicated in Figure 9.4. Since the destination must be able to recompute the hashed value using the secret shared with the source, the ICV performed at the source must exclude any fields in the IP packet that might change. IPsec AH does this by requiring that the source set these mutable fields to a known value prior to the secure hash computation. Mutable, yet unpredictable fields include the Type Of Service (TOS) byte, flags, the Time To Live (TTL) field, and the header checksum, which the source zeros out for purposes of the ICV computation. A mutable, yet predictable value is the destination address when the IP source routing option is present. In this case, the source substitutes the eventual destination address from the source route when doing the ICV computation. The source sets the Authentication Data field to zero as well before computing the ICV. Of course, the source uses the original values of the mutable fields when it forwards the packet to the next hop. The receiver performs the same substitution prior to calculating its own version of the ICV. If the ICV values match, then the receiver has authenticated the sender as well as the integrity of the IP header and higher-layer data.

As described in Chapter 7, the AH ICV secure hash computation supports integrity and authentication because it is a digital signature using a shared secret key. As of 1999, the IETF had specified two methods for the ICV keyed–Hashing Message Authentication Code (HMAC) [RFC 2104]. RFC 2403 documents the usage of Message Digest version 5 (MD5), and RFC 2404 describes the use of Secure Hash Algorithm version 1 (SHA-1) by either AH and ESP. The IPsec SA establishment protocol allows the addition of other hash functions, but a base implementation should meet both of these standards in order to be considered interoperable.

Encapsulating Security Payload (ESP)

As described earlier, IPsec ESP can also be used in either transport or tunnel mode. Figure 9.5 illustrates the ESP overhead field usage in these two modes for the case of IPv4, as specified in RFC 2406. Similar to the AH protocol, the difference between the tunnel and transport modes is whether the payload contains the original IP header or not, respectively. Like AH, the ESP header contains the SPI and an anti-replay sequence number field. The SPI field indicates the encryption and authentication algorithms used for a security association between the ESP source and destination. ESP can employ encryption and authentication separately or together, but must employ at least one of these functions. Unlike AH, the Next Header field is part of the packet trailer but has the same interpretation. In addition, the ESP trailer pads the packet payload to support block

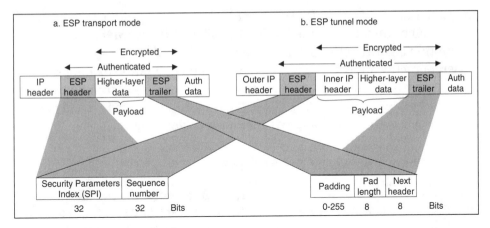

Figure 9.5   IPsec ESP packet format.

mode cryptographic algorithms as well as align the Next Header field on a 32-bit boundary. Furthermore, the source may use the padding field to disguise the length of the higher-layer data field. Finally, the last field is optional and contains a variable amount of Authentication Data when present. This field is computed in a manner similar to that of the AH protocol, except the calculation covers only the fields indicated in the figure. In particular, note that the computation does not involve the IP header with fields that may be changed by the IP network or the authentication data itself. This avoids the complexity of processing mutable fields, but eliminates the AH feature of authenticating the source IP address in the outermost header.

The most important additional function that ESP provides over AH is that of confidentiality through encryption using a secret key shared between the source and destination. ESP uses symmetric cryptographic algorithms, which achieve the best performance for the reasons described in Chapter 7. IPsec ESP encrypts only the payload plus the ESP trailer, which is the higher-layer data plus trailer in transport mode, as shown in Figure 9.5a, or the innermost IP header plus the higher-layer data and trailer in tunnel mode, as shown in Figure 9.5b. The SA establishment protocol determines the encryption algorithm utilized by ESP. If the negotiated algorithm is null, then ESP applies no encryption. If the authentication option is selected, then encryption is performed first. Since the outermost IP header is not encrypted, the processing for mutable fields performed in the AH authentication data calculation is not necessary. When ESP encryption is used in tunnel mode, the actual source and destination of the packet are kept confidential, which addresses a traffic analysis security attack. RFC 2406 requires that an ESP implementation support the Data Encryption Standard Cipher Block Chaining (DES CBC) crypto-graphic algorithm, as specified in RFC 2405 and 2451 as well as a null encryption algorithm [RFC 2410]. The choice of DES CBC represents the general practice in IETF standards to give implementation examples that require cryptographic technologies that are free and clear from copyright or patent issues [Kaufman 99]. However, the ESP standard is readily extensible for use with a wide range of encryption algorithms.

Useful Combinations of AH and ESP

There are a number of ways that enterprises can combine the use of AH and ESP to meet different needs [Kaufman 99; RFC 2401; Stallings 98a]. This section briefly discusses some of these with reference to the scenarios shown in Figure 9.6, which illustrate use of AH and ESP protocols in either the tunnel or transport modes to connect hosts and security gateways. Originally, ESP was targeted to perform encryption and AH to perform authentication. Because ESP provides most of the functions of AH, a host-to-host SA that uses transport mode AH in combination with transport mode ESP, while possible, is not typical. However, the configuration shown in Figure 9.6a, where use of ESP with optional authentication in conjunction with AH, makes sense. Since transport mode AH authenticates the source host's IP header, it prevents source IP address spoofing. As noted earlier transport mode ESP employing the authentication option does not provide this capability.

In a configuration where a host generates transport mode ESP packets, an intervening security gateway may utilize tunnel mode AH to provide a security perimeter that conceals the identity of the actual source and desti-

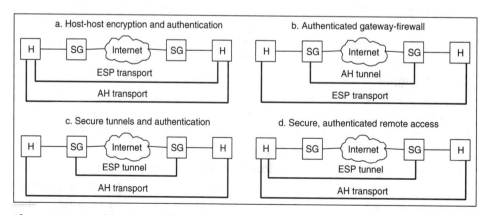

Figure 9.6 Combinations of IPsec AH and ESP.

nation hosts, as shown in Figure 9.6b. This design also authenticates the sending security gateway, which restricts address spoofing and higher-layer protocol forgery to a remote LAN secured by the sending security gateway. The firewall can then filter a list of the outer IP addresses corresponding to the security gateways in an enterprise VPN. This makes external attacks difficult. Most security techniques, except transport mode IPsec, don't protect against internal security compromises. Use of tunnel mode AH can be a useful mechanism to identify from which enterprise location internal attacks originate.

Another possible mode is that the hosts use transport mode AH, but the security gateways utilize tunnel mode ESP, as illustrated in Figure 9.6c. Usually, security gateways encrypt all traffic traversing the public Internet between secured enterprise sites, thereby providing confidentiality. Because the original source and destination IP addresses are part of the encrypted payload in tunnel mode ESP, traffic analysis by anyone outside of the security perimeter established by security gateways is impossible. Also, AH authenticates the sender as well as the integrity of the payload, again addressing the problem of security problems within secured enterprise sites.

Another important use of IPsec protocols is that of secure authenticated remote access, which may be performed using the configuration shown in Figure 9.6d. The use of tunnel mode ESP with encryption between the remote host and the security gateway is similar to the solution offered by the Point-to-Point Protocol (PPTP) described in Chapter 8. Here, ESP can encrypt the data and provide authentication of the tunneled host IP address header to the security gateway. Transport AH mode provides for authentication of the remote host to the destination host across a secured LAN when the data is in the clear in the enterprise LAN. Again, this prevents man-in-the-middle types of attacks within the enterprise's secured LAN.

WHO CAN YOU TRUST?

Don't assume that the public Internet is the only place from where hackers, crackers, thieves, and saboteurs may try to attack sensitive information and applications in an enterprise. Sometimes the greatest threat can come from within a secured enterprise LAN itself. Someone penetrating the physical security of an enterprise to gain access to an internal terminal, a careless employee hooking up a dial-up line to his or her computer at work, or a disgruntled employee can be serious security threats. A security gateway or firewall does nothing against this type of internal attack. If the information is extremely sensitive, encryption and authentication on a host-to-host basis is the only solution.

Internet Key Exchange (IKE)

In addition to providing a flexible, extensible framework for enabling various encryption techniques, the IPsec protocol suite also defines an automated solution for the difficult problem of key management. The solution targets scalability in a global sense using the X.509-based digital certificate technique described in Chapter 7. Its formal name is Internet Key Exchange [RFC 2409], but the solution is called IKE for short because it's much easier to say IKE than it is to remember the two protocols that perform IPsec key management. The first protocol is the Internet Security and Key Management Protocol (ISAKMP), which defines a framework consisting of a set of open-ended semantics and syntax for a cryptographic exchange between two parties to establish trust and exchange secret keys [RFC 2408]. ISAKMP is a conversational protocol that supports a broad range of negotiation dialogs between parties establishing a security association. The second, called Oakley, is a specific cryptographic exchange for establishing trust based on the Diffie-Hellman (DH) key exchange, described in Chapter 7, with several additions that overcome the known weaknesses of this technique. As specified in RFC 2412, Oakley provides a precisely specified key management protocol that fits within the ISAKMP-defined framework. We briefly summarize the important parts of Oakley, since it is an implementable example of the generic ISAKMP framework. The reader interested in more detail should consult the referenced RFCs, or see Kaufman (99), Kosiur (98), or Stallings (98a).

Oakley has several modes: main, aggressive, and quick [RFC 2412]. The main mode involves the exchange of a larger number of messages and information, but provides the highest level of security. At the other end of the scale, quick mode involves the exchange of fewer messages with less information, but has looser security. Oakley defines the use of main mode or aggressive mode to first establish an ISAKMP SA. Main mode has five optional features: stateless cookie exchange, Perfect Forward Secrecy (PFS) for the keying material, secrecy for the identities, PFS for identity secrecy, and use of signatures (for nonrepudiation). The initiating and responding parties can use any combination of these options. The aggressive mode does not provide secrecy for the identity of the parties, but does support stateless cookie exchange, PFS for the key information, and signature options defined for the main mode. The aggressive mode involves the exchange of three messages instead of the five used in main mode to achieve a similar result at the expense of not keeping the identities of the parties secret. We first define several new concepts employed by ISAKMP and Oakley, then describe the aggressive mode as an example.

A *cookie* is an implementation-dependent bit string, for example, a cryptographic hash function applied to a periodically changed secret, the local and remote IP addresses, and the local and remote UDP ports. Cookies must be stateless, expire periodically, and be reproducible only by the creator of the original cookie. Cookies provide a weak address-validation mechanism that prevents an attacker from trying to clog a host with useless processor-intensive work involving Diffie-Hellman key exponentiation. The *group name* identifies the size of the integers, the arithmetic operation, the prime number p, and the generator element g used in the Diffie-Hellman computations (see Chapter 7).

Figure 9.7 illustrates the three Oakley messages exchanged between an Initiator (I) and a Responder (R) to establish an authenticated secret key. The first message generated by the initiator begins with a set of values encrypted with the initiator's private key. These are the initiator's cookie, the message type, the group name, the Diffie-Hellman parameter $X = g^x$ modulo p computed using a locally generated random number x and a proposed set of encryption, hashing, and authentication options for the initial SA. The NIDP field indicates that the remaining fields are not encrypted, and because this information block contains the unencrypted initiator and responder identities (i.e., ID(I) and ID(R)), aggressive mode does not provide confidentiality for the identities of the communicating parties. Oakley also employs a randomly generated number, called a *nonce*, indicated as Ni in the figure, to protect against replay attacks. Finally, the initiator signs the fields indicated by shading in the figure using its private key Ki.

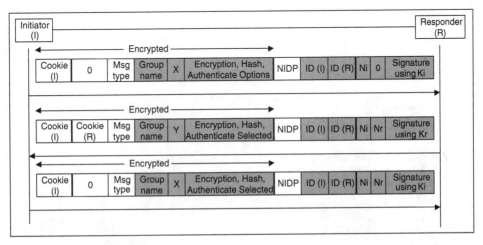

Figure 9.7 Oakley aggressive mode key exchange.

Upon receipt of this message, the responder adds its own cookie, the Diffie-Hellman parameter $Y = g^y$ modulo p using a locally generated random number y and a selection from the set of encryption, hashing, and authentication options proposed by the initiator. It adds its own randomly generated nonce Nr and signs the shaded fields using its private key Kr. It encrypts the portions of the message indicated in Figure 9.7 and returns this message to the initiator. If the initiator accepts the selections made by the responder, then it acknowledges it with the message indicated in the figure. The negotiation can actually continue with the initiator proposing options until the responder selects an acceptable set. Now the initiator and responder have a shared secret key using the Diffie-Hellman algorithm as follows: $K = XY = g^{xy}$ modulo p. Once this secret key is in place, additional message exchanges can occur securely to exchange parameters necessary to establish AH and ESP security associations using the ISAKMP message structure defined in RFC 2407.

Oakley relies on public-key digital certificate technology described in Chapter 7 to provide authentication of the initiator and responder identities encrypted using their public keys. The IETF is actively working on the definition of a Public Key Infrastructure (PKI) to solve this problem [Ibe 99; Perlman 99]. The design involves a hierarchy of Certificate Authorities (CAs), illustrated in Figure 9.8. At the bottom of the tree of trust, end users interface with a CA that may be run by an enterprise, an ISP, or a third party. There may be different levels of CA between the user and a Policy Certifi-

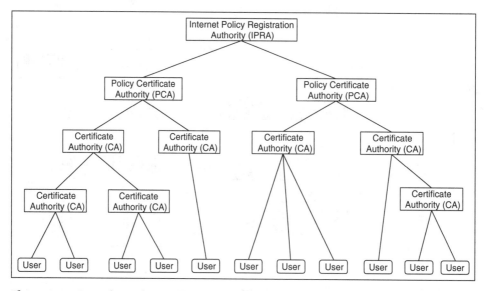

Figure 9.8   Tree of trust for certificate authorities.

cate Authority (PCA). PCAs are responsible for signing the certificates of lower-level CAs. At the root of the tree is a single Internet Policy Registration Authority (IPRA) that signs the PCA certificates. This hierarchical model enables cross certification of CAs in a scalable manner. Two leading vendors offering PKI key management capabilities in 1999 were Entrust and Verisign [Cosine 99]. The total cost of ownership per certificate ranged from $400 to $750 per year, depending on the total number of certificates.

This completes our coverage of the protocols involved in IP-based VPNs using the encryption, hashing, and signature techniques described in Chapter 7. The remainder of this chapter describes two other techniques for making IP-based networks virtual and private. The first of these involves extensions to the BGP protocol. The second builds upon the connection-oriented MPLS capability automatically configured using information exchanged between edge routers using BGP.

BGP Extensions in Support of VPNs

As described in Chapter 6, *The Internet Protocol Suite*, the Border Gateway Protocol (BGP) is the exterior routing protocol used between ISPs in the Internet. Also, in many cases, enterprise sites use BGP exchange reachability information with an ISP, perform load balancing, and automatically recover from failed access links. Several other extensions or uses of BGP provide additional capabilities that may be of use to some enterprises. The first of these is the BGP optional transitive communities attribute defined in RFC 1997 [Huston 98]. BGP requires that networks transmit the communities attribute to the next network, even if that network does not support the attribute. A BGP *community* is a group of destinations that share some common property, as identified by a 32-bit number. The first 16 bits identify the Autonomous System (AS) number of the network supporting the community, with that AS administering the last 16 bits of the community number. The network administrator defines communities to which each destination belongs. By default, every destination belongs to the public Internet community unless otherwise configured. Another concept used in BGP is that of a *confederation*, which is a set of BGP-capable routers that create a single advertisement to the remainder of an AS. This is an optional BGP extension [RFC 1965] used within larger ISP networks to reduce the number of BGP sessions [Huston 98] and consequently improve scalability.

A range of BGP community attributes are reserved to identify communities that have global significance. These are: NO_EXPORT, NO_ADVERTISE, and NO_EXPORT_SUBCONFD. An AS receiving a route with the

NO_EXPORT communities attribute must not advertise that route outside its community. An AS receiving a route with the NO_ADVERTISE communities attribute must not advertise that route to other BGP peers, even those within its own community. An AS receiving a route with the NO_EXPORT_SUBCONFD communities attribute must not advertise that route to external BGP peers, even those within its own confederation. BGP speakers may use the communities attribute to control which routing information it accepts, prefers, or distributes to neighbors.

The most well known and widely used communities attribute is NO_EXPORT, illustrated by the example shown in Figure 9.9. The example shows interfaces identified by CIDR IPv4 address prefixes for the public Internet (e.g., p.s/16) and two communities (e.g., p.r.x/24). Both community X and community Y have their ports configured with the NO_EXPORT BGP community attribute. The dashed lines indicate the reachable address prefixes advertised by BGP Update messages over iBGP between the routers supporting these interfaces. The advertisements indicated at the bottom of the figure reflect the normal operation of the public Internet where every address prefix received is advertised out onto every other interface. This includes the iBGP sessions to the two communities, as shown in the middle of the figure. However, since the two communities are configured for no address exportation outside their own community, their address prefixes are advertised only to interfaces within their own community. However, note that each community still has full knowledge of the reachability of public Internet prefixes and the associated BGP attributes.

The communities attribute prevents advertisement of routes in only one direction—namely, the reachability of the virtual private communities is not advertised to the public Internet or other communities. If the imple-

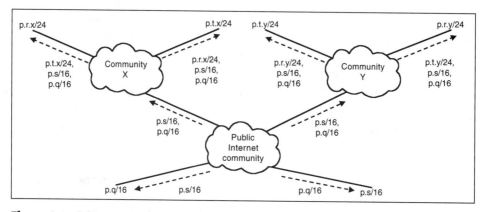

Figure 9.9 BGP community–controlled advertisement.

mentation uses a single forwarding table per router, then the ISP network may still forward traffic to these communities if they receive packets with the correct address. This is not really security, but obscurity instead. An important observation here is that enforcement of BGP community attributes requires a separate forwarding table for each port on a router. This, in fact, is a foundational requirement for designs implemented within a single ISP router shared across multiple enterprise VPN sites. Although no standard exists for such a virtual router at the time of this writing, we describe a proprietary example with reference to documentation available in the public domain as an example of this technique in the next section.

BGP-Controlled MPLS VPN

This section summarizes the important aspects of a general architecture for VPNs constructed on top of a homogeneous MPLS backbone network controlled by an extended version of BGP, as described in RFC 2547. Theoretically, multiple service providers could operate this backbone network. However, the situation in which a single provider offers this type of service will likely occur before multiple providers do so, much as has been the situation for frame relay and ATM service provider VPN solutions. Figure 9.10 shows the generic architecture and shorthand terminology used in the following description. A *Customer Edge* (CE) router represents a *site* on a VPN, which is a set of IP addresses reachable without use of the backbone. A site may be geographic or may represent an access link from a private enterprise network. Typically, different enterprises own and operate the CEs, as indicated by the shading in Figure 9.10. Each CE physically connects to a *Provider Edge* (PE) router and may connect to multiple PE routers for resiliency. The IP address prefixes that are reachable via a CE site may correspond to the physical interface or may consist of a number of logical interfaces that are considered *virtual sites*, created, for example, by frame relay, ATM, or Ethernet virtual LANs. We use the term *site* to refer to a physical or logical interface. A site may belong to one or more VPNs. The VPN identifier must be unique to the service provider(s) supporting the VPN service and, preferably, would be globally unique [RFC 2685]. Each PE router can support multiple CE router sites and must have a separate forwarding table for each site. The PE router has a shared forwarding table for reaching the public Internet. Finally, within the service provider MPLS backbone, Provider (P) switch/routers interconnect the PE routers using MPLS label switching.

Enterprises administer CE routers, which exchange routing information only with the PE routers and not other CE routers. This is more scalable

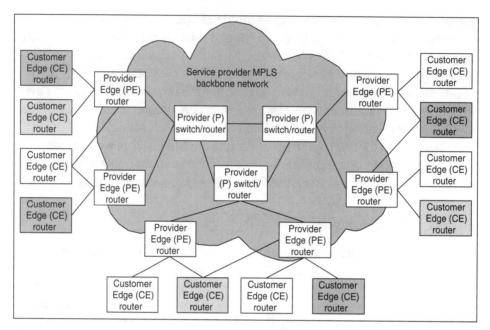

Figure 9.10 BGP/MPLS architecture and terminology.

than the tunneling approaches described earlier, where every enterprise router peers with many other routers. The routing protocol operating between the CE and PE routers may use static configuration, Routing Interchange Protocol (RIP), Open Shortest Path First (OSPF), or BGP. The service provider administers the PE and P routers. The CE routers never see the routing message interchange between PE and P routers. PE routers exchange messages using an extended iBGP protocol. Interchanges between PE and P routers use an interior routing protocol, such as OSPF or IS-IS, in concert with an MPLS Label Distribution Protocol (LDP). In this design, the backbone provider routers have no knowledge of the VPN service, which makes this solution quite scalable [Rekhter 98; Rekhter 99]. This strict partitioning of administration and routing in conjunction with the implementation of a separate forwarding table for each site within the PE routers is the foundation of this provider-based VPN service. This occurs because the PE router can forward traffic on a site-by-site and VPN-specific basis. Note that the presence of a separate forwarding table in the PE router for each VPN identifier allows sites in different VPNs to use overlapping address spaces. This is an important capability when IPv4 addresses are difficult to obtain and are becoming ever more scarce. The essence of the solution is in how the routing protocol fills in these separate forwarding tables. Let's look at simple examples of completely separate intranets and a partially overlapping extranet to illustrate the structure and use of the per-site forwarding tables in the PE routers and the label-switching tables in the backbone provider P switch/routers.

Figure 9.11 shows a simple example of two CEs, belonging to enterprises A and B, connected to two PE routers. Two P switch/routers interconnect the PE routers in the network backbone. The figure shows the forwarding table that operates on the packet on the input side of each PE and P port, with the first column denoting the index into the table. The table on a PE router port connecting to a CE site uses the IP Destination Address (IP DA) as an index into the table to determine an interface number (IF) and two MPLS labels (L1 and L2). The innermost label (L2) is unique within the PE router to the site, and the outermost label (L1) corresponds to the Label Switched Path (LSP) connecting to the PE router that is the destination for the IP DA for that enterprise VPN. If the destination interface is local to the PE router, then the L1 and L2 fields are not used and the packet is switched to the interface IF identified in the table. The PE router port connecting to a provider switch/router (P) looks at the received innermost label (L2) and routes this to a particular interface. This works because the ingress lookup added the proper label. The P switch/router forwarding tables operate only on the outermost MPLS label (L1). The input label (L In) determines the outgoing interface (IF) and the label to use on output to that interface (L Out). If the L Out column contains a dash, then the outermost label is stripped off before forwarding the MPLS

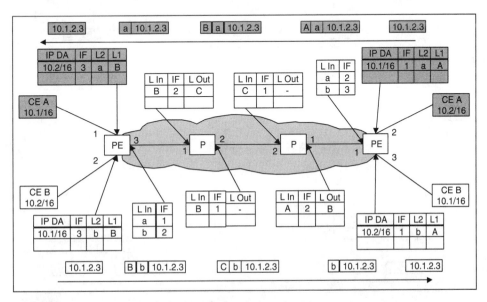

Figure 9.11   Intranet BGP/MPLS example.

packet. Notice that this occurs on the connections from the P switch/ router to the PE router. The sequence of packets at the top of the figure shows how these tables switch a packet from CE A 10.2/16 to the host with IP address 10.1.2.3 at CE A 10.1/16. In a similar manner, the sequence of packets at the bottom of the figure shows how these tables switch a packet from CE B 10.2/16 to the host with IP address 10.1.2.3 at CE B10.1/16.

Figure 9.12 shows a simple example of an extranet with limited connectivity. In an extranet application, the sites that are allowed to communicate must have unique addresses, which the following example illustrates. As in the previous example, the A and B sites are part of separate intranets; however, sites CE A 11.2/16 and CE B 12.2/16 are also allowed to communicate, thereby forming an extranet. The population of the forwarding tables allows this communication via entries in the IP prefix forwarding tables in the PE routers for these sites, as well as the MPLS trunk-side forwarding table. The packet flow trace at the top of the figure shows the flow from CE A 11.2/16 to CE B 12.2/16, and the trace at the bottom of the figure shows a flow in the opposite direction.

These tables are relatively complex, even for these simple networks. Obviously, manually filling out such tables is not scalable and is error-prone. The real power in the design described in RFC 2547 is the manner in which extensions to BGP [RFC 2283] automatically configure these tables. Before describing the operation of this protocol, let's first look at

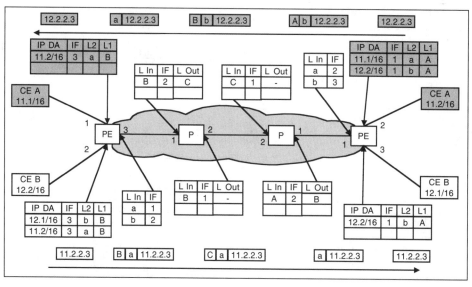

Figure 9.12   Extranet BGP/MPLS example.

the desired result for intranet and extranet connectivity and define some additional terminology.

Figure 9.13 shows two representations of an extranet VPN involving sites from three enterprises identified by the letters A, B, and C followed by a site number. The first is a Closed User Group (CUG) model similar to that described in Chapter 4, *Early Connection-Oriented VPNs—X.25 and Frame Relay.* The second uses connections, such as frame relay, ATM, or a tunneled protocol. Here, as shown in Figure 9.13a, all sites are part of an overall VPN X, and they are further subdivided as being part of one of six VPN identifiers, corresponding to all of the possible regions in a Venn diagram. Figure 9.13b depicts an alternative, equivalent representation of the site connectivity between the same three enterprises. This representation clearly shows that the sites in enterprises A, B, and C have complete full-mesh connectivity via solid lines. Dashed lines show the interenterprise connectivity equivalent to that of the CUG representation. The virtual connection representation requires specification of 102 connection endpoints, whereas the CUG representation requires specification of VPN membership using assignment of only 45 VPN identifiers. For an intranet-only configuration, the CUG requires on the order of n configurations, compared with on the order of n^2 configurations in a virtual connection or tunnel-based design.

The BGP/MPLS VPN technique implements the CUG representation in a rather flexible way. First, the network administrator assigns at least one Route Distinguisher (RD) to each site. RFC 2547 specifies a 7-byte RD. The combination of the RD and the IPv4 prefix is called the VPN-IPv4 address prefix. At a minimum, the RD must make the IPv4 prefix of the site unique.

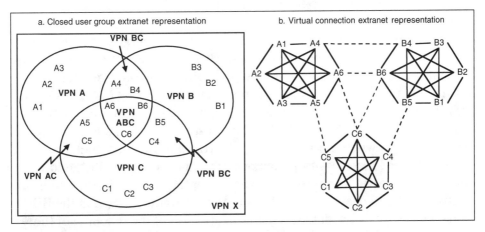

Figure 9.13   Representations of extranet connectivity.

An RD can also be used to advertise different attributes for the same destination, which can be quite useful in extranets, as described later. The combination of the RD and the site's IPv4 address is therefore unique, and can be advertised to the PE routers using extended iBGP along with the standard BGP attributes described in Chapter 6. Note that the RD does not imply any VPN membership or routing policy. It simply guarantees unique addresses and provides for the flexibility to associate multiple policies with a particular site.

Several additional attributes that provide VPN support are advertised in BGP Update messages. Two important ones that implement the CUG intranet and extranet capability are the Target VPN and Origin VPN attributes. The *Target VPN* attribute defines the set of sites to which a PE router must distribute iBGP Update messages, as these sites may be part of an intranet or extranet. Although similar to the 2-byte BGP community attribute previously described, the Target VPN has an 8-byte identifier range [RFC 2685]. In a homogeneous intranet, only the Target VPN attribute is necessary. The Target VPN attribute is VPN X in the example of Figure 9.13a. The *Origin VPN* attribute provides additional information that PE routers use to determine subdivisions of an intranet or extranet connectivity. Specifically, sites ignore routes advertised via iBGP that do not have the same Origin VPN as they do in their configuration. The Origin VPN attribute corresponds to the VPN identifiers A, B, C, AB, AC, BC, and ABC in Figure 9.13a. Service provider control of the assignment of the target and origin VPN attributes delivers security comparable to a connection-oriented VPN protocol, such as frame relay or ATM.

Several protocols work together to automatically fill in the forwarding tables in the PE routers and P switch/routers, as illustrated in Figure 9.14. First, the PE routers are logically connected by iBGP. The adjacency of PE routers in an iBGP sense is determined via configuration and need not necessarily be full mesh if enterprise sites are not present on every PE router. Furthermore, proven techniques such as BGP route reflection and confederations can scale the iBGP portion of the VPN infrastructure. The net result is that iBGP transfers the attributes and addressing information, either configured at each site or learned dynamically from the customer router, to every other site in the VPN. As in standard BGP, it is then a local policy decision whether to accept an advertised route and which route to select if the PE receives more than one advertisement for a VPN address prefix. This creates an association with the enterprise VPN's IPv4 address prefix and the IP destination address of the PE router carried in the BGP update message. Now all that remains is creation of the mapping of the inner and outer MPLS labels.

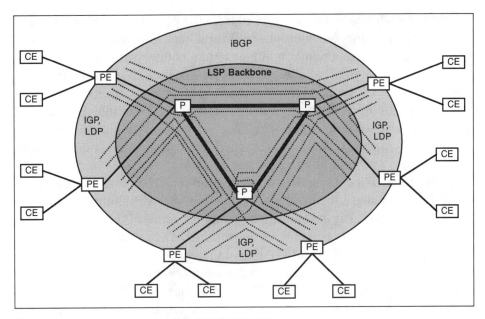

Figure 9.14 Protocols supporting BGP/MPLS VPNs.

The association of VPN connectivity with the innermost label involves the PE router using iBGP to distribute a unique MPLS label associated with the each unique VPN-IPv4 prefix that it knows about. Next, the PE routers use either an automatic MPLS Label Distribution Protocol (LDP) or manual provisioning to create the necessary associations between a MPLS Label Switched Path (LSP) and the PE IP addresses advertised via IGP. This results in a mesh of LSPs associated with the innermost label over the core P switch/routers that fully interconnects the PE routers supporting a shared set of VPNs, as shown via the dashed lines in the center of Figure 9.14. Ideally, the provider should do this with knowledge of customer traffic patterns and pending installations. Now the PE router has all the necessary information to fill in the forwarding tables facing the CE router and the P switch/router. The automatic LDP or manual provisioning sets up the full mesh of LSPs associated with the outermost label in the backbone P switch/routers, as shown by thick lines in the figure. This aspect of the design achieves significant scalability in comparison with single-level VC-based connection-oriented networks like frame relay. A similar concept exists with virtual path trunking in ATM. The PE routers use the innermost labels distributed via iBGP within the outermost labels to send packets to only the correct VPN, as determined by configuration of the target and origin VPN iBGP attributes.

This network-based solution differs from the connection-oriented frame relay, ATM, and tunneled solutions in several important ways. First, in a connection-oriented network, multiple virtual connections must be made from each CE site to other sites, as many as a full mesh. In the BGP/MPLS design, the PE routers share the full mesh of LSPs in the backbone between multiple VPNs, thereby achieving statistical multiplexing and more predictable traffic engineering. Second, much of the provisioning of a connection-oriented network is avoided. For example, in a fully meshed network with n sites, adding a new site in a connection-oriented network requires the addition of $n - 1$ new connections. On the other hand, in a BGP/MPLS network, after configuring the new site with the target and origin VPN attributes, the automatic protocols take care of the rest.

On the surface, at least, a parallel exists here between the overlay voice PBX implementations over private lines and network-based voice VPN solutions compared with the IP-based overlay solutions and the foregoing virtual private IP network-based solution. This analogy is valid in the context of connectivity between enterprise sites. Recalling the discussion from Chapter 3, *Circuit-Switched VPNs*, enterprises first installed overlay networks of PBXs because they were less expensive than public telephone service. However, the advent of competition changed the economics, and now most enterprises employ service provider–supplied solutions for voice networking. If history repeats itself, then service provider offerings of IP-based VPN solutions may well become an important aspect of enterprise VPNs as an IP-aware evolution of the connection-oriented VPN solution space—it is too early to predict at this point. However, there are several important differences between voice and IP VPNs. First, the virtual partitioning offered by the BGP/MPLS service ends at the customer edge router. Additional authentication and encryption requires use of IPsec protocols to provide security within an enterprise LAN. Furthermore, the use of secured tunneling protocols is essential for dial-in access. Finally, use of network-based VPN technologies will initially be limited to a single provider until such time that providers use the same equipment and administer it consistently.

Principal Applications

We've described a lot of protocols and techniques so far. How do enterprises actually use VPN technologies and protocols in real-world applications? How does an IP VPN relate to access to the public Internet? Are there any security issues involved in such an environment? To answer these questions, let's look at a few typical IP VPN deployment scenarios that involve the technologies and protocols covered so far.

BEWARE OF GEEKS BEARING GIFTS

A common ploy that hackers like to try is to install a Trojan horse or trapdoor program in a host through an Email attachment, diskettes, or a Web download. Once so compromised, a host inadvertently becomes a transit point that hackers employ to conceal their identity. Hackers persistently scan hosts connected to the Internet for such Trojan horse programs. The user of the computer may not even be aware that his or her computer is being used surreptitiously. In fact, historically, computer crimes often go undetected, and even if detected, often go unreported [Sieber 86; Kabay 98]. The rapid adoption of *always-on* Internet access technologies poses an even greater opportunity for hackers and therefore a greater risk for enterprises. The emergence of consumer-grade firewall products may be a partial answer to this problem.

Secured VPN Access and the Public Internet

Any host that simultaneously has access to secure resources within an enterprise and the public Internet is a serious security risk. If a compromised host is attached to a secured enterprise LAN using a tunneling protocol between the host's VPN software and a Security Gateway (SG) and the public Internet at the same time, then it becomes a pathway into the secured enterprise LAN for a hacker, as shown in Figure 9.15a. Two solutions are possible here. First, the enterprise provides VPN software so the user cannot access the public Internet, but can access *only* enterprise VPN resources, when using a secured tunnel. Although this method is secure, it can be rather restrictive for some enterprise applications that require access to both the VPN and public Internet access. A better solution is to have any traffic destined for the public Internet first traverse the tunnel into the secured enterprise LAN and then traverse the enterprise firewall (see Chapter 7) to the public Internet, as shown in Figure 9.15b. This solution provides enterprise users access to VPN resources while using the firewall to keep attackers who may enter from the public Internet away from sensitive enterprise resources. This design allows an enterprise site to act as the firewall-protected gateway to the Internet as accessed by other LANs over secured tunnels.

A number of variations on this basic theme exist [Brown 99; Fowler 99; Kosiur 98]. One such variation reverses the position of the security gateway and the firewall in Figure 9.15b. This secures access to the firewall-protected LAN, but exposes the security gateway to attacks from the Internet. Some scenarios combine the functions of routing, firewalls, and

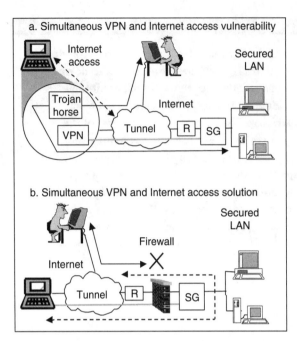

Figure 9.15   Simultaneous VPN and Internet access.

security gateways into a single implementation that reduces costs by minimizing the number of boxes at each enterprise site. Another cost-cutting design places security gateways on only those enterprise resources that absolutely require the highest level of security, with the firewall providing the only protection for the remainder of the resources. Other configurations require the use of Network Address Translation (NAT), as defined in Chapter 7, if the enterprise employs private IP addresses. Finally, don't forget that IPsec allows the use of encryption and authentication on a host-to-host basis, offering the highest level of security focused on precisely the applications that require it most.

Typical IP VPN Deployment Scenarios

A number of VPN designs are possible using the protocols and architectures described in this book. This section describes two typical designs that illustrates some of the trade-offs that enterprise application requirements and traffic patterns drive. Figure 9.16 illustrates the first scenario, which is oriented toward an enterprise with a hierarchical traffic pattern with many branch sites homing to a few headquarters sites. The branch sites use frame relay or ATM PVCs to access the headquarters site, which has a firewall that creates a Demilitarized Zone (DMZ) between itself and a

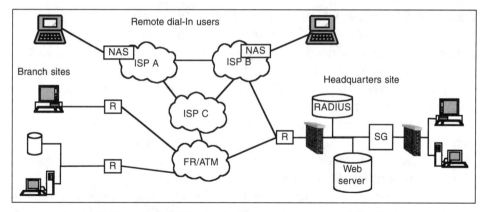

Figure 9.16 Hybrid FR/ATM, IP hierarchical VPN design.

security gateway. The enterprise deploys a RADIUS server for securing dial-in access via communication with Network Access Server (NAS) devices deployed in multiple ISPs in the DMZ. An enterprise often places the public Web server in the DMZ, sometimes further enhancing security by placing a more restrictive firewall between the secured LAN and the DMZ. In this configuration, the security gateway works only with the remote dial-in users. The headquarters site in this example is dual-homed for reliability purposes via a direct connection to ISP B and a FR/ATM PVC to ISP C. As analyzed in Chapter 8, this design makes the most sense when the enterprise traffic pattern is hierarchical.

Figure 9.17 illustrates a pure IP-based VPN design that has a cost structure essentially independent of the traffic pattern. Here, every site has a firewall and security gateway so that any site may directly access the Internet or any other site. Furthermore, we show the RADIUS server, Web server, and extranet database located at three separate sites. Dial-in users

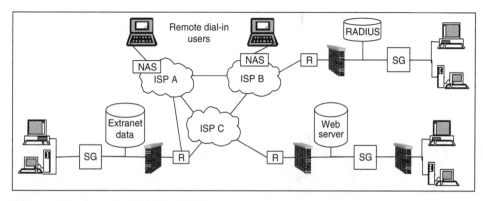

Figure 9.17 Pure IP distributed VPN design.

are secured using the RADIUS authentication server and the security gateway as previously described. This design also reduces access costs since traffic for the Internet need not traverse the firewall at only the headquarters site, as shown in the hierarchical example. Sites may also be dual-homed to different ISPs or to different sites within the same ISP for resiliency purposes, as necessary. This design is better suited to extranet applications since communication via the public Internet is more interoperable and rapidly deployable than any other communication service, with the possible exception of telephony. However, telephony does not support the range of multimedia services of which IP is capable.

We've now covered a broad range of VPN-enabling architectures, technologies, and protocols. How does one decide what is best for a particular enterprise? What are the next steps that a network designer should take? Are there other techniques and solutions that should be avoided or carefully watched? Will the public Internet become the medium of choice for constructing VPNs, or will service provider-based networks capture the emerging VPN market? Although no one can answer any of these questions with certainty, the next and final chapter surveys opinions and projections from industry experts, trendsetters, and crystal-ball gazers. This, then, is the jumping-off point into the exciting, yet uncertain, future of VPNs.

The Future of VPNs

**You must learn from the mistakes of others. You can't
possibly live long enough to make them all yourself.**
—Sam Levenson

This chapter covers the future of VPNs from several points of view. First,
there is the practical aspect of determining the specific steps that an enterprise should take toward a VPN. This involves detailed requirement collection, alternative analysis, migration planning, and implementation. Another
dimension is that of technology, protocols, and standards. This involves
trend analysis regarding which of the currently available technologies protocols will become the dominant standard and therefore deliver cost-
cutting and productivity-enhancing benefits to enterprise applications. The
final viewpoint involves trying to foresee the future in the rapidly evolving
world of Internet-driven networking and is therefore the most interesting,
but also the most speculative.

Planning and Implementing a VPN

Establishing a set of goals and establishing a plan to meet them is critical
to success in most human endeavors, and virtual private networking is no
exception. The steps here are similar to those of any large-scale project.
First, collecting requirements, drivers, and needs is necessary research to

establish goals. Next, developing several candidate designs and analyzing them in the harsh light of commercial business reality is a crucial step. A VPN may not be right for the enterprise under consideration at this time, and timing is important. Finally, if the decision is to implement a new type of VPN, or migrate existing private network applications to a VPN, the work is not done. Detailed planning and a well-thought-out migration strategy are essential for an enterprise to achieve the goals set out at the beginning of the process. This section summarizes these steps, giving references for the reader interested in more detail.

Collecting Requirements and Establishing Goals

A number of enterprises have already implemented VPNs of the types described in this book. A good starting point is to look at an enterprise that is similar to yours in some way, and read case studies, papers, and books about what worked and what did not. However, be aware that the needs of each enterprise are unique and different; therefore, basing a decision on others' experiences, while helpful, is not sufficient to guarantee delivery of maximum benefit. Important areas of requirements collection are analysis of potential security threats and essential performance metrics. Formulating a threat model and considering what would happen if important information were stolen, made public, or corrupted is an essential step [Brown 99; Kaufman 99]. Determining the performance required by applications is also important. Consider what would happen if a site is disconnected for a long period. Assess what the impact of network congestion would be. Discriminate between nice-to-have performance and what is absolutely necessary—this can make quite a difference in qualifying network designs and their eventual cost.

Although a generic framework may not apply to all enterprises, there are some helpful points of view when categorizing types of requirements. One way to analyze VPN requirements is to consider the community of interest and access methods [Cisco 99; Fowler 99]:

- Cost-effective remote and mobile user access
- An infrastructure for intranets that keeps resources secure within a single enterprise
- An infrastructure for extranets for controlling resource sharing between two or more enterprises

As described in Chapter 8, *Dial-In Access and Multiprotocol Tunneling VPNs*, some fundamental trade-offs exist. The crossover points regarding enterprise dial-in versus ISP-provided access services are strongly dependent on the number of users that require dial-in access and the type as well as amount of activities that these users conduct. In general, a remote user population that generates bursty activity during relatively long-duration sessions is a good candidate for ISP access. A critical piece of information in making the business justification here is analysis of current expenses. If the enterprise currently owns access servers and uses long-distance telephone service, then collect telephone bills for at least the past year to set a tangible cost reduction goal. Also, identify the trend in remote access usage and factor in any plans for new sites either domestically or internationally. Using IP-based remote access VPN technology can often result in significant cost savings when compared with international telephone call charges [Fowler 99].

Often an enterprise already has one or more current intranets constructed out of private lines or connection-oriented VPN technologies, such as X.25, frame relay, and/or ATM. Collect the information about these current networks, their annual expenditures in terms of equipment purchases, service provider fees, and any other operating expenses. This becomes the baseline for a comparison analysis of network design alternatives. Also, collect information about the applications running on these networks, the utilization statistics, and performance requirements. If a driving requirement for the enterprise is extranet connectivity other than that provided by traditional telephony, then an IP-based solution is one of the few choices available. However, since the IPsec standards are relatively new, an environment where a few large enterprises work with a number of small to medium-sized enterprises has been a successful model for extranet deployment, as discussed later in this section.

Another important dimension for assessing requirements and setting goals is the size of the enterprise [Cisco 99; VPNet 99]. Small enterprises with less than 100 employees often use ISP services anyway for access to the public Internet. Therefore, an IP-based VPN is often a natural candidate for an Internet-savvy small enterprise. Medium-sized enterprises with less than 1,000 employees are also often prime candidates. If such a venture is in a high-growth mode, then turning over the task of running an Internet-based network to an outsourcing company or a service provider allows the enterprise to focus on its principal mission. This is particularly true if international communication is a significant part of the budget. Exceptions among midsized enterprises might be those whose core competency is communication networking or those with demanding performance requirements. A private line or connection-oriented network may be the only solution that meets the stringent requirements that some enterprises demand. Large enterprises have the most choices. These organizations are often of such scale that justification of specialized staff to run any type of communication network is possible. The critical issue here is whether an enterprise wants to focus on developing this expertise or outsource it to another company. As the complexity of running a VPN increases, many corporations choose the outsourcing alternative.

Analyzing Alternatives and Decision Making

With the enterprise's requirements and goals in hand, the next step is to develop several design approaches. Here, creativity and due diligence in the development of technology options is essential. A network designer should strive to have at least two options for comparison purposes. Understanding how to think about these options is the principal purpose of this book and the many references cited herein. When interviewing candidate equipment suppliers and/or service providers, ask questions. If a vendor or service provider cannot take the time to answer questions prior to the sale, be wary about the level of postsale support that would be available. Consider using a formal Request For Information (RFI) or Request For Proposal (RFP) to get responses and price quotes in writing. An alternative is to outsource the development of alternatives and analysis to experts. For example, traffic analysis and optimal network design are challenging tasks that only the largest of enterprises can typically afford to perform inhouse. If you have the time and resources, get several bids for this important activity before making a decision. Plan for success in the design process. Envision the impacts of growth, new capacity-hungry and QoS-aware applications, and the evolving, increasingly Internet-centric business environment.

A significant challenge is accurately quantifying the cost and schedule of a new network for comparison with the cost structure of one or more existing networks. Accurate assessment of the benefits side of the business case can also be challenging. Try to be as specific as possible, putting values and schedules to cost savings. Be somewhat conservative when preparing the business justification for a new or markedly changed network infrastructure, because it is human nature to underestimate the resources and time required in many endeavors. Bosses seldom fire people for spending less than the budgeted amount or delivering a project early. Yet don't be overly conservative, because this may cause missed opportunities. Seek out peer reviews and comparable case studies in recently published periodicals, books, or Web sites if the business case does not prove profitable at first. Also, look at major factors that would change the crossover point in a trade-off analysis. These will be important factors to track after a successful network implementation. Use business cases developed by a vendor, an outsourcing supplier, or a service provider as input to your decision process, but don't rely on this as the sole input. For examples see AT&T(99), Checkpoint(99), Cosine(99), Data Fellows(99), Lombard(98), Shiva(99), and TimeStep(99). Realize that a business case developed by a potential supplier usually puts matters in the best possible light for that supplier. See Chapter 8 for some examples of business case analyses that strive to be more comprehensive and critical.

Don't forget that the cost of running a communication network continues long after installation is complete. Consider the entire life-cycle cost in your analysis. In your planning, account for the period during which multiple parallel networks will exist. The cost of operating a complex IP-based overlay VPN can be significant for a small enterprise. Compare estimates of performing such management functions in-house to fees charged by outsourcing providers. Outsourcing is often a lower-risk alternative, albeit at a somewhat higher cost than a medium-sized to large enterprise that develops a VPN core competency itself can achieve. Of course, an enterprise can choose to outsource only parts of the overall task—design alternative development, business case analysis, network planning, network migration, and operation—or else outsource the entire VPN life cycle. Beware: Increased outsourcing means decreased control. Carefully choose your outsourcing supplier. If your first choice fails to perform, you might need to change suppliers, which can be expensive and disruptive.

Migrating and Operating the New Network

Once you've decided on the technology, architecture, and network design that are best, you need to develop a detailed plan for migrating from the current network state to the desired end state [Brown 99; Fowler 99]. A good idea is to start with a trial network first, preferably using non-mission-critical traffic. Such a pilot network allows verification of assumptions and migration plans, as well as a final check on the true operating costs and schedules that will be achieved. If you are using an outsourcing partner, the trial network gives the enterprise an early look into that experience.

After successful completion of a pilot network, migrate other applications and networks in phases whenever possible. Plan to leave any prior production networks up in parallel during the migration period in case unforeseen problems arise. If a problem does occur and you have to roll back to the old network, you will be glad that you took this precaution, even if it extends the period required to achieve a return on the initial investment. Start with the minimal set of VPN features necessary at first. Turn on new features and capabilities, let the network stabilize, and get your operations staff familiar with the new environment before moving on to the next phase. Only after operations and the user community have confidence in the new VPN technology should an enterprise remove the old network.

Once the new network is up and running, an enterprise must be committed to purchasing software upgrades, scheduling training, and performing preventive maintenance on the VPN. For connection-oriented VPNs, this involves monitoring the service provider virtual connections for reliability and QoS. An enterprise must also track traffic levels and make cost-effective choices regarding virtual connection orders to realize the benefits. For IP-based VPNs, maintenance of the security-related aspects of the network is of paramount importance [Brown 99; Kosiur 98]. For sensitive information, use the strongest encryption allowed by law in the country where that part of the network operates. Establish good physical security policies, enforce selection of difficult-to-compromise passwords, and train the user community in good security practices [Fowler 99; Kaufman 99; Kosiur 98]. Keep close track of all laptops and their security status. A lost or stolen laptop can open an express lane into the heart of an otherwise secure network.

Network management is frequently overlooked in the planning and business justification phases and can consequently be a negative surprise in the realized cost-benefit once the new network is in operation. Don't try to skimp on up-front costs by not purchasing a vendor's or service provider's network management software or services. Configuration and monitoring of security gateway, firewall, and network address translation functions are critical to the operation of an IP-based VPN [Brown 99; Kosiur 98]. Standard management interfaces and protocols end up being the least common denominator and are often years behind what vendors and providers can offer with proprietary solutions. Network management standards are usually late for good reason—network managers cannot define management protocols until the engineers have completely defined the things that require management! In a multivendor environment with mature technologies, standards are essential. In this case, look to a systems integrator to supply these systems instead of building your own, unless your enterprise is in the business of developing network management systems.

Learn from What Others Have Done

Unless your enterprise is the first to try a new technology, protocol, or architecture, there will likely be case studies available for review. A frequently documented extranet case study is the Automotive Network eXchange (ANX) [Minoli 99; Fowler 99]; see the ANX Web site at www.anxo.com for more information. This extranet VPN involves a few large enterprises (automotive manufacturers) and a significant number of small to medium-sized enterprises (their suppliers). Initiated by the Automotive Industry Action Group (AIAG) in 1994, the IPsec-based ANX network had Chrysler, Ford, and General Motors as the founding network participants. These companies and other major automotive manufacturers utilize parts and services from a large number of common Original Equipment Manufacturers (OEMs), such as Bosch, Delta, Fisher, ITT, and TRW. Following the completion of successful trials in 1997 and 1998, ANX launched into production in November 1998. By the end of 1999, ANX had nearly 500 registered trading partners. As an example of a quantifiable goal achievable by an extranet, the AIAG estimates that a Collaborative Planning, Forecasting, and Replacement (CPFR) tool running over the ANX network may save up to $1,200 per vehicle. This savings results from a reduction of the delivery cycle time of parts and supplies and the associated inventory levels.

The ANX architecture is based on a set of interconnected Certified Service Providers (CSPs), Certified Exchange Point Operators (CEPOs), and Certificate Authority Service Providers (CASPs), to which ANX Trading Partners (TPs) subscribe, as illustrated in Figure 10.1. Telcordia (formerly Bellcore) has been chosen as the ANX overseer, which awards certification to CSPs and CEPOs. The ANX service quality certification categories are the following: network service features, interoperability, performance, reliability, business continuity and disaster recovery, security, customer care, and trouble handling. ANX has also specified the International Computer Security Association (ICSA) to certify IPsec-compliant equipment.

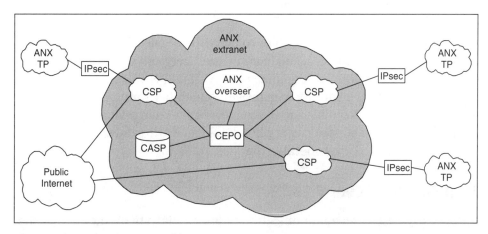

Figure 10.1 ANX extranet architecture.

Additional references for more information are www.aiag.org/anx and www.icsa.net. Equipment that has the ICSA stamp of approval is a good place to start when looking for IPsec-compliant vendors.

This network is effectively a partitioned set of interfaces running on top of the public Internet infrastructure offered by the selected set of certified commercial ISPs [Kirchoff 96]. It replaces the prior complex arrangement of physical and logical connections between trading partners with one logically administered, cryptographically secured connection to the ANX extranet. Choice of the TCP/IP protocol suite provides access to a broad range of file transfer, Electronic Document Interchange (EDI), Email, and other application software, as well as networking technologies discussed in Chapters 7 through 9. This is especially important in the automotive industry where computer-based techniques are increasingly used in every stage of the design, manufacturing, delivery, and maintenance aspects of the business.

Although the benefits of ANX apply primarily to medium-sized to large enterprises in the automotive industry, the drive toward interoperability will benefit other industry segments in the longer term. We now turn from the practical aspects of planning and implementing a network in the near term to gazing a few years into the future. Natural sets of questions arise regarding the evolution and adoption of technologies and services that have similar capabilities. In particular, the relative market share of these technologies will obviously impact the economies of scale and consequently the cost basis that an enterprise will realize using that technology.

Technology, Protocol, and Standards Directions and Trends

Technology is an important enabler to meet the needs of enterprises. The search for the holy grail of a single converged network solution continues now with IP as the foundation, instead of ATM and N-ISDN as in past visions. The IP-based solution has proven scalability for connectionless services; however, a significant challenge lies ahead in adapting IP to become capable of supporting application-level traffic and QoS requirements in a standard interoperable manner.

Will One Size Ever Fit All?

In the early 1990s, telecommunication industry analysts predicted that the ATM-based protocol suite would do everything and usher in the information age. However, the emergence of the killer applications of Email and Web browsing changed all that. Instead, the world flocked to the networking technology developed by government funding over three decades. Now, the same industry analysts tout the IP-based protocol suite as the solution that will do everything and usher in the information age. Looking back in time, the advocates of narrowband ISDN made similar claims in the 1970s.

Will one telecommunication solution ever meet all the needs of the diverse environment created by the action and interaction of human enterprise? Will one solution displace all others? The answer is, probably not; the history of technology sets a number of contrary precedents. AM radio efficiently uses spectrum, but cannot deliver the higher-quality audio that the less efficient FM radio can. Multiple formats for recording and playback of audio and video have existed since their inception. Monopolies on computers and operating systems do not last forever. Witness IBM's fall from dominance and the ascension of Microsoft, Intel, and Cisco. Although telephony eventually replaced telegraphy, voice communication and video broadcasts never replaced distribution of the written word via postal mail, newspapers, and books. People still travel as much as they ever did despite the availability of videoconferencing. However, each innovation in telecommunication changes the way people and enterprises work together. The innovations ushered in by the IP-based suite of protocols simply raise the bar even higher for the next wave of networking technology, whatever that may be.

One thing is certain, however: The tremendous popularity of IP has slowed down the pace of innovation in the IETF. Old-timers wish for the good old days when fewer people were involved, there was little commercial focus, and innovation was a cooperative effort. Now, politics, business, naivete, and even personality consistently impede progress. These are all symptoms of large, successful bureaucratic organizations. However, one thing the IETF does have in its favor is a fundamentally different operating paradigm than that used by many other standards bodies—namely, "rough consensus and running code" [Kowack 97].

Riding the Wave of Internet Growth

In Chapter 6, *The Internet Protocol Suite*, we described the technical reasons that the Internet has scaled so well. In order to truly appreciate how well the connectionless design of IP has scaled historically, Figure 10.2 plots the number of hosts [Hobbes 99] and the number of BGP route entries [Telstra 99] in an ISP router from 1995 through 1999. Note that these plots

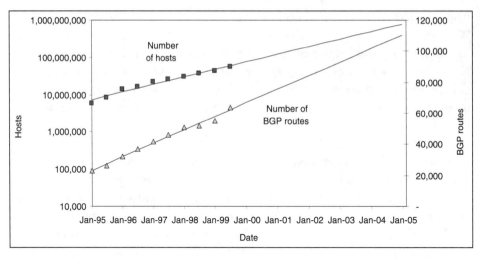

Figure 10.2 Internet hosts and routing entries.

are on different scales. The number of Internet hosts is plotted against a logarithmic scale on the left, while the number of BGP route entries is plotted against a linear scale on the right. The solid line projects these trends out another five years. The historical growth rate for the number of hosts is exponential, with a 60 percent growth from year to year. On the other hand, the number of BGP route entries grew in a linear manner, increasing on average by less than 10,000 entries per year. Since the BGP routing message interchange and processing required are proportional to the number of route entries and not the number of hosts, the connectionless infrastructure of the Internet still has a significant amount of scalability. Although the connectionless routing aspect of the Internet appears ready to sustain these rapid growth rates, there are several other areas where change will be necessary to meet continuing growth and increasing demand for performance. A significant challenge is simply responding to the huge demand. The overall capacity required in ISP backbones is growing at a rate faster than that of the user population, because the community of interest increases with the population and more users now have higher-speed access facilities. Furthermore, new applications such as voice, audio, and video create more traffic on the Internet.

Although the routing table size has scaled well, the overall capacity of routing and switching equipment has had difficulty keeping pace with demand. The Internet routing protocols run best over single links connecting adjacent nodes. These link speeds were 10 Gbps in the year 2000. Beyond this level of traffic, ISPs must perform additional traffic engineering to split the load across multiple parallel links. This design, unfortunately, causes packet reordering and degrades TCP performance [Bennett 99]. However, higher-speed links alone will likely not be the final answer. Either improved TCP implementations that more effectively handle reordering or network designs that make many parallel links look like one larger link will be necessary.

Another important issue is the matter of addressing. Theoretically, IPv4 has more than 4 billion host addresses available. However, practically, the number is much lower because the grouping of addresses by prefix that yields the aforementioned scalability leads to much less than full utilization of the address space. As evidence of this fact, many enterprises cannot get enough IPv4 address prefixes and instead employ private addresses using Network Address Translation (NAT), as described in Chapter 7, *Building Blocks for IP-Based VPNs—Security, Quality, and Access*. The longer-term solution, developed by the IETF, is, of course, the IPv6 header that expands the address field size from 4 to 16 bytes, offering a huge increase in the number of potential addresses. In order to appreciate how large this number is, we point out that IPv6 has sufficient range to address each atom of every living organism on earth! Of course, the widespread adoption of IPv6 will likely occur only after major applications, such as Microsoft and AOL Web browsers, support it. In response to the looming tidal wave of demand, the industry has established the IPv6 Forum. It intends to address the practical issues of migration and the impact of administering this huge address space so that the scaling properties exhibited by the Internet continue well into the twenty-first century. See www.ipv6forum.com for more information.

Routing protocols have another scalability challenge that is often more restrictive than the number of table entries. The flooding operation involved in a link-state routing protocol produces significant transients of message processing during certain network events. This effectively constrains the number of nodes that can exist within a single IGP domain. A way of scaling such a network is to partition it into multiple hierarchical domains. Currently, the OSPF and IS-IS IGP protocols support two levels of hierarchy. This affords significant scalability; however, networks containing even more nodes require more levels of hierarchy [McDysan 00]. The ATM PNNI protocol [ATMF PNNI 1.0] supports multiple levels of hierarchy, but requires careful network design to avoid processor overload during connection establishment [Felstaine 99]. The experience gained in hierarchical ATM networking will likely be another area that IP routing will use to meet this challenge in scalability [Li 99].

The Inevitable Delivery of QoS over the Internet

IP QoS will become a reality because of the trailblazing efforts of frame relay and ATM, not despite them [Crowcroft 99; McDysan 00]. A significant challenge for the connectionless IP paradigm is that of guaranteeing capacity at an acceptable level of quality. As an increasing number of enterprises require support for business-quality voice, video, and mission-critical applications, the IP infrastructure must evolve to this changing demand profile. In earlier chapters, we described several of the approaches developed to date to address these issues. Chapter 5, *Modern Connection-Oriented VPNs—ATM, MPLS, and RSVP,* described how MultiProtocol Label Switching (MPLS) is an IP-aware evolution of ATM. In effect, the initial deployments of MPLS are a protocol-agnostic traffic engineering underlay to IP that is more effective than ATM within an ISP backbone [Adwuche 99; Li 99]. MPLS promises a potential future evolution path for scalable evolution of QoS in the Internet using label stacking, which, as described in Chapter 5, is an extension of ATM virtual paths. Service provider–delivered solutions than combine the traffic engineering of MPLS with the scalability of connectionless routing as described in Chapter 9, *IP Security-Enabled and Routing-Controlled VPNs*, may become a significant VPN technology in the future.

Chapter 5 also described the Resource reSerVation Protocol (RSVP), which is a protocol developed so that applications can signal requests for capacity and quality. However, the processing required for RSVP is even greater than that of connection-oriented protocols like ATM for long-duration voice and video sessions, since the sender must refresh the request periodically. Alternatively, other session-oriented protocols, such as the Session Initiation Protocol (SIP) being defined for IP telephony, could be used to generate an implied request for capacity and quality as well [Gibson 99a]. These protocols still have per-connection-oriented processing and therefore could not be supported in large aggregates in a connectionless backbone. They work best in an architecture that distributes processing as close to the host as possible. The policy information could be stored locally within a node or accessed remotely via a protocol, such as the Common Open Policy Service (COPS) protocol being developed by the IETF [Boyle 99].

A promising approach involves moving the connection- or session-oriented functions to the very edge of the network and using simple connectionless functions in the core. As described in Chapter 7, the marking of each packet using differentiated service (diffserv) codepoints at the edge of the network can be done based on traffic and quality requests signaled by the end user or the enterprise edge router. The edge node within the ISP network can then perform policing and policy enforcement, and then use a diffserv codepoint to simply represent the net result of applying these complex functions. The backbone nodes within the core then operate on the diffserv codepoints, possibly using a relatively small set of class-based queues with thresholds, as described in Chapter 5. Alternatively, diffserv codepoints or other signaling information could be mapped to MPLS Label-Switched Paths (LSPs) that have different quality and traffic levels [Gibson 99b]. Backbone nodes could also apply different functions based on protocol type—for example, using Random Early Detection (RED) for TCP to provide a form of graceful degradation in the face of congestion.

Figure 10.3 graphically depicts how these concepts could work together in an interconnected ISP network supporting enterprise intranet or extranet connectivity in the near future. Starting in the lower left-hand corner, an enterprise site comprising a QoS-aware set of clients, servers, and databases implements QoS in some manner. Since standards are not complete, many enterprises use a bandwidth manager to perform this function [Higgins 99]. The planned rollout of an RSVP-based Windows 2000 and NT 5.0 by Microsoft sets the stage for a standards-based QoS-aware LAN environment. Enterprise sites securely connect to an edge router in a QoS-aware ISP through a firewall and a router that may implement various security gateway features. The enterprise and ISP routers perform access-level protocols, such as RSVP, diffserv marking, or analysis of session signaling, such as SIP to deliver QoS on the access facilities. Within the QoS-aware ISP network, edge routers aggregate the access requests over an MPLS backbone comprising high-performance, large-capacity Label-Switched Routers (LSR). QoS-aware ISPs could interconnect using MPLS LSRs or routers.

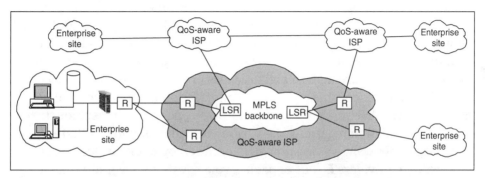

Figure 10.3   Scalable QoS architecture for the Internet.

One of the most beguiling challenges is that of delivering the required capacity for aggregates of sessions across the backbone of a connection-less network. This occurs naturally in connection-oriented protocols, but has been handled by traffic engineering based on historical usage patterns in many ISP networks. Promising developments in the areas of using actual traffic measurements to automatically adjust routing will initially be vendor-proprietary developments [Drake 99]. However, it is likely that enterprise users will drive the service provider industry to a standard interoperable solution.

Expansion of Applications and Services

The network infrastructure is not the only thing that an enterprise can out-source to another party. Although the virtual sharing of a public network was the focus of this book, another set of emerging technologies supports virtualization of higher-layer applications and services in an outsourcing environment. Starting in 1999, a new breed of company called an Application Service Provider (ASP), aims to provide what an enterprise typically had to perform itself in the past [Turner 99]. The ASP concept is an evolution of the time-shared computing data center of the 1970s updated to the twenty-first century Internet-aware new world. An ASP can achieve economies for an enterprise because it collocates the application-hosting server farms on an ISP network backbone. By being collocated on a back-bone, ASPs reduce access charges when compared with server farms hosted on an enterprise site. However, note that ASPs can support only commodity applications, because the economy of scale derives from pro-viding the same application to many enterprises. ASPs also give the hosted applications the reliability and physical security of a classical telephone company central office, including power backed up by battery and genera-tor in the event of extended power outages. The hosted applications that are supported extend beyond the long-offered Web hosting into traditional mainframe programs supported by an IT organization, such as those used by human resources departments. Viewed in another way, an ASP is an extension of outsourcing into higher layers of the layered computer com-munications protocol stack. For more information on this emerging tech-nology, see the ASP industry consortium Web page at www.aspindustry.org and the information regarding the various providers identified there.

Another important service now being offered by many traditional and new service providers is that of packet voice switched over alternative access networks. The principal areas of industry focus are Voice over IP

(VoIP) and Voice over Digital Subscriber Line (xDSL) technologies. Beginning in the mid-1990s, enterprises constructed private voice networks using frame relay and ATM to connect PBXs via virtual connections. Soon thereafter, equipment also supported VoIP. In our terminology of VPNs discussed in Chapter 1, *Introduction and Overview*, these all would have been private networks. What is changing now is that carriers are beginning to trial the implementation of media gateways within their networks that connect directly to the traditional telephone network, as described in Chapter 5 [Willis 99]. The quality of packet voice approaches the standard set by traditional telephony, although the additional delay introduced by packetization is unavoidable. A QoS-aware IP backbone is necessary to realize the best quality. However, history has shown that enterprises will accept a reduction in voice quality if the price discount is deep enough. For example, many enterprises moved to satellite communications for voice in the 1980s because it was cheaper, although the long delays made interactive conversation difficult. Nevertheless, a number of challenges exist for IP telephony [Reimers 99]. These include scalability, reliability, and feature content as compared with the PBX- and public telephone network-based systems that many enterprises employ today. Some enterprises are deploying ATM-based solutions because they are mature and address these issues.

A significant challenge that these alternative technologies supporting voice must meet is standardization of signaling and control protocols. In the IP telephony space, there are two competing signaling protocols. The older standard derived from N-ISDN is usually referred to as H.323 [ITU H.323], although a number of other ITU-T Recommendations define various aspects of the protocol suite. The newer standard is defined by the IETF and is known as the Session Initiation Protocol (SIP) [RFC 2543]. Although many of the earlier IP telephony implementations are based on H.323—for example, Microsoft's NetMeeting—the number of SIP implementations is increasing. One area where these two standards align is at the media encapsulation layer, because both use the Real-Time Transport Protocol (RTP) and Real-Time Control Protocol (RTCP) summarized in Chapter 7.

VPNs in the Twenty-first Century

We are now at the end of our story about VPNs. What will the future hold? Although no one can say with certainty, this section presents selected thoughts published by industry experts that make predictions, give cautions, or attempt to foresee fundamental changes in direction in the application of VPNs by enterprises.

Lessons of the Marketplace

IP-based VPNs were the rage of the trade press in the late 1990s. The hype has cooled off somewhat now, and the market forecasts are not as aggressive. This is a commonly encountered technology adoption trend in any new business [Moore 91], as illustrated in Figure 10.4. The figure depicts the relative market share according to the classical bell curve. Starting from the left-hand side, technology enthusiasts and then visionaries make up a small early market. Every new technology encounters a critical point in the market adoption cycle, which Geoffrey Moore calls the *chasm*, as indicated in the figure. Here, pragmatists want to see sound business benefits before adopting the new technology or moving away from ones that are already delivering sound benefits. Modern IP-based VPN technologies are at the point of crossing the chasm and testing adoption by the mainstream market. Moore refers to this phase as moving from the bowling alley to being inside the tornado [Moore 95]. The bowling alley is a period of niche-based adoption driven by compelling customer needs. In the case of IP-based VPNs, the ANX network is a good example of this phase. The tornado is the period when the mass market rapidly adopts the new paradigm. For IP-based VPNs, the tornado period will likely arrive early in the

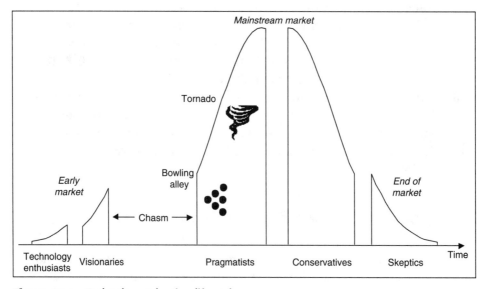

Figure 10.4   Technology adoption life cycle.

twenty-first century. However, when the tornado period does arrive, pricing becomes extremely important, which is good news for enterprises. Also, the tornado phase often results in either a dominant player gaining even more market share or the emergence of a new player if the technology shift or paradigm is radical enough.

If we integrate the market adoption stages depicted in Figure 10.4, the result is the classical S curve of market adoption. Frame relay and ATM have crossed their chasms and moved through their bowling alley and tornado phases, and have now entered into the conservative and pragmatic phases. As would be expected, the revenue growth rates for frame relay and ATM services have been declining, yet are still positive, since they have already captured many of the markets that they will ever penetrate. On the other hand, the markets for voice VPNs, X.25, and private lines are relatively flat or even declining in some regions of the world. These technologies are approaching the end of the market phase. The market views such mature products as a commodity, on which price alone is the principal decision factor.

The latest IP-based VPN technology is poised now to grow rapidly, depending on how quickly it moves through the tornado. Not every technology will make it—as seen in Chapters 8 and 9, the early proprietary tunneling technologies may be largely overtaken by standards-based solutions. There is significant overlap between IPsec and the L2TP tunneling protocol as well. Finally, many of the first IP-based VPN solutions were overlay technologies. As discussed in Chapter 9, network-based solutions may prove to be more cost competitive than these overlay solutions for some enterprise applications.

Sustaining and Disruptive Technologies

Sometimes it is difficult to distinguish the madman from the visionary. A useful business model categorizes technological changes as either sustaining innovation or disruptive technology [Christensen 97]. A sustaining innovation fosters improved product performance through technological change, which may be quite complex. On the other hand, disruptive technology often simply combines older technologies and may actually worsen product price performance in the short term. The dilemma results because sustaining innovation often outstrips the market demand for price performance, while the disruptive technology improves over time and displaces the older, increasingly less justified solution delivered by sustained innovation. Although the author of this model has not applied this analysis directly to telecommunications, some interesting parallels exist. The closest is that of the computing industry, where the mainframes from IBM gave way to the minicomputers from DEC, which were then supplanted by microcomputers [Moore 99]. The move to different scales of computers was a disruptive technology change that resulted in dramatic shifts in market share in the computing market. A recurring theme across many industries is that the dominant players also change as a result of disruptive technological change, while sustaining innovations tend to leave incumbent players in place.

So how does this model apply to the VPN technologies studied in this book? First, the IP-based VPN solutions described in Chapters 8 and 9 qualify as a disruptive technology because they are basically an assembly of existing techniques as an overlay to a public (or shared) IP-based network. Initially, these solutions may not have the best price performance for certain enterprise applications and traffic patterns. However, the economy of scale of a QoS-aware Internet built atop MPLS will likely change these economic considerations early in the twenty-first century and replace the ATM-based infrastructure that many ISPs deployed in the late 1990s [Stephens 98]. Furthermore, the complex QoS and traffic management features of ATM have proven difficult for many enterprises to implement. A solution automatically coupled to the IP-based application that makes it easy for enterprises to administer policy may well be what the marketplace requires. An open question is whether an overlay or network-based solution will deliver the lowest overall life-cycle price performance to the enterprise.

Another potentially disruptive technology will be the emerging datacentric wireless communication networking techniques and associated application software. A promising approach is the Local Multipoint Distribution Service (LMDS) [Brown 99; Skoro 99]. Essentially a cellular network for data, LMDS can deliver capacity at rates up to 155 Mbps, as compared with rates of 8 to 64 kbps delivered over conventional telephony-based wireless networks. Since LMDS can be deployed quickly, it may well be an attractive access alternative for enterprises that are not near the locations where service provider fiber-optic cables run. On the downside, since LMDS operates at millimeter waveband frequencies, it is susceptible to rain fade and poor performance during periods of high humidity. This may limit the deployment of LMDS in certain geographic regions or applications that cannot tolerate downtime during rainy periods. Another important area will be wireless LANs, which have a set of advantages and disadvantages. Rewiring an enterprise building is an expensive proposition that wireless LANs avoid. Additionally, wireless LANs can significantly improve productivity by giving employees access to important resources from wherever they may be located within an enterprise facility. The risk involves security issues, because wireless communication makes eavesdropping so much easier. Here IPsec technology will likely play a significant role.

Of course, there will be a number of sustaining innovations necessary to continue the growth and continuing price performance improvements of IP-based VPNs [Brown 99; Kosiur 98]. As mentioned earlier in this chapter, ISPs need larger and faster routers and switches in order to build a scalable, QoS-aware Internet in the near future. In addition, as the sophistication of hackers increases, the power of cryptographic protection must also keep pace. Furthermore, a cost-effective Public Key Infrastructure (PKI) is fundamental to the IPsec paradigm. Most experts predict that Moore's law regarding the doubling of price performance for electronics every 18 months will continue for the foreseeable future. Sophisticated technologies, such as molecular-level integrated circuits and photonic computing, may be necessary to sustain this trend; however, these techniques are being actively researched in the industry.

Changing Role of the Enterprise in Society

Some telecommunication analysts predict that the optoelectronic network of the future will look something like today's Internet, but some aspects may not be recognizable at all due to disruptive technological innovations. However, the most subtle, yet possibly the most far-reaching, impact may be neither business nor technological, but societal. One significant impact on the future of VPNs may come from government involvement. As discussed in Chapter 7, government regulation and concerns regarding encryption technology already pose a significant challenge for multinational enterprises. As discussed in Chapter 8, one of the greatest social benefits of VPNs may be that of telecommuting. If information workers can productively apply their skills from their homes, then many social benefits may result. Traffic congestion on highways and public transportation systems may decline. The quality of life would also improve for those telecommuters because they could spend more time with their families. However, those who are pioneering these new technologies will likely realize such benefits last, since they must still attend face-to-face meetings and travel around the world in the development of these new and innovative solutions [Naisbitt 82].

The sweeping changes of the Internet-powered information age may have implications [Cairncross 97] that reach even further. Although the majority of people communicated via television and the telephone in 1995, the rapid growth of host computers connected to the Internet, as summarized earlier in this chapter, will change this situation within a few decades if current trends continue. The price of telephone service in the United States is no longer distance dependent. Similarly, a planetwide communication infrastructure girdled by fiber-optic networks should deliver this same distance insensitivity to video and any other application that human beings can conceive. The compelling visual nature of television became the opiate of the masses in the latter half of the twentieth century. However, even with hundreds of channels available on many cable systems, many viewers rue the fact that they frequently find nothing worth watching. Therefore, a pent-up demand exists for an increased array of selections and even video-on-demand services—if the price is right. The worldwide embrace of the Internet will do more than any other technology has done in the past to shrink planetary distances that previously separated cultures, commerce, and companies.

Glossary

AAL (ATM Adaptation Layer) A collection of protocols that transforms input data streams into a sequence of 48-byte payloads within ATM cells. Currently, four AAL types are defined. AAL1 supports constant-bit-rate connection-oriented traffic. AAL2 supports real-time variable-bit-rate traffic. AAL3/4 supports connectionless and connection-oriented variable-bit-rate traffic. AAL5 supports connection-oriented variable bit-rate traffic.

ABR (Available Bit Rate) A service category defined by the ATM Forum that supports variable-bit-rate traffic with feedback control. The ABR standard defines several control mechanisms that allow a network to control a sender's transmission rate between a Minimum Cell Rate (MCR) and a Peak Cell Rate (PCR).

Access concentrator See **RAS** (**Remote Access Server**).

ACK (Acknowledgment) A response that indicates reception of a transmitted message.

AH (Authentication Header) One of the two IPsec protocols, the other being the Encapsulating Security Payload (ESP). AH provides data origin authentication, packet integrity, protection from replay attacks, and a tunneling capability.

AIN (Advanced Intelligent Network) A Telcordia- (formerly Bellcore) defined architecture and set of protocols for implementing circuit-switched, telephony-oriented advanced services and VPNs.

ANSI (American National Standards Institute) The American telecommunications standards organization. See www.ansi.org for more information.

Application proxy   A type of firewall that controls external access by operating at the application layer.

ARP (Address Resolution Protocol)   The discovery protocol used by host computer systems to establish the correct mapping of Internet-layer addresses, also known as IP addresses, to Media Access Control (MAC)–layer addresses.

ARPA (Advanced Research and Projects Agency)   A U.S. federal research funding agency often credited with initially deploying the network that led to the Internet.

AS (Autonomous System)   A collection of networks administered by a common organization. An autonomous system describes a set of networks that share a common external policy. See **BGP**.

Asymmetric cryptosystem   A configuration in which the sender employs an encryption key that is different from the one used by the receiver. See **Public key cryptography**.

ATM (Asynchronous Transfer Mode)   A connection-oriented switching and multiplexing standard that uses fixed-length data cells of 53 bytes, consisting of a 5-byte header and a 48-byte payload. The small, fixed cell size supports high-speed switching and introduces a controlled amount of jitter. ATM is asynchronous in the sense that, unlike TDM, the transmission of cells requires no synchronization to a reference clock.

ATM Forum   An industry-organized group of manufacturers, carriers, and customers that define specifications for ATM-based equipment and services. See www.atmforum.com for more information.

ATM service categories   A set of categories that define QoS parameters, traffic parameters, and the use of feedback. These are: CBR, rt-VBR, nrt-VBR, UBR, and ABR.

Authentication   The process of ensuring that the source of data is indeed who it claims to be. See **Biometrics**, **CHAP**, **PAP**, and **X.509 certificate**.

B Channel (Bearer Channel)   Refers to full-duplex Integrated Services Digital Network (ISDN) TDM service operating at 64 kbps.

BECN (Backward Explicit Congestion Notification)   A notification signal used in frame relay and ATM that is passed backward to the originator of traffic warning of a congested point in the network along the path to the destination. This notification occurs explicitly in the Frame Relay frame header or is defined in the ATM Resource Management (RM) cell.

Best-effort service   A service that has no associated QoS specifications for delay, loss, or jitter.

BGP (Border Gateway Protocol)   An Internet routing protocol used to pass routing information between different Autonomous Systems (AS). BGP passes network-layer address reachability information, the path by which this reachability was determined, and a number of attributes. Routers apply local policy to BGP messages to select the route to network-layer address prefixes.

Biometrics   Use of unique human physical traits, such as fingerprints, retinal scans, or speech recognition, in the authentication process.

B-ISDN (Broadband Integrated Services Digital Network)   An ITU-T-defined set of standards for integrated transmission, switching, and multiplexing of data, audio, and video. B-ISDN has three logical planes: user, control, and management. The user plane provides the basic service as determined by control plane signaling. All three planes use a common ATM layer that operates over a variety of physical layers.

BRI (Basic Rate Interface)   An N-ISDN standard supporting circuit-switched TDM communication at speeds of up to 128 kbps.

Broadcast   The process of sending a communication from one source to multiple destinations.

Brute-force attack   A form of cryptanalysis where the attacker uses all possible keys or passwords in an attempt to crack an encryption scheme or login system.

CA (Certificate Authority)   A trusted third party that associates a public key with proof of identity by producing a digitally signed certificate. See **X.509 certificate**.

CAC (Connection Admission Control)   An algorithm that determines whether a device accepts or rejects a connection request. Generally, CAC algorithms accept requests only if enough capacity and buffer resources exist to establish the connection at the requested quality of service (QoS) without impacting connections already in progress.

CBC (Cipher Block Chaining)   A mechanism used in coordination with symmetric key bulk encryption algorithms (such as DES) to encrypt arbitrarily long strings of data. CBC works by using the results of previous DES operations over portions of the same message as part of the data used to encrypt future portions to make cryptanalysis more difficult.

CBR (Constant Bit Rate)   An ATM service category that corresponds to a constant bandwidth allocation for a traffic flow. It supports circuit emulation, as well as continuous bitstream traffic sources, such as voice, video, or telemetry data.

CCS (Common Channel Signaling)   A telephony-originated technique that uses a shared control signaling channel that is separate from the individual bearer channels.

CCS7 (Common Channel Signaling System Number 7) An ITU-T-defined common channel signaling standard used in telephony and ISDN. It provides NNI signaling and communication with Intelligent Network (IN) components used in telephone networks. The North American variant is called SS7.

CDV (Cell Delay Variation) An ATM QoS parameter that measures the variation in transit time of a cell over a Virtual Channel Connection (VCC). For applications that are jitter-sensitive, this is a critical service parameter.

CDVT (Cell Delay Variation Tolerance) A parameter that specifies the depth of the Peak Cell Rate (PCR) leaky bucket in the Generic Cell Rate Algorithm (GCRA). Effectively, CDVT defines how many back-to-back cells can exist at the line rate in a conforming connection.

CHAP (Challenge Handshake Authentication Protocol) A secure login procedure for dial-in access that avoids sending a password in the clear by using cryptographic hashing. Contrast with **PAP (Password Authentication Protocol)**.

CIDR (Classless Inter-Domain Routing) The commonly used Internet addressing paradigm that passes both the network prefix and a mask of significant bits in the prefix. CIDR supersedes the earlier paradigm of class-based routing, where a mask of significant bits implied the prefix.

CIR (Committed Information Rate) A frame relay traffic management term describing a minimum access rate at which the service provider commits to provide the customer for any given Data Link Connection Identifier (DLCI).

Circuit switching A connection-oriented technique based on either time- or space-division multiplexing and switching providing minimal delay, guaranteed capacity, and privacy of information transfer via physical separation.

CLP (Cell Loss Priority) A single-bit field in the ATM cell header that indicates the discard priority. A CLP value of 1 indicates that an ATM switch can discard this cell during periods of congestion.

CLR (Cell Loss Ratio) An ATM QoS metric defined as the ratio of lost cells to the number of transmitted cells.

Confidentiality Protecting data or traffic patterns from unauthorized disclosure. Encryption is often used to provide confidentiality.

Connectionless A method of communication whereby each component of the communication is handled separately by the network. Connectionless networking does not require establishment of a connection prior to communication of data.

Connection-oriented   A method of communication that requires establishment of a connection by management procedure or signaling prior to transmission of data from the sender to the receiver.

Controlled-Load Service   A service profile defined within the Integrated Services architecture with traffic level measured according to the token bucket. The profile offers a service-level equivalent to an unloaded network.

COPS (Common Open Policy Service)   A TCP-based request-response protocol that a network element can use to refer decisions to a remote policy decision point.

CPE (Customer Premises Equipment)   Equipment deployed on a customer's site. A carrier may offer CPE as part of a service, or a customer may own CPE.

Cryptanalysis   Process of analyzing encrypted data with the goal of recovering the plaintext without knowledge of the cryptographic key.

Cryptography   The discipline of designing and implementing protocols and procedures that enhance the overall security of document storage, retrieval, and transmission. Cryptographic techniques are typically used to add confidentiality, integrity, and/or authentication to messages or documents.

Cryptosystem   A combination of encryption, decryption, authentication, and key management algorithms that delivers confidentiality, integrity, authentication, and nonrepudiation.

CTD (Cell Transfer Delay)   An ATM QoS metric that measures the one-way transit time for a cell to traverse a Virtual Channel Connection (VCC) between two measurement points, typically the source and destination.

CUG (Closed User Group)   A technique of assigning sets of user addresses to groups that are allowed to communicate. By assigning users to multiple groups, intranet and extranet connectivity can be constructed. X.25, frame relay, ATM, firewalls, and BGP all use this concept.

Datagram   See **packet** and **(UDP) User Datagram Protocol**.

DE (Discard Eligible)   A bit field defined within the frame relay header that informs a switch that this frame can be discarded when congestion occurs.

Decryption   The inverse of the process of encryption, formally defined as the transformation from ciphertext to plaintext.

Delay   The amount of time it takes for a data packet to traverse the network from its source to its destination. Also called *latency*.

Denial-of-service attack   A situation in which an attacker floods a system with messages that prevents it from performing other services.

DES (Data Encryption Standard)   One of the oldest symmetric key bulk encryption mechanisms in current use. DES uses a 56-bit key, which many experts regard as too short to adequately protect critical data. See **Triple Data Encryption Standard (3DES)**.

DHCP (Dynamic Host Configuration Protocol)   A protocol that allows end-system computers to automatically obtain an IP host address, subnet mask, and DNS information.

Differentiated Services   A service architecture that applies a per-hop service response to a packet, based upon the contents of the TOS byte in the IP packet header.

Diffie-Hellman (DH) encryption   An asymmetric public-key cryptosystem that provides for the secure exchange of secret keys over a public network, such as the Internet.

Digital certificate   See **X.509 certificate**.

Digital signature   A field associated with a message or document that validates the integrity of the contents. A user generates a digital signature with his or her private key. Therefore, any user can verify the sender's identity and the signed message by retrieving that user's public key in a signed digital certificate from a Certificate Authority (CA).

Digital Subscriber Line (DSL)   A transmission technology that allows transfer of data at higher speeds than those offered by modem communication over the same twisted-pair technology used by telephony. The general notation is xDSL, where the character x denotes a specific standard for the transmission rate in each direction between the user and the network.

Dijkstra algorithm   Also referred to as Shortest Path First (SPF), it is a single-source, shortest-path algorithm that computes all shortest paths from a single point of reference based on a single link metric. Both the Open Shortest Path First (OSPF) and Intermediate System to Intermediate System (IS-IS) routing protocols use this algorithm.

DLCI (Data Link Connection Identifier)   A frame relay address significant only to the local physical interface. In general, the DLCI differs at the endpoints of a frame relay virtual connection.

DNS (Domain Name Service)   A protocol used to support the hierarchical resolution of host names to IP addresses (and vice versa) on the Internet.

DOI (Domain of Interpretation)   An IPsec term describing the set of protocols and parameters negotiated by Internet Key Exchange (IKE) in the establishment of a Security Association (SA).

DS0 (Digital Signal Level 0)   A term used in North America to refer to a single TDM channel operating at 64 kbps.

DS1 (Digital Signal Level 1)   A North American framing standard for transmitting TDM at 1.544 Mbps.

DS3 (Digital Signal Level 3)   A North American framing standard for transmitting TDM at 44.736 Mbps.

E.164   An ITU-T-defined numbering plan for public voice and data networks containing up to 15 digits. The public switched telephone network (PSTN) uses E.164 addressing.

E1   An ITU-T framing standard for transmitting TDM at 2.048 Mbps.

E3   An ITU-T framing standard for transmitting TDM at 34.368 Mbps.

EAP (Extensible Authentication Protocol)   An IETF standard means of extending PPP authentication protocols, such as PAP and CHAP, to include additional authentication data (e.g., biometric data).

EFCI (Explicit Forward Congestion Indication)   A field in the ATM cell header that indicates to the destination that congestion was encountered.

Encapsulation   The protocol mechanism of carrying one protocol over another. Tunneling protocols use encapsulation.

Encryption   A security mechanism used to transform data from an intelligible message (plaintext) into an unintelligible message (ciphertext) using cryptographic algorithms employing a key to provide confidentiality. *Decryption* recovers the plaintext from the ciphertext using a cryptographic key.

End system   A device that terminates an end-to-end protocol. Also called a *host*.

ESP (Encapsulating Security Payload)   One of the two IPsec protocols, the other being the Authentication Header (AH). ESP supports a range of services, including encryption, some authentication functions, tunneling, and protection from replay attacks.

Ethernet   The IEEE 802.3 and ISO set of standards define operation of a LAN protocol at 10, 100, and 1,000 Mbps. Ethernet operates over coax, twisted-pair, and fiber-optic physical media.

Extranet   A computing and network infrastructure supporting controlled communication between a set of cooperating enterprises.

FECN (Forward Explicit Congestion Notification)   A notification signal used in frame relay passed forward to the destination of traffic from a congested point in the network along the path to the destination.

Firewall   A device that operates on received packets at the periphery of a secure network to prevent unauthorized access to important resources. A firewall may examine and/or operate on network-, transport-, and even application-layer information in performing this function.

Flow   A sequence of packets from a single source all addressed to the same remote application. If the application uses TCP or UDP, the same source and destination IP address, as well as identical source and destination port addresses, characterize a flow.

Fragmentation   A process whereby a device breaks an IP packet into smaller packets, or fragments, that are less than or equal to the Maximum Transmission Unit (MTU) size of a link.

Frame relay   Based on the X.25 and HDLC standards, an ITU-T-defined standard for connection-oriented packet switching operating at Layer 2 for efficiently forwarding packets based on the Data Link Connection Identifier (DLCI) field in the frame header.

FRF (Frame Relay Forum)   An industry organization that specifies implementation agreements for frame relay equipment and protocols. See www.frforum.com for more information.

FTP (File Transfer Protocol)   A TCP-based, transaction-oriented file transfer protocol used in TCP/IP networks.

Gbps (Gigabits per second)   A rate equivalent to 10^9 bits per second.

GCRA (Generic Cell Rate Algorithm)   An ATM specification for testing conformance of offered ATM traffic to a set of parameters (see **CDVT**, **MBS**, **PCR**, **SCR**). Equivalent to the leaky bucket algorithm. An arriving cell is conformant if the bucket defined by the traffic parameters has enough remaining space to add the cell.

Guaranteed Service   An Integrated Services service class that provides an upper bound on delay for a traffic load specified by token bucket parameters.

Hashing   A one-way transformation of a variable-length message into a fixed-length message. A good hashing function makes a reverse transformation difficult. A cryptographic hashing function, also called a Message Authentication Code (MAC), uses a secret key when performing the one-way transformation.

HDLC (High-level Data Link Control)   A bit-oriented, synchronous data link–layer protocol developed by the International Standards Organization (ISO). HDLC provides an encapsulation mechanism for transporting data on synchronous serial links using framing characters and Cyclic Redundancy Check (CRC) error detection.

Header   Protocol-specific information associated with a payload that forms a protocol data unit.

HMAC (Hashed Message Authentication Code)   Use of a cryptographic hashing function with a Message Authentication Code (MAC).

Hop   The passage of a data packet from one network switching or routing element to the next.

Host   A workstation, PC, or end system that terminates an end-to-end protocol.

HTTP (HyperText Transfer Protocol)   A TCP-based application-layer protocol used for passing information between Web servers and Web clients.

iBGP (Internal BGP, Interior BGP)   Use of BGP to carry exterior routing information between edge routers within a single administrative routing domain, eliminating the need to redistribute exterior routing to interior routing. iBGP refers to a specific use of BGP and is not a separate protocol.

ICMP (Internet Control Message Protocol)   A network-layer protocol that provides feedback on errors and other information pertinent to IP packet handling.

ICV (Integrity Check Value)   An IPsec AH hash value calculated over data and utilizing some private or secret key material that allows the receiver to validate the integrity of a packet.

IEEE (Institute of Electrical and Electronics Engineers)   A worldwide engineering standards body for the electronics industry. See standards.ieee.org for more information.

IETF (Internet Engineering Task Force)   An organization that develops and specifies protocols and Internet-related standards, generally at the network layer and above. These include routing-, transport-, application-, and session-layer protocols. See www.ietf.org for more information.

IGP (Interior Gateway Protocol)   Historical term referring to a routing protocol used within an Autonomous System (AS).

IKE (Internet Key Exchange)   An IPsec protocol framework that defines the means for hosts to securely negotiate and exchange identification, algorithms, and keys. Specific protocols include ISAKMP and Oakley.

IN (Intelligent Network)   An ITU-T-defined architecture and set of protocols that supports value-added telephony services allowing separation of functions using standard interfaces. See **AIN**, **SCP**, and **SSP**.

Integrated Services   A framework defined by the IETF that supports QoS, resource sharing, packet-drop specification, provision-for-usage feedback, and a Resource ReserVation Protocol (RSVP).

Integrity   A process that ensures received data has not been modified.

Internet   A reference for the loosely administered collection of interconnected networks around the world that share a common addressing structure using IP.

Intranet   Refers to the interior of a private network, which either is not connected to the global Internet or is controlled in some way such that access to certain resources is limited to users within a single enterprise. Intranet also refers to the Web-based computing infrastructure of a single enterprise.

IP (Intelligent Peripheral)   An Intelligent Network (IN) component that implements specialized services, such as a voice response system.

IP (Internet Protocol)   The network-layer protocol used in the Internet standardized by the IETF. IP is a connectionless protocol that provides addressing, routing, security, fragmentation and reassembly, and support for QoS in the packet header.

IPng (IP next generation)   See **IPv6 (Internet Protocol version 6)**.

IPsec (IP security)   A set of IETF standards that defines a suite of security protocols that provide confidentiality, integrity, and authentication services. See AH, ESP, ISAKMP, and IKE.

IPv4 (Internet Protocol version 4)   The version of the Internet Protocol in wide use today.

IPv6 (Internet Protocol version 6)   The version number of the IETF standardized next-generation Internet Protocol (IPng) proposed as a successor to IPv4.

ISAKMP (Internet Security Association Key Management Protocol)   An extensible protocol-encoding scheme that complies to the Internet Key Exchange (IKE) framework for establishment of Security Associations (SAs).

ISDN (Integrated Services Digital Network)   See **N-ISDN**.

IS-IS (Intermediate System to Intermediate System)   A link-state routing protocol for connectionless Open Systems Interconnection (OSI) networks, similar to Open Shortest Path First (OSPF). ISO standard 10589 documents the IS-IS protocol specification.

ISO (International Standards Organization)   An international organization for standardization, based in Geneva, Switzerland, that establishes voluntary standards. The documents produced by the ISO are termed *International Standards*. Well known for the seven-layer OSI Reference Model (OSIRM). See www.iso.ch for more information.

ISP (Internet Service Provider)   A supplier that provides transit for client network or individual user IP traffic, access to the public Internet, and other optional services.

ITU (International Telecommunications Union)   A United Nations treaty organization, previously called the Consultative Committee for International Telegraphy and Telephony (CCITT). The ITU Telecommunications standardization sector (ITU-T) defines standards for N-ISDN, frame relay, B-ISDN, IP, and a variety of other transmission, voice, and data-related protocols. See www.itu.int for more information.

IXC (Inter-eXchange Carrier)   A public carrier providing connectivity between Local Exchange Carriers (LECs).

Jitter   The perturbation of interpacket arrival times compared to the interpacket transmission times of the original sequence. Also known as *delay variation*. See **CDV (Cell Delay Variation)**.

Kbps (Kilobits per second)   Data transfer speed of 10^3 bits per second.

Kerberos   A session-oriented key distribution and authentication technology developed at MIT that provides security services to hosts over an insecure network.

Key   A digit string used by a cryptographic algorithm to produce ciphertext.

Key escrow   The controversial practice of safely storing a copy of a private or secret key so that a trusted authority can recover protected data or act in the interest of crime prevention or national security.

L2F (Layer 2 Forwarding)   A protocol developed by Cisco that tunnels higher-layer protocols over IP employing encryption to implement VPNs. See **L2TP**.

L2TP (Layer 2 Tunneling Protocol)   An IETF standardized protocol used primarily for support of dial-in connections. A successor to the proprietary Microsoft PPTP and Cisco L2F protocols, L2TP gives mobile users the appearance of being on a enterprise LAN.

LAN (Local Area Network)   A local communications environment, typically constructed with privately operated wiring and communications facilities.

Layer 1   Commonly used to describe the physical layer in the OSI Reference Model. Examples include the copper wiring or fiber-optic cabling that interconnects electronic devices.

Layer 2   Commonly used to describe the data link layer in the OSI Reference Model. Examples include Ethernet, frame relay, and ATM.

Layer 3   Commonly used to describe the network layer in the OSI Reference Model. Examples include IP and Novell's Internet Packet eXchange (IPX).

LDAP (Lightweight Directory Access Protocol)   A subset of the ITU-T X.500 directory access protocol optimized for TCP/IP networking.

Leaky bucket   See **GCRA (Generic Cell Rate Algorithm)**.

LEC (Local Exchange Carrier)   A communication services provider, such as a monopoly telephone network or an independent telephone company, constrained by government regulations to provide services within a localized geographic region.

LSA (Link-State Advertisement)   A process and message format that conveys information concerning the local node and the state of local links that allow each node to construct the overall topology of the network. Most interior routing protocols use LSAs (e.g., OSPF, IS-IS, and PNNI).

MAC (Medium Access Control) A protocol defined by the IEEE that controls workstation access to a shared transmission medium. The MAC sublayer interfaces to the Logical Link Control (LLC) sublayer and the Physical layer. Examples are 802.3 for Ethernet and 802.5 for Token Ring.

MAC (Message Authentication Code) A standard that uses DES Cipher Block Chaining (CBC) to produce a digital signature.

Man-in-the-middle attack Scenarios in which a malicious user can intercept messages and insert other messages that compromise the otherwise secure exchange of information between two parties.

maxCTD (maximum Cell Transfer Delay) An ATM QoS metric that measures the transit time for a cell to traverse a virtual connection between two measurement points.

Mbps (Megabits per second) Data transfer rate of 10^6 bits per second.

MBS (Maximum Burst Size) An ATM traffic parameter used in conjunction with the Sustainable Cell Rate (SCR) that describes the number of cells that may be transmitted at the peak rate as determined by the GCRA leaky bucket algorithm.

MCR (Minimum Cell Rate) An ATM traffic parameter related to the Available Bit Rate (ABR) service. The network varies the allowed cell rate of an ABR connection between the MCR and the PCR using Resource Management (RM) cells.

MD4, MD5 (Message Digest) Commonly employed versions of hashing algorithms that produce a fixed-length message digest.

MPLS (MultiProtocol Label Switching) A switching technique that forwards packets based on a fixed-length label inserted between the link and network layer or use of a native Layer 2 label, such as frame relay or ATM. Similar to frame relay and ATM in function, MPLS differs from these protocols by virtue of its tight coupling to IP routing protocols.

MTU (Maximum Transmission Unit) The maximum size of a data frame that can be carried across a data link layer. Every host and router interface has an associated MTU related to the physical medium to which the interface is connected; an end-to-end network path has an associated MTU that is the minimum of the individual-hop MTUs within the path.

Multicast A communication service that delivers a single information flow to multiple destinations.

NAP (Network Access Point) A point at which Internet Service Providers (ISPs) interconnect.

NAS (Network Access Server) See **RAS (Remote Access Server)**.

NAT (Network Address Translation)   The process of converting from one IP address space to another. Enterprises often employ NAT to share a few public IP addresses among many private IP addresses.

NBMA (Non-Broadcast Multi-Access)   A network that does not support broadcast, yet provides multiple points of access. Examples are X.25, frame relay, and ATM.

N-ISDN (Narrowband Integrated Services Digital Network)   An ITU-T-defined set of standards that encompasses operation over TDM at the DS1/E1 rate and below. N-ISDN interworks with traditional telephony standards.

NNI (Network-Node Interface, Network-Network Interface)   A generic term that refers to the interface between two switches or two networks in frame relay and ATM networking standards.

Nonrepudiation   A process of ensuring that a user cannot later deny that he or she sent a message.

nrt-VBR (non-real-time Variable Bit Rate)   One of two variable-bit-rate ATM service categories in which timing information is not crucial. Generally used for delay-tolerant applications with bursty characteristics, such as packet data.

Oakley protocol   A mechanism for cryptographic key exchange specified by ISAKMP that uses an embellished version of the Diffie-Hellman key exchange algorithm.

OC (Optical Carrier)   Fundamental unit in the SONET (Synchronous Optical Network) hierarchy. OC indicates an optical signal and n represents increments of 51.84 Mbps. Thus, OC-1, -3, -12, -48, and -192 equal optical signals of 51, 155, 622, 2,488, and 9,953 Mbps, respectively.

OSI (Open Systems Interconnection)   The seven-layer protocol architecture developed by the ISO in the 1980s as a standard to enable multivendor interoperability. Now primarily of historical interest since TCP/IP has emerged as the de facto standard that meets the interoperability objective.

OSPF (Open Shortest Path First)   An interior routing protocol that uses a link-state protocol coupled with the Dijkstra shortest path–selection algorithm.

Outsourcing   The business arrangement whereby one organization performs functions for another. For example, an enterprise may outsource its network, its LAN, or even its applications.

Packet   A set of information composed of a header and payload. The header contains sufficient information for a packet-switching network to transfer the packet to the destination and perform any services requested by the user.

Packet switching   A technique that segments user data into fixed or variable-length units called *packets*, composed of a header and a payload. The network operates on the fields in the header in a store-and-forward manner to reliably transfer the packet to the destination.

PAP (Password Authentication Protocol)   A protocol that allows peers connected by a PPP link to authenticate each other using the simple exchange of a username and password.

Password   A string of letters, digits, and other characters used as a basic level of authentication in many systems.

Path message   An RSVP message generated by the data source that describes the characteristics of the data flow.

PBX (Private Branch eXchange)   A circuit switch owned by a single enterprise that may perform value-added features, such as abbreviated dialing, caller identification, and conference calling.

PCM (Pulse Code Modulation)   A telephony standard for converting analog signal levels into digital values for transmission using Time Division Multiplexing (TDM).

PCR (Peak Cell Rate)   An ATM traffic parameter used in conjunction with CDVT that determines whether traffic conforms to a peak rate defined by the GCRA leaky bucket algorithm. In general, the peak rate may be less than the access line rate.

PDH (Plesiochronous Digital Hierarchy)   A legacy Time Division Multiplexing (TDM) technique for carrying digital data. *Plesiochronous* means nearly synchronous, as opposed to truly synchronous transmission systems defined by the SONET and SDH standards.

PGP (Pretty Good Privacy)   A protocol that supports encryption and digital signatures. Authentication is determined using a web-of-trust model, as opposed to the hierarchical distribution of certificates in IPsec.

PNNI (Private Network-to-Network Interface)   The ATM Forum specification for the hierarchical distribution of topology information among switches in an ATM network to allow for the computation and establishment of virtual connections. The topology distribution protocol is similar to link-state routing protocols. The specification also includes a signaling protocol to establish connections using source-defined and alternate routing.

PoP (Point of Presence)   A physical location on a carrier or service provider network at which a user can connect.

PPP (Point-to-Point Protocol)   A data link protocol used on dial-in and remote access links. PPP operates over a wide range of physical- and link-layer protocols. It also supports a number of authentication protocols, such as PAP, CHAP, and EAP.

PPTP (Point-to-Point Tunneling Protocol)   A widely used proprietary protocol developed by Microsoft and other vendors. Intended primarily for dial-in and remote user access. The IETF-defined L2TP protocol standard supports many of the functions in PPTP.

PRI (Primary Rate Interface)   An N-ISDN standard supporting circuit-switched TDM communication at speeds of up to 2.048 Mbps internationally (1.536 Mbps in North America) in increments of 64 kbps.

PSTN (Public Switched Telephone Network)   A generic term referring to the public telephone network commonly used by ordinary telephones, PBXs, modems, and facsimile machines.

Public-key cryptography   An asymmetric cryptosystem in which the sender uses a private key and the receiver uses a widely known public key.

Public Key Infrastructure (PKI)   A system of Certificate Authorities (CAs) and registration authorities that use digital certificates to distribute public keys and authenticate parties engaged in secure communications.

PVC (Permanent Virtual Connection)   A permanently established virtual connection, usually configured via administrative means.

QoS (Quality of Service)   A set of metrics that define the quality delivered to a specific connection, flow, access circuit, or other aspect of a user's communication network service.

RADIUS (Remote Authentication Dial-In User Service)   An IETF standardized protocol that supports authentication, management, and accounting for remote and dial-in users. An enterprise may run a RADIUS server that uses shared Remote Access Server (RAS) resources provided by an ISP.

RAS (Remote Access Server)   Devices that provide dial-in network access to users over telephone or ISDN lines. These devices provide modem pools and implement PPP protocols with dial-in users, employing authentication protocols like PAP or CHAP. An RAS device may have authentication data stored within it or on a remote server using a protocol like RADIUS.

RED (Random Early Detection)   A congestion-avoidance algorithm that randomly discards packets when the queue depth in a router exceeds a predetermined threshold. This action implicitly signals the onset of congestion, and TCP senders throttle back their transmission window.

RFC (Request for Comments)   RFCs are documents produced by the IETF for the purpose of documenting IETF protocols, operational procedures, and other related information.

RIP (Routing Information Protocol) RIP is a classful, distance-vector, hop-count-based, interior-routing protocol. Although declared historical by the IETF, a version 2 specification is being developed to add the CIDR capability.

Routing The process of calculating the forwarding table based on network topology information determined from link-state advertisements (LSAs) and/or BGP update messages.

RSA (Rivest Shamir Adleman) A proprietary public-key cryptosytem (named after the inventors) used in the Secure Sockets Layer (SSL) in Web browsers.

RSVP (Resource reSerVation Protocol) An IP-based protocol used for communicating application QoS and capacity requirements to intermediate transit nodes in a network. RSVP uses a soft-state refresh mechanism to maintain path and reservation state in each node in the reservation path.

RTCP (Real-Time Control Protocol) An IETF standard that controls and monitors RTP sessions and provides for the measurement of performance.

RTP (Real-Time Transport Protocol) Part of the TCP/IP suite, RTP operates over UDP and conveys sequence numbers and timestamps between packet video and audio applications. Used in VoIP and Web-based audio and video playback applications.

RTT (Round-Trip Time) The time required for data traffic to travel from its origin to its destination and back again.

rt-VBR (real-time Variable Bit Rate) One of the two variable-bit-rate ATM service categories in which timing information is critical. Generally used for delay-intolerant applications with bursty transmission characteristics, such as packet voice, audio, and video.

SA (Security Association) An IPsec term that defines the protocols and keys that a pair of endpoints will use to accomplish secure communication. See **SPI (Security Parameters Index)**.

SCP (Service Control Point) An Intelligent Network (IN) architectural component that is a remote processor and database. It is invoked by using transactions generated by a Service Switching Point (SSP).

SCR (Sustainable Cell Rate) An ATM traffic parameter that characterizes a bursty source. It defines the maximum allowable rate for a source in terms of the Peak Cell Rate (PCR) and the Maximum Burst Size (MBS).

SDH (Synchronous Digital Hierarchy) ITU-T-defined standard for the physical layer of high-speed optical transmission systems. Similar to SONET in terms of transmission speeds; however, differences in overhead functions make these systems incompatible. See **STM (Synchronous Transfer Module)** for the definition of standard rates.

SDLC (Synchronous Data Link Control)   A serial, bit-oriented, full-duplex, link-layer communications protocol developed by IBM for SNA that was a precursor to HDLC.

SG (Security Gateway)   An IPsec term for the point at which either the Authentication Header (AH) and/or Encapsulating Security Payload (ESP) tunnel mode is implemented.

SHA (Secure Hash Algorithm)   A U.S. government National Institute of Standards and Technology (NIST) standardized hashing function. The current version is SHA-1.

SIP (Session Initiation Protocol)   An IETF standardized protocol for initiating a session or allowing a mobile user to register a name association with an IP address. Used for initiating Voice over IP (VoIP) communication sessions.

SLA (Service-Level Agreement)   A contract between a network service provider and a subscriber that quantifies the minimum level of service that the provider must deliver without supplying some form of rebate.

SLIP (Serial Line IP)   An early link layer protocol that supported dial-in access to the Internet. It has largely been superseded by PPP.

Smart card   A hardware-based authentication scheme implemented on a credit card—size device that contains a microprocessor implementing the authentication algorithm.

SNA (Systems Network Architecture)   The name used to refer to a collection of networking technologies invented and deployed by IBM throughout the 1970s and early 1980s to interconnect mainframes and peripheral devices.

Sniffer   Applications and devices that can examine all traffic on a LAN segment and either store it for later analysis or perform some amount of interpretation of the information.

SNMP (Simple Network Management Protocol)   A User Datagram Protocol (UDP)-based network management protocol used predominantly in TCP/IP networks. SNMP can be used to monitor, poll, and control network devices.

Soft state   A self-administered state that times out and removes itself unless periodically refreshed. See **RSVP**.

SONET (Synchronous Optical Network)   A Bellcore- and ANSI-defined North American standard for high-speed fiber-optic transmission systems. Has equivalent transmission rates to the ITU-T SDH, but the overhead usage is incompatible. See **OC** and **STS** for the definition of standard rates.

SPI (Security Parameters Index)   A value carried in AH and ESP protocols to enable the receiving system to select the security association (SA) under which a received packet will be processed. The combination of a destination address, a security protocol, and an SPI uniquely identifies an SA.

SS7 (Signaling System Number 7)   The North American variant of Common Channel Signaling (CCS). See **CCS7**.

SSL (Secure Sockets Layer)   A security protocol designed to serve as a shim between TCP and a session-layer protocol (originally and most popularly HTTP). SSL is a flexible mechanism that allows for the selection of mutually satisfactory security protocols and modes, as well as the security identification of one or both parties utilizing a public key attached to an X.509 public-key certificate.

SSP (Service Switching Point)   An Intelligent Network (IN) architectural component that interfaces to subscribers and other IN components. See **IP, SCP, STP**.

STM (Synchronous Transfer Module)   STM-N is the basic unit of SDH (Synchronous Digital Hierarchy) defined in increments of 155.52 Mbps. The variable N represents multiples of this rate. Commonly encountered rates are STM-1 at 155.52 Mbps, STM-4 at 622.08 Mbps, STM-16 at 2.488 Gbps, and STM-48 at 9.953 Gbps. In general, an STM-N payload may contain multiple lower-speed payloads. The notation STM-Nc indicates concatenation of the TDM payload to operate as a single high-speed bit stream.

STP (Signal Transfer Point)   A packet switch commonly used in telephone networks to support the Common Channel Signaling 7 (CCS7) protocol for connecting components in the Intelligent Network (IN).

STS (Synchronous Transfer Signal)   STS-N is the basic unit of the SONET multiplexing hierarchy defined in increments of 51.84 Mbps. Commonly encountered rates are STS-3 at 155.52 Mbps, STS-12 at 622.08 Mbps, STS-48 at 2.488 Gbps, and STS-192 at 9.953 Gbps. Usually, STS is viewed as an electrical signal to differentiate it from the SONET optical signal level designated as OC-N. In general, an STS-N payload may contain multiple lower-speed payloads. The notation STS-Nc indicates concatenation of the TDM payload to operate as a single high-speed bit stream.

SVC (Switched Virtual Connection)   A virtual connection dynamically established in response to signaling and released in response to signaling or a failure condition.

Symmetric cryptosystem   A configuration whereby the sender and receiver both employ the same secret encryption key. See **DES (Data Encryption Standard)**.

T1   A four-wire transmission repeater system for operation at 1.544 Mbps. Also used to refer to a DS1-formatted digital signal. See **DS1 (Digital Signal Level 1)**.

T3   Another name used to refer to a DS3-formatted digital signal. See **DS3 (Digital Signal Level 3)**.

TACACS (Terminal Access Controller Access Control System)   A proprietary Cisco protocol that performs remote authentication and accounting. Similar to RADIUS.

Tbps (Terabits per second)   Transmission rate of 10^{12} bits per second.

TCP (Transmission Control Protocol)   A transport-layer protocol that provides reliable session-oriented establishment of logical host-to-host connections over an IP network. TCP implements an efficient packet acknowledgment system that assures applications of an error-free, properly ordered byte stream. Many of the popular application-layer protocols, such as HTTP, Telnet, and FTP, run over TCP.

TDM (Time Division Multiplexing)   A multiplexing method, developed initially for economic reasons in telephone networks, that is now the basis of digital data communication networks. TDM aggregates multiple simultaneous circuits over a single high-speed channel by assigning an individual time slot to each circuit.

Telnet   A TCP-based terminal-emulation protocol used in TCP/IP networks, predominantly used for logging into remote systems.

Token bucket   A traffic-monitoring scheme that uses a stream of tokens flowing into a bucket of fixed capacity to determine whether an arriving packet conforms to the traffic parameters specified by the token rate and the bucket depth. If an arriving packet finds sufficient tokens in the bucket, then it is conformant and removes that quantity of tokens from the bucket. Otherwise, an arriving packet is deemed nonconforming and does not remove any tokens from the bucket. RSVP uses the token bucket definition. It is similar in result, yet different in implementation, to the leaky bucket algorithm.

TOS (Type Of Service)   A 1-byte field in the IP packet header designed to contain values that indicate how each packet should be handled in the network. The diffserv standard redefines usage of this byte.

Triple Data Encryption Standard (3DES)   Adds security to the DES algorithm by performing the operation three times with different subkeys.

Trojan horse   A program with a hidden purpose that compromises security in some way.

TTL (Time To Live) A field in an IP packet header that indicates how long the packet is valid. The TTL value is decremented at each hop; when the TTL equals 0, the packet is usually discarded because it has exceeded its maximum hop count.

Tunneling A process that carries one protocol over another using encapsulation, but also creates a logical connection with additional processing between endpoints. This additional processing may provide authentication, encryption, or other services. L2F, L2TP, PPTP, and IPsec all support tunneling.

UBR (Unspecified Bit Rate) An ATM Forum–defined service category for best-effort traffic. The UBR service category provides no QoS guarantees.

UDP (User Datagram Protocol) A transport-layer protocol that provides a minimal set of services for transporting application data in IP datagrams for delivery to a complementary application running on a remote host. Unlike TCP, UDP supports no error checking, packet acknowledgment, or virtual session control. Therefore, applications that employ UDP are simple request-response applications, such as DNS or SNMP, or those that require real-time performance, such as RTP for transport of voice and video.

UNI (User-Network Interface) An interface between a user and a network as defined in frame relay and ATM specifications.

UPC (Usage Parameter Control) A reference to the implementation of leaky bucket-based traffic policing done at a User-Network Interface (UNI). See **GCRA**.

VBR (Variable Bit Rate) A generic term for sources that transmit data in an intermittent or bursty manner. The ATM Forum divides VBR into a real-time and non-real-time (rt-VBR and nrt-VBR) service categories in terms of QoS requirements. See also **nrt-VBR** and **rt-VBR**.

VC (Virtual Connection, Virtual Circuit, Virtual Call, Virtual Channel) A generic term used to refer to a connection-oriented data service, such as X.25, frame relay, or ATM.

VCC (Virtual Channel Connection) An end-to-end connection between two ATM devices. Sometimes referred to as a VC. A VCC may be permanent (PVC) or switched (SVC).

VCI (Virtual Connection Identifier) Used in conjunction with the VPI, it is a field in the ATM cell header that identifies the local end of an ATM Virtual Channel Connection (VCC). In general, the VCI (and the VPI) may differ at the endpoints of a VCC.

VoIP (Voice over IP) A series of complementary technologies designed to provide telephony-style voice service on top of an IP network. VoIP is of interest to people trying to leverage their existing network infrastructure, as well as those looking for a potentially more cost-effective alternative to circuit switching.

VPC (Virtual Path Connection)   A connectivity path between two end systems across an ATM switching fabric. Sometimes referred to as a VP. A VPC can carry several VCCs within it. A VPC may be permanent (PVC) or switched (SVC).

VPI (Virtual Path Identifier)   A field in the ATM cell header that identifies the local end of an ATM Virtual Path Connection (VPC) or Virtual Channel Connection (VCC). In general, the VPI may differ at the endpoints of a VPC or VCC.

VPN (Virtual Private Network)   A network that shares resources with other VPNs but provides privacy. Privacy can mean not only confidentiality and integrity, but separation of capacity as well. Several means exist to implement VPNs, as covered in this book: circuit switching, connection-oriented packet switching, and technologies overlaid on a shared connectionless IP network infrastructure. The overlay technologies include Network Address Translation (NAT), firewalls, tunneling protocols, security gateways, and network-based routing solutions.

WAN (Wide Area Network)   A network environment in which the elements of the network are located at significant distances from each other and typically uses carrier facilities.

WDM (Wavelength Division Multiplexing)   A communication technique whereby multiple digital bitstreams modulate different optical wavelengths to share a single fiber-optic strand.

Window   The technique of establishing the number of frames or packets that can be outstanding (unacknowledged) before the source can transmit again. Examples of windowing protocols are X.25 and TCP.

WWW (World Wide Web)   The global collection of Web servers, interconnected by the Internet, that use the HyperText Transfer Protocol (HTTP).

X.25   An ITU-T-defined standard for connection-oriented packet switching that operates at Layer 3 on an end-to-end basis and Layer 2 on a hop-by-hop basis.

X.509 certificate   A document containing public-key material combined with fields identifying the owner and issuer of the certificate. The Certificate Authority (CA) digitally signs this document to ensure validity of the contents.

References

[ADSL Forum] ADSL Forum, *ADSL Forum Home Page*, http://www.adsl
.com/adsl/.

[Adwuche 99] D. Adwuche, "MPLS and Traffic Engineering in IP Networks," *IEEE Communications*, December 1999.

[ANSI T1.105] ANSI, *Telecommunications—Synchronous Optical Network (SONET)—Basic Description Including Multiplex Structures, Rates, and Formats*, T1.105-1995.

[ANSI T1.617] ANSI, *ISDN—Signaling Specification for Frame Relay Bearer Service for Digital Subscriber Signaling System Number 1 (DSS1)*, T1.617-1991, October 1991.

[ANSI T1.617] ANSI, *ISDN—Signaling Specification for Frame Relay Bearer Service for Digital Subscriber Signaling System Number 1 (DSS1) (Protocol Encapsulation and PICS)*, T1.617a-1994, January 1994.

[ANSI X9.17] ANSI, *Financial Institution Key Management (Wholesale)*, ANSI X9.17-1995.

[AT&T 94] AT&T, "AT&T Implements City Pair Pricing for Accunet T1.5 IOC Service," July 18, 1994, www.att.com/press/0794/940718.bsb.html.

[AT&T 99] AT&T, "Virtual Private Networks and the Enterprise: A Market Assessment," Broadband Publishing, www.vpdn.com, 1999.

[ATMF PNNI 1.0] ATM Forum, *Private Network-Network Interface Specification Version 1.0*, af-pnni-0055.00, March 1996.

[ATMF TM 4.0] ATM Forum, *ATM Forum Traffic Management Specification, Version 4.0*, af-tm-0056.000, April 1996.

[Awdeh 94] R. Awdeh, H. Mouftah, "Survey of ATM Switch Architectures," Computer Networks and ISDN Systems, Number 27, 1995.

[Baker 97] R. Baker, *Extranets*, McGraw-Hill, 1997.

[Baran 64] P. Baran et al., "On Distributed Communications," RAND Corporation, 1964, www.rand.org/publications/rm/baran.list.html.

[Bear 76] D. Bear, *Principles of Telecommunication—Traffic Engineering*, Peter Petringus Ltd., 1976.

[Bennett 99] J. Bennett, C. Partridge, N. Shectman, "Packet Reordering Is Not Pathological Network Behavior," *IEEE/ACM Transactions on Networking*, December 1999.

[Bertsekas 92] D. Bertsekas, R. Gallager, *Data Networks—Second Edition*, Prentice-Hall, 1992.

[Black 95a] U. Black, *The X Series Recommendations*, McGraw-Hill, 1995.

[Black 95b] U. Black, *Frame Relay Networks*, McGraw-Hill, 1995.

[Black 95c] U. Black, *ATM: Foundation for Broadband Networks*, Prentice-Hall, 1995.

[Boyle 99] J. Boyle, R. Cohen, D. Durham, S. Herzog, R. Rajan, A. Sastry, "The COPS (Common Open Policy Service) Protocol," IETF, draft-ietf-rap-cops-07.txt, August 1999.

[Briere 90] D. Briere, *Virtual Networks—A Buyer's Guide*, Artech, 1990.

[Brown 99] S. Brown, *Implementing Virtual Private Networks*, McGraw-Hill, 1999.

[Cairncross 97] F. Cairncross, *The Death of Distance*, Harvard Business School Press, 1997.

[Cantelon 92] P. Cantelon, *The History of MCI—The Early Years 1968–1988*, Heritage Press, 1992.

[Cerf 74] V. Cerf, R. Kahn, "A Protocol for Packet Network Interconnection," *IEEE Transactions on Communications*, May 1974.

[Checkpoint 99] "Redefining the Virtual Private Network," www.checkpoint.com, 1999.

[Chorafas 90] D. Chorafas, H. Steinmann, *Intelligent Networks—Telecommunications Solutions for the 1990s*, CRC Press, 1990.

[Christensen 97] C. Christensen, *The Innovator's Dilemma—When New Technologies Cause Great Firms to Fail*, Harvard Business School Press, 1997.

[Cisco 99] Cisco, "Intranet/Extranet VPNs Making a Case for Secure, Cost-Effective Managed Network Services," www.cisco.com, 1999.

[Coffman 98] K. Coffman and A. Odlyzko, "The Size and Growth Rate of the Internet," *First Monday*, October 1998, www.firstmonday.dk/.

[Comer 95] D. Comer, *Internetworking with TCP/IP Vol. I: Principles, Protocols, and Architecture*, Prentice-Hall, 1995.

[Cosine 99] Cosine Networks, "Moving into the Cloud: The Case for Network-Based VPNs," 1999, www.vpdn.com/content/vpnbackground/default.asp#WhitePapers.

[Crowcroft 99] J. Crowcroft, M. Handley, I. Wakeman, *Interworking Multimedia*, Morgan Kaufmann, 1999.

[Cypser 78] R. Cyspser, *Communications Architecture for Distributed Systems*, Addison Wesley, 1978.

[Data Fellows 99] Data Fellows, "Total Cost of Ownership in Data Security," www.datafellows.com, July 1999.

[de Prycker 95] M. de Prycker, *Asynchronous Transfer Mode—Solution for Broadband ISDN*, Prentice-Hall, 1995.

[Diffie 76] W. Diffie, M. Hellman, "New Directions in Cryptography," *IEEE Transactions on Information Theory*, November 1976.

[Drake 99] J. Drake, "Traffic Engineering Using Smart Connections," Fore Systems, UUnet MPLS Workshop, 1999.

[Feit 98] S. Feit, *TCP/IP—Signature Edition*, McGraw-Hill, 1998.

[Felstaine 99] E. Felstaine, R. Cohen, "On the Distribution of Routing Computation in Hierarchical ATM Networks," *IEEE/ACM Transactions on Networking*, December 1999.

[Ferguson 98] P. Ferguson, G. Huston, *Quality of Service*, Wiley, 1998.

[Flanagan 97] T. Flanagan, E. Safdie, "Internet Security Primer, Applied Technologies Group," www.techguide.com/, 1998.

[Floyd 93] Floyd, V. Jacobson, "Random Early Detection Gateways for Congestion Avoidance," *IEEE/ACM Transactions on Networking*, August 1993.

[Fowler 99] D. Fowler, *Virtual Private Networks*, Morgan Kaufmann, 1999.

[FRF 12] Frame Relay Forum, *Frame Relay Fragmentation Implementation Agreement*, FRF.12, December 15, 1997.

[FRF 3.1] Frame Relay Forum Technical Committee, *Multiprotocol Encapsulation Implementation Agreement*, FRF 3.1, June 1995.

[Gibson 99a] M. Gibson, J. Crowcroft, "Use of SIP for the Reservation of QoS Guaranteed Paths," draft-gibson-sip-qos-resv-00.txt, October 1999.

[Gibson 99b] M. Gibson, "The Management of MPLS LSPs for Scalable QoS Service Provision," draft-gibson-manage-mpls-qos-00.txt, October 1999.

[Goralski 95] W. Goralski, *Introduction to ATM Networking*, McGraw-Hill, 1995.

[Goralski 97] W. Goralski, *SONET*, McGraw-Hill, 1997.

[Goralski 99] W. Goralski, *Frame Relay for High-Speed Networks*, Wiley, 1999.

[Hafner 98] K. Hafner, M. Lyon, *Where Wizards Stay Up Late: The Origins of the Internet*, Touchstone, 1998.

[Higgins 99] K. Higgins, "Priority Traffic," *Internet Week*, September 20, 1999.

[Hobbes 99] R. Hobbes, "Hobbes' Internet Timeline," 1999, v4.2http://www.isoc.org/guest/zakon/Internet/History/HIT.html.

[Huitema 95] C. Huitema, *Routing in the Internet*, Prentice-Hall, 1995.

[Huston 99] G. Huston, *ISP Survival Guide*, Wiley, 1999.

[Ibe 99] O. Ibe, *Remote Access Networks and Services—The Internet Access Companion*, Wiley, 1999.

[IEEE 802.1D] IEEE, *ANSI/IEEE Standard 802.1D—Local and Metropolitan Area Networks, Part 3: Media Access Control (MAC) Bridges*, IEEE, 1998.

[Insight 96] Insight Research Corporation, *Private Line Services 1996–2001*, June 1996.

[ITU G.702] ITU-T, *Digital Hierarchy Bit Rates*, Recommendation G.702, 1988.

[ITU G.707] ITU-T, *Network Node Interface for the Synchronous Digital Hierarchy (SDH)*, Recommendation G.707, 1996.

[ITU G.711] ITU-T, *Pulse Code Modulation (PCM) of Voice Frequencies*, Recommendation G.711, 1988.

[ITU H.323] ITU-T, *Packet-Based Multimedia Communications Systems*, Recommendation H.323, February 1998.

[ITU I.211] ITU-T, B-ISDN Service Aspects, Recommendation I.211, March 1993.

[ITU I.356] ITU-T, *B-ISDN ATM Layer Cell Transfer Performance*, Recommendation I.356, October 1996.

[ITU I.363.1] ITU-T, *B-ISDN ATM Adaptation Layer Specification: Type 1 AAL*, Recommendation I.363.1, August 1996.

[ITU I.363.2] ITU-T, *B-ISDN ATM Adaptation Layer Specification: Type 2 AAL*, Recommendation I.363.2, September 1997.

[ITU I.363.3] ITU-T, *B-ISDN ATM Adaptation Layer Specification: Type 3/4 AAL*, Recommendation I.363.2, August 1996.

[ITU I.363.5] ITU-T, *B-ISDN ATM Adaptation Layer Specification: Type 5 AAL*, Recommendation I.363.5, August 1996.

[ITU I.370] ITU-T, *Congestion Management for the ISDN Frame Relaying Bearer Service*, Recommendation I.370, 1991.

[ITU I.371] ITU-T, *Traffic Control and Congestion Control in B-ISDN*, Recommendation I.371, 1996.

[ITU I.610] ITU-T, *B-ISDN Operation and Maintenance Principles and Functions*, Recommendation I.610, November 1995.

[ITU Q.700] ITU-T, *Introduction to CCITT Signalling System No. 7*, Recommendation Q.700, March 1993.

[ITU Q.922] ITU-T, *ISDN Data Link Layer Specification for Frame Mode Bearer Services*, Recommendation Q.922, 1992.

[ITU Q.931] ITU-T, *Digital Subscriber Signalling System No. 1 (DSS 1)—ISDN User-Network Interface Layer 3 Specification for Basic Call Control*, Recommendation Q.931, March 1993.

[ITU Q.933] ITU-T, *ISDN Signaling Specification for Frame Mode Bearer Services*, Recommendation Q.933, 1991.

[ITU Q.1201] ITU-T, *Principles of Intelligent Network Architecture*, Recommendation I.312/Q.1201, October 1992.

[ITU Q.1211] ITU-T, *Introduction to Intelligent Network Capability Set 1*, Recommendation Q.1211, March 1993.

[ITU Q.1213] ITU-T, *Global Functional Plane for Intelligent Network CS-1*, Recommendation Q.1213, October 1995.

[ITU Q.1214] ITU-T, *Distributed Functional Plane for Intelligent Network CS-1*, Recommendation Q.1214, October 1995.

[ITU Q.1215] ITU-T, *Physical Plane for Intelligent Network CS-1*, Recommendation Q.1215, October 1995.

[ITU Q.1218] ITU-T, *Intelligent Network Interface Specifications for Capability Set 1*, Recommendation Q.1218, October 1995.

[ITU Q.1219] ITU-T, *Intelligent Network User's Guide for Capability Set 1*, Recommendation Q.1219 April 1994.

[ITU Q.1221] ITU-T, *Introduction to Intelligent Network Capability Set 2*, Recommendation Q.1221, September 1997.

[ITU X.25] ITU-T, *Interface between Data Terminal Equipment (DTE) and Data Circuit-Terminating Equipment (DCE) for Terminals Operating in the Packet Mode and Connected to Public Data Networks by Dedicated Circuit*, Recommendation X.25, October, 1996.

[ITU X.509] ITU-T, *Information Technology—Open Systems Interconnection—The Directory: Authentication Framework*, Recommendation X.509, August 1997.

[Kabay 98] M. Kabay, "ICSA White Paper on Computer Crime Statistics," ICSA, 1998, www.icsa.net/library/research/.

[Kaufman 99] E. Kaufman, A. Newman, *Implementing IPsec: Making Security Work on VPNs, Intranets, and Extranets*, Wiley 1999.

[Keshav 98a] S. Keshav, R. Sharma, "Issues and Trends in Router Design," *IEEE Communications Magazine*, May 1998.

[Keshav 98b] S. Keshav, *An Engineering Approach to Computer Networking*, Addison-Wesley, 1998.

[Kirchoff 96] D. Kirchoff, "Making the Connection," www.aiag.org/anx, 1996.

[Kleinrock 64] L. Kleinrock, *Communication Nets: Stochastic Message Flow and Delay*, McGraw-Hill, 1964.

[Kleinrock 75] L. Kleinrock, *Queuing Systems Volume I: Theory*, Wiley, 1975.

[Kosiur 98] D. Kosiur, *Building and Managing Virtual Private Networks*, Wiley, 1998.

[Kowack 97] G. Kowack, "Internet Governance and the Emergence of Global Civil Society," *IEEE Communications*, May 1997.

[Kozik 98] J. Kozik, W. Montgomery, J. Stanaway, "Voice Services in Next-Generation Networks: The Evolution of the Intelligent Network and Its Role in Generating New Revenue Opportunities," *Bell Labs Technical Journal*, October–December 1998, www.lucent.com/ideas/perspectives/bltj/oct-dec1998/pdf/paper08.pdf.

[Kumar 98] V. Kumar, T. Lakshman, D. Stiliadis, "Beyond Best Effort: Router Architectures for the Differentiated Services of Tommorow's Internet," *IEEE Communications Magazine*, May 1998.

[Lamberelli 96] L. Lambarelli, "TM Service Categories: The Benefits to the User," circa 1996, www.atmforum.com/atmforum/service_categories.html.

[Leida 98] B. Leida, "A Cost Model of Internet Service Providers: Implications for Internet Telephony and Yield Management," M.S. thesis, MIT, 1998, www.nmis.org/AboutNMIS/Team/BrettL/contents.html.

[Leiner 98] B. Leiner, V. Cerf, D. Clark, R. Kahn, L. Kleinrock, D. Lynch, J. Postel, L. Roberts, S. Woolf, "A Brief History of the Internet," www.isoc.org/internet/history/brief.html.

[Leonard 99] A. Leonard, "We've Got Mail—Always," *Newsweek*, September 20, 1999.

[Levine 99] D. Levine, "Let Your Fingerprint Be Your Password," *Internet Week*, June 7, 1999.

[Li 99] T. Li, "MPLS and the Evolving Internet Architecture," *IEEE Communications*, December 1999.

[Lombard 98] S. Lombard, L. Cramer, S. Torres, *Virtual Private Networking: Maximizing Network Performance while Reducing Costs*, Applied Technologies Group, www.techguide.com, 1998.

[Lyon 91] T. Lyon, "Simple and Efficient Adaptation Layer (SEAL)," ANSI T1S1.5/91-292, August 1991.

[McDysan 00] D. McDysan, *QoS and Traffic Management in IP and ATM Networks*, McGraw-Hill, 2000.

[McDysan 94] D. McDysan, D. Spohn, *ATM: Theory and Application*, McGraw-Hill, 1994.

[McDysan 98a] D. McDysan, D. Spohn, *Hands-On ATM*, McGraw-Hill, 1998.

[McDysan 98b] D. McDysan, D. Spohn, *ATM Theory and Applications—Signature Edition*, McGraw-Hill, 1998.

[Medin 99] M. Medin, J. Rolls, "The Internet via Cable," *Scientific American*, October 1999.

[Meinel 99] C. Meinel, "How Hackers Break In . . . and How They Are Caught," *Scientific American*, October 1998.

[Microsoft 97] Microsoft, *Understanding Point-to-Point Tunneling Protocol (PPTP)*, 1997, www.microsoft.com/ntserver/commserv/techdetails/prodarch/understanding_pptp.asp.

[Microsoft 98] Microsoft, *Virtual Private Networking: An Overview White Paper—DRAFT*, 3/18/98, www.microsoft.com/ntserver/commserv/techdetails/overview/vpnovw.asp.

[Minoli 97] D. Minoli, *Internet & Intranet Engineering—Technologies, Protocols, and Applications*, McGraw-Hill, 1997.

[Minoli 98a] D. Minoli, E. Minoli, *Delivering Voice over IP Networks*, Wiley, 1998.

[Minoli 98b] D. Minoli, E. Minoli, *Delivering Voice over Frame Relay and ATM Networks*, Wiley, 1998.

[Minoli 99] D. Minoli, A. Schmidt, *Internet Architectures*, Wiley, 1999.

[Moore 91] G. Moore, *Crossing the Chasm*, Harper Business, 1991.

[Moore 95] G. Moore, *Inside the Tornado*, Harper Business, 1995.

[Moore 99] G. Moore, P. Johnson, T. Kippola, "The Next Network," *Forbes*, February 22, 1999.

[Naisbitt 82] J. Naisbitt, *Megatrends*, Warner, 1982.

[Naugle 99] M. Naugle, *Illustrated TCP/IP*, Wiley, 1999.

[Newsweek 99] "The Dawn of E-life," *Newsweek*, September 20, 1999.

[Odlyzko 98] A. Odlyzko, "Data Networks Are Lightly Utilized, and Will Stay That Way," October 7, 1998, www.research.att.com/~amo/doc/networks.html.

[Onvural 93] R. Onvural, *Asynchronous Transfer Mode: Performance Issues*, Artech-House, 1993.

[Pecar 93] J. Pecar, R. O'Connor, D. Garbin, *Telecommunications Factbook*, McGraw-Hill 1993.

[Perlman 92] R. Perlman, *Interconnections*, Prentice-Hall, 1992.

[Perlman 99] R. Perlman, "An Overview of PKI Trust Models," *IEEE Network*, November/December 1999.

[Reimers 99] B. Reimers, "The Bumpy Road to IP," *Internet Week*, August 16, 1999.

[Rekhter 98] Y. Rekhter, *BGP/MPLS VPNs (Overview)*, UUnet International Workshop on MPLS, 1998, http://info.uu.net/ads/techconf/presentations/.

[Rekhter 99] Y. Rekhter, *BGP/MPLS VPNs*, UUnet International Workshop on MPLS, 1999.

[RFC 768] J. Postel, *User Datagram Protocol*, IETF, RFC 768, August 1980.

[RFC 793] J. Postel, *Transmission Control Protocol*, IETF, RFC 793, September 1981.

[RFC 1055] J. Romkey, *A Nonstandard for Transmission of IP Datagrams Over Serial Lines: SLIP*, IETF, RFC 1055, June 1988.

[RFC 1106] R. Fox, *TCP Big Window and Nak Options*, IETF, RFC 1106, June 1989.

[RFC 1112] R. Braden, *Requirements for Internet Hosts—Communication Layers*, IETF, RFC 1122, October 1989.

[RFC 1123] R. Braden, *Requirements for Internet Hosts—Application and Support*, IETF, RFC 1123, October 1989.

[RFC 1323] V. Jacobson, R. Braden, D. Borman, *TCP Extensions for High Performance*, IETF, RFC 1323, May 1992.

[RFC 1332] G. McGregor, *The PPP Internet Protocol Control Protocol (IPCP)*, IETF, RFC 1332, May 1992.

[RFC 1334] B. Lloyd, W. Simpson, *PPP Authentication Protocols*, IETF, RFC 1334, October 1992.

[RFC 1483] J. Heinanen, *RFC 1483: Multiprotocol Encapsulation over ATM Adaptation Layer 5*, IETF, RFC 1483, July 1993.

[RFC 1490] T. Bradley, C. Brown, A. Malis, *Multiprotocol Interconnect over Frame Relay*, IETF, RFC 1490, July 1993.

[RFC 1492] C. Finseth, *An Access Control Protocol, Sometimes Called TACACS*, IETF, RFC 1492, July 1993.

[RFC 1510] J. Kohl, C. Neuman, *The Kerberos Network Authentication Service (V5)*, IETF, RFC 1510, September 1993.

[RFC 1518] Y. Rechter, T. Li, *An Architecture for IP Address Allocation with CIDR*, IETF, RFC 1518, September 1993.

[RFC 1519] V. Fuller, T. Li, J. Yu, K. Varadhan, *Classless Inter-Domain Routing (CIDR): an Address Assignment and Aggregation Strategy*, IETF, RFC 1519, September, 1993.

[RFC 1591] J. Postel, *Domain Name System Structure and Delegation*, IETF, RFC 1591, March 1994.

[RFC 1598] W. Simpson, *PPP in X.25*, IETF, RFC 1598, March 1994.

[RFC 1619] W. Simpson, *PPP over SONET/SDH*, IETF, RFC 1619, May 1994.

[RFC 1631] K. Egevang, P. Francis, *The IP Network Address Translator (NAT)*, IETF, RFC 1631, May 1994.

[RFC 1633] R. Braden, D. Clark, S. Shenker, *Integrated Services in the Internet Architecture: An Overview*, IETF, RFC 1633, June 1994.

[RFC 1634] M. Allen, *Novell IPX Over Various WAN Media (IPXWAN)*, IETF, RFC 1634, March 1994.

[RFC 1661] W. Simpson, *The Point-to-Point Protocol (PPP)*, IETF, RFC 1661, July 1994.

[RFC 1662] W. Simpson, *PPP in HDLC-like Framing*, IETF, RFC 1662, July 1994.

[RFC 1701] S. Hanks, T. Li, D. Farinacci, P. Traina, *Generic Routing Encapsulation (GRE)*, IETF, RFC 1701, October 1994.

[RFC 1702] S. Hanks, T. Li, D. Farinacci, P. Traina, *Generic Routing Encapsulation over IPv4 Networks*, IETF, RFC 1702, October 1994.

[RFC 1771] Y. Rechter, T. Li, *A Border Gateway Protocol 4 (BGP-4)*, IETF, RFC 1771, March 1995.

[RFC 1817] Y. Rekhter, *CIDR and Classful Routing*, IETF, RFC 1817, August 1995.

[RFC 1883] S. Deering, R. Hinden, *Internet Protocol, Version 6 (IPv6) Specification*, IETF, RFC 1883, December 1995.

[RFC 1884] R. Hinden, S. Deering, *IP Version 6 Addressing Architecture*, IETF, RFC 1884, December 1995.

[RFC 1885] A. Conta, S. Deering, *Internet Control Message Protocol (ICMPv6) for the Internet Protocol Version 6 (IPv6)*, IETF, RFC 1885, December 1995.

[RFC 1886] S. Thomson, C. Huitema, *DNS Extensions to Support IP Version 6*, IETF, RFC 1886, December 1995.

[RFC 1889] H. Schulzrinne, S. Casner, R. Frederick, V. Jacobson, *RTP: A Transport Protocol for Real-Time Applications*, IETF, RFC 1889, December 1996.

[RFC 1965] P. Traina, *Autonomous System Confederations for BGP*, IETF, RFC 1965, June 1996.

[RFC 1973] W. Simpson, *PPP in Frame Relay*, IETF, RFC 1973, June 1996.

[RFC 1990] K. Sklower, B. Lloyd, G. McGregor, D. Carr, T. Coradetti, *The PPP Multilink Protocol (MP)*, IETF, RFC 1990, August 1996.

[RFC 1994] W. Simpson, *PPP Challenge Handshake Authentication Protocol (CHAP)*, IETF, RFC 1994, August 1996.

[RFC 1997] P. Traina, Ravi Chandrasekeran, *BGP Communities Attribute*, IETF, RFC 1997, August 1996.

[RFC 2001] W. Stevens, *TCP Slow Start, Congestion Avoidance, Fast Retransmit, and Fast Recovery Algorithms*, IETF, RFC 2001, January 1997.

[RFC 2043] A. Fuqua, *The PPP SNA Control Protocol (SNACP)*, IETF, RFC 2043, October 1996.

[RFC 2065] D. Eastlake, C. Kaufman, *Domain Name System Security Extensions*, IETF, RFC 2065, January 1997.

[RFC 2097] G. Pall, *The PPP NetBIOS Frames Control Protocol (NBFCP)*, IETF, RFC 2097, January 1997.

[RFC 2104] H. Krawczyk, M. Bellare, R. Canetti, *HMAC: Keyed-Hashing for Message Authentication*, IETF, RFC 2104, February 1997.

[RFC 2118] G. Pall, *Microsoft Point-to-Point Compression (MPPC) Protocol*, IETF, RFC 2118, March 1997.

[RFC 2125] C. Richards, K. Smith, *The PPP Bandwidth Allocation Protocol (BAP)/The PPP Bandwidth Allocation Control Protocol (BACP)*, IETF, RFC 2125, March 1997.

[RFC 2131] R. Droms, *Dynamic Host Configuration Protocol*, IETF, RFC 2131, March 1997.

[RFC 2138] C. Rigney, A. Rubens, W. Simpson, S. Willens, *Remote Authentication Dial In User Service (RADIUS)*, IETF, RFC 2138, April 1997.

[RFC 2153] W. Simpson, *PPP Vendor Extensions*, IETF, RFC 2153, May 1997.

[RFC 2211] J. Wroclawski, *Specification of the Controlled-Load Network Element Service*, IETF, RFC 2211, September 1997.

[RFC 2212] S. Shenker, C. Partridge, R Guerin, *Specification of Guaranteed Quality of Service*, IETF, RFC 2212, September 1997.

[RFC 2283] T. Bates, R. Chandra, D. Katz, Y. Rekhter, *Multiprotocol Extensions for BGP-4*, IETF, RFC 2283, February 1998.

[RFC 2284] L. Blunk, J. Vollbrecht, *PPP Extensible Authentication Protocol (EAP)*, IETF, RFC 2284, March 1998.

[RFC 2341] A. Valencia, M. Littlewood, T. Kolar, *Cisco Layer Two Forwarding (Protocol) L2F*, IETF, RFC 2341, May 1998.

[RFC 2364] G. Gross, M. Kaycee, A. Li, A. Malis, J. Stephens, *PPP Over AAL5*, IETF, RFC 2364, July 1998.

[RFC 2381] M. Garrett, M. Borden, *Interoperation of Controlled-Load Service and Guaranteed Service with ATM*, IETF, RFC 2381, August 1998.

[RFC 2401] S. Kent and R. Atkinson, *Security Architecture for the Internet Protocol*, IETF, RFC 2401, November 1998.

[RFC 2402] S. Kent and R. Atkinson, *IP Authentication Header*, IETF, RFC 2402, November 1998.

[RFC 2403] C. Madson, R. Glenn, *The Use of HMAC-MD5-96 within ESP and AH*, IETF, RFC 2403, November 1998.

[RFC 2404] C. Madson, R. Glenn, *The Use of HMAC-SHA-1-96 within ESP and AH*, IETF, RFC 2404, November 1998.

[RFC 2405] C. Madson, N. Doraswamy, *The ESP DES-CBC Cipher Algorithm with Explicit IV*, IETF, RFC 2405, November 1998.

[RFC 2406] S. Kent and R. Atkinson, *IP Authentication Header*, IETF, RFC 2406, November 1998.

[RFC 2407] D. Piper, *The Internet IP Security Domain of Interpretation for ISAKMP*, IETF, RFC 2407, November 1998.

[RFC 2408] D. Maughan, M. Schertler, M. Schneider and J. Turner, *Internet Security Association and Key Management Protocol (ISAKMP)*, IETF, RFC 2408, November 1998.

[RFC 2409] D. Harkins and D. Carrel, *The Internet Key Exchange (IKE)*, IETF, RFC 2409, November 1998.

[RFC 2410] R. Glenn, S. Kent, *The NULL Encryption Algorithm and Its Use with IPsec*, IETF, RFC 2410, November 1998.

[RFC 2411] R. Thayer, N. Doraswamy and R. Glenn, *IP Security Document Road Map*, IETF, RFC 2411, November 1998.

[RFC 2412] H. Orman, *The OAKLEY Key Determination Protocol*, IETF, RFC 2412, November 1998.

[RFC 2419] K. Sklower, G. Meyer, *The PPP DES Encryption Protocol, Version 2 (DESE-bis)*, IETF, RFC 2419, September 1998.

[RFC 2451] R. Pereira, R. Adams, *The ESP CBC-Mode Cipher Algorithms*, IETF, RFC 2451, November 1998.

[RFC 2472] D. Haskin, E. Allen, *IP Version 6 over PPP*, IETF, RFC 2472, December 1998.

[RFC 2474] K. Nichols, S. Blake, F. Baker, D. Black, *Definition of the Differentiated Services Field (DS Field) for the IPv4 and IPv6 Headers*, IETF, RFC 2474, December 1998.

[RFC 2475] S. Blake, D. Black, M. Carlson, E. Davies, Z. Wang, W. Weiss, *Architecture for Differentiated Services*, IETF, RFC 2475, December 1998.

[RFC 2509] M. Engan, S. Casner, C. Bormann, *IP Header Compression over PPP*, IETF, RFC 2509, February 1999.

[RFC 2543] M. Handley, H. Schulzrinne, E. Schooler, J. Rosenberg, *Session Initiation Protocol (SIP)*, IETF, RFC 2543, March 1999.

[RFC 2547] E. Rosen, Y. Rekhter, *BGP/MPLS VPNs*, IETF, RFC 2547, March 1999.

[RFC 2582] S. Floyd, T. Henderson, *The NewReno Modification to TCP's Fast Recovery Algorithm*, IETF, RFC 2582, April 1999.

[RFC 2597] F. Baker, J. Heinanen, W. Weiss, J. Wroclawski, *Assured Forwarding PHB Group*, IETF, RFC 2597, June 1999.

[RFC 2598] V. Jacobson, K. Nichols, K. Poduri, *An Expedited Forwarding PHB*, IETF, RFC 2598, June 1999.

[RFC 2620] B. Aboba, G. Zorn, *RADIUS Accounting Client MIB*, IETF, RFC 2620, June 1999.

[RFC 2621] G. Zorn, B. Aboba, *RADIUS Accounting Server MIB*, IETF, RFC 2621, June 1999.

[RFC 2637] K. Hamzeh, G. Pall, W. Verthein, J. Taarud, W. Little, G. Zorn, *Point-to-Point Tunneling Protocol*, IETF, RFC 2637, July 1999

[RFC 2661] W. Townsley, A. Valencia, A. Rubens, G. Pall, G. Zorn, B. Palter, *Layer Two Tunneling Protocol L2TP*, IETF, RFC 2661, August 1999.

[RFC 2685] B. Fox, B. Gleeson, *Virtual Private Networks Identifier*, IETF, RFC 2685, September 1999.

[RFC 2686] C. Bormann, *The Multi-Class Extension to Multi-Link PPP*, IETF, RFC 2686, September 1999.

[RFC MPLS] E. Rosen, Y. Rekhter, D. Tappan, D. Farinacci, G. Fedorkow, T. Li, A. Conta, *MPLS Label Stack Encoding*, IETF, draft-ietf-mpls-label-encaps-07.txtREF, 1999/09/16.

[Russell 95] T. Russell, *Signaling System #7*, McGraw-Hill, 1995.

[Ryan 98] J. Ryan, "WDM: North American Deployment Trends," *IEEE Communications Magazine*, February 1998.

[Saunders 96] S. Saunders, *The McGraw-Hill High-Speed LANs Handbook*, McGraw-Hill, 1996.

[Schneier 95] B. Schneier, *Applied Cryptography: Protocols, Algorithms, and Source Code in C*, Wiley, 1995.

[Schneier 99] B. Schneier, J. Kelsey, D. Whiting, D. Wagner, C. Hall, N. Ferguson, *The Twofish Encryption Algorithm*, Wiley, 1999.

[Shiva 99] "The Value of a VPN to Your Company," www.shiva.com, 1999.

[Sieber 86] U. Sieber, *The International Handbook on Compuer Crime*, Wiley, 1986.

[Simoneau 97] P. Simoneau, *Hands-On TCP/IP*, McGraw-Hill, 1997.

[Skoro 99] J. Skoro, "LMDS: Broadband Wireless Access," *Scientific American*, October 1999.

[Stallings 98a] W. Stallings, *Cryptography and Network Security—Principles and Practice, Second Edition*, Prentice-Hall, 1998.

[Stallings 98b] W. Stallings, *High-Speed Networks—TCP/IP and ATM Design Principles*, Prentice-Hall, 1998.

[STD 0051] W. Simpson, *The Point-to-Point Protocol (PPP)*, STD 0051, IETF, July 1994.

[Steenstrup 95] M. Steenstrup, *Routing in Communication Networks*, Prentice-Hall, 1995.

[Stephens 98] R. Stephens, P. Johnson, "IP, Therefore I Am: The Race to Network-Aware Services," www.nextgenerationnetworks.com, October 19, 1998.

[Tannenbaum 81] A. Tannenbaum, *Computer Networks*, Prentice-Hall, 1981.

[Tannenbaum 96] A. Tannenbaum, *Computer Communications, Third Edition*, Prentice-Hall, 1996.

[TeleChoice xDSL] Telechoice, "The Telechoice Report on xDSL On-line," www.telechoice.com/xdslnewz/.

[Telstra 99] Telstra, "Internet BGP Table," www.telstra.net/ops/bgptable.html, December 1999.

[Thompson 97] K. Thompson, G. Miller, R. Wilder, "Wide-Area Internet Traffic Patterns and Characteristics," *IEEE Network*, November/December 1997.

[TimeStep 99] TimeStep, *The Business Case for Secure VPNs*, 1999, www.timestep.com/downloads/secure_vpn_business_case.pdf.

[Turner 99] M. Turner, "Migrating to Network-Based Application Services," *Business Communications Review*, February 1999.

[USDC 98] "The Emerging Digital Economy," U.S. Department of Commerce, April 1998.

[van Bosse 98] J. van Bosse, *Signaling in Telecommunication Networks*, Wiley, 1998.

[VPNet 99] VPNet, "Managed VPN Services: Market Opportunity and Paths to Implementation," www.vpnet.com, 1999.

[Wagner 97] R. Wagner, E. Engelmann, *Building & Managing the Corporate Intranet*, McGraw-Hill, 1997.

[Whyte 99] W. Whyte, *Networked Futures*, Wiley, 1999.

[Wilder 98] F. Wilder, *A Guide to the TCP/IP Protocol Suite*, Artech House, 1998.

[Willis 99] D. Willis, "Voice over IP: The Battle Heats Up," www.nwc.com, March 8, 1999.

Index